PLUNDERING AFRICA'S PAST

THE CARTER LECTURES
CENTER FOR AFRICAN STUDIES
UNIVERSITY OF FLORIDA, 1993

PLUNDERING AFRICA'S PAST

edited by
PETER R. SCHMIDT & RODERICK J. McINTOSH

INDIANA UNIVERSITY PRESS ◆ BLOOMINGTON & INDIANAPOLIS
JAMES CURREY ◆ LONDON

Published in North America by Indiana University Press,
601 North Morton Street, Bloomington, Indiana 47404
and in Great Britain by James Currey Publishers,
54B Thornhill Square, Islington, London N1 1BE.

© 1996 by Indiana University Press

The paper used in this publication meets the minimum
requirements of American National Standard for Information
Sciences—Permanence of Paper for Printed Library Materials,
ANSI Z39.48-1984.

Manufactured in the United States of America

Library of Congress Cataloging-in-Publication Data
Plundering Africa's Past / edited by Peter R. Schmidt and Roderick J.
McIntosh.
  p. cm.
  Includes bibliographical references and index.
  ISBN 0-253-33040-8 (cl. : alk. paper). —ISBN 0-253-21054-2 (pa :
alk. paper)
  1. Africa, Sub-Saharan—Civilization.   2. Archaeological thefts—
Africa, Sub-Saharan.   3. Art thefts—Africa, Sub-Saharan.
I. Schmidt, Peter R. (Peter Ridgeway), date.   II. McIntosh,
Roderick J.
DT352.4.P55   1996
967—dc20   95-50698

1   2   3   4   5   01   00   99   98   97   96

British Library Cataloguing in Publication Data
  A catalogue record for this book is available from the British Library

  ISBN 0-85255-738-8 (paper)
  ISBN 0-85255-739-6 (cloth)

CONTENTS

CONTENTS

ILLUSTRATIONS

PREFACE

Those of us who have devoted our lives to the study of the African past are alarmed by current trends that are systematically and inexorably obliterating the material manifestations of the continent's heritage. This degradation of the African past is not a new process, for it dates back to colonial looting of African shrines and royal treasuries. But its contemporary severity is linked to big capital investment in Europe, America, and Japan in the antiquities of Africa. The demand created by foreign avarice, often closely tied to arrogant display of exotic items for status purposes, is leading directly to the mining of thousands of ancient sites in Africa. The mother lode in this instance consists of terra-cottas, beads, and other precious objects that embody the spirit and creativity of the African past.

Students of African history, anthropology, and art learn of the glorious accomplishments, for example, of ancient Ghana and Songhai, as well as Great Zimbabwe. Their lessons are only partial lessons, however, for they consist of information derived from fragmentary documentary evidence, oral traditions, and a little archaeology. Because most of the African past is not accessible through documentary record, archaeology provides one of the few options, along with historical linquistics (which provides a large picture), to build a more complex and more finely nuanced history of ancient times. Thus, the potential for archaeology to contribute to the writing of better informed ancient African history is immense.

Under current conditions and trends, this potential will not be realized. The complexities and importance of African contributions to global civilization are being rudely and shockingly interrupted and ended by the looting of traditional storehouses, archaeological sites, and museums. Unless the international community joins with concerned African colleagues to expose and arrest these depredations, there will be little knowledge to add to the historiography of the African past in the future.

Historians, archaeologists, and art historians are among the most deeply concerned by these disquieting trends. As then-president of the Society of Africanist Archaeologists, I worked to bring together in 1990 these different concerned constituencies at the biennial meeting of the Society to share their knowledge and to declare their determination to do something practical to stop the degradation of the African past. Out of that meeting came a very determined and practical set of resolutions that addressed ways to counter the illicit trade in African antiquities. I remember clearly the depth of alarm and concern expressed during the plenary session, and then rushing to my office and drafting the resolutions that we later unanimously adopted.

While the impact of those resolutions had measurable results (McIntosh, this volume), we also recognized that these issues remained remote and mostly unrecognized by other scholars and by the public; knowledge was restricted to those who were actively involved in African fieldwork or museum work and had occasion to witness problems firsthand. To be sure, the problems were of interest to thousands of African historians and students of African history as well as to policy makers in governments and non-government organizations around the world. The crisis was so pressing, so severe, that it demanded further hearings.

The concerns and the question of diminishing time for the preservation of Africa's past led us to the Carter Lecture Series as a possible venue for intense and thorough airing of the issues. The Carter Lecture Series has been conducted since 1986 by the Center for African Studies at the University of Florida to address precisely such issues that threaten the welfare of the African continent. It also incorporates the philosophical position that an open discussion of the issues with significant contributions from African colleagues will often lead to practical and reasonable solutions.

With this in mind, I organized a lecture series aimed at exposure of and remedies for the plundering and disappearance of the African past for April 1993. Representatives were invited from Zambia, Cameroon, Kenya, Tanzania, Nigeria, and Mali to provide a variety of African views and arguments. Scholars were invited from the United States and Mexico (to gain a comparative perspective), as was an investigative journalist from Belgium who has devoted several years of effort to an exposé of the illicit trade in antiquities between Mali and Europe. One of the most important constituencies represented was the United States government. In particular, two representatives from the United States Information Agency were present to share an important diplomatic success—the negotiation of a formal accord between the United States and Mali that designated a broad range of artifacts as materials prohibited for import into the United States. Also very important to the success of the discussions was the participation of the Chief of the International Standards Section, Physical Heritage, UNESCO; she helped to provide a more international scope to our debates.

This book results from the 1993 Carter Lectures. It is, we think, a profoundly disquieting document in its detailed accounts of how and why Africa's past is being plundered. Perhaps one of the most significant results of the book is the clear and poignant voices of African colleagues who are calling their governments and indigenous institutions to account. Accountability starts at home, they are saying, and there is a disturbing amount of evidence for state incompetence and complicity in the theft of artifacts and in the destruction of sites.

The messages held in this book will disturb historians. They should be equally upsetting to government policymakers in the Western world and in Africa as well as in non-government organizations. And, these messages may awaken the student of Africa who hopes that he or she may play a role in constructing a more positive and complete history of the continent. We do not have to continue along the dreadful path that we currently follow. This book sets out many positive alternatives that can be pursued to arrest the senselessness of museum thefts, organized gangs plundering ancient sites, and corrupt officials selling off heritage sites to the highest foreign bidder for a new tourist hotel. We must not remain compliant in the face of such offenses. There are alternatives, and this book charts the course for action to arrest the current trends.

ACKNOWLEDGMENTS

Our thanks go to all those who assisted in the organization of the 1993 Carter Lecture Series at the University of Florida. Special thanks go to Delores Collier, who made most of the travel arrangements. Additional financial support came from the Center for African Studies and the Foundation for African Prehistory and Archaeology (FAPA). Ronald Cohen, as chairman of the Carter Lectures Committee, lent his enthusiastic support to the project throughout. James Ellison and Patricia Miller both assisted in editorial matters, with Patricia Miller taking up last-minute details before submission. We are grateful for the comments of two anonymous readers. Our sincere thanks also to Kent Schneider of the U.S. Forest Service, who provided important financial support for the travel of African participants in the Carter Lectures.

PETER SCHMIDT
GAINESVILLE, FLORIDA

PLUNDERING
AFRICA'S
PAST

1

THE AFRICAN PAST ENDANGERED

Peter R. Schmidt and Roderick J. McIntosh

Brent bounded ahead of Togola and McIntosh, leaping over the deep craters and trenches left by looters who had plundered the site. Brent quickly ran to a particularly deep hole at the edge of the site and waved frantically for the others to join him. As they approached, they saw clouds of dust. Then heads emerged from the hole. Brent had caught three looters in the act.

A Belgian investigative journalist, Michel Brent, was visiting the floodplain of Mali's Inland Delta in the company of two archaeologists with years of experience in one of the most heavily plundered regions of Africa. They had invited the journalist to see what one of the archaeologists, Téréba Togola, considered to be the most extensively looted site in his country. For Togola and his American collaborator, Roderick McIntosh, stumbling upon the looters in action suddenly transformed the destruction of Mali's past from outrage in the abstract to the dilemma of suppression of a concrete act of wrongdoing.

The dilemma illustrates the complexity of the network of actors and their motivations that makes the pillaging so difficult to eradicate. These looters were not evil, faceless criminals wielding grotesque picks; rather, they were the poorest of the local peasants, with the wasted calves and tattered clothes seen all too often in rural Mali. The dilemma was that all three observers immediately felt pity and sympathy for the peasant looters, who form the lowest tier of the network of pillagers and traffickers. No longer could all the actors in the looting drama—laborers, local antiquities procurers, European traffickers, American collectors—be viewed as manifestations of the same faceless evil.

This plunder in a remote region of Mali is not uncommon in Africa. Although archaeologists, art historians, and museum researchers are keenly aware of similar degradation of African antiquities elsewhere in Africa, the extent and seriousness of the plunder remain concealed to most inside and outside of the academic world. The systematic dismantling of Pre-Columbian monuments has a longer exposure, more visibility, and widespread condemnation, but the situation emerging in Africa is no less serious. In many ways it may be worse because of the poverty and civil strife that exacerbates and accelerates the destruction of the past. This story from Mali is not unique; every researcher has at one time witnessed or heard reliable testimony about the looting of ancient sites and the illegal removal of important cultural objects from Africa. Every researcher with such direct knowledge feels frustration and a sense of isolation. What legal recourse is available to combat these offenses against the past? Are there other colleagues and institutions that share our outrage, that have developed means to begin to cripple the networks organized to plunder and market Africa's past?

These questions have been considered at several professional meetings over the past five years, with some successes, particularly at the 1990 Society of Africanist Archaeologists biennial meeting held in Gainesville, Florida and the 1995 congress of the Panafrican Association of Prehistory and Related Studies held in Harare, Zimbabwe. These meetings brought together scholars of various disciplines who discovered that they shared common concerns and fears and found that they could speak with a common voice about the future of African antiquities. At the 1990 SAfA meetings and at the Panafrican Congress this common determination took the form of a series of resolutions that spoke to our obligation to oppose the illicit trade in African antiquities in all its forms and manifestations, including the collusion of thermoluminescence laboratories in dating ancient terra-cotta artifacts looted from archaeological sites. Once these resolutions were shared with other professional societies (McIntosh 1991; *The African King* 1990), other frustrated scholars came forward to add their voices. The airing of these resolutions was a major weapon in the successful fight, two years later, to end the dating of Inland Niger Delta terra-cottas by the Oxford thermoluminescence laboratory (Inskeep 1992). By 1993 it was apparent that further action was necessary. A critical number of scholars, government officials, and investigative journalists were prepared to share their intersecting views and to document the structure and negative impact of the illicit trade in African antiquities.

The Carter Lecture Series has as its mission the dissemination of knowledge about critical issues facing the continent. It was, therefore, appropriate to organize a Carter Lectures conference focused on the plunder of Africa's past that included diverse perspectives, most importantly from Africa but also from scholars based in the United States. These academic voices needed balancing with those who had firsthand experience as government policymakers and officers charged with implementation of antiquities laws. It was also important to highlight African concerns because several fundamental questions arise out of this discussion: Whose heritage is valued, and what is not valued? Since most valuation appears to come from the West, we felt it was central to the discourse to learn what valuation is being placed on objects by Africans concerned with this expression of the past. In our view, it was also necessary to include those who had tried to bring the looting of Africa to the attention of lay audiences and public officials. We are aware, if the lessons from North America are taken into account, that our efforts to curb the illicit trade in Africa hinge on enhanced public concern and involvement.

Much of what was addressed in the Carter Lectures and in this book remains outside of the public knowledge and outrage, principally because news about plunder in Africa and even in the United States is generally overlooked. A U.S. champion of antiquities protection, Senator Pete Domenici of New Mexico, recently remarked on the looting of a twenty-acre Pueblo site containing 250 rooms. "The media did not relay word of this tragic theft to the world. Where is the hue and cry about the theft of archaeological artifacts? Where are the reporters and the cameras alerting the public to this loss? Where are the commentators explaining the impact of this loss on our society?" If the looting of a major archaeological site draws little or no attention in this media-obsessed society, then it is not difficult to imagine the dimensions of the problem in Africa, where there is virtually no dissemination of archaeological knowledge. In Africa there is relatively little debate about the systematic destruction of cultural heritage. Senator Domenici, who comes from a small state with large disfranchised minority populations, is aware that plundering of the past deprives populations of their human right to a cultural heritage.

Such a human right is fundamental. This perspective emerged in the conference as an essential philosophical underpinning to strategies designed to destroy the power relations that allow the rape of the African past. The protection of civil and political human rights against the abusive exercise of asymmetrical power relations is, according to the Universal Declaration of Human Rights, not inherently more important for human well-being than the right to a cultural identity. Though various scholars assign primacy to political and civil rights, it is increasingly apparent from the codification of human rights within both United Nations and African covenants that the right to a cultural heritage is now a widely accepted legal principle. Claims for human dignity under this right may prove to be the most powerful means to challenge abuses against cultural heritage perpetrated by governments and groups of individuals operating with official or tacit approval of governments.

One of the few avenues of recourse against the illicit trade in antiquities has been the UNESCO convention of 1970.[1] It is clear that two decades of attempts to implement this instrument have met with very limited success. One notable exception to this pessimistic assessment is the 1993 accord between Mali and the United States. Also, the United States and El Salvador recently (1995) concluded a broad ban on the unauthorized import of all pre-Columbian antiquities, an action undertaken under the aegis of the 1970 UNESCO convention. However, such conventions alone are insufficient. They are often seen by Western states as intrusive into the domain of property law, and, moreover, the powerful interests controlling the illicit trade show themselves very effective in opposing the implementation of these agreements. As well, several European countries, France and the United Kingdom most notably, that otherwise champion political and civil rights have steadfastly refused to become party to the international heritage conventions. This situation may change soon. As of late 1995, the French instrument of ratification of the 1970 UNESCO convention has been passed by the Assemblée Nationale and signed by President Mitterrand; final action has, however and inexplainably, been held up by the Foreign Ministry. Given the acknowledged failures of the UNESCO convention to curb the trade, the Carter participants felt that it was important to develop alternative legal strategies that encompass universal principles under which claims can be made for the right to participate in a cultural heritage.

This position is not without disagreement. Lyndel Prott, in her capacity as UNESCO's chief representative on cultural property, believes that such human-rights claims should not be made unless there is every reason to believe that they will be legally successful (Prott, this volume). Peter Schmidt, on the other hand, takes a view more compatible with the social sciences and argues that change and transformation of power relations must be seen in terms of process (Schmidt, this volume; Nagan 1993). The making of the human-rights claim sends a notice to those exercising power against the group being disfranchised that the human right to a cultural past is being reclaimed. The claiming process is an essential ingredient in establishing the legitimacy of the right (Nagan 1993; Cohen 1993). Rights not claimed go unrecognized, without response and acknowledgment from those engaged in the abuse. Another justification of such claims, regardless of the legal counterarguments, is that time is running out for Africa's past. We cannot wait to debate the fine points of the legal arguments and must proceed with a legal perspective on human rights that allows us to bring the greatest possible influence against those engaged in the deprivation of the right to a cultural heritage in Africa.

When might such a claim be an appropriate strategy? One necessary element is significant scale; that is, discrimination against entire ethnic groups and regional degradation of antiquities that affect the cultural heritage of discrete groups of people are obvious conditions that make such claims more powerful and easier to pursue before international tribunals and public opinion. Several examples come to mind. Kusimba (this volume) writes about current prejudice against the Swahili in contemporary Kenya. He explains how this prejudice is translated into the erasure of Swahili cultural heritage. By the argument we follow here, an affront to the right of the Swahili people to participate in a cultural life is carried out by government officials who facilitate and participate in the sale of traditional Swahili sites, including ancient ruins, to foreigners and development institutions. Destruction of the ancient ruins inevitably follows soon after land alienation.

An example of a rights violation at the national scale is seen in Mali, where there is ongoing and wholesale looting of many hundreds if not thousands of terra-cotta statuettes from archaeological sites and from family shrines. This is not a new phenomenon. The extraction of these objects from Mali is suspected from the first year (1893) of French penetration into the Inland Niger Delta (McIntosh, this volume). A more expansive human-rights argument can be used to reclaim a "lost" national heritage currently held in the museums of Europe and the United States. A human-rights claim to recover this looted past may be justified under the principle that continued deprivation of these objects denies Malian peoples their right to a cultural heritage.

Several essays in this volume illustrate the larger malaise in international relations as expressed in failures to acknowledge the illicit trade and to attempt its arrest. A dissection of the structure of the pillaging and illicit export network at work in Africa reveals the corrosive effect of power asymmetries among nations: a tangled web of corruption, profit, and selective blindness on the part of officials in Africa and in the West. Karoma, Mturi, and Kusimba (this volume) document the losses suffered by an entire nation when its officials turn their backs on their preservation mission, either for lack of manpower or due to neglect at all levels of the state, or because they have been co-opted by the agents of tourist development. One particularly egregious example of official complicity is documented by Karoma at Kilwa, a UNESCO World Heritage site on the southern coast of Tanzania (Karoma, this volume). Kilwa is an isolated site with only infrequent contact with the central antiquities office in the capital, Dar es Salaam, and the antiquities officers in charge of the site have little contact with supervisors. Karoma shows that such neglect by the agency responsible for protection has led to the subversion of the conservation mission at Kilwa. By the effective use of photographs, Karoma documents the antiquities officers' destruction of the site they are charged with protecting. He shows that stones from the ruins are being mined under the gaze of these officials, who then use some of them for the construction of their own homes.

If this tale of direct official involvement in site destruction upsets our expectations about the ethical standards of antiquities protection, it is no less serious than other official neglect witnessed in Tanzania. Mturi, for several decades instrumental in the preservation of Tanzanian sites in his capacity as director and chief conservator of antiquities, exposes forms of official neglect that lead to the widespread destruction of cultural resources. Mturi's concern is directed to the remarkable rock paintings of central Tanzania, where there are virtually thousands of important and unique rock-art sites, most of which remain unrecorded. This spectacular rock art, popularized by Mary Leakey's important book *Africa's Vanishing Art* (1983), is quickly disappearing. A prominent UNESCO consultant has determined that the area, found to contain the most important collection of rock art outside of France's Paleolithic caves, and to be perhaps even older, qualifies to be a World Heritage site. Such a designation would allow special technical and financial assistance in preserving these priceless resources.

Even though UNESCO found subsequent to its 1976 general conference that the rock-art sites of Tanzania would qualify for an international campaign to study and preserve them, there had been no Tanzanian government reaction as of 1993. A detailed plan for a documentation campaign was prepared in 1986. Yet in 1993 nomination forms to place the rock-art sites on the World Heritage List remained unsubmitted. Meanwhile, Mturi observed that between UNESCO's 1980 field assessment and his own assessment in 1992 there had been an alarming rate of destruction of rock art, by both natural agency and human activities. This confirms other independent assessments and suggests that official neglect is the principal reason why Tanzania is only a decade or so away from the final disappearance of its extraordinary rock art. This will be a loss for all of humankind, a loss of global importance.

The bold commentaries by Karoma, Kusimba, and Mturi mark an important departure for African scholars, who in the past have tended to blame the West for lack of help and for primary complicity in the erosion of Africa's cultural resources. This is not to say that the West is not deeply complicitous. In fact, the chapters by McIntosh and Brent describe the web of networks in which auction houses, art journals, thermoluminescence laboratories, and museums contribute to and service an obscure but scandalous form of commerce.

The networks that move African art and antiquities through the international marketplace may be less mature than those that deal in pre-Columbian art, but, like the latter, the illicit traffic out of Africa remarkably parallels the international drug trade. At the lowest and least remunerated tier are the peasant diggers. They sometimes work freelance during the agricultural off-season. Increasingly, they

are organized by dealers from nearby small towns into (full-time) corps number-
ing in the scores or hundreds. They may be given only their meals, with a small
commission paid by the piece. The local dealers often are kin to the important
African traffickers in the capitals, who may send young male relatives to Europe
to sell art directly to museums or collectors. More frequently, the principal African
dealers establish exclusive commercial relationships with owners of galleries in
Europe (and to a lesser extent in the United States), thereby saving the Western
dealer the inconvenience of having to travel to rural regions and the greatly
feared risk (however remote) of imprisonment in an African jail.

The owners of relatively few galleries, principally in London, Paris, Brussels,
and several Swiss cities, do the majority of distribution to collectors, museums,
and other galleries further removed from the source. These primary galleries take
the principal risk as the illicitly-obtained pieces cross international frontiers. By
way of compensation, these gallery owners enjoy the greatest price markup.
As in the case of efforts to interdict the international narcotics trade, those who
handle material crossing countries' borders would be most vulnerable to coordinated efforts by police, customs officials, and international law-enforcement
agencies, such as Interpol. The primary galleries provide the fabricated documentation that often accompanies looted art and antiquities. They cultivate the friend-
ship of major collectors and try to join the boards of public-trust museums or try
to control "Friends of the Museum" organizations. Their role is to facilitate the
unemcumbered, unremarked-upon movement of illicit art—in other words, to
"launder" the art.

They are thereby in a position to manipulate the prices and the volume of art,
always ensuring that they are in control of investment-grade materials. They also
know who in the academic world is willing (for a fee) to provide letters of authentication and validation, which thermoluminescence laboratories are willing (again
for a fee) to run date determinations on pieces with unverifiable origin, and which
art journals are willing to accept highly lucrative gallery advertising for art from
any source, no questions asked. The academics, scientists, and publishers who
provide these services are, ironically, the import nations' counterparts of the peasant producers. They are vital to the trade but (claim to be) ignorant of the true
prices the pieces ultimately will attain. They sell their honor for considerably less
than the thirty pieces of silver that it may cost the runners to subvert various customs and police officials on African frontiers and, undoubtedly, also on the Western sides of the frontier.

If corruption and eroded ethical standards typify European institutions and individuals engaged in the illicit trade as exposed in Brent's chapter, then an appropriate balance is reached in the chapters by Karoma, Kusimba, Nkwi, and Jegede
that expose the corruption within African institutions, both governmental and
traditional. Corruption in Africa is often the by-product of culture change when
indigenous institutions invested with the stewardship of sacred objects fail to
meet their traditional mission. Nkwi poignantly illustrates the consequences of
the collapse of the *kwifoyn*, a secret society in the Kom kingdom of Cameroon that
is charged with the curation of sacred, royal, and ritual regalia. *Kwifoyn* was once
based on the recruitment of commoner youth into the service of the king. Western

education, however, diminished the number of *kwifoyn* guards and eroded their associated values of guardianship to such a level that the most powerful and symbolic object in Kom, the *Afo-a-Kom*, was stolen from the *kwifoyn* storehouse. The theft of this sacred embodiment of the Kom nation created a collective identity crisis among all Kom and threatened the foundation of royal legitimacy. Although subsequently recovered in 1973 through the intercession of concerned scholars and a philanthropist, the sacred statue then faced severe problems of stewardship upon its return to Kom kingdom. While a comprehensive remedy for curation was not forthcoming, Nkwi does show how the conscious reconstruction of the *kwifoyn* institution by the king led to its revitalization during the 1980s and reestablished a new ethos of curation—a possible model for other African cultures seeking to recuperate similar local institutions once invested with curatorial responsibilities. However, until such institutions come to grips with the need for economic incentives for those entrusted with curation, it is likely that even revitalized cultural values will erode in the face of powerful economic inducements from the foreign marketplace.

The Kom experience of revitalizing an important curatorial institution at the local level is also a possible model for the reconfiguration of more modern museums in Africa—that is, those that have developed out of a European tradition of acquisition, research, and exhibition of objects disassociated from living cultures. It came as a surprise to conference participants that so much discussion focused on African museums. But it became very clear that the sad condition of African museums constitutes one of the deepest concerns in the conservation of objects with cultural and historical value. Out of this discussion arose the realization that the mission of the African museum is undergoing a serious reevaluation in the minds of our African colleagues (Musonda, jegede, this volume), who are increasingly searching for vital indigenous perspectives for the treatment and use of cultural objects as well as for legitimate economic incentives that overwhelm temptation for corruption and theft.

dele jegede provides us with an insider's view of the hemorrhaging of Nigeria's museums, attributing this to reasons including but also beyond economic depression and corrupt inducements from the West. The museums just do not function. He relates why in Nigeria the museum is alien to the needs and sensibilities of the people, who see it as a distant, disembodied government agency. This characterization of the museum as mortuary and government shrine stands in stark contrast to the values of indigenous shrines (filled with objects of interest to the art trade) that evoke intimacy, accessibility, reverence, and community. He and others, such as Posnansky and Drewal, argue for a reconfiguration of the African museum that is more in keeping with local capacities and cultural needs. One of the reasons for rampant theft from African museums, thinks Posnansky, is related to the failure of museum personnel to understand and relate to the values attached to the objects that they curate and display. Were they socialized or trained in a way that appreciates the meanings of the objects they touch and care for, such appreciation would provide the foundation for stewardship that precludes theft. But as we have already argued, museum personnel will continue to be corrupted under the economic exigencies of most African states until there are reasonable economic alternatives to underpin their curation. A decent standard of living is the only way to ensure the loyalty of museum staff.

The European display of African objects provides a complementary perspective on the alienation of people from the African objects they view. Musonda, who works with museums in Zambia, believes that Western museums fabricate stories about African material culture for which they do not have certain contextual information pertaining to function and symbolic significance. Musonda suggests that such depictions defeat the mission of the museum to educate and further distances the European observer from African cultures. After all, African cultures have never been viewed as animating and informing such objects but simply as the place from which such objects are harvested.

Samuel Sidibé, director of the National Museum in Mali, argues that the current plundering of Mali has its genesis in the European collection missions that continued unabated right up to the very end of colonialism. His chapter makes an important connection between former museum acquisitions policies (which can most kindly be called rapacious) and contemporary practices among all but the most scrupulous public-trust institutions. Sidibé shows how the plundering of the Malian past gained legitimacy under the colonial practice of "collecting missions." These ventures, sponsored by a diverse range of public and private institutions, harvested sacred and royal objects—often by trickery and downright theft—to fill the museums of Europe (in this case, France). He effectively establishes a connection between these past pillages of Malian heritage with the contemporary scene of systematic plunder of ancient sites. In effect, a tradition of pillage is the European legacy—once official, now commercial.

Now driven by commercial interests, the scale of looting in Dogon villages and in the tells of the Inland Niger Delta of Mali is shocking in the numbers of looters involved and the totality of the losses. As Sidibé and Brent both observe, whole villages and encampments of immigrant workers are mobilized for the open and systematic excavation of very large sites, paid for and organized by dealers in the antiquarian trade. If this offends our sensibilities, consider the fate of the National Museum of Somalia in Muqdisho and in Hargeysa (Brandt and Mohamed, this volume). The contents of both museums were completely looted. What was not looted at the New National Museum in Muqdisho, such as archaeological artifacts stored in bags, was thrown into the streets. But not only conditions of civil war lead to such terrible consequences. The stripping of the ethnographic collections from the Hargeysa museum in northern Somalia is paralleled on a lesser scale by the systematic theft, orchestrated by European (in this case, German) academics, of the ethnographic collections of the National Museum of Tanzania in Dar es Salaam. Collusion and corruption are as destructive as mortars. We feel compelled to ask if, within this bleak diagnosis, there are any positive alternatives that can be taken to reshape the mission of African museums and their effectiveness as keepers of the past.

Museums in Africa have looked outside for their clientele and intellectual paternity. By servicing primarily the expatriate community, these museums have been unable to develop exhibitions that elicit local interest. Local tastes differ and are not always predicable by Western expectations. For example, Drewal (this volume) cites the successful exhibit on the history of bicycles in Burkina Faso,[2] positively received because it was a topic that was immediate and personal to most people. This experience illustrates the potential that community interest has for creating stronger bonds and identity between people and museums in Africa. The leakage that causes jegede, LaGamma, and Drewal to despair can be prevented by more appropriate and culturally sensitive programs. The usual case today is a training system based on apprenticeship in foreign museums or on short-term tutorials in centers using Western methods and techniques. Posnansky and jegede advocate a reversal; apprenticeships should be in the village or with work groups practicing traditional modes of craft production. This training approach, set within the living culture, engenders an appreciation for and identity with the objects, an essential form of partial insurance (the remainder being economic incentives) against economic temptations to sell museum collections to the highest bidder.

It is appealing to many African and Western scholars searching for alternatives to the failed policies of museums in Africa to embrace local solutions that appear to be more sensitive to material objects that are significant to cultural heritage. Yet there are dangers and disadvantages in a wholesale acceptance of local solutions. Nkwi's intimate familiarity with the plight of the *Afo-a-Kom* in Cameroon leads to an important insight about the potential incapacity of local institutions to adequately curate objects in their care. The return of the *Afo-a-Kom* to the Kom kingdom precipitated the positive reform of the institution of *kwifoyn*, but even a revitalized *kwifoyn* did not satisfy even minimal international standards of curation for this important artifact. After eleven years in storage within the king's chambers, the *Afo-a-Kom* was in tatters when it was brought out in 1984 for an international tour. Likewise, other sacred regalia were stacked randomly and indiscriminately on the floor in the storage room. If there is a conflict between local customs in handling objects (as in this instance) and national and international standards, is the local practice the one which should prevail? Past experience shows that the imposition of international standards results in the alienation of local participants, suggesting that any program introducing change must also learn from and amplify local values. With the participation of student apprentices from museums or universities it is possible to introduce low-tech treatments that complement the sensibilities and goals of local curators. But a deeper issue here is what incentive there is for the *kwifoyn* of Kom to curate royal and other regalia. Until the *kwifoyn* members can devise ways to develop economic incentives—because their potential members simply have too many other attractive alternatives—how can they prevent one of their number or one of the princes from stealing and selling the regalia (Nkwi, this volume)?

There are some hopeful experiments. The government of Mali, grappling for effective responses to the looting crisis, has developed a plan of action that directly engages museum and antiquities staff in rural community life. This outreach program taps into local networks of preservationists and advocational historians proud of the region's past. Using participatory anthropological methods, the members of Missions Culturelles travel to three of the most heavily plundered areas. They have been charged by the culture ministry to listen to and learn from local experts about traditional values that can be adapted to the national preservation program. In its infancy, this innovative approach recognizes that a centralized program directed from the capital city will be ineffective, while at the same time it adopts a communicative posture (and quiet monitoring) that incorporates local attitudes and behavior into any plan that may be developed by national authorities.

All of these issues encapsulated in the crisis of museums are examples of a larger issue that has emerged in all the chapters in this volume: Who defines cultural heritage? The case studies that we have highlighted provide chilling examples of the runaway destruction of Africa's past. What are the power relations that come into play in defining what is culturally important and what is not? What would induce those who feel they are powerless to make the effort to preserve artifacts or sites? Why do hundreds of Malians participate in the looting of ancient sites? If the preservation of these antiquities is not important to them, who is setting the agenda? For whom will the past of Mali be preserved, if it is preserved at all? Many of the papers touch on issues related to these questions, such as minority interests in conflict with national hegemonic development policies.

Our initial story about the tattered Malian peasants as innocent common laborers in the employ of urban dealers and ultimately European art investors captures the forces at work in impoverished nations where *any* job is a good job. Their looting is clearly at odds with Western academic sensibilities and with the national interest, but what has the state done for these local peasants? We see in several examples from the East African coast that the state is all too often the agent of displacement of local peoples. Even if national or expatriate researchers make good-faith efforts at inventory and assessment, how often is this knowledge shared with the local population? All people want to take pride in their own pasts. Often, however, neglect by the state (or active complicity of the state's agents) opens the local field to the ravages of those international forces that view art and antiquities as investment and commodities. Moreover, official neglect undermines trust and understandably leads local people to believe that preservation is not valued.

One of the obstacles to developing a local sense of pride and immediate identity with the objects of the past is the absence of a historical imagination that ties the living and sometimes diverse populations to those who came before them. Responsible dissemination of archaeological interpretation and visible publications can stimulate interest in the past and pride that the local past has national or even global importance. Such historical imagination has come to evoke a new ethos of protection to the ancient tells of Jenne-jeno. And, it is important to emphasize, this has been accompanied by a burgeoning cottage industry of tourist guides who make their living by making representations about Jenne-jeno's past. While it is apparent that economic incentives play a key role in the development of popular interest in and dissemination of Jenne-jeno's ancient history, it is not without problems. Some of the local guides involved in this informal sector are also tied to the illicit trade in archaeological objects. Islamic city elders, local preservationists, and the cultural mission personnel are trying to organize the tour guides to better develop tourism, thus enticing them away from the illicit trade. The locals have become the guardians of the past.

We cannot assume, however, that even with respectful efforts to engage the local community in the preservation and conservation of cultural resources, groups and individuals will respond to the national mission. Mturi shares his frustration at government's failure to involve local participants in the planning and continuation of the Bagamoyo Conservation Project in Tanzania. While the project organizers held seminars for local officials and building owners, the response has been limited and a government-initiated idea for an association of owners interested in restoring their buildings has languished because of insufficient local initiative and participation. In spite of one attempt to convert a building to a guest house, the project has stalled. The economic advantages of restoration remain hidden to the local community and not surprisingly disinterest prevails.

Mturi identifies several problems in making the Bagamoyo Project a success. Local attitudes are based on the idea that any action to conserve historic Bagamoyo is a government responsibility, a syndrome of dependency that inhibits local involvement. Once involved, government often fails to follow through on the most basic issues. The failure of the Antiquities Unit to maintain a small park and the restored German blockhouse contiguous to it leads Mturi to conclude that if the agency does not professionally manage this particular monument, it will again revert to a state of disrepair. The underlying message to local residents in this instance is one that contradicts other government efforts to involve local owners in restoration. Good intentions to elicit local engagement and investment in a national project to conserve Tanzania's cultural heritage are meaningless if the agency responsible neglects the past over which it has stewardship.

Tensions between local practices and beliefs and national agendas for conservation and ideological use of cultural resources present a difficult problem throughout the continent. They are vividly illustrated in the chapter by Wilson and Omar, who discuss attempts by the National Museums of Kenya to preserve the ruins on Pate Island in the Lamu Archipelago. The Pate ruins are an extensive and rich record of the growth of Swahili civilization along the East African coast as well as the source of important archaeological evidence for an indigenous first-millennium A.D. culture that appears to have laid the foundation for the more complex trading society that followed. However, the peasants who live on Pate are first concerned about their livelihood; they use stones from the ruins to build their houses (similar to the Kilwa phenomenon), and they cultivate tobacco among the ruins. Wilson and Omar agree that it is difficult to argue that the Kenyan government should prevent cultivation in the ruins and thus deprive people of making money from a minor cash crop under conditions of limited economic opportunities and restricted land. Yet the people of Pate continue to harvest materials from the ruins to build houses, an activity that eventually will erase any aboveground vestiges of the ancient civilization. How can a balance be reached, with both the national and local economic interests being satisfied? These are difficult questions. But the longer we wait to seek answers, as in the case of the Tanzanian rock paintings, the closer we come to having both the issues and the cultural resources disappear altogether.

The tensions between government cultural policy and local needs are expressed in other ways. Government encouragement and sponsorship of development schemes often runs counter to legislation to prevent the destruction of heritage sites. This contradiction between development interests and conservation interests within government is a well-known phenomenon in Western countries, especially in the United States, where interagency conflicts over development plans were common during the 1970s before explicit procedures were devised to assess the impact of government-sponsored and -approved development on cultural resources.

Kusimba provides some jarring examples of the negative impact of development interests in Kenya. His observations about Gulu, a walled site destroyed in late 1992 by local businessmen, show the extent of the problem. The lack of manpower and the absence of monitoring at Gulu meant that the systematic mining of its distinctive surrounding walls for building rock (likely used in the walls of a new hotel nearby) went unnoticed for months. Gulu's virtual disappearance represents the voracious appetite of tourist development as well as the failure of the National Museums to develop a capacity to work with local populations, both foreign and non-Swahili, to monitor and beneficially utilize the archaeological ruins in their midst.

In their defense, the cultural heritage managers along the Kenyan coast are currently overwhelmed by development aimed at tourism. Is there any remedy for that area? Or is it symptomatic of what we can expect to happen in Zanzibar, mainland Tanzania, coastal Ghana, coastal Mozambique, and elsewhere? It is clear that under current conditions the development of coastal properties will continue to erase the Swahili past. Incentives such as tax relief for protection of ancient properties by developers has yet to be considered. The potential for an integrated tourism that utilizes the cultural resources in the midst of hotels and bars is enormous and might well add economic diversity to investment in the area while preserving the past. While archaeo-tourism is not without its negative impacts—much as eco-tourism among the giant redwoods of northern California is not without its deleterious effects—at this stage in the destruction of Kenya's past the presence of tourists at these ruins would be a boon. It would raise the visibility of these resources both internationally and among Kenyans, who would see firsthand the economic value that lies in their effective preservation.

When we survey the art trafficking scene, it sometimes appears that little that is constructive can ever come of the relations between developing and wealthy nations. Even the high hopes and soaring rhetoric that accompanied the 1970 drafting of the UNESCO convention have been deflated. Of the major art-importing nations, only the United States has ratified the convention. It did so only in 1983, after the moneyed dealers and museums lobby had for some time blocked ratification debate in the Senate and in the House of Representatives with misleading arguments of "foreign tampering" with principles of private property. Of the nations of greater Africa, all of which are at risk, only twenty have become state parties to the convention as of 1995. Several that suffer particularly from the hemorrhaging of their past—Ghana, Zimbabwe, and Ethiopia are the most obvious examples—have not yet become signatories.

To the satisfaction of the concerned world, however, one nation that long resisted this obligation has now become, arguably, the world leader in the effort to redefine mutual respect among nations. A popular uprising in Mali recently overthrew a brutal, dictatorial regime that was heavily involved in the transport of ancient Inland Delta terra-cotta art across its own borders. The people of Mali elected as president an archaeologist, Alpha Oumar Konaré, who unhesitatingly directed his government to make Africa's first request to the United States for an emergency ban on the import of broad classes of antiquities. After months of painstaking effort by the Malian culture ministry and museum officials, working in tandem with the head of the U.S. embassy's cultural mission, Bill Crowell (La-Gamma, this volume), a formal request for action was forwarded to the Cultural Property Advisory Committee, administered by the USIA. The committee carefully scrutinized the request under an enabling legislative mandate (Papageorge Kouroupas, this volume). Upon the recommendation of the committee, on September 23, 1993, the United States and Mali formally entered into a novel and inclusive bilateral partnership for the suppression of the antiquities traffic.

Before the Malian request, the United States had received and acted affirmatively upon five Latin American requests, but these were rather restricted either in the region to be protected or in the class of material covered. A sixth request by Canada is sweeping in its demand for import controls on virtually all archaeological and ethnographic materials, but action on this demand was delayed while the somewhat less-inclusive Malian request was considered. The Mali–United States bilateral accord is therefore a prototype. It is conceptually innovative because it addresses artifacts that are still in the ground. The prototype served its purpose: since the 1993 Mali–United States accord, a similarly inclusive accord was signed between the Unites States and El Salvador.

The Mali–U.S. accord is not retroactive. It does not address Malian antiquities already in the United States. Rather, Mali and the United States have addressed art and artifacts still in the ground, *in situ* material for which the scientific potential of excavation in context can be preserved (McIntosh, Togola, and McIntosh 1996). The hoped-for effect is that the agreement will suppress the market for materials ripped out of archaeological context. The import restrictions are inclusive in that all archaeological materials from the Late Stone Age (Neolithic) to the eighteenth century are covered. Significantly, the accord explicitly goes beyond cultural property defined as "art." It also includes the handicrafts of everyday life as well as all ancient materials from the nearby caves of the Dogon region. The region covered is not limited to the (already significant) 120,000 square kilometer floodplain of the Inland Delta but extends significantly upstream along the Niger River and into neighboring regions. The accord thus sets the principle of inclusiveness against the argument of dealers and other moneyed interests that only a narrow scope on import bans protects national legal sovereignty. The United States timed the announcement of the accord to honor Mali on its National Day, a symbolic courtesy that conveyed a welcome message of mutual respect from one of the world's most privileged nations to one of the world's newest democracies.

LaGamma and Papageorge Kouroupas strongly imply in their contributions to this volume that U.S. foreign service officials have long yearned for just such a prototype as a model to demonstrate a good-faith willingness to work with other nations to draft analogous instruments to protect the past. Since September 1993, the accord has been used by the United States and by other signatories of the 1970 convention to ask non-signing nations to reconsider their reluctance to become state parties. Switzerland is reportedly about to sign, a major breakthrough among European states associated with the illicit trade (Papageorge Kouroupas, pers. comm.). France, too, has begun procedures for formal ratification. This is a first step. Other nations will closely observe the equally important steps taken by both Mali and the United States to implement the accord effectively.

Lest we forget, such accords are just words without the goodwill and co-operation necessary for implementation. On both the U.S. and the Malian sides there must be education of customs and law-enforcement officials. There must be a network of archaeologists, art historians, and museum professionals willing to identify stolen pieces and to give their time to training. Embassy personnel in Bamako and in Washington must communicate and work hard for interdiction. The Mali–United States bilateral accord unambiguously puts in place the *intention* to prosecute. The next, most visible step toward effective implementation will be the indictment of dealers moving Inland Delta antiquities across the U.S. border, which will send a clear message to those engaged in the illicit trade. We believe that one excellent example of the effectiveness of such an aggressive approach is seen in the U.S. Park Service's prosecution of those who have looted protected sites in the national parks of the Southwest United States and Alaska. Successful prosecution has profoundly deterred looter activity. There is no question that a well-publicized and vigorously prosecuted court case will send the strongest message to those engaged in the trade that their activities will be punished. As well, it will send a message to other African nations that solutions are available and that a more-coordinated effort will lead to successful interdiction and sup-pression of the trade.

RESOLUTIONS

From the first day, participants in these Carter Lectures were aware that this was the first forum that had so thoroughly inquired into all dimensions of Africa's plundered and disappearing past. During discussions it became apparent that the participants were united in their desire that the conference also be a forum for practical action. There was a palpable sense that the issues were so critical to the protection of Africa's past that it was important to go beyond scholarly dis-course and to set out an agenda for action that was compatible with our scholarly concern.

Several participants had found the set of resolutions concerning the illegal art trade drafted at the 1990 annual meeting of the Society of Africanist Archaeolo-gists to be a useful document to share with colleagues in other disciplines and to show to officials in African countries as evidence that not everyone was cowed or complacent in the face of the looting of the African past. Several of the governmental and nongovernmental officials, Lyndel Prott of UNESCO in particular, had had long experience with drafting resolutions of international scope. The Carter Conference participants quickly agreed that the conference should end with an attempt to reach consensus on recommendations for practical action.

In the end, such agreement was achieved with alacrity. All participants were asked to submit what they believed to be the most critical issues to be addressed. The suggestions were then collated, edited, and formatted by the conference organizers. A session was then chaired by C. M. Kusimba at which the draft resolutions were read, reworded, and voted upon. All were accepted unanimously.

Anyone who shares the concerns discussed in this book may find the following resolutions useful to share with colleagues and others who despair of the future of the African past.[3]

Recognizing that all the world's peoples have a fundamental human right to participate in cultural life, and

Recognizing the human right to a cultural identity and heritage and affirming our intention to campaign for these cultural rights, especially in cases of their repeated violation, and

Recognizing the power of mobilizing shame to draw attention to violations of cultural heritage,

We *professional archaeologists, anthropologists, art historians, artists, and museologists resolve*:

1) To actively lobby governments to become signatories to international conventions designed to arrest the illicit removal of cultural resources, such as the 1970 UNESCO convention and the UNIDROIT draft, and to adopt effective implementing legislation;

2) To assist African authorities in preparing notifications of stolen cultural property to appropriate international organs such as UNESCO and Interpol, and in applying for protection under the U.S. Cultural Properties Implementation Act;

3) To exchange information on standards of ethical behavior through our professional bodies and to police those standards effectively;

4) To find out other bodies, such as the American Museums Association, with whom we can form alliances;

5) To work closely with the media and to use films such as *The African King* to ensure the widest and most forthright exposure of individual participants in the illicit trade, of site destruction, of the illicit trade in objects, and of the fate of individual objects and to establish a newsletter on current problems;

6) To sponsor educational workshops to train customs officials, police, faculties of law, judicial staff, and cultural administrators and to make available our professional expertise to law-enforcement agencies for the identification of illegally exported heritage resources;

7) To assist African institutions through Western universities and museums, particularly in the efforts of regional centers to strengthen and expand training of archaeologists and museologists for central and local postings;

8) To produce scholarly work concerning cultural heritage in clear, straightforward language and to have it disseminated in languages understood by the people most affected;

9) That Western and African museologists will work together to improve interpretations of African items in Western museums;

10) To pressure international aid programs and agencies to adhere strictly to their own internal regulations requiring impact assessments, mitigation of damage, and publication of plans;

11) To work to have heritage sites, and especially religious sites actively used by local communities, protected in national and local management plans, national legislation, and international instruments; and,

12) To encourage concerned and aware lovers of art and heritage to become patrons and protectors of that heritage.

Furthermore, the persons making these resolutions also make the following Recommendations:

1) That African nations put into place pan-African mechanisms to monitor and to help nonmember nations in implementing international conventions on cultural-heritage management and on the suppression of the illicit trade in art and antiquities. These mechanisms should be used to investigate and to publicize failures to apply and enforce such conventions;

2) That aid-granting agencies, such as the U.S. Agency for International Development, NORAD (Norwegian aid agency), and DANIDA (Danish aid agency), as well as international development bodies, such as the World Bank or the International Monetary Fund, should

i) mandate assessments and mitigation of archaeological and ethnographic resources affected by projects as well as publish results of such studies; and

ii) contract such work to universities and institutions in the countries concerned to build up their facilities, staff exposure, and training experience;

3) That specific curricula to address heritage management be incorporated into university degree programs and that these curricula be disseminated to every tier of African national education;

4) That all multinational corporations engaged in industrial, agricultural, or other developments disturbing the landscape should be subject to the same requirements as international donor agencies;

5) That the director-general of UNESCO be invited to give priority assistance to countries whose cultural heritage is subject to extreme danger because of civil or international armed conflict and, in particular, send a mission to Somalia as soon as possible to assess possible remedies for the serious condition of that country's cultural heritage.

These resolutions and recommendations will be brought to the attention of other international organizations, such as UNESCO, the International Council of Museums (ICOM), the International Council on Monuments and Sites (ICOMOS), the International Centre for the Study of the Preservation and the Restoration of Cultural Property in Rome (ICCROM), and to professional societies, such as the Arts Council of the African Studies Association (ACASA), the African Studies Association (ASA), the Society of Africanist Archaeologists (SAfA), and the Archaeological Institute of America (AIA), among others.

NOTES

1. Hereafter referred to as the 1970 UNESCO convention; the full title is the Convention on the Means of Prohibiting and Preventing the Illicit Import, Export, and Transfer of Ownership of Cultural Property.

2. Drewal in turn cites Ravenhill 1992.

3. These resolutions were endorsed unanimously by the participants in the 10th meeting of the Panafrican Association of Prehistory and Related Studies, Harare, June 1995.

REFERENCES

The African King. A film distributed by Pilgrim Pictures, Ltd., London. 1990.

Cohen, Ronald. "Endless Teardrops: Prolegomena to the Study of Human Rights in Africa." In *Human Rights and Governance in Africa*, ed. R. Cohen, G. Hyden, and W. Nagan, 3–38. Gainesville: University Presses of Florida and Center for African Studies, 1993.

Inskeep, Ray. "Making an Honest Man of Oxford: Good News for Mali." *Antiquity* 66, 250 (1992): 114.

McIntosh, Roderick. "Resolved: To Act for Africa's Historical and Cultural Patrimony." *African Arts* 24, no. 1 (1991): 18–22, 89.

McIntosh, Roderick J., Téréba Togola, and Susan Keech McIntosh. "The Good Collector and the Premise of Mutual Respect among Nations." *African Arts* 28, 4 (1996): 60–69, 110–12.

Nagan, Winston. "The African Human Rights Process: A Contextual Policy-Oriented Approach." In *Human Rights and Governance in Africa*, ed. R. Cohen, G. Hyden, and W. Nagan, 87–108. Gainesville: University Presses of Florida and Center for African Studies, 1993.

2

THE HUMAN RIGHT TO A CULTURAL HERITAGE

AFRICAN APPLICATIONS

PETER R. SCHMIDT

The prevailing normative view of human rights assigns most of them to the civil and political domain. Human rights are commonly associated with conflict between individuals and states that abuse rights through the denial of free speech, through torture, or through incarceration without due judicial process. Such abuses form a common part of the relationship of many peoples with totalitarian states determined to keep power at whatever expense. The exercise of arbitrary power in Africa, typically by political leaders who have usurped and come to represent state power, has become all too common a part of modern African history (An-Naʿim and Deng 1990; Shepherd and Anikpo 1990).

Given the serious need to build more effective mechanisms for the protection of civil and political rights in Africa, is it then frivolous or irrelevant to suggest that the right to a cultural past is as important for one's well-being as the right to a fair trial, to freedom of assembly, or to unfettered religious expression? Such civil and political rights are at the center of upholding human dignity, and their importance has gained recognition through conflict over their violation and the development of legitimate claims for their protection. Much may be learned from the process in which civil and political rights claims emerge, gain legitimacy, and are applied to the benefit of the world community (Cohen, Hyden, and Nagan 1993). This process is all the more important in light of thinking that asserts that economic, social, and cultural rights are second-class rights—more difficult to agree to and not yet universally acknowledged.

Upon further inquiry, it is evident that any assertion that civil and political rights are more important ignores an understanding of how rights arise out of claims and come to be legitimated. Vital rights do not exist unless claimed. The claiming process develops out of individual and group needs to reclaim human dignity, a quality that cannot be attached to any particular right of subordinate or superior quality. The circumstances out of which a claim arises—namely, the denigration of human dignity—determine the moral force and acceptance of the rights claim.

The post–World War II era witnessed the emergence of a panoply of individual rights and freedoms demanded as a response to the abuses experienced during the war (United Nations 1980; Prott and O'Keefe 1984). These rights were first declared as part of the United Nations Charter, which promotes fundamental human rights as the foundation for world peace. By 1948 the Universal Declaration of

Human Rights had developed a comprehensive rendering of both political and other human rights. That document's article 27 contains the first explicit reference to cultural rights, the right to participate in the cultural life of the community. Equally important is article 22, which introduces economic, social, and cultural rights as indispensable for human dignity and the free development of personality. Such rights are to be realized by national effort and international cooperation. That declaration is tempered, however, by the realization that resources of each state and the international community may limit efforts in this direction.

Shortly after the human-rights commission finished the draft of the Universal Declaration, it began work on a draft of a covenant that addressed the issue of implementation and also included provisions on economic and cultural rights. A General Assembly resolution of 1950[1] poignantly stated that civil and political rights are interconnected and interdependent with economic, social, and cultural rights and that, "when deprived of economic, social, and cultural rights, man does not represent the human person whom the Universal Declaration regards as the ideal of the free man" (United Nations 1980). As implementation of the rights was attempted, this position eroded somewhat; within two years the two categories of rights had been separated into two international covenants. In 1966 the Covenant on Civil and Political Rights went to the General Assembly for adoption along with an optional protocol that established the machinery for handling complaints from individuals. The Covenant on Economic, Social, and Cultural Rights included no optional protocol, thus suggesting that rights claims in this domain would be more difficult to effect.

Not until 1976 were the covenants ratified and entered into force. The preamble to both instruments used similar language, affirming once again the equality of the different rights (United Nations 1980). The presence of measures for implementation of civil and political rights signaled at least a relative priority in the process of implementation. As for cultural rights, the right to participate in cultural life was reaffirmed. The sole elaboration pertaining to cultural heritage stated that it was necessary to ensure that the conservation of culture be obtained to fulfill this right.

THE HISTORICAL BACKDROP TO THE PRESERVATION OF CULTURE

During the twenty-eight-year hiatus between the Universal Declaration and the ratification of the covenants in 1976, the United Nations Educational, Scientific, and Cultural Organization (UNESCO) took up the mandate to preserve world cultural heritage, mostly in response to a series of General Assembly resolutions seeking to expand the scope and involvement of UNESCO with human-rights issues in cultural heritage. In 1966 the Declaration of the Principles of International Cultural Cooperation was proclaimed by the general conference of UNESCO; this document asserts that "Each culture has a dignity and value which must be respected and preserved" (United Nations 1980:102). Although not part of a human-rights covenant, the declaration and a number of other formal positions that followed over the next decade both in UNESCO and through General

Assembly resolutions fill out and give form to the human-rights statements made in various covenants and declarations. Meanwhile, UNESCO was promulgating the Convention on Ownership of Cultural Property, in 1970 (hereafter the 1970 convention),[2] and the Convention Concerning the Protection of the World Cultural and Natural Heritage, in 1972. None of these attempts to preserve world cultural heritage was explicitly tied to human rights until 1973, when the General Assembly responded to a report by UNESCO's, director general on culture and human rights by passing a resolution that expressed concern over the preservation and enrichment of national cultures and ways of life. The text specifically requests the preservation and restoration of places and buildings that serve as media for cultural transmission. The document also strongly encourages educational approaches that employ cultural heritage to enable every individual to use cultural values for advancement. An emphasis on the preservation of cultural and moral values and the cultural environment was also abstracted from *Human Rights and Scientific and Technological Developments.* a 1973 report by Rene Maheu, then the director general of UNESCO.

Maheu focused on spiritual values and their linkage to the preservation of a cultural environment when he presented his report to the General Assembly on October 31, 1973:

> A landscape, shaped and fashioned by those who have worked on it over the ages, not governed soley [*sic*] by strictly utilitarian aims but also following practices depending on cultural standards—religious, moral or aesthetic—more or less consciously observed. "Cultural environment" and "background to life," then, mean the same thing. But in fact it is much more than a background. It is a universe, as essential to the human condition as nature itself. Through the play of the symbols, more or less explicit in it according to our degree of cultural development, it constitutes, at one and the same time, a fund of ideas and values embodied in materials and forms from which our spiritual life derives the resources needed for its daily sustenance and motion, its breath of life, and also a mirror which, by constantly reflecting back to us our deep attachments, changing tastes or varying moods, prompts us and helps us to express ourselves and thereby, in our turn, to create. (Maheu 1973:21)

These qualities appeal to moral sensibilities and historical meaning. They are eloquent and compelling and helped to set the standard within UNESCO and other institutions for clarifying the importance of preserving the material cultural environment, whether a culturally constituted landscape or a district in a town. While Maheu helped to set the tone and direction of preservationist sentiments in UNESCO, his vision was limited and did not extend beyond elements such as architectural features that continue to figure in the lives of people today.

For several decades, archaeology has played a significant role in the recovery of ancient history, especially in circumstances where local historical knowledge has been erased by colonialism and modernization. Archaeology has become all the more important in the construction of history in Africa, where written history is relatively abbreviated and most African heritage remains buried in the earth.

Such a view is some distance from Maheu's, and that distance may help to explain why the historical contextualization that archaeology provides has remained a hidden quality in concerns over the preservation of cultural values. Maheu made the following remarks about archaeology in the same report: "We must not be deceived . . . by the present craze for archaeology which, in most cases, is no more than a taste for anachronistic exoticism which, just like the flights of imagination prompted by the conquest of space, is essentially a response to a need for escape the very reverse of true culture" (Maheu 1973:9).

This peculiar view of archaeology—with its emphasis on the exotic and anachronistic—betrays a fundamental misunderstanding of ancient objects and the values associated with them. Archaeology as we know it today can document the historical contexts in which objects were made, used, and discarded or finally applied. In place of this richer historical fabric we observe a kind of presentism and a set of values that stress creativity and invention—attributes that come to be attached to objects under the general philosophical position that exposure to such objects will stimulate creativity and innovation in the future. This is a noble position, but it implicitly accepts the absence of context, the most powerful means to communicate processes of creativity and innovation. We see the last clear expression of this interpretation in a 1976 report to the General Assembly by the UNESCO director general, who asserts that "the right to culture obliges public authorities to create the social and economic conditions which permit the effective exercise of this right," and that the material products of cultural systems, when preserved, provide the inspiration for future creativity (United Nations General Assembly A/31/111).

During the early 1970s the question of repatriation of cultural items to the country of origin also arose in General Assembly debates. This issue obviously intrudes into the relations of African and Western states, particularly against the background of the removal of cultural property under the repressive conditions of colonialism. The United Nations has addressed this question in numerous resolutions since 1973, when the issue was first brought to the General Assembly by Zaïre (Bourgi, Colin, and Weiss 1987). The major thrust of this debate is one that focuses on depredations in the past, although it does invoke general references to human rights. For example, the early United Nations resolutions pertaining to the restitution of cultural property refer to fundamental human rights, as does a resolution adopted by the Eighteenth General Conference of UNESCO (18C/Res. 3. 428). Restitution is also closely interwoven with ideas about national liberation and the recovery of cultural identity (Bourgi, Colin, and Weiss 1987). Nonetheless, restitution becomes less certain as a result of statutes of limitation and is complicated by issues of retroactivity.

UNESCO has since adopted a pragmatic attitude toward the return and restitution issue by working toward the reassembly of dispersed heritages when such cultural property has a fundamental significance for spiritual values and cultural heritage. This is accomplished primarily through bilateral agreements encouraged and sponsored under UNESCO's international conventions, if they apply to the countries concerned.

APPROACHES TO THE PROTECTION OF CULTURAL HERITAGE

At the risk of being misunderstood, I want to explore the consequences of these approaches to the protection of cultural heritage. Such perspectives focus on the object—virtually without exception removed from its archaeological context—as the major concern. Within UNESCO such concern has been expressed through organized attempts to return works of art and manuscripts, for example, to countries of origin. In addition, UNESCO has focused on the development of instruments, such as the 1970 convention, that create legal devices among states to interdict the illicit trade in antiquities. These essential and important devices are designed to inhibit and to disrupt illicit activities, but they are devices aimed at particular objects—individual artifacts and clusters of artifacts that have been determined to have significance. In theory, in the long run such an approach restricts the market and leads to the diminution of heritage-site destruction.

But these approaches seem to have lost sight of human-rights issues. The question of a human right to a cultural heritage is lost in a plethora of procedures at the expense of higher-order principles. Twenty years ago, when the General Assembly was searching for more clearly stated linkages between human rights and cultural heritage, they received Director General Maheu's discourse on the important and essential associations between the material cultural world and its centrality to the human condition. This report, however, failed to speak thoroughly on issues of human rights. In fact, the report simply makes fleeting references to (or perhaps, more accurately, only pays lip service to) cultural preservation and human rights. Because Maheu's report apparently set the course for subsequent UNESCO directions, human rights were not elevated to a point of explicitly tying the well-being of the cultural/material past to the well-being of contemporary populations.

If we have lost our way in the Western world, then perhaps we can look for some guidance from human-rights developments in Africa. An examination of the often maligned Banjul Charter, otherwise known as the African Charter on Human and Peoples' Rights, adopted unanimously by African heads of state in 1981, reproduces almost verbatim the concept of the right to participate in the cultural life of the community drawn from the Universal Declaration and the Covenant on Economic, Social, and Cultural Rights. However, the third paragraph of article 17 sets out a distinctive African rendering of cultural rights that amplifies the principles that we are trying to bring to the surface: "The promotion and protection of morals and traditional values recognized by the community shall be the duty of the State."

This is one of the most explicit renderings of cultural rights to highlight traditional values, a concept that readily incorporates cultural heritage. But the Banjul Charter adds another article that explicitly ties cultural identity to heritage: "All peoples shall have the right to their economic, social, and cultural development with due regard to their freedom and identity and in the equal enjoyment of the common heritage of mankind" (Peter 1990: article 22, paragraph 1). It is encouraging to see that African states have increased the formal scope of rights recognition to encompass cultural heritage.

In many human-rights covenants, rights are expressed both as individual and as those that the state should promote and protect. In article 17 of the Banjul Charter, state action is called upon, an approach that reflects the communitarian structure of the charter. Stronger rights are those specifically vested in the individual, an approach that Fernyhough (1993) convincingly argues is common to African societies, contrary to the predominant view that African rights are normally vested in the group or community. The Banjul statement of rights, stressing as it does socialist principles paralleling approaches once popular in Eastern Europe, puts the responsibility of cultural-rights protection on the state.

When protected in this way, cultural rights may be destined to become victims of a state's self-interest when conflict arises between the state's economic or political interests and a community's cultural heritage sensibilities, for example. The interests of a local community often do not coincide with those of the state. Moreover, as the state is an arbitrary and artificial construct, it is to be expected that it may not incorporate sensitivity to the cultural heritage of communities and individuals within communities. This distancing of state interests from heritage interests tends to be amplified when contemporary populations are physically removed from their ancestors' ancient residences. Kusimba (this volume) vividly exposes the avarice and incompetence of state authorities who are following large economic rewards in areas no longer settled by descendants of the ancient Swahili, in this instance by permitting development for tourism and ranching schemes in the midst of the most sensitive historic areas in Kenya.

Another scenario that might easily arise under such conditions has occurred over the last several years in Tanzania: In 1988 some Muslims decided to build a new secondary school on the Kunduchi ruins, a gazetted site[3] north of Dar es Salaam. When informed of the destruction of archaeological remains, the responsible state authorities did not intercede with an order to stop and relocate the project. Two possible explanations for the lack of state action to protect the site are fear that opposition to the Islamic community over the project was a politically dangerous venture and the belief that construction of an Islamic structure on a traditional Islamic site was a natural and acceptable historical process. It is also quite plausible that the responsible officials in the Ministry of Lands (which knowingly and improperly issued the permit) personally profited from the venture. Although bureaucratic incompetence may well be a key ingredient in state failure to act in defense of heritage resources, the absence of state identity with local heritage issues is an underlying deficiency in a system that invests primary responsibility in the state to protect the human right to a cultural past.

Recognizing that the state and its appointed authorities are rarely reliable agents for cultural protection is therefore critically important. In the face of the failure of local remedies in the instances of Kunduchi and the coastal littoral in Kenya, individuals can initiate claims within communities or concerned interest groups. Thus, the Banjul Charter creates some unique opportunities for the protection of the human right to a cultural heritage, although it is an alternative not without problems. As Hyden (1993) notes, the commission has limited powers of investigation and its inability to prosecute makes it a "toothless tiger." While developing states have myriad potential interests, particularly economic, that conflict with the promotion and protection of cultural rights, the Banjul Charter provides one of the clearest avenues to seek redress for the violation of cultural rights in case the state fails to curtail their denigration.

Individual claims may be made directly to the African Commission on Human and Peoples' Rights, but only after exhausting all local remedies. Such caveats are common language but can be used by a state to deny the validity of a claim by its people. However, the claimants will have elevated the issue to the point of negotiation among the commission, the secretariat, and the state concerned—a process in which exposure begins to trigger public embarrassment and shame (see McIntosh, this volume). As all African states are party to this instrument, such approaches are immediately available under conditions where other avenues have failed to curtail or prevent pillaging or wanton destruction (Kusimba, this volume).

The failure to address questions of pillaged and willfully destroyed cultural heritage as human-rights violations has seriously hampered attempts to stop the illicit international trade in antiquities and activities such as the organized mining of sites that feed artifacts into that trade. Instead we are trapped in an approach that is bogged down by a focus on particular assemblages of artifacts, by cumbersome and extensive diplomatic negotiations to effect bilateral agreements, and by the lack of participation of many Western and African countries in the UNESCO convention of 1970 (Prott, this volume). Meanwhile, the pillaging of sites in Africa continues to accelerate to a point where whole containers filled with archaeological artifacts regularly find their way to Europe (Brent, this volume).

NEW DIRECTIONS FOR CULTURAL HERITAGE RIGHTS

The human right to participate in culture has come to incorporate the idea that such participation includes a cultural identity explicitly tied to cultural heritage. This proviso has appeared on all human-rights lists since the approval of the Universal Declaration of Human Rights in 1948. It has come to be refined and elaborated, as already noted, in subsequent declarations, including the African Charter on Human and Peoples' Rights of 1981. While human rights claims based on cultural integrity are now being made by minority cultural groups in various parts of the world, the human right to a cultural heritage has not yet been claimed on a national or a global scale, with charges of violations of the right leveled against a state by individuals or by a state against another state. The time for nationalizing or globalizing African human-rights claims to cultural heritages is clearly upon us.

It is important to understand the process by which principles for rights are created and how they gain sufficient acceptance to eventually translate into legislation and action against those who violate them (Nagan 1993; Cohen 1993). Nagan and Cohen have argued that this kind of processual analysis demands that we discover those patterns of social alienation that create or germinate claims for human rights. The social alienation in this instance is the physical removal of material remains of cultural pasts to an alien environment, a process that strips such objects of all historical meaning and their potential to educate.

Prott (this volume) argues persuasively that the weakness of applicative international procedures makes many generalized human rights prescriptions unrealistic. However, my position here, following Nagan, is that a process-oriented view of human rights goes beyond a dichotomy between moral rights and legal rights to which Prott apparently adheres. Human rights are meant to "bind" the sovereign (state). If there is no consent by the sovereign, then human rights are not law but a kind of positive morality, a position consistent with modern legal theory (Nagan, pers. comm., 1994). Some human-rights claims are honored, some are not. Precisely because some human-rights declarations are weak without enforcement procedures (Prott, this volume), it is essential to build a political culture in which human-rights claims can be contested *in whatever arena* is available. This is the process that leads to validated rights—issuing from a political culture in which such expectations are derived from active claiming of human rights. Rights not claimed are rights not legally validated, defined, or enforced.

Given the current awareness of social alienation and the potential of human-rights claims, how do such claims come to be recognized and acted upon by those world bodies invested with such responsibility? First, aggrieved parties and outside critics, such as Amnesty International, the Society for Africanist Archaeologists, and the World Archaeological Congress, must campaign for them. One strategy would be to direct attention to the violation of the human right to a cultural heritage when African states fail to protect heritage sites and even participate in their destruction. For example, the repeated failure of Kenyan authorities to act against the destruction of protected sites along the Swahili coast clearly falls within this category of claims (Kusimba, this volume). It is essential that such a claim be initiated by the aggrieved individuals or groups within Kenya, perhaps working in concert with external critics to bring the claim either to the African commission or to the United Nations through the Committee on Economic, Social, and Cultural Rights established in 1987. One of the first findings of the new committee is that individual rights in the covenant are seen as legal rights and are being reviewed in their implementation as such (Ramcharan 1989:43). This encouraging trend suggests that these rights are moving closer to civil and political rights in recognition and implementation.

Such a strategy may have the advantage of bringing to the surface the failures of African states to pass adequate antiquities legislation and to invest in an infrastructure that provides protection to heritage sites. In countries where educational capacity and resources are available to address such problems, human-rights claims could focus attention on heritage issues and cause preventive action to be taken. However, an internal approach may be flawed, especially when poor countries without sufficient developmental capacity are targeted or when only one part of the human-rights problem—the failure of the African state to provide protection—is addressed.

Another untested and potentially more powerful approach is available: a formal human-rights claim made by one or more African states against European states (all having ratified the pertinent covenants) that currently allow the free passage of African antiquities defined (through other bilateral agreements under the UNESCO convention) as illicit. Traders in antiquities who operate out of Europe create much of the demand that sustains the plundering of sites in countries such as Mali and Ghana. European states such as Belgium that allow their citizens to abuse Malian and Ghanaian human rights by the unsanctioned importation of cultural heritage are implicated in such abuse. Mali, Ghana, or both countries could file a formal complaint with the United Nations Committee on Economic, Social, and Cultural Rights seeking investigation into such abuses for further action. State-to-state human-rights complaints are a legitimate procedure in human-rights law if the states are party to the same covenant—for example, Sweden's complaint against Turkey over its abuse of Kurdish human rights (Paul Magnarella, pers. comm., 1992).

It is critical that a more diverse strategy be devised for the protection of world heritage rights. The strategy must include the escalation of human-rights claims regarding cultural heritage to the level of state-to-state complaints. The procedure itself, or the threat of the procedure, would apply a powerful moral force on European states that are participating in human-rights abuses against African peoples. Such a move would precipitate diplomatic efforts to find resolutions or, failing that, at least bring "unwelcome publicity and denunciation" or the "mobilization of shame" (McIntosh, this volume). The application of such a strategy may accelerate the ratification and implementation of the UNESCO convention and the passage of stronger domestic laws.

It is apparent that the UNESCO convention of 1970, despite its good intent and positive accomplishments, does not elicit participation in the convention or provide the means to arrest the illicit trade in African antiquities over the next several decades. As long as key Western states are slow to ratify the convention, the goal that every state "become increasingly alive to the moral obligations to respect its own cultural heritage and that of all nations" will not be realized; the goal of working together in international cooperation for the protection of cultural heritage will also not be reached. We must, sadly, confront the failure of the UNESCO convention of 1970 to carry the burden of the human right to a cultural heritage. The numerous redundant resolutions calling for better participation of states in the 1970 convention at the 1982 UNESCO World Conference on Cultural Policies held in Mexico City are an index to the frustrations inherent in its implementation (UNESCO 1982). It is extremely disquieting to note that, only nine years after Director General Maheu's presentation of a report that at least made philosophical links between human rights and cultural heritage, there was no mention of human-rights issues at Mexico City. Can the African past await protection under these conditions?

We may perhaps find some hope in the recent bilateral accord between the United States and Mali, if it successfully inhibits the illegal movement of antiquities between these two countries (LaGamma, Papageorge Kouroupas, this volume). But even if containers full of artifacts are returned to countries such as Ghana by the use of the UNESCO convention or by other legal devices, such artifacts are meaningless except for their inherent aesthetic values. Ripped from their contexts, they symbolize only the failure of the world community to escalate the conflict between avarice and the right to a cultural heritage into the arena of human-rights violations. The recovery and restitution of cultural property concerns itself with past wrongs, which are difficult to document and to place on the anvil of conflict from which human-rights claims are forged.

CONCLUSION

The slow birth of a human right to a cultural heritage has been witnessed over a three-decade process of definition and elaboration of the concept in human-rights lists. While debate still prevails over its efficacy and that of cultural rights in general vis-à-vis civil and political rights, there is no doubt about its widespread recognition as a right that is fundamental to the human condition. All the same, the right has not gained acceptance, because debate and conflict over its proper status in society has not become an instrumental part of our social life.

If colonization was the first stage in the West's denigration of the African past, then the erasure of Africa's cultural heritage that is occurring today is the second. The responsibility for the disappearance of Africa's cultural heritage also rests on the African state. All too often we witness the direct complicity of the state in the destruction of heritage resources (see Kusimba, this volume; Karoma, this volume; Mturi, this volume). The systematic destruction of Africa's past is now beginning to stimulate reflection, reaction, and awareness that activities such as the mining of sites for terra-cotta artifacts in Mali or Ghana imperil the capacity of present and future individuals to create and innovate from the lessons contained in the past. From awareness grows action; from action, human-rights claims.

It is also clear that while human-rights claims to a cultural heritage are only in their earliest period of gestation, they are so compelling and so serious that responsible and democratic leaders of Africa, such as Alpha Konare of Mali, are putting such concerns at the top of their national agendas. Cultural heritage as a human right can only be legitimized by action that obtains its universal application in law. It deserves a global campaign, for not only is the cultural heritage of Africa under threat, but so too is the cultural heritage of all peoples.

NOTES

1. Resolution 421 E (V) of December 4, 1950.

2. The full title is the Convention on the Means of Prohibiting and Preventing the Illicit Import, Export, and Transfer of Ownership of Cultural Property.

3. A gazetted site or monument is one that has been formally documented and recognized as historically significant and worthy of protection and efforts at preservation and has therefore been entered into a national registry of sites to be protected by the state.

REFERENCES

An-Na'im, Abdallahi Ahmed, and Francis M. Deng, eds. *Human Rights in Africa*. Washington, D.C.: The Brookings Institution, 1990.

Bourgi, Albert, Jean-Pierre Colin, and Pierre Weiss. *International Aspects of Cultural Rights.* Paris: UNESCO, 1987.

Cohen, Ronald. "Endless Teardrops: Prolegomena to the Study of Human Rights in Africa." In *Human Rights and Governance in Africa,* ed. R. Cohen, G. Hyden, and W. Nagan, 3–38. Gainesville: University Presses of Florida and Center for African Studies, 1993.

Cohen, Ronald, Goran Hyden, and Winston Nagan, eds. *Human Rights and Governance in Africa.* Gainesville: University Presses of Florida and Center for African Studies, 1993.

Fernyhough, Timothy. "Human Rights and Precolonial Africa." In *Human Rights and Governance in Africa,* ed. R. Cohen, G. Hyden, and W. Nagan, 39–73. Gainesville: University Presses of Florida and Center for African Studies, 1993.

Hyden, Goran. "The Challenges of Domesticating Rights in Africa." In *Human Rights and Governance in Africa,* ed. R. Cohen, G. Hyden, and W. Nagan, 256–80. Gainesville: University Presses of Florida and Center for African Studies, 1993.

Maheu, Rene. "Human Rights and Scientific and Technological Developments." Report to the General Assembly, October 31, 1973.

Nagan, Winston. "The African Human Rights Process: A Contextual Policy-Oriented Approach." In *Human Rights and Governance in Africa,* ed. R. Cohen, G. Hyden, and W. Nagan, 87–108. Gainesville: University Presses of Florida and Center for African Studies, 1993.

Peter, Chris Maina. *Human Rights in Africa: A Comparative Study of the African Human and People's Rights Charter and the New Tanzanian Bill of Rights.* New York: Greenwood Press, 1990.

Prott, Lyndel, and P. J. O'Keefe. *Law and the Cultural Heritage.* Oxford: Professional Books, Ltd., 1984.

Ramcharan, B.G. "Economic, Social, and Cultural Rights: UN and Third World Dimensions." In *Human Rights, Development and Foreign Policy: Canadian Perspectives,* ed. I. Brecher. Halifax: Institute for Research on Public Policy, 1989.

Shepherd, George W., Jr., and Mark O.C. Anikpo. *Emerging Human Rights: The African Political Economy Context.* New York: Greenwood Press, 1990.

United Nations. *United Nations Action in the Field of Human Rights.* New York: United Nations, 1980.

United Nations General Assembly. "Preservation and Further Development of Cultural Values." A report of the Director-General of UNESCO to the General Assembly, August 24, 1976.

UNESCO. *Cultural Rights as Human Rights.* Studies and Documents on Cultural Policies, no. 3. Paris: UNESCO, 1970.

———. *World Conference on Cultural Policies: Final Report.* Paris: UNESCO, 1982.

3

SAVING THE HERITAGE

UNESCO'S ACTION AGAINST ILLICIT TRAFFIC IN AFRICA

Lyndel V. Prott

Illicit traffic in cultural property is a worldwide problem, affecting almost every culture. Works of art stolen from museums in Western Europe; archaeological sites ruined by the destruction of clandestine excavation; locally treasured works taken from village churches in newly accessible Eastern Europe and long vulnerable Latin America; monumental sites mutilated by the removal of sculptures, at present especially evident in Cambodia and Nepal; items of decor, furniture, and collectibles stolen from private collectors and historic houses; objects taken from museums during looting in the wake of armed conflict—all these phenomena are part of a huge problem, always serious but currently of epidemic proportions.

The problem for sub-Saharan Africa is particularly difficult, as it is for many traditional communities. In numerous African countries, significant cultural objects remain in their traditional communities, lacking the protection of even minimal security systems and of strong local belief systems that formerly would have made it inconceivable for a member of that community to cooperate in the removal of a cultural object of importance.

Although museums exist, they are not generally supported by a strong museological culture that ensures proper financing, a sure place in the activities of the community of that state, or even a degree of interest that would ensure proper management of the collections (Posnansky, this volume). For many Africans, objects removed from the local community and placed in a museum are dead objects, lacking the significance in use that made them important elements in indigenous life.

Many African cultural objects have had a ritual significance that protected them until twentieth-century changes weakened belief systems and made it possible for some Africans to regard the pieces as commercial objects. A large proportion of African artifacts, though they may be connected with a particular ceremony, are not connected with a monumental complex, which may make tracing their origin even more difficult than for antiquities and sculptures (in itself a very hard task). Most objects in the illicit trade come from previously undocumented contexts.

Finally, illicit trade often seriously affects the present life of the community, not just in economic terms because of the loss of items that might have attracted tourists and therefore brought economic benefits, but also because of the loss of the best examples of a cultural tradition to inspire younger artists, resulting in the deterioration of artistic skills and disparagement of local culture. Tourism itself often contributes to the estrangement of Africans from their own cultures, as visitors are content with "airport art" that has the right dimensions to survive a charter air flight and to fit a suitable niche in a Western home, thus adding a further pressure to the loss of traditional forms.

LEGAL PROTECTION

UNESCO has actively attempted to assist states in stopping the drain of cultural resources away from those who made them and into collections that may be accessible to the wealthy of the industrialized world, but are certainly not available to the members of traditional communities.

The exportation that occurred in colonial days has already created an imbalance between holdings of cultural objects of traditional communities in European museums and those left at the source. To address this imbalance, UNESCO has established the Intergovernmental Committee for Promoting the Return of Cultural Property to Its Countries of Origin or Its Restitution in Case of Illicit Appropriation. This committee's work is inspired by a 1978 appeal of the director general of UNESCO (annex I) in which he called for the return to their countries of "at least the art treasures which best represent their culture, which they feel are the most vital and whose absence causes them the greatest anguish." This appeal, rarely cited, is worthy of particular attention, for it shows careful consideration of all the relevant factors.

Despite this appeal, few returns have been made. A great deal of material was returned from Belgium to Zaïre before the establishment of the committee. Subsequently, some of these objects reportedly appeared on the international market. Some returns have been made by private collectors (notably a collection of Gabon), but by and large little has happened. As of 1993, no African state had brought a case to the committee. Zambia has sought to do so regarding the Broken Hill skull, but because the United Kingdom, where the skull is now, does not belong to UNESCO, the committee has no jurisdiction to act.

The committee has attempted to increase its effectiveness. Its members devised an appropriate claim form and then, finding the form's interpretation difficult, designed guidelines that included many examples (UNESCO and cod. CC-86// WS/3). Perhaps so much detail has deterred states from making claims: As of 1993, only seven cases had been brought before the committee. Claims have been made by Ecuador, Jordan, Iran, Iraq, Greece, and Turkey (two claims). It is notable that no African states have filed claims, not even Nigeria and Ghana, which were active in United States debates on this issue and whose difficulties in obtaining the repatriation of objects by existing methods are on record (Eyo 1986:203; Staunton and McCartney 1981:15). The scarcity of claims may well result from a lack of resources, from a certain skepticism about the effectiveness of such initiatives in relation to the amount of work required, or from a "lack of stamina" for the necessary follow-up, as the first chair of the committee suggested (Prott and O'Keefe

1989). Whatever the case, the countries that have had a successful return program have done so with the substantial help of institutions in the former holding states, e.g., Zaïre (Belgium), Indonesia (Netherlands), Papua New Guinea (Australia and New Zealand), and Vanuatu (Australia).

It must be noted that the material taken in colonial days often was more culturally valuable than that being taken now. Consider, for example, the taking of material in Benin by a British punitive raid in 1897 (jegede, this volume). When others sought to destroy the prestige and dignity of an African society, the objects that most symbolized its culture and that were most valued were taken. However, it has long been clear that there will be considerable reluctance to return objects to a country when other objects are continually moving out and the returns are therefore negated by further losses. For this reason, among others, the committee takes a close interest in UNESCO's efforts to stop the present illicit trade.

Arguments for and against repatriation are many. In disentangling the arguments, which are conflicting and of different levels and areas of discourse, legal arguments as to property, prescription, and retroactivity cannot be regarded as valid, since they emanate from one legal system (that of the acquirer) and can be balanced by equally valid arguments from the legal system of the despoiled country (Prott and O'Keefe 1989:830–55). By whose legal system should the taking or the present legal status of the object be judged? I disagree with Peter Schmidt that the legal issues of statutes of limitation and retroactivity are relevant factors in determining these issues. The appropriate principles for the resolution of claims for repatriation are cultural, not legal (Prott and O'Keefe 1989:863–94). The dearth of serious professional discussion and of claims over the last few years is surprising.

THE 1970 UNESCO CONVENTION

UNESCO was the first body to enact an international legal instrument to counter the illicit trade, although efforts to do so go back at least to 1919 (Prott and O'Keefe 1989:708–25). The 1970 UNESCO Convention on the Means of Prohibiting and Preventing the Illicit Import, Export, and Transfer of Ownership of Cultural Property (Prott and O'Keefe 1989:726–801; Fraoua 1986) is not free of defects. However, it does remain the only viable international instrument on the subject and has had great influence in changing public opinion on this issue.

The convention had a tortuous drafting history, which explains some of the anomalies in the text. All but two articles come from a draft prepared by the UNESCO secretariat that conformed to the rather general drafting practice of the civil law. Articles 7 and 9 were taken from an alternative draft proposed by the United States and show the much more detailed drafting style of the common law. Partly for these reasons, the convention is subject to differing interpretations. The United States, for example, in effect applies only the provisions of articles 7 and 9, subject, in the case of article 9, to a further internal procedure (an application to the U.S. Cultural Property Advisory Committee). A number of other states regard these articles only as more specific provisions to general rules spelled out in articles 3, 6, and so forth.

Whatever view one takes of the breadth of the convention, it is noteworthy that the United States has at least attempted to enforce it and has administered its implementing legislation seriously. However, I am not aware of any case where the legislation has been applied to cultural objects from Africa; the *Afo-a-Kom*, a wooden carving said to represent the spirit of the Kom people, was returned from the United States to Cameroon in 1966, before the drafting of the convention (Nkwi, this volume; Merryman and Elsen 1987:56–57). Argentina can be regarded as an importing state, for it has major collectors who buy in international markets. However, it has no export control for its own cultural heritage and I am not aware of any case where it has applied the convention to cultural property illegally exported from another state party to the convention. Australia and Canada, on the other hand, are both parties to the 1970 convention. These two countries see the problem from both sides, with collectors, including the museum community, buying abroad as well as buying sensitive indigenous and early colonial material of such great importance to their respective national cultural heritages that some of it must be kept within the country.

The attitude of other major art trading states is of interest. Switzerland,[1] long reputed to be one of the safe havens for the trading of illicitly acquired objects, announced in 1993 that it will become a party to the 1970 convention and is undertaking legislative changes to enable it to do so. The United Kingdom announced some time ago that it did not intend to become a party. Reunited Germany has not become a party, although the Democratic Republic of Germany was a party until unification. Italy, Greece, Portugal, and Spain, all countries with major problems of looting of sites and theft, are parties to the convention, but as of late 1995 no other European state has yet acceded, although the French and Dutch governments have been considering the matter closely.

It is easy to criticize the lack of enthusiasm of collector states for measures that will hamper the freedom of their citizens to acquire whatever cultural goods are on the market. However, it is notable that the majority of African countries, who have the most to gain from becoming parties to the convention, have not joined. Although Algeria, Angola, Burkina Faso, Cameroon, the Central African Republic, Côte d'Ivoire, Egypt, Guinea, Libya, Madagascar, Mali, Mauritania, Mauritius, Niger, Nigeria, Senegal, Tanzania, Tunisia, Zaïre, and Zambia are all parties to the convention, Benin, Burundi, Chad, the Congo, Equatorial Guinea, Gabon, the Gambia, Ghana, Guinea-Bissau, Kenya, Lesotho, Liberia, Malawi, Mozambique, Namibia, Rwanda, Sierra Leone, Somalia, South Africa, Sudan, Swaziland, Togo, Uganda, and Zimbabwe are not.

The reasons for market and collector states' reticence are clear and range from the profound to the venal. Many states have a firm belief in the free circulation of goods as a fundamental tenet of their economic and legal systems. To make an exception for cultural objects goes against the belief that all goods are fundamentally objects of commerce. In practice, the art trade brings in very large amounts of foreign currency in a country such as the United Kingdom, and it is the avowed aim of the British government to maintain London as the capital of the world art trade. Diligent checking of sources will limit the acquisition of dubious materials and will make the process of acquisition of legally traded material more complex and time consuming. The difficulty of being a federal state has been mentioned (although Australia, Brazil, Canada, the former Czechoslovakia, India, Mexico, Pakistan, the former Yugoslavia, and the old Soviet Union all are or have been parties with federal constitutions in force). The rights of citizens to private property, sometimes subject to constitutional guarantees, have been said to prevent a state from entering obligations that would require a government to deprive citizens of objects when their ownership would normally have been recognized by the existing legal rules of the state (e.g., acquisition of a cultural object illegally exported from another state or, in some systems, bona fide acquisition of a stolen cultural object). The argument is also made that many objects are better cared for and more secure in a collection in a wealthy state than they would be in their place of origin.

These reasons all have counterarguments. Treating cultural objects like any other object of commerce is in fact negating the practice of large parts of the community that treat them in a noncommercial way—churches, museums, and collections. Archaeologists and anthropologists see the destruction such attitudes cause to the cultural fabric of the communities with which they work. Federal states have found it possible to become parties to the convention. It is not easy, but where the will is present, solutions can generally be found for federal problems. Provided laws are publicized and applicable prospectively, there is no deprivation of property, since the objects to which the new rule applies have not yet become the property of citizens. Although Africans tend to dismiss the argument about security and care of objects as self-serving, some objects that have been returned to developing states reportedly have seriously deteriorated or have been destroyed, and others have resurfaced on the international market. If a strong stand is to be taken in the Western market, a state must show that it has proper standards of care (though these need not be exactly the same as those in wealthy Western museums).

It would not be fair to pretend that improved control over the illicit trade will not require self-denial on the part of the wealthier museums and collectors. Those who want better control must persuade these groups that self-denial is justified by portraying graphically the destruction caused by the illicit trade and confronting the many arguments used to camouflage the real incentive to refrain from international cooperation on the issue.

The reasons why African states have not joined the convention are perhaps more complex. In some states the persons most responsible for preservation of cultural property may not be fully aware of the convention and its advantages. Other countries may believe that there is little point in becoming a party when only one major market has done so. For those states that have looked more closely at the convention and its workings, there may be difficulties of professional resources. For example, in one country (not in Africa but with similar problems for its traditional communities) a lawyer examined the convention and believed that complex legislation would be necessary, although existing legislation seemed adequate in my view. After this first brief examination, the convention was laid aside in favor of more pressing and apparently less complicated matters. In such cases, UNESCO will send an expert to assist in the preparation of legislation, as happened in Gabon, for example. The problem of finding a place in the legislative agenda remains. States that have already given high national priority to the problem of illicit traffic, such as Nigeria, have also become parties to the convention. Other African states share the problem of many Western democracies: cultural legislation is very often at the bottom of the list of legislative priorities.

Although the problem of illicit traffic has received considerable attention, and the special legal issues to which it gives rise have resulted in a growing body of specialization among Western lawyers, few African lawyers possess a detailed knowledge of the field. An attorney from Nigeria and one from Swaziland have each written an article (not yet published) on the topic, and there are no doubt drafters of legislation who have had some experience with the local law, but it is not easy to find someone to state the African case and argue for the evolution of national and international law in terms persuasive to lawyers on other continents.

UNESCO gives technical assistance other than legislative expertise. For example, it publishes notices of stolen cultural property at the request of a state party and distributes it to all other signatories. Advice is also given on U.S. decisions to restrict imports of particular foreign cultural property—by late 1995, the United States had distributed five such notices pertaining to Latin American nations and only one (Mali) relating to Africa. In addition, UNESCO publishes national legislation on the protection of movable cultural heritage, covering more than seventy-five states so far. One UNESCO publication summarizes the laws of more than 140 countries regarding the export of cultural objects, and another publication explains the steps that states can take to control the illicit trade (Prott and O'Keefe 1988; Prott and O'Keefe 1983).

UNESCO also organizes regional seminars on illicit traffic in cultural objects. The first for southern African was held in Arusha, Tanzania in 1993, and followed a successful seminar, held by the International Council of Museums, "What Museums for Africa?" in Benin, Ghana, and Togo in November 1991. A major concluding conference, directed at the highest level decision-makers in sub-Saharan Africa, was held in Bamako, Mali, in October 1994. Its principal objective was to ensure that expert recommendations would be translated into government policies, thus engaging all levels of administration in the protection of national heritage items.

Many African countries lack good communication between different arms of government. For example, police in many African countries deny that illicit traffic in cultural property is a problem, while cultural administrators simultaneously claim that it is a serious one. Similarly, customs services in many of these countries regard prevention of illicit traffic in cultural property as a low priority. Likewise, if the appropriate minister is not properly briefed or is not as powerful as other ministers, the necessary legislation will receive little parliamentary time.

UNIDROIT PRELIMINARY DRAFT CONVENTION ON STOLEN OR ILLEGALLY EXPORTED CULTURAL OBJECTS

The UNESCO convention cannot deal with problems of private law, because, strictly speaking, UNESCO has no mandate in this area. Yet some crucial aspects in private law shelter the illicit trade, most notably the protection accorded in many legal systems to the bona fide purchaser. Bona fides are in many cases presumed, thereby protecting the acquirer, because the original owner of a stolen object would have to prove lack of bona fides, which is difficult. Although this principle is seen as fundamental to many legal systems, sufficient consensus existed to try to change the rule for stolen cultural objects. Even France, which enshrined this principle in its 1806 civil code, was willing to take this step in view of the terrible losses by theft from its own cultural heritage.

UNESCO understood the need for changes in private law to complement the principles of the 1970 convention. In 1984 it therefore asked the International Institute for the Unification of Private Law (UNIDROIT), based in Rome, to take up the issue of cultural heritage and private law. Chapter 2 of the UNIDROIT Convention on Stolen or Illegally Exported Cultural Objects, adopted on 24 June 1995, provides that stolen objects must be returned and that compensation will only be given where the acquirer has used a high degree of diligent inquiry. This provision is intended to alter the widely accepted practice among collectors and dealers of not rigorously checking the provenance of objects. It has been standard practice for dealers and auctioneers not to name their vendors and for buyers not to question the credentials of sellers. If buyers risk losing objects if they fail to inquire, then this practice should change, as sales are unlikely to take place unless information is given. In this respect the UNIDROIT convention should have an important impact on the flow of illegally acquired cultural objects. Although the UNIDROIT convention speaks of return, its most important contribution may be preventive. By threatening return if proper inquiries are not made, it hopes to change art market practices and make illegally trafficked goods unsaleable.

Another problem arose from the failure of many systems to apply foreign public laws, including those controlling export. Although some countries with European-style legal systems do so (Australia, Greece, Italy, New Zealand, Portugal, and Spain, all parties to the UNESCO convention), regarding cultural property, many others do not, as was shown by the refusal of the English House of Lords to order the return to New Zealand of the Taranaki panels which had been illegally exported.[2] However, a trend has recently developed of states applying mandatory foreign public laws (Prott 1989:219–317). The UNIDROIT convention has taken note of this phenomenon by providing for the return of illegally exported objects where their removal affects certain important interests, such as the physical preservation of the object or its context, the integrity of a complex object, or scientific information, provisions that clearly cover dismemberment of monuments and clandestine excavation. In addition, UNIDROIT would require the return of objects used in a living culture, a criterion that would certainly include the *Afo-a-Kom*.

The UNIDROIT convention thus deals with some of the most difficult issues remaining doubtful or unresolved after the adoption of the 1970 UNESCO convention. For the eighty-two parties to the 1970 convention, it represents a step toward greater protection of their movable cultural objects. For important market states that have expressed their support for the principles of the UNESCO convention but have not joined, the UNIDROIT convention provides an instrument for the same purpose in a form that should not present difficulties of interpretation.

Despite the obvious importance of this new draft to African states, few sent representatives to the negotiations. Nigeria and Senegal (the only African countries to join UNIDROIT), Angola, Benin, Burkina Faso, Mali, Mauritius, and Zimbabwe took part. Of course, when negotiations are held in Europe (in this case Rome, the headquarters of UNIDROIT), the expense of four separate visits over three years will considerably strain national budgets. A number of African representatives to UNIDROIT negotiations have been members of their diplomatic mission in Rome—that is, not necessarily experienced either in preservation of cultural heritage or in the legal issues related to it. While they can therefore report on the negotiations, it is hard for them to intervene and take stances on sometimes obscure areas of law. More were represented at the full diplomatic conference which adopted the text: Angola, Burkina Faso, Cameroon, Côte d'Ivoire, Gabon, Guinea, Madagascar, Mali, Mauritius, Nigeria, Senegal, South Africa, and Zambia were all present, and, among the Arab-speaking African states, Egypt, Libya, Morocco, and Tunisia. It is to be hoped that African states will support the UNIDROIT convention and that it will provide an avenue for the return of cultural property from those countries who were not party to the UNESCO convention but will join the UNIDROIT convention. So far only Burkina Faso, Guinea, and Zambia have signed.

While early indications showed that European states would be interested in the UNIDROIT convention, the situation has become a little clouded since the adoption of the Directive of the European Community on the return of cultural property within the community. All took part in the negotiations. France and Italy have signed the convention, but most of the other states abstained from voting on the final text.

A U.S. expert, John Merryman of Stanford University, participated in the group that formulated the first draft of the UNIDROIT text, and a U.S. delegation attended each of the three subsequent meetings of governmental experts that have studied and amended it. However, it is clear that the dealer community in the United States will fight hard against U.S. participation in the convention (*The Art Newspaper*, 21 September 1991, 26–29). As in the case of the U.S. acceptance of the UNESCO convention, this international instrument will not be accepted unless the U.S. archaeological and anthropological community lobbies as effectively for its views as the dealers lobby for theirs.

REGIONAL AND BILATERAL SCHEMES

Since 1983 the Commonwealth Secretariat, London, has been working on a scheme for the mutual recognition of export controls on cultural property. Many African countries are members of this body. Although all but one of the members of the Commonwealth favor the scheme, the United Kingdom has been unwilling to adopt it. Now that it has undertaken obligations toward European states in this respect, however, it may wish to reconsider its moral obligations toward Commonwealth countries. African states could only gain from such an agreement.

The United Nations Institute for the Prevention of Crime and Rehabilitation of Offenders, with the help of UNESCO, has formulated a draft model bilateral treaty on cultural heritage. Bilateral agreements also exist between the United States and El Salvador, Guatemala, Peru, and Mexico. However, except for the 1993 Mali-U.S. accord, African countries have not entered into bilateral agreements, and in view of the time and professional resources that would be needed for such negotiations, it is hardly surprising. It clearly is in the interest of African states to use a multilateral procedure where possible.

INTERNATIONAL COOPERATION

Beyond and beside the legal instruments in force there are networks for international cooperation. Interpol issues notices of stolen cultural objects for constituent national police forces. However, the vast majority of requests for this kind of assistance are from European states, although most African states are members of the Interpol system. UNESCO likewise issues notices of stolen cultural objects for members of the 1970 convention and forwards them to other states party to it. Of the twenty-four notices issued by UNESCO to 1995, only one was for an African country (objects stolen from the Museum of Jos, Nigeria) although another (also for Nigeria) is in preparation. One of these items was subsequently located in Switzerland, seized by the Swiss police, and ultimately returned to Nigeria (LaGamma, this volume).

The International Foundation for Art Research, in New York, keeps a database of stolen cultural property and shares its information with the London-based Art Loss Register. These registers should be searched by prospective buyers; the UNIDROIT draft provides that unless such a search is made, compensation will not be paid to an acquirer who has had to return a stolen cultural object. However, this system will not work for African countries unless they report their losses and can provide detailed information and photographs to enable identification.

Annex 11 of the Customs Cooperation Council's 1977 International Convention on Mutual Assistance for the Prevention, Investigation, and Repression of Customs Offences foresees assistance in the control of smuggling of works of art, antiques, and other cultural property. However, it is not known how much use has been made of this provision by African countries.

Although the United Kingdom is not party to the 1970 UNESCO convention, on April 1, 1984, its major dealers and auction houses adopted a Code of Practice for the Control of International Trading in Works of Art, based on the principles of that convention. However, this action does not offer a great deal of comfort to African states because foreign states cannot invoke the code the same way they can invoke obligations under an international convention or a bilateral treaty, although breaches of the code could be exploited in the media to create shame, as McIntosh proposes (this volume). There have, in any event, been several controversies over the administration of the code (Prott and O'Keefe 1989:553–54).

The code resembles a gentlemen's agreement and is administered in the United Kingdom by a committee representing the signatories. The Confédération Internationale des Négociants en Oeuvres d'Art has adopted the same code, adapted where necessary, but it is not clear whether controversial cases have been discussed and whether there is an effort to police its application.

Most importantly the International Council of Museums adopted a code of ethics in 1986 that includes the following statements in article 3(a):

> Museums should recognize the relationship between the marketplace and the initial and often destructive taking of an object for the commercial market, and must recognize that it is highly unethical for a museum to support in any way, whether directly or indirectly, that illicit market.
>
> A museum should not acquire, whether by purchase, gift, bequest, or exchange, any object unless the governing body and responsible officer are satisfied that the museum can acquire a valid title to the specimen or object in question and that in particular it has not been acquired in, or exported from, its country of origin and/or any intermediate country in which it may have been legally owned (including the museum's own country) in violation of that country's laws.

A number of important museums in Australia, New Zealand, the United Kingdom, and the United States have adopted acquisitions policies in line with this code.

INTERNAL AND REGIONAL COOPERATION

Much could be done to strengthen internal and regional cooperation between African countries. Although such cooperation could already be organized through the UNESCO convention, not all the African states whose cooperation would be necessary are parties to it. It is evident that there are some regional hubs through which virtually all the illicit traffic of neighboring countries passes. Regional cooperation of police and customs services is not well organized to enforce the export control laws of neighboring states, in stark contrast to the Directive of the European Community, in which fifteen states have agreed to return illegally exported cultural objects from other community states.

DEFECTS IN SYSTEMS OF PREVENTION AND RETURN

In addition to the gaps in national legislative protection, in coordination of national police, customs, and cultural services, in regional cooperation, and in international participation, the biggest single problem for return of cultural property (and hence for deterring buyers from acquiring illegally traded objects) is the lack of adequate identification. Where return procedures exist for stolen cultural goods, precise identification is essential. Returning an object requires a clear description in terms that make identification possible (dimensions, material of composition, color, character, any distinguishing features such as damage or markings) as well as good photographs, preferably from several angles. The return of the object to Jos was possible because these elements were present. But not all museums in Africa are properly inventoried. And what about objects held in villages? There are several important facts to recall here. A special procedure under the U.S. Cultural Property Implementation Act (PL 97-446) applies to cultural property stolen from a museum or a religious or secular public monument or similar institution provided that such property is documented as appertaining to the inventory of that institution. There will clearly be many cases where important cultural objects in Africa are not in an institution and many where they are not inventoried.

Of course, legal actions regarding theft occur in most jurisdictions. But to succeed in such an action, the claimant must prove that the object in the hands of the defendant is the same piece that was stolen, often a difficult proposition. In a case in the English courts, for example, the Indian government brought evidence of the style of an idol, its metallurgical composition, and even the termite tracks over its surface to prove that it was the missing idol from a suite of twelve excavated illegally at the same time.[3] The New Zealand government was able to provide identity through a photograph showing a spademark on a set of carvings it claimed.[4] Both objects had been accompanied by fictional documents of provenance.

The difficulties of proving identity have suggested to many states the possibility of avoiding the problem by claiming return because of illicit export. If all categories of a certain object—for example, all antiquities—are subject to export control, and the object is found in another country without an export license, then it should be possible to claim it. There are two problems with this solution. First, most countries, except those party to the 1970 UNESCO convention, do not enforce the export controls of other states. Second, because it is usually not possible to discover the date of illicit export, the acquirer will always claim that it was exported before the date of the legislation, and because the burden of proof is on the claimant, such claims are generally difficult to conclude.

These problems are compounded for the objects produced by clandestine excavation. Almost certainly they have not been catalogued (though the case of theft from legal excavations should not be overlooked). In such a case it becomes impossible to identify the object as having been illegally exported from the claimant state since the date of controlling legislation. In a Canadian case the judge held that there was no evidence that the Nok sculpture concerned had been exported since the date of imposition of export control, even though export control had existed since 1924 and the remains of the Nok culture had not been discovered until 1943.[5]

The United States has provided in its legislation and practice for the imposition of import restrictions on archaeological and ethnological materials when the cultural heritage of the country concerned is in jeopardy from pillage. This procedure has been applied in many cases, but the only one in Africa has been in Mali (Papageorge Kouroupas, this volume). In general, the import restrictions have been applied to specific materials from specific areas, such as cultural artifacts from the southwest region of El Salvador; antique textiles from Coroma, Bolivia; Moche artifacts from the Sipan archaeological areas of Peru; and so on. (In 1995 the United States and El Salvador concluded the first comprehensive, countrywide ban on the import of pre-Columbian objects.) The government of the country concerned must apply, but many states do not have the expertise and the resources to prepare a detailed dossier that the committee would find overwhelming. Of course, countries can receive help from professionals from other states who understand the culture concerned, the deprivations caused by illicit traffic, and the U.S. role in this situation. But the requirements of the U.S. legislation are very much like the standard form and guidelines for its completion prepared by the Intergovernmental Committee for Promoting the Return of Cultural Property to Its Countries of Origin or Its Restitution in Case of Illicit Appropriation—the bureaucratic procedures required are sufficiently daunting to discourage those who want to have objects returned.

What can be done? The single most significant action would be a massive program of inventories. Museums have the programs and the personnel, but generally not in sufficient numbers in Africa. Consequently, the Western museum community must assist local programs and train more African professionals in inventory techniques; and volunteers, amateurs, students, and whatever other resources are available will be needed to photograph as much material as possible.

There is no reason why cultural property must be kept in institutions, unless of course that is the considered choice of the Africans themselves. In Papua New Guinea, for example, there is a register of national treasures, which includes important objects kept in the villages. Museum staff from Port Moresby has embarked on field trips into the most remote areas, cataloguing and photographing important ethnological and artistic items. The village people keep the objects as long as they are in use or are believed necessary to the life of the people, but it is explained to them how important the object is and that it cannot be sold or given away except to the national museum. Sadly, the museum staff once found itself following a dealer delivering a different message (fortunately, in this case, without success). If the villagers no longer want the responsibility of the object, then the museum takes it into its care. But proper care in the museum also depends on having enough well-trained professional staff to catalogue and conserve it and on having good museum security.

For the problem of clandestine excavation there is no easy solution. The new UNIDROIT Convention on Stolen or Illegally Exported Cultural Objects provides that clandestinely excavated objects be treated as stolen. However, proving the identity, origin, and date of illegal excavation remains difficult and it may still be easier to proceed under the provisions of illegal export since proof of illegal export (absence of an application for permission to export) may be easier.

Because the legal tracking of such objects is so difficult and so rarely successful, the best hope of minimizing the loss of illegally excavated material is a wide-ranging educational campaign and the promotion of ethical acquisition policies. In this respect, the best weapon is that of media investigation and exposure utilizing the social pressure of shame. Brent and McIntosh (this volume) provide good examples of the effectiveness of such pressure. A Swiss group of volunteers for aid to Third World countries has investigated and published (the Declaration of Berne) and continues to bring to public notice the involvement of dealers in Switzerland in the trade and has been instrumental in the Swiss government's decision to become party to the 1970 UNESCO convention. Of course, where archaeological resources are known, as much inventory work should be done as is possible.

DEVELOPMENT OF THE LAW

Much has yet to be done to create a satisfactory framework for the protection of the cultural heritage of the developing countries. The outlines, however, exist. Article 1 of the UNESCO Declaration of the Principles of International Cultural Cooperation of 1966 provides that each culture has a dignity and value that must be respected and preserved, and every people has the right and the duty to develop its culture. Article 7 reads "Cultural co-operation shall be carried on for the mutual benefit of all the nations practicing it. Exchanges to which it gives rise shall be arranged in a spirit of broad reciprocity." It is clear that previous exchanges have been overwhelmingly against the interests of African states, which not only have lost the most significant parts of their heritage but also have not often been exposed to the artistic accomplishments of other cultures. H. Abranches (1983) comments, for example, that in the whole of black Africa it is impossible to find a single museum of Asian art, a good gallery of modern impressionism, or any collection of Greek sculpture, Aztec pottery, or Slav silverware.

Further arguments can be derived from a number of other international legal instruments, such as the 1966 United Nations Covenant on Economic, Social, and Cultural Rights (Prott 1988), but none of these documents will be of much use unless the legal infrastructure is also put into order in the state of origin. For example, the 1956 UNESCO Recommendation on International Principles Applicable to Archaeological Excavations has many provisions on the management of archaeological resources, including the declaration of state ownership of the archaeological subsoil, but many states have not yet implemented them. Other UNESCO instruments are also applicable, but again, participation by African states is below the norm.

In 1981 the Organization of African Unity adopted the Banjul Charter on Human and Peoples' Rights, which includes the right to develop a culture (article 22.1), also mentioned in the UNESCO Declaration of the Principles of International Cultural Cooperation (article 15.1.c). The Universal Declaration of the Rights of Peoples, a nongovernmental statement put together at a conference at Algiers in 1976, went much further and provided for a right to respect for cultural identity (article 2); the right of minority peoples to respect for identity, traditions, language, and cultural heritage (article 19); the right of a people to its own artistic, historical, and cultural wealth (article 14); and the right of a people not to have an alien culture imposed upon it (article 15). These latter formulations have not been adopted in any legal instrument. It is clear that the development of culture, in building on its own traditions, must have some access to the best of that tradition: the preservation of an essential core of a cultural heritage within the country is essential to that development. Much needs to be done to spell out the content of cultural rights, which are only sketchily described in existing legal documents (Prott 1988).

However, I do not agree with Schmidt that human-rights issues have become "lost in a plethora of procedures." This view ignores the debate that has emerged about peoples' rights within UNESCO and the hostility expressed by predominantly Western human-rights scholars to proclamations of broad statements of rights without the establishment of corresponding procedures (Brownlie 1988:14–15). Such antagonism results partly from thoroughgoing skepticism about the effectiveness and lack of precision of such general statements and also from the important division between claims for rights (moral rights) and established rights (legal rights). If the claim for a right is assumed to create a legal right, there is danger that an expansive principle will be regarded as established in law and that the hard process of defining the right, locating the agent to ensure its observance, and establishing remedies for its breach will not be undertaken. "No right without a remedy," an old saw of English common law, had sound reasoning behind it. It follows that Ronald Cohen's analysis (1993) of the way that human rights emerge, on which Schmidt bases his study, may be regarded as accurate in political science or moral philosophy, but has dangers when misread as legal analysis.

I have tried to show elsewhere (Prott 1988) the variety of possible interpretations of formulations of cultural rights in the African charter and elsewhere. Work should not cease on adequately formulating cultural rights, but developments must occur on the procedural side if a right is to have any practical effect. It is not realistic to expect that the proclamation of a human right to heritage will immediately, or even in the short term, affect the illicit trade. In view of the lack of use of the Intergovernmental Committee for Promoting the Return of Cultural Property to Its Countries of Origin or Its Restitution in Case of Illicit Appropriation, despite its considerable political profile at its establishment, African states are unlikely to complain of breach of human rights against European states regarding illicit traffic in cultural goods. The dealer lobby is extremely influential in the European states, and many African states depend on aid programs financed by those countries.

CONCLUSION

How can we take the heat out of the international market for African cultural objects? We can deter by ensuring that purchasers check provenance, and that if they do not, they will have to return the object without compensation (UNIDROIT). We can deter by encouraging multilateral agreements to respect other cultural heritages and provide procedures for return (UNESCO convention, UNIDROIT) and by lobbying hard to have them accepted by wealthy collecting countries. We can encourage African states to become parties to the UNESCO convention and, in due course, to the UNIDROIT convention. We can educate the market in wealthy countries by every means available, especially the media, about the cost to states of origin of their collecting passion. We can encourage self-denying ordinances, such as the International Council of Museums Code of Ethics, and ethical acquisition policies for museums in wealthy countries. We can donate time and resources to assist African states with inventories, conservation, applications under existing procedures, and museum security. We can assist African states in educating their peoples about the need to retain cultural property. And we can assist African countries in training enforcement officers and in coordinating national and regional action.

NOTES

1. Switzerland has been implicated in many well-known cases, such as *Attorney General of New Zealand v. Ortiz* ([1982] 1 Q.B. 149; [1982] 3 W.L.R. 571 (CA); [1983] 2 W.L.R. 809 (H.L.) [England]) in which Maori carvings from New Zealand were held by a collector in Switzerland; *Autocephalous Greek Orthodox Church of Cyprus and the Republic of Cyprus v. Goldberg and Feldman Fine Arts, Inc.* (717 F.Supp. 1374 [1989] aff'd 917 F.2d 278 [1990]), in which mosaics stolen from Kanakaria in northern Cyprus appeared at the free port of Geneva; and the case of the artifact stolen from the Jos Museum, Nigeria, found when offered for auction in Switzerland (LaGamma, this volume).

2. *Attorney General of New Zealand v. Ortiz*, see note 1.

3. *Union of India v. Bumper Development Corporation* (unreported decision, Q.B.D. 17 February 1988) (England).

4. *Attorney General of New Zealand v. Ortiz*, see note 1.

5. *R. v. Heller* (1983) 27 Alta. L.R.(2d 346); (1984) 51 A.R. 73 (Q.B.) (Canada).

REFERENCES

Abranches, H. *Report on the Situation in Africa* (UNESCO Doc. CLT83/CONF.216/3, 1983. Report to the Intergovernmental Committee for Promoting the Return of Cultural Property to Its Countries of Origin or Its Restitution in Case of Illicit Appropriation).

Brownlie, I. "The Rights of Peoples in Modern International Law." In *The Rights of Peoples,* edited by J. Crawford, 1, 14–15. Oxford: Clarendon Press, 1988.

Cohen, R. "Endless Teardrops: Prolegomena to the Study of Human Rights in Africa." In *Human Rights and Governance in Africa,* ed. R. Cohen, G. Hyden, and W. Nagan, 3–38. Gainsville: University Presses of Florida and Center for African Studies, 1993.

Eyo, E. "A Threat to National Art Treasures: The Illicit Traffic in Stolen Art." In *The Challenge to Our Cultural Heritage: Why Preserve the Past?* ed. Y. R. Isar. Paris: UNESCO, 1986.

Fraoua, R. "Convention concernant les mesures à prendre pour interdire et empêcher l'importation, l'exportation, et le transfert de propriété illicites des biens culturels." UNESCO Doc. CC-86/WS/40, 1986.

Merryman, J. H., and A. E. Elsen. *Law, Ethics, and the Visual Arts,* 56–57. Philadelphia: University of Pennsylvania Press, 1987.

Myles, K. "The Needs and Problems of a Particular Country—Ghana." In *Lost Heritage,* edited by I. Staunton and M. McCartney, 15. London: Commonwealth Arts Association, 1981.

Nagan, Winston. "The African Human Rights Process: A Contextual Policy-Oriented Approach." In *Human Rights and Governance in Africa*, eds. R. Cohen, G. Hyden, and W. Nagan, 87–108. University Presses of Florida and Center for African Studies, 1993.

Prott, L. V. "Problems of Private International Law for the Protection of the Cultural Heritage." In *Recueil des cours de l'académic de droit international de La Haye.* 217, 1989.

———. "Cultural Rights as Peoples' Rights in International Law." In *The Rights of Peoples*, ed. J. Crawford, 93–106. Oxford: Clarendon Press, 1988.

Prott, L. V., and P. J. O'Keefe. National Control of Illicit Traffic in Cultural Property. UNESCO Doc. CLT-83/WS/16, 1983.

———. *Handbook of National Regulations Concerning the Export of Cultural Property.* Paris: UNESCO, 1988.

———. *Law and the Cultural Heritage: Vol. III—Movement.* London: Butterworths, 1989.

Staunton, I., and M. McCartney, eds. *Lost Heritage.* Report of the Symposium on the Return of Cultural Property. 21 May 1981. London: Commonwealth Arts Association, 1981.

4

JUST SAY SHAME

EXCISING THE ROT OF CULTURAL GENOCIDE

RODERICK J. MCINTOSH

Just how should an archaeologist respond to the truly horrific destruction of historical and scientific data? Just how bad must things become before one resorts to personal violence, or the discipline rises up into collective violence? What other, more constructive steps can be taken? The illicit commerce in African art and antiquities is, increasingly, horror in the making. One of the contributors to this volume, Michel Brent, has exposed the particularly nightmarish case of the looted ancient terra-cotta and metal arts of the Middle Niger of Mali (Brent 1993, 1994a, 1994b). This essay[1] will focus on recent events in the commerce in Malian antiquities as illustrative of some of the problems—and reasons for cautious hope—that are just now appearing in other domains of African art and antiquities.

Five years ago there was very little cause for optimism. The looting of sites providing these terra-cottas and the growth of the international market in which these pieces circulated appeared to continue on the geometric if not exponential course they had assumed since the late 1960s or early 1970s. However, a series of shaming episodes (and a good deal of steady effort by academics and others resolved to take action) has checked if not reversed this pessimism.

One of these shaming episodes has come to be called the Dutch chainsaw massacre. This episode has affected almost every tier of the looting network and so helps in understanding the structure of that network. Most importantly, this episode shows the effects of exposure to public scorn on the complicitous. The purpose of this contribution is not to make yet another restatement of the academic argument that pillaged pieces, even if later displayed in museums for scholars to study, are by the very act of removal from archaeological sites rendered of negligible knowledge value. I take it as a given, with Paul Bator, that

> an antiquity without a provenance—even if perfectly preserved—is of limited historical significance; if we do not know where it came from, it can provide only limited scientific knowledge of the past. The preservation of archaeological evidence thus requires not only that objects as such be protected from destruction or mutilation, but, further, an opportunity to study and record exactly where and how each object was buried and how it related to other objects. (Bator 1983:25)

I take this statement as a point of departure for the true purpose of what follows here: to argue that collectors' and traffickers' protestations that their actions save art from destruction from the elements and contribute to spreading widely the knowledge of other peoples are just so much cynical camouflage for a conspiracy to pillage a country's heritage for profit.

Similarly, I will not review the history of Western collectors' interest in African art (see, among others, Steiner 1994:4–7), nor of intellectual fashions in the analysis of that art (Steiner 1994:11–144). Rather, you will see my reason for guarded optimism as we trace the responses and ramifications that broke like ripples over the smooth pond of complicitous silence in the collecting and art scholarship world following the television showing of a single shaming documentary film. You will see why I feel that all those of good faith who are truly horrified by this insult to science and to national heritage can coordinate in effective action— armed with the trowel, the pen, or even the chain saw—under the banner of "JUST SAY SHAME."

The title, of course, is a play on the failed anti-drug slogan of the Reagan-Bush years. The international structure of the illicit art trade and the illicit drug trade are remarkably similar (McIntosh, Togola, and McIntosh 1996). But the "Just Say No" campaign was destined to fail because far too many drug consumers and drug traffickers lived so wretchedly that they had nothing to lose if caught by the authorities. In the case of the art market, consumers and those who service the traffic have a great deal to lose—vast sums of money and their good names. Sidibé (this volume) speaks to the heart of the argument of using public exposure to shame to diminish the illicit traffic in antiquities. He quite correctly states that such commerce is built upon a foundation of secretive trust (and of warped honor) among thieves. Shame erodes trust, which is why the behavior of almost every actor in the present market can be changed by shaming arguments—and by shame's obverse, pride.

But before moving on to the Dutch chainsaw massacre, I will relate how bad the Middle Niger cultural genocide had become—so bad that I almost resorted to violence.

A CLOSE CALL FOR ENTWISTLE'S WINDOWS

Before 1977, scores, hundreds, perhaps even thousands of terra-cottas had been looted from archaeological sites near the historic Malian town of Jenne. Not one had come from a scientifically excavated and dated context. Art historical studies of style, vague oral traditions, and a series of some 240 highly problematic thermo-luminescence dates generated some consensus among art historians that these objects dated largely from the fifteenth through eighteenth centuries; few, if any, came from earlier than the fourteen century (de Grunne 1980:26–27, 52; Nesmith 1984:64; Stoneham 1980:282).

Susan Keech McIntosh and I conducted the first excavations at the site of Jenne-jeno in 1977 (McIntosh and McIntosh 1979, 1980). In a unit named Mound 2, a terra-cotta and a suite of associated ceramics had been built into the floor of a

structure. The walls of this house or place of ceremony were purposefully collapsed and the building abandoned. Charcoal, probably from a short-lived shrub,
was incorporated into the floor nearby and was radiocarbon dated to between the
eleventh and late thirteenth centuries. We realized the importance of having a
Middle Niger terra-cotta in dated, controlled context, so we published the find
in *African Arts* (McIntosh and McIntosh 1979) before the site report appeared. The
radiocarbon dates for the site had not yet been published or communicated in any
form, but when my complimentary copy of the journal arrived, the back cover
bore an advertisement for a Middle Niger terra-cotta, offered by Entwistle's gallery in London. The piece for sale was described as follows: "This important
twelfth-century terra-cotta sculpture of an ancestral couple was excavated in the
Djenne district of Mali, West Africa."

I was enraged by the implications that would be clear to anyone with even
passing interest in this art. Readers would think that either we had colluded with
the London dealer to boost the value of the advertised piece (and there was some
correspondence on this point in a later issue of *African Arts*),[2] or the journal editors had divulged this information to one of their long-standing advertisers. I believe the latter was the case. I was so enraged that I cycled to the Cambridge
railway station, bought a ticket for London, and was halfway there before my resolve to throw a brick through Entwistle's shop window wavered.

TERRA-COTTAS AND THE ANCIENT MIDDLE NIGER SOCIETIES

For some time after this incident I could not abide the thought of art historians. In
my mind, and quite unfairly, art historians were little better than the journals,
such as *African Arts*, in which they published. Furthermore, Mali was doing very
little to stop the looting of archaeological sites. The wife of then President Musa
Traoré and her brother, the head of Douane, were deeply implicated by rumor in
the export of this art out of the country (Leveau 1994:78). Art dealers in Brussels,
Paris, and New York and auction houses such as Sotheby's were openly dealing in
this art. Prices rose incredibly: by rumor, a piece that would have fetched $7,000 to
$8,000 in the mid-1970s could command a price in the low hundreds of thousands
by the mid-1980s. It seemed that no one in Mali or in the West cared about the
situation except for a few apoplectic archaeologists. The situation was one of abid-
ing pessimism. But I realize now that, already, things were beginning to change in
Mali, within the discipline of art history, and within the very structure of the art
market. To understand how these changes have become the source, now, of my
guarded optimism, let me briefly digress to the historical and archaeological
processes that gave birth to these Middle Niger terra-cottas (McIntosh 1989, 1992;
McIntosh and McIntosh 1986, 1988; S. K. McIntosh 1995).

Until the later 1970s, we were utterly ignorant of the context and dates of this
art. We were ignorant also of the communities that produced it. We now realize
that long-distance trade and urbanism began a thousand years earlier than previous historical wisdom had accepted. Indeed, the floodplain of the Middle Niger is
now considered home to one of the world's great, indigenous, and underived

urban civilizations. One of these cities, Jenne (including ancestral Jenne-jeno), is on the UNESCO list of major World Heritage sites.

The terra-cottas have been important to understanding the social and political evolution of this extinct Middle Niger society. The art has given society three dimensions. We as yet do not know much about the rituals, religion, and belief system in which the terra-cottas functioned.[3] That information will come as the context of more pieces is discovered. But the very variety of forms and locations of the terra-cottas suggests that the religion was not a monolithic state cult with a restricted pantheon of gods and in which production of sacred art was jealously guarded by a despot.

Theories about the origins of preindustrial cities in the Old World predict the presence of just such a despot and just such a state cult (McIntosh 1991a). The city is not so much a place as a revolution. In this view, the city is an appendage of a coercive state, itself the culmination of a long evolution of centralized political control over a highly stratified population. The city is home to the elite. But what about Middle Niger cities, where there is as yet little evidence of a stratification by wealth or prestige and less still of despotic control mechanisms? Jenne-jeno had a stable settlement (prospering for a millennium and a half) with a large population (probably between fifteen and fifty thousand), providing services and manufacturing for an economically integrated hinterland. Jenne-jeno satisfies the classic definition of a preindustrial city—less the despot.

We must, of course, create an alternative hypothesis to the vertical-control, coercive model. Art joins a cluster of other archaeological evidence, all circumstantial, to be sure. These data suggest that the Middle Niger urban population was highly stratified horizontally but not under the thumb of a despot. By A.D. 800 (to take an arbitrary date) multiple craft and production groups or corporations had evolved over almost a millennium. Burial practices exploded, reinforcing the impression of a highly complex society. The cities themselves lack temples, citadels, palaces—those monuments to an ideology of permanency of an entrenched elite. The cities are clusters of mounds that most likely housed separate occupation specialists. Art in its variety of contexts and forms reinforces the view of urban heterogeneity.

In fact, art constitutes a major prop for the hypothesis that urbanism at places like Jenne-jeno represents a long, indigenous history of specialization and segmentation of a population with multiple, competing, overlapping, and in some senses mutually overriding claims to authority. But dates and contexts are known for just a fraction of the terra-cottas claimed to have a Middle Niger provenance.

When the whole corpus of Middle Niger terra-cottas is inserted into the equation of social and political evolution, the conclusion of explosive social variability is almost inescapable. The Middle Niger terra-cottas appear to assist social cohesion and consensus-making in ways similar to those found by Hays (1993:81, 88), who looks cross-culturally at explosions of art in societies undergoing dramatic aggregation and horizontal complexity but remaining bereft of vertical-control hierarchies. This art apparently burgeoned at about the time Islam penetrated the Sahel. Does this represent a reaction of traditionalists against an intrusive, exclusionary religion that would prohibit not just representations of humans but of the very gods these terra-cottas may depict? Or, as was the case in several West African masking traditions, did the initial days of syncretistic Islam stimulate a wealth of representational art? Do the horsemen, which some art historians claim date to the end of this tradition, depict a cavalry-bred elite coincident with the great second millennium imperial states of Mali and Songhai (Bathily 1989; Brooks 1993)?

And what of geographical variability? The majority of the looted pieces are claimed to be from the Jenne-Mopti region and, indeed, most documented looting has taken place there. But looted pieces in related styles are reported from the Macina (near Ténékou) and the Guimbala (Erg de Bara, north of Lake Débo). Some have come from the habitation mounds and tumuli of the lakes region, including many bronzes in a parallel style (Nesmith 1984). How were these objects related to the terra-cottas in the aesthetic and belief systems? There is a wealth of other painted symbols in pots, art in appliqué, and even phalli. Without the context that allows the relation of these pieces to the terra-cottas in time and space, we just do not know their connection. That relationship is presumably the key to an eventual interpretation of the beliefs about the sacred world and codes of aesthetics of this extinct society.

The ring of questions could expand almost infinitely. What about the similarities of this art with that of the so-called Sao region of the southern Lake Chad plain, contemporaneous but fifteen hundred kilometers to the east? And what of the similarities of some pieces from Jenne-jeno with Nok heads—in this case at a very great temporal remove? As long as the only source of this art is butchered sites, we will never know. True, there are those who still offer the bankrupt argument that looted, context-bereft art can still provide knowledge to scholars. But this argument becomes significantly less defensible with the evidence from the more voluminous market in pre-Columbian antiquities that scholarly use of illicit art means tacitly justifying the means by which the pieces are obtained and demonstrably contributes to acts of thievery (see Alexander 1990; Coe 1993).

As long as antiquities are removed for profit, with no regard for the knowledge about the producing society that they can provide, these questions cannot be answered. The problem is gargantuan. The best pieces fetch obscene prices. Vast sums change hands at the upper (import country) tiers of the market. Yet only derisory sums trickle into the local economy in exchange for this massive destruction of local and national heritage. The danger for archaeology is immediate. Once a site has been looted, the original context cannot be reconstructed, even that of the data (such as animal bones, potsherds, hearths, and house walls) left behind. In some areas of the Middle Niger, as Sidibé estimates (this volume), 80 to 90 percent of the sites have some evidence of looting.[4] There is immediate danger of losing primary data concerning this original urban civilization before really even beginning to investigate it.

Even for the most callous academic art historian (who otherwise could not be bothered with the animal bones, or the political life of the artists), the art available on the market must be viewed as a miserable sample of ancient Middle Niger art. (Surely even that art historian feels a responsibility to the society's aesthetic corpus as a whole.) The looted art on display in museums or in touring private collections represents a cull of the "best." But who is doing the culling? The majority of legitimate archaeological pieces from sites such as Jenne-jeno are headless or separated heads. Yet museums and private collections are filled with whole statuettes. These tend to be better made and probably conform to someone else's standards of high art—or perhaps to standards of salable art (for a discussion of how dealers and collectors manipulate the aesthetic and commodity value of African art, see Steiner 1994:13, 158–64). One can imagine dealers' difficulties when they try to unload onto most European or American collectors some of the crude, seemingly haphazardly made, and filth-covered statuettes that serve important ritual purposes in Malian ethnographic situations, such as the *boli* of Bamana Komo cults. I suspect that animals, indeterminate subjects, and geometric and abstract symbols are underrepresented in terra-cotta.

THE DUTCH CHAINSAW MASSACRE

Even the best, museum-quality pieces are culled so that a controlled number circulate through the market in a manipulated flow, thus maintaining demand and even increasing that demand, and hence prices. The view that dealers and collectors have constructed a market for profit and that all other values are expendable is a basic premise of *The African King* (1990).

"Massacre" is the academic community's (gleeful) verdict on the international fallout from the documentary film *The African King*, by the Utrecht social anthropologist Walter Van Beek, which was shown on British and Dutch television to devastating effect. This film is not a unique instance of action taken against the illicit art trade—indeed, it is just one of several—but it bloodied several tiers of the market and, therefore, is useful in understanding the structure of the market and the vulnerability to shame of those who occupy those various tiers.

Van Beek contrasts the self-satisfied, naked acquisitiveness of the cultural elite from the nations that import objects with the pillage of Jenne-region archaeological sites, repositories of a national heritage. The European apologists for the trade recorded on this film, the collectors and dealers, the museum directors and laboratory scientists, are interchangeable with their American or Japanese counterparts. The art really could just as easily be pieces looted from Bali, Copan, or the Agora.

In keeping with the chainsaw imagery, the art market might be seen as a tree. Healthy, this tree would represent the vital cultural heritage of the people of Mali. Ancient art is integral to the structure of that tree, because knowledge by the peoples of Mali of their artistic heritage serves, in Bator's terms, as a mirror of their inner consciousness, "intimately tied to the existence and awareness of a sense of community" (1983:28). This splendid corpus of ancient art enables Malians to demonstrate that they are the inheritors of an urban civilization on a par with those of contemporary Mesoamerica or the early first millennium B.C. Aegean.

However, the tree is rotting in several places. Figure 4-1 shows the places of infestation, indicating the participants in the illicit commerce in Malian antiquities.[5]

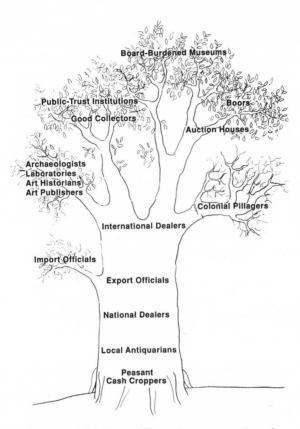

Figure 4-1. The "Tree of Shame," a representation of
the rot that has infested the illicit commerce in Malian
artifacts. Each infestation is labeled with the names of
participants in the illicit trade.

Whether their role is direct or indirect, all participants in the antiquities market
take part in cultural genocide. Each was exposed, in one form or another, by *The
African King*. With characteristic good humor, Van Beek has kindly consented to
his depiction as a wood nymph who will eradicate the disease.

The film shows how rot infests the entire tree. Where that art should be most
visible and accessible to the public, the tree wears a crown of withered leaves. The
pollution is caused by museums swayed from their public-trust mission by manipulated boards and, especially, by the collectors-for-profit and power whom
Jaime Litvak King devastatingly describes as "destructive, snobbish, tax-haven-
seeking boors" (1989:207). Let there be no doubt about the fundamental values of
the boors. Collecting art in the international arena has always involved showing
power—personal and national—over others. Many self-justificatory statements
by the collectors and Western dealers in *The African King* show this indisputably
to be the case. It will come as no surprise that a major collector, Michel Leveau of
the Dapper Foundation in Paris, uses rank nationalism to justify buying certifi-

Figure 4-2. The wood nymph (Professor Van Beek, who produced the film *The African King*) cutting down the "Tree of Shame."

ably looted Malian (ex–Afrique Occidentale Française) antiquities, "Pour éviter que cette collection ne parte, elle aussi, pour les Etats-Unis"[6] (1994:78). This is a variation on the theme of "we stole it, so it belongs to us."[7] Those collectors are serviced by the rotten boughs of the art market, the international auction houses and the international dealers, particularly those fronted by private galleries in Brussels, Paris, and London. The rotten boughs prop up one another: one of the most prominent collectors, Count Baudouin de Grunne of Belgium, is the father of the former director of the tribal arts division of Sotheby's, Bernard de Grunne. But that very interconnectedness makes these players in the sad drama of Mali's looted heritage that much more vulnerable to tarnished reputation, leading to loss of prestige and credibility when one of their coconspirators is shown to have engaged in shameful behavior.

The film devastates the other supports to the trade: the scientist adding value to looted pieces by dating or authenticating them, import and export country officials who allow the trade to flourish under their noses, and the dealers and antiquarians at the source. *The African King*, as a vehicle of shame, and other recent shaming incidents have in a very real sense begun to excise the rot. The lesson is twofold. First, the rot is so pervasive and the tree's boughs are so interwoven that anyone having any contact with the pillaged art, however fleeting or disinterested, must be aware that his or her actions may have unintended consequences. Second, all those profiting and gaining power from art are legally and morally vulnerable. Shame has already had an effect that I never would have predicted, even five years ago.

ROT AT ALL TIERS

Middle Niger terra-cottas have been removed to Europe in quantity for many decades. Indeed, oral tradition in Jenne claims that the process began at the first moment of colonial penetration in 1893.[8] According to oral tradition, the first official decree of the commander of the French forces, Col. Archinard, was to gather together all the town's elders in front of the mosque. They were required to surrender all terra-cotta statuettes in their families' possession—and the figures promptly disappeared. Apocryphal or not, the story shows that, in the minds of locals, the looting is not a recent phenomenon and that it is indubitably associated with the Western presence in their town. Indeed, hundreds of statuettes probably traveled to Europe as colonial perks, hence the depiction of a branch called colonial pillagers. This branch is withered and atrophied due to the end of colonialism. It has not fallen off entirely because of the repatriations claims outstanding for much African art exported during the colonial period.

This art as an inflation-proof, gilt-edged investment is a relatively recent development. This is the domain of the boors, who generally have no interest in the art as art or who may have begun with curiosity about the art but were soon perverted by the monetary inflation of their collection's worth and by the thrill of power over others (in this case, over a whole sovereign nation) by the act of acquisition. One sees a perfect illustration of this in the case of the collector de Grunne in *The African King*. His collection was the world's largest, but it began not for love of the terra-cottas but purely by chance as part of an exchange for a Cameroonian mask (see Brent 1994b:28–29). As de Grunne states during his interview in that film, "Collection is an investment."

Intimately linked with the boors are board-burdened museums. Particularly in the United States, the trash-bond decade of the 1980s saw many museums taken over by business people, who see their mission as running the museum solely as a business, with acquisitions as investments and power as their bottom line. These changes in the philosophy of running museums affected art and antiquities prices and accession policies across the board. Michael Coe's description of the pre-Columbian situation beginning in the 1960s applies perfectly to Africa. "The marketplace underwent a profound change due, on the one hand, to a quantum jump in the commercial exploitation of archaeological remains in the Maya area, and on the other, to a cabal of collectors and art appraisers who began to abuse the U.S. tax laws regarding charitable donations to educational institutions" (1993:272). To the directors of these board-burdened museums, arguments of responsibility to the public trust or curation of world heritage are alien. In the Dutch version of the film, a director of a Dutch museum argues that he must acquire Malian terra-cottas because everyone else is doing so. In other words, commodities become inflation-proof investments when everyone wants them.

The boors and board-burdened museums are out on a limb that deserves to whither like the denuded colonial pillagers branch nearby. Since the screening of *The African King*, and, I believe, in part because of the publicity of the film, things became too hot for de Grunne *père*. He sold his collection to the Fondation Dapper in Paris, which has subsequently tried to justify their accession of this and other looted antiquities by claiming that their collection ethic forbids dealing in archaeological material (a patent absurdity) and which has contested Brent's reports of the profit on the sale made by de Grunne (Leveau 1994:77, 78 in response to Brent 1994a:51; see also Brent 1994b:35). The Fondation Dapper tried to reinvest the collection by publishing a glossy catalogue written by a willing academic. As of late 1995, they have been unable to find art historians willing to collaborate.

The public shame produced by journalistic exposés, coordinated moral pressure brought to bear by right-thinking officials and scholars, and the "coercive activity of prevention and deterrence" (Bator 1983:26) can affect even the most crass players in the art market. In *The African King* you can see that the boors and the international dealers who serve them are already scared. Indeed, the film concentrates on the duplicitous manipulations of information that form the fundamental strategy of the latter. They want no photos, no records of locations of finds. The art must be *introuvée* with no demonstrable origin and certainly without a date of removal from the ground or across national frontiers. As Van Beek says in the film, the boors must remain "as vague as possible about their movements, vagueness bordering on amnesia." They fear imprisonment in the source countries, prosecution and impoundment in their own countries, and evaporating profits if their art becomes too dangerous to handle in the rarefield world of the tony auction houses and dandified collector elite. Resistance will no doubt be strong; the boors and international dealers have vast sums at stake.

And the international dealers have much to dread. If anyone harbors any charitable thoughts about dealers selflessly bringing lost art to public visibility, saving it from the elements and neglect in the source countries (see also Bator 1983:21–22), the film should erase such illusions: One dealer tried to justify his actions by saying, "Napoleon brought back treasures from his conquests. . . . What you really need is for [Africans] to become mature enough to set up the whole thing . . . to set a legitimate business." When Van Beek points out that the dealer is arguing that Africans should organize themselves to protect themselves against the dealers, the dealer agrees.

This kind of arrogance removes the illusion that, at base, the boorish collectors, international dealers, and, for that matter, the source-nation dealers are in the business for the art. The trade is about the power of possession and about the power that comes with wealth. Although before the overthrow of Traoré the enforcement of Mali's laws against export of these terra-cottas was terribly lax, now the threat of prison hangs over everyone involved in looting and transport. As de Grunne *père* says of the uneasy collusion of national dealers and local officials at the time of the film: "It's badly organized and [there is] also a blacklist. If you don't take measures to protect yourself, you can have a lot of trouble."

Not immune to shame, also, are the auction houses, which face increasing numbers of legal challenges (Greenfield 1989:246–48). Sotheby's, Christie's, and the like trade on profits and on their good reputation. Since the screening of *The African King*, de Grunne has left his position at Sotheby's and the art scene completely and now works for a trade journal about computers. The art community view is that a monster auction he organized failed miserably. African art which he authenticated, valued, and priced failed to fetch his anticipated sums. He and Sotheby's were shamed. Despite his intimacy with his father's collection and those of his circle of friends, despite his accreditation with a Yale Ph.D (research based in part on his father's collection), the shaming effect of publicity about the failed sale had its effect.

Here is where the international community can step in. In his thoughtful study of the art market, Bator comes to the conclusion that it would be "difficult to think of economic rewards that could plausibly be used to protect archaeological sites or other public monuments. . . . What is needed, therefore, is the coercive activity of prevention and deterrence" (1983:26). National dealers and antiquarians serve as "hatchet men for their foreign counterparts" (jegede, this volume) in the rape of their own country. Exposure will not be straightforward, as Brent, Téréba Togola (an archaeologist with the Malian Institut des Sciences Humaines), and I found when we surprised peasant looters at work at a Middle Niger archaeological site thirty kilometers from Jenne (McIntosh 1994:33). Although frightened of prison, the looters were even more frightened of the consequences to themselves or to their families if they revealed the name of the local antiquarian who employed them. The traffic in antiquities is a mean business in which only the ruthless thrive. The international community must encourage the national government to find the local antiquarian in that well-appointed house in Mopti, clearly identified in *The African King*, and make an example of him. Just a few prison sentences on both sides of the export- import frontier can be powerful lessons.

The African King has an explicit shaming lesson (if slightly inaccurate) for those I have called import officials and an implicit criticism of the Malian export officials. In the first case we have good news, and in the latter, excellent news. I include as an import official everyone involved in the formulation of policy and implementation of laws concerning the import of illegally obtained art. The film is incorrect in saying that no Western nations have ratified the 1970 UNESCO conventions; in March 1983 President Ronald Reagan signed the ratification papers. The United States joins only Italy, Argentina, Canada, and Australia among the developed world nations (Brent 1994b:27–28). But implementation on a country-by-country basis (except for a few emergency cases, including the 1993 U.S.-Mali ban on Niger Valley imports) has previously been stalled by powerful interests.

The logjam has been jostled, if not completely freed, by a formal request by the Malian government for a sweeping bilateral agreement between the United States and Mali. As this is the very first request from Africa and the first from any country to treat antiquities and ethnographic pieces expansively, the process was undertaken deliberately. The implications of this accord shall constitute the closing optimism of this chapter. It is important to recognize that this is a 180 degree turn from the Malian government's position before the 1991 overthrow of the despot Traoré. Mali's action will incite other African nations to make analogous requests. Serious action by the United States (including increasing customs and police training) must surely eventually shame our Western and Japanese counterparts to reform national legislation, to ratify the 1970 UNESCO convention, and to train import officials at all levels from embassy staffs to customs police. Similar efforts must be made to change attitudes among all levels of export officialdom to conform to the moral example presented by Malian President Konaré, an archaeologist. The first step must begin with those local officials, judges, heads of gendarmerie posts, and civil administrators (préfets and sous-préfets) who turn a blind eye to the trade to avoid offending local antiquarians, who are often the wealthiest, most influential members of their communities.

To match the potential of pressure on the import officials, the international community can strengthen the resolve of public-trust institutions (as opposed to the board-burdened museums) to resist purchases of illegally exported art. Some, such as the University Museum of the University of Pennsylvania, have had, since the early 1970s, explicit accession policies excluding such material. Good collectors, who truly love and respect the art and who see themselves as part of a joint enterprise with archaeologists, art historians, and historians, can increase our knowledge and appreciation of extinct societies. What museum wants the bad publicity of a Euphronius Krater (Meyer 1973:87–93) or Lydian treasure (Greenfield 1989:301–05)? Surely the J. Paul Getty Museum wishes it had never bought the now infamous Getty Kouros (Bianchi 1994; Elia 1994). Most collectors see their purpose as noble. Education, persistent reminders, and a dedication to bring these consumers into a community of action with scholars and art devotees can indeed change the mission of these public-trust institutions from collecting to preserving (Papageorge Kouroupas, this volume). As Maria Papageorge Kouroupas correctly states, preservation occurs through aggressive canons of accession, including insistence upon documentation of origin and legality of export, before acquisition. After all, these public-trust institutions and collectors willing to share their fortune with the public are the players who can perhaps educate the greatest numbers of the Western public to the issues of art and antiquities as national and global heritage and to issues of national heritage as a fundamental human right. These institutions, then, are the import-side counterparts of national museums in export countries that are properly dedicated to preservation, local public education, and presentation of national history to the rest of the world (Wilson and Omar, this volume).

Education, pride of one's place in history, and a sense of a common purpose with one's compatriots can demonstrably affect the peasant cash croppers exploited for their labor by the local antiquarians. In *The African King*, the Mopti antiquarian had a stable of sixteen Dogon working for food and for a commission on individual pieces (see also Brent 1994a:50). In a Sahelian sector of a struggling nation like Mali, who can fault a local farmer for needing help to feed his family? Around Jenne, the archaeological mounds are considered to be monuments to a pre-Islamic past; before the excavations at Jenne-jeno, the occupants of modern Jenne cared little about the site.

However, *The African King* tells only part of the story of looting in the Jenne region. To be sure, all sites in the region are under threat. Jenne-jeno itself had been badly pillaged well before the first excavations in 1977 and that pillaging continued, somewhat abated, before our return in 1981. By that date, however, we had begun to publish in French in popular journals (such as *Geo-France, Topic, UNESCO Courier, Afrique Histoire,* and *Jeune Afrique*) and to send those articles to friends and members of the citizens' preservation organization, Les Amis de Jenne. By the time of our next visit to Jenne, in 1986, the increase of looting at Jenne-jeno had effectively ceased and preservation of the site has continued throughout the rapacious early 1990s (except, curiously, for a narrow slice of the northwestern periphery of the mound). There is general agreement in Jenne and at the Institut des Sciences Humaines that this preservation of Jenne-jeno has resulted entirely from vigilance by Jenneans.[9] Although the problem may simply have been pushed into the hinterland, this success proves that local pride can, with proper education, be turned to preservation. In Jenne, the government is planning to establish a local museum and to control the flow of tourists to Jenne-jeno (for two views on using a nation's past as a tourist draw, see Kusimba, this volume, and King 1989).

Short of major ongoing excavations funded by international agencies, the monetary situation of the peasant cash croppers remains unaddressed. Perhaps this is not the concern of the archaeological, museum, and art communities, but what if all those diggers turned to the fabrication of statuettes? Surely a significant number could make fair copies. That would then satisfy the market of occasional tourists who would simply like a souvenir of their pleasant stay in Mali. If, however, all those who serviced the market by authenticating, valuing, and dating the art refused to provide those services for pieces lacking export licenses, a major industry of fakes could potentially knock the bottom right out of the market in terracottas. As Coe describes the pre-Columbian situation, "There is hardly a public or private collection in the world without fakes. Faking is to collecting what weeds are to gardening, with similar destructive effects: I know of cases in art evaluation where detection of forgery has turned Olmec objects valued at more than $20,000 into $20 souvenir items" (1993:275). Even now, dealers in Malian terra-cottas are falling out among themselves and claiming many famous pieces to have been forgeries (Brent 1994b:31). There are rumors that forgers even irradiate their pieces to artificially increase the age of terra-cottas to be dated by thermoluminescence (Samuel Sidibé, pers. comm., 1992). Such are the rumors that can rend the gossamer web of confidence linking the providers and consumers of looted antiquities.

This then leads to our last players in the market, those who service the trade even though they have heard all the counterarguments. *The African King* ends with a shameful interview with a director of one of the art-market servicing laboratories, Professor Michael Tite of the Oxford University Research Laboratory for Archaeology and the History of Art. Tite makes the baldest justification for running thermoluminescence dates without question, arguing the strangling effects on science of Thatcherite economics and proposing business in the service of academic research. The film appeared on British television soon after the Society of Africanist Archaeologists, at its 1990 Gainesville meeting, passed a resolution to ban the thermoluminescence dating of illicitly exported pieces (McIntosh 1991b). The public airing of the film initiated a letter-writing campaign by archaeologists, coordinated by Ray Inskeep of Oxford and Chris Chippindale, editor of *Antiquity*, to shame the Oxford University Committee for Archaeology into action (Chippindale 1991:6–8; 1992:827–28; Dembélé and Van der Waals 1991; Inskeep 1992). The timing was perfect. The University Committee for Archaeology passed a resolution prohibiting the lab from treating West African objects without export papers. Dating and authentication will no longer be undertaken for private individuals or commercial salesrooms and galleries.

This incident represents one victory against mercenary science; two more triumphs have occurred on the art historical front. The longtime editor of *African Arts* reflected and helped to set the moral standard for a generation of art historians who treated art as masterpieces rather than as social documents. Such scholars believed that knowledge of art derives from a kind of cultured empathy (*verstehen*, in historicist terms—McIntosh 1992; see Coe 1993:272–73), rather than from analysis, a separate but integrated branch of social history. There has recently been a sea change in Africanist art history and a passing of the reins of the discipline to a newer generation. One of the newer generation, Henry Drewal, writes in this volume about a joint archaeological–art historical foundation to support investigation, preservation, academic publication, and public education regarding African sites and monuments. Earlier generations would not have taken such initiative.

The art historical sea change has swept over *African Arts*, as it has over many other art publishers. The membership list of the editorial consulting board is a who's-who of the new generation. The journal now publishes articles on the nature of the art market, on the authentication of African art, and on the very definition of art.[10] Now we can hope the *African Arts* board will debate their policy for accepting advertising. A previous generation of art publishers would never sacrifice its splendid art photographs, even if printing of those plates had to be funded by the acceptance of advertising for looted pieces. The new generation has few delusions about the complicitousness of that stance.

Archaeologists have not traditionally been less willing to service the trade by making the self-deluding argument that "objects coming through the market were worthy of scholarly study" (Coe 1993:288). Prehistoric archaeology is enduring a decade of intense introspection about the manipulation of the past. Even before the 1980s, there has been a sense of collective shame about the actions of the disciplinary fathers, such as Schliemann and Layard, or of the contemporary brother Africanist Duncan Mathewson in the treasure-hunting employ of Mel Fischer. Shame and a real effort at collective awareness have not always led to consensus on practical action.

In *The African King*, the Dutch archaeologist Van der Waals says, "One could say that Jenne-jeno has been virtually a disaster for archaeology—because it was only after the dig at Jenne-jeno that statuettes became objects of prestige and, therefore, sought after by European collectors and it threatens all the sites here." Yet not

much later he co-authors the statement "Désormais, autour de Djenné par example, les populations ne sont plus indifférentes aux pillages perpétrés à côté
de leurs villages: c'est le cas de Djenné-Djeno pour laquelle la menace actuelle
est plutôt l'érosion"[11] (Dembélé, Schmidt, and Van der Waals 1993:231). The statement in the film is a bit disingenuous, because the looting and export were voluminous long before the first season at Jenne-jeno, 1977. That year Jacqueline Evrard
published a massive dissertation on Middle Niger terra-cottas in various Belgian
collections. The bulk of the de Grunne collection was assembled before then.
During a visit in 1973, Merrick Posnansky encountered local antiquarians, who
identified themselves as agents of de Grunne and were collecting statuettes at
Jenne.[12]

Rather, Steiner (1994:7) presents the more plausible explanation that inflation
in prices for all African art and antiquities (not just the Middle Niger terra-cottas)
and expansion in looting are linked to the growing dearth of authentic pieces on
the market after the heavy exodus of masks and ritual objects from the continent
in the 1960s and 1970s. In a variation on this explanation, other Africanist art historians with an intimate knowledge of the museum scene believe that demand for
African art was a wagon hitched to the engine of demand for fine collectible investment art of that period and the 1980s (Kate Ezra and Philip Ravenhill, pers.
comm.). I know of no art historian who believes that legitimate publication causes
looting, although it may identify pieces later to be stolen from local museums.

Publication of the Jenne-jeno statuettes found in radiocarbon-datable contexts
fits Prott's injunction (this volume): publish to protect. Should we not dig? Should
we not publish? Drewal (this volume) also argues that publishing safeguards the
art and archaeology. Doing so breaks the chain of enforced ignorance about the
date and place of the find and about its travels from original context to some sterile
glass cage. The answer by all Malian and Senegalese who have seen *The African
King* is that we must do both—more excavation, more publication. Without excavation and the archaeological discovery of the unwritten accomplishments of
Africa's past, Western paternalism can continue to pass off the prehistory of the
continent as a pale reflection, a derived and secondary aping of processes and developments that took place in other, more paramount parts of the globe. From research at Jenne-jeno, Dia, Timbuktu, from several years of Dutch research around
Mopti and Diafarabé (Dembélé, Schmidt, and Van der Waals 1993), and recent
work by students in the Méma (Togola 1993), it is now known that the southern
Middle Niger was the seat of an early, original, and underived urban civilization.
Must the under-appreciation of the African past be perpetuated to save its antiquities from plunder?

Or is there another way? What is to be done by an archaeologist who wants simultaneously to add to knowledge through research and to take steps against the
illicit art market? The Society of Africanist Archaeologists has recommended that
new sites be inventoried and published without identifying their exact location.
This solution is difficult because many of the models and paradigms employed
to demonstrate the urban character of a city depend upon the geometry of site
hierarchies in the central site's hinterland. Without maps of those hierarchies, the
argument is weakened. Wilson and Omar (this volume) explain the importance of

site inventories for complete and appropriate preservation legislation. There are, however, ways to abstract and modify those maps and models.

I close with two final points of optimism. At the request of Mali, the U.S. Information Agency has recently drafted a bilateral agreement for the protection of a broad spectrum of archaeological materials from the Middle Niger and Dogon country (Kaufman 1994; Papageorge Kouroupas, this volume; U.S. Information Agency 1992). This import ban goes far beyond previous limited region- or class of artifact-specific agreements with El Salvador, Bolivia, Peru, and Guatemala. Second, the United States and thirty-three other member states of the International Institute for the Unification of Private Law have redrafted a treaty to improve co-operation among countries seeking the return of illegally exported and excavated objects ("U.S., Other Nations Redraft Policy" 1994). Shame is one weapon against the felons. Legal measures are needed also. As in the story of the Benin objects imported to Switzerland recounted by LaGamma in this volume, well-meaning individuals such as art historians and embassy personnel often simply lacked guidance and precedents to help their efforts to right obvious wrongs. The international community is slowly coming around. Let us hope the example of the Malian-U.S. bilateral agreement shames more European countries and Japan into ratifying the 1970 UNESCO convention.

Let us hope the implementation legislation is promulgated speedily and that it has real teeth. Let us hope that the judicial powers will prosecute high-visibility cases. The rot that infects the appreciation of the archaeological and aesthetic accomplishments of Africa's past can only thrive in the shadows. When the prime actors in the sad drama of the commerce in Africa's heritage, and their base philosophy, greed, and contempt for Africans are exposed to the light of shame, they and their corrupting games will wither away.

NOTES

1. My title is taken from Brent 1994a:50.

2. Letter from Michael A. Coronel, *African Arts* 12 (August 1976), 6.

3. Unfortunately, the one major attempt by an art historian to divine the rituals in which the terra-cottas were used, Grunne 1987, has serious flaws. See the critique in McIntosh 1992:147–48.

4. A Dutch team of archaeologists (Project Togué) mapping sites in a two thousand square kilometer region north and east of Jenne found that 45 percent of the sites had evidence of pillaging and 2 percent were disfigured over 70 percent or more of their surface area (Dembélé, Schmidt, and Van der Waals 1993:231).

5. This figure is an amplification of an anatomy of the illicit antiquities network published in McIntosh and McIntosh 1986: fig. 48. See also Coe 1993: fig. 1.

6. "To ensure that this collection, too, does not slip away to the United States." (My translation.)

7. The author hopes that these and other nationalistic ejaculations are the product of individuals feeling themselves besieged and under pressure to find any argument to justify participation in the looting network. What better demonstration that possession of art is power and that the movement of stolen art across national frontiers maps the relative power of nations (McIntosh, McIntosh, and Togola 1989:75)?

8. Oral traditions collected by the author, Susan Keech McIntosh, and Hama Bocoum from several sources in Jenne in 1977.

9. Consensus reached at the February 1994 meeting of Les Amis de Jenne, called by Boubarcar Diabe, head of the ISH Mission Culturelle à Djenné.

10. See the autumn 1995 issue of *African Arts*, in which the 1993 U.S.-Mali accord is debated.

11. "However, around Jenne for example, the local populations do not act with indifference toward the pillage perpetrated next to their villages; that is the case for Jenne-Jeno, for which the menace now is erosion, rather than looting." (My translation.)

12. A statement made during the question period after this paper was read at the Gainesville conference.

REFERENCES

The African King [film]. London: Pilgrim Pictures, 1990.

Alexander, Brian, "Archaeology and Looting Make a Volatile Mix." *Science* 250, no. 4984 (November 23, 1990):1074–75.

Bathily, A. *Les portes de l'or: Le royaume de Galam (Sénégal) de l'ère Musulmane au temps des négriers (VIIIe-XVIIIe siècles)*. Paris: Harmattan, 1989.

Bator, Paul M. *The International Trade in Art*. Chicago: University of Chicago Press, 1983.

Bianchi, Robert Steven. "Saga of the Getty Kouros." *Archaeology* 47, no. 3 (May/June 1994):22–23.

Brent, Michel. "Afrique: le pillage continue." *Le Vif/L'Express* 2167 (January 1993):34–37.

———. "Le Grand Pillage du Mali." *Le Vif/L'Express* 2218 (January 15, 1994a):48–52.

———. "The Rape of Mali." *Archaeology* 47, no. 3 (May/June 1994b):26–31, 34–35.

Brooks, George. *Landlords and Strangers: Ecology, Society and Trade in Western Africa, 1000–1630*. Boulder, CO: Westview Press, 1993.

Chippindale, Christopher. "Editorial." *Antiquity* 65, no. 246 (March 1991):3–11.

———. "Editorial." *Antiquity* 66, no. 253 (December 1992):823–30.

Coe, Michael D. "From *Huaquero* to *Connoisseur*: The Early Market in Pre-Columbian Art." In *Collecting the Pre-Columbian Past*, ed. Elizabeth Hill Boone, 271–90. Washington, D.C.: Dunbarton Oaks, 1993.

Dembélé, Mamadi, Annette M. Schmidt, and J. Diderick Van der Waals. "Prospection de sites archéologiques dans le delta intérieur du Niger." In *Vallées du Niger*, 218–32. Paris: Editions de la Réunion des Musées Nationaux, 1993.

Dembélé, Mamadi, and J. Diderick Van der Waals. "Looting the Antiquities of Mali." *Antiquity* 65, no. 249 (December 1991):904–05.

Elia, Richardo. "A Corruption of the Record." *Archaeology* 47, no. 3 (May/June 1994):24–25.

Evrard, Jacqueline. "Archéologie Ouest Africaine: Les figures en terre cuite du Mali—Description morphologique et essai de typologie." Mémoire de Licence, Université Catholique de Louvain, 1977.

Greenfield, Jeanette. *The Return of Cultural Treasures*. Cambridge: Cambridge University Press, 1989.

Grunne, Bernard de. *Terres cuites anciennes de l'Ouest Africain*. Louvain-la-Neuve: Institut Supérieur d'Archéologie et d'Histoire de l'Art, 1980.

———. "Divine Gestures and Earthly Gods. A Study of the Ancient Terracotta Statuary from the Inland Niger Delta in Mali." Ph.D. diss., Yale University, 1987.

Hays, Kelly Ann. "When Is a Symbol Archaeologically Meaningful? Meaning, Function, and Prehistoric Visual Arts." In *Archaeological Theory: Who Sets the Agenda?* ed. Norman Yoffee and Andrew Sherratt, 81–92. Cambridge: Cambridge University Press, 1993.

Inskeep, R. R. "Making an Honest Man of Oxford: Good News for Mali." *Antiquity* 66, no. 250 (March 1992):114.

Kaufman, Jason E. "L'Héritage Cultural Africain Menacé." *Le Journal des Arts* (April 1994):25.

King, James Litvak. "Cultural Property and National Sovereignty." In *The Ethics of Collecting Cultural Property*, ed. Phyllis Mauch Messenger, 199–208. Albuquerque: University of New Mexico Press, 1989.

Leveau, Michel. "Sur l'art Africain [Controverses]." *Le Vif/L'Express* (May 13, 1994):77–78.

McIntosh, R. J. "Ancient Terra-cottas before the Symplegades Gateway." *African Arts* 22, no. 2 (1989):74–83, 103–04.

———. "Early Urban Clusters in China and Africa: The Arbitration of Social Ambiguity." *Journal of Field Archaeology* 18 (1991a):199–212.

———. "Resolved: To Act for Africa's Historical and Cultural Patrimony." *African Arts* 24, no. 1 (1991b):18–22, 89.

———. "From Traditional African Art to the Archaeology of Form in the Middle Niger." In *Dall'archeologia all'arte tradizionale Africana*, ed. G. Pezzoli, 145–51. Milan: Centro Studi Archeologia Africana, 1992.

———. "Plight of Ancient Jenne." *Archaeology* 47, no. 3 (1994):32–33.

McIntosh, R. J., and S. K. McIntosh. "Terra-cotta Statuettes from Mali." *African Arts* 12, no. 2 (1979):52–53, 91.

———. "Dilettantism and Plunder: Dimensions of the Illicit Traffic in Ancient Malian Art." *UNESCO Museum* 149 (1986):49–57.

———. "From *Siècles Obscurs* to Revolutionary Centuries in the Middle Niger." *World Archaeology* 20, no. 1 (1988):141–65.

McIntosh, R. J., S. K. McIntosh, and Téréba Togola. "People Without History." *Archaeology* 42, no. 1 (1989):74–80, 107.

McIntosh, R. J., T. Togola, and S. K. McIntosh. "The Good Collector and the Premise of Mutual Respect among Nations." *African Arts* 1996.

McIntosh, S. K., ed. *Excavations at Jenné-jeno, Hambarketolo, and Haniana (Inland Niger Delta, Mali), the 1981 Season.* University of California Publications in Anthropology, No. 20. Berkeley: University of California Press, 1995.

McIntosh, S. K., and R. J. McIntosh. *Prehistoric Investigations in the Region of Jenne, Mali.* Cambridge Monographs in African Archaeology, no. 2. Oxford: BAR, 1980.

Messenger, Phyllis Mauch. *The Ethics of Collecting Cultural Property.* Albuquerque: University of New Mexico Press, 1989.

Meyer, Karl E. *The Plundered Past.* New York: Atheneum Press, 1973.

Nesmith, Fisher. "The Jenne Bronze Question." *African Arts* 17, no. 3 (May 1984):64–69, 90.

Steiner, Christopher B. *African Art in Transit.* Cambridge: Cambridge University Press, 1994.

Stoneham, D. "Quelques datations par thermoluminescence de terre cuites du delta intérieur du Niger." In *Terres cuites anciennes de l'Ouest Africain*, ed. Bernard de Grunne, 276–82. Louvain-la-Neuve: Institut Supérieur d'Archéologie et d'Histoire de l'Art, 1980.

Togola, Téréba. "Archaeological Investigations of Iron Age Sites in the Méma Region (Mali)." Ph.D. diss., Rice University, 1993.

"U.S., Other Nations Redraft Policy." *Federal Archaeology Report* 7, no. 1 (Spring 1994):17.

U. S. Information Agency. "Curbing Illicit Trade in Cultural Property: U.S. Assistance under the Convention on Cultural Property Implementation Act." Washington, DC, 1992.

5

A VIEW INSIDE THE ILLICIT
TRADE IN AFRICAN ANTIQUITIES

MICHEL BRENT

TRANSLATION: BRUNO CASSIERS AND KATE GOFF

What follows is a rather personalized report of evidence collected during a
six-month investigation for the Belgian newsweekly for which I work, *Le Vif/
L'Express* (for other results of this investigation see Brent 1993). This investigation led me to discover the darker sides of the clandestine trade in works of art.
During the investigation, I came into contact with major collectors of African art,
specialized art merchants, museum directors, art restorers, and dealers. I hardly
need to point out that in this field—the illicit trade of African antiquities—there
are no statistics whatsoever, no verifiable figures, and few trustworthy scientific
studies. Every piece of information one gathers must be considered as a piece of a
puzzle; however, these pieces of information can, of course, be checked against
one another.

True investigatory journalism would necessarily begin with several questions
about how this trade is organized and driven. Who takes part in it? When did it
originate? How do these objects leave Africa? How do they arrive in Europe and
America? Who are the intermediaries? Just who profits from this traffic? And can
we assess its real extent?

I do not think it is possible to answer these questions with any real degree of accuracy. The vast network that has worked so actively to plunder the African heritage during the past twenty-five years and even before operates in such a secret
way that no definitive statement can be made concerning the real extent of this
trade and responsibility cannot be apportioned fairly among the parties that have
a hand in it. It is quite clear, however, that these appalling practices deserve
to be condemned, that these underground networks should be penetrated by
the authorities, and that the international community should strive to dismantle
them. At any rate, it became clear to me, doing this research, that many people—
scientists, merchants, art critics, experts, crafts people, and dealers—do know
what is going on, but they are not prepared to talk about the trade or about their
contribution to the networks by which the art leaves Africa, at least not if they
think they will go on record.

Since it is difficult, perhaps impossible, to draw a good overall portrait of the
situation, I prefer to illustrate the problems with specific cases before attempting
to draw any conclusions. Each of these case stories, in its own way, reveals a great
deal about the prevailing manner in which this illicit trade is conducted.

The first case situation occurred in Holland. In July 1992 customs officers in the port of Rotterdam inspected a container that had just arrived from Ghana. Why did they choose to inspect that particular container when hundreds of them travel through the port each day? They did so simply because there was a flagrant discrepancy between the declared value (5,000 gulden, or 2,650 U.S. dollars) and the size of the container. The customs officers opened the container and discovered two hundred terra-cotta statuettes carefully packed in straw. As they were incapable of assessing the value of these objects themselves, they made the excellent decision to call the director of the Leiden Rijksmuseum voor Volkenkunde, Rogier Bedaux, to conduct an evaluation. On examining the cargo, Bedaux discovered that among the two hundred statuettes destined for the tourist trade, there were eighty-four objects of Koma (northern Ghana) origin, probably dating from the seventeenth century. Each of these Koma statuettes could be worth approximately $10,000, which brings the total value of the haul to $840,000. The police seized the statuettes, but the Dutch Ministry of Justice could do very little from that point on because Holland had not ratified the 1970 UNESCO Convention on the Means of Prohibiting and Preventing the Illicit Import, Export, and Transfer of Ownership of Cultural Property. The best the authorities could do was to fine the importer, a Utrecht antiques dealer, on the grounds that he had submitted a false declaration of value. If the Ghanaian government had not intervened, the dealer would have been able to retrieve his booty after having simply paid the fine.

The dealer failed because Rogier Bedaux contacted the Ghanaian embassy in Brussels immediately after he identified the eighty-four statuettes. Robert Badu, the Ghanaian consul, himself quite aware of the kind of traffic that occurs, telephoned the Dutch Ministry of Justice. Badu urged the ministry to retain the objects long enough for him to introduce a civil lawsuit against the antiques dealer. In fact, this was the only course of action still open to the consul in his attempt to retrieve the statuettes.

In the end, the affair was resolved by the lawyers for the two parties, who reached a bizarre compromise. To recover the works of art and repossess a part of its heritage stolen from the country, Ghana gave the Utrecht dealer written assurance that he would still be able to travel to Ghana and would not, once there, be prosecuted for the illegal export of objects of art. This assurance was given, of course, on the condition that the antiques dealer would not resume his illegal trading activities. In a 1992 interview Badu told me that the Ghanaian authorities estimate the value of the clandestine export of antiquities to be several million dollars each year. He also told me that during the Komaland statuettes affair, he had asked Interpol in Holland for help but never received any response. He also told me that the Utrecht antiques dealer had already returned to Ghana on two occasions—as a simple tourist, of course! As to the Komaland terra-cottas, they have been returned to Ghana.

I chose this particular story as an introduction to the illegal traffic in art objects because it reveals several of the major problems faced by African authorities in their attempt to eradicate this traffic. First, is it not shocking, indeed humiliating, for a government official to be forced to accept a compromise in which the guilty party is declared free to enter and leave that country at will after having broken its laws? The humiliation is doubled because this accommodation with a criminal is made in order to retrieve objects of deep cultural significance to the official's country. Ultimately, such humiliations abound because European states have not bothered in the past twenty-five years to ratify the 1970 UNESCO convention that concerns the preservation of humanity's heritage.

This particular example of the stolen Komaland statuettes is revealing on two further points: First, if antique dealers import African objects by the container, there is little doubt that business is booming. Second, in spite of the measures taken by some African authorities to stop this traffic, it is still possible (through bribes, for example) to circumvent many African customs controls.

The second case I will describe underlines another difficulty faced by those many African officials who take seriously their charge to stop this cultural hemorrhage: African geography. The territories are immense, the network of roads is precarious, and borders are easily permeated. All these factors favor the development and expansion of clandestine digs and make control of such criminal excavation particularly difficult, if not impossible.

In December 1989, Samuel Sidibé (interview, January 7, 1993), director of the National Museum of Mali, was told of a clandestine excavation in which more than two hundred people were working and camping on a permanent basis. This dig was at Thial, a village located near Tenenkou, in the Middle Niger some three hundred miles north of Bamako. When, a few weeks later, he traveled to the site himself (mission report no. 0336/DNAC rédigé en date du 24 mai 1990 par Mamadi Dembele, chef de mission) he realized the extent of the damage being done. More than two acres had been excavated. Huge pits had been dug, and side galleries had been tunneled in which at least one man died because they were not shored up. The extent of the work indicated that it had been going on for months, and it could be presumed that any work of art found there had already left the country. Indeed, Sidibé learned a few days later that a few terra-cotta objects from the Tenenkou site had already made their way to Paris and were being sold for an average price of $5,300 each. In this case, as in the previous one, the African authorities took steps. They arrested some of the suspects and convinced the local villagers that it would be in their own interest to keep works of art in the country and have nothing to do with the dealers.

Sidibé told me that the whole affair had begun with the chance discovery by a farmer of a terra-cotta statuette probably dating back to the sixteenth century. This find had provoked a rush of antique dealers from Mopti to the site. Sidibé hoped that measures already taken would stem the flow of objects, but he also pointed out how difficult it is to control a territory covering half a million square miles.

For several reasons, I would like to comment a little further on the case of the Tenenkou terra-cottas. First, this is probably one of the few cases for which we have firsthand information concerning an entire clandestine network, from the villagers at the dig, through the export network, all the way to the great museums. Second, we know the identity of the dealers and the collectors implicated in this traffic. One can see clearly in this case (as in all instances of looting of cultural heritage) that they are at the origin of the boom in the trade in terra-cotta statues. Third, we know how the objects were removed from Mali, and we know what financial gains have been made and by whom. Finally, some significant people have been prepared to talk about this case, and, as a result, a few journalists have been able to investigate it in some depth.

Discovered in the 1930s (Veillard 1940), the Malian terra-cottas began to be studied by a handful of scientists, chiefly Roderick and Susan McIntosh, who worked at the Jenne-jeno site in 1977, 1981, and 1994. Several years before these legitimate excavations began, a Belgian collector of primitive art, Count Baudouin de Grunne, bought a small series of these terra-cottas from a friend, Willy Mesdagh, who was also the owner of a large collection of African art. This was to be the beginning of the world's most important collection of African terra-cotta statues, now known as the de Grunne collection. How did de Grunne know from which dealers in Mali to purchase new statuettes even before legitimate excavations began at these sites?[1] How did this man, the mayor of one of Brussels's communes, manage to acquire so many items when laws were already in force in Mali prohibiting the export of antiquities? De Grunne—who has probably never even asked himself what damage he was doing to Mali's heritage—answered the question when he was interviewed in 1990 by a Dutch social anthropologist, Walter Van Beek, for the making of the film *The African King*.[2] According to information de Grunne freely gave Van Beek, several dealers, among them Philippe Guimiot, Emile Deletaille, and Alain de Monbrison, established links with antique dealers in Mopti during their frequent trips to Mali. The Mopti dealers would inform the Europeans of any interesting finds and the objects could then be shipped to Europe or the United States. Thus began this network. According to one of my sources, who asked not to be named, the gang pretended to be in the mango business to avoid arousing suspicion with their frequent trips to Mali.

But how did the items leave Mali? One of the Mopti dealers was later interviewed by Van Beek, who posed as a potential buyer while concealing a tape recorder. This so-called antiquarian told Van Beek there would be no problem at all with customs, as the officers were his friends. By this, I believe he meant that the customs officials were bribed. They would inspect his hand luggage but would not even open his suitcases. And how did the Mopti dealer get hold of the terra-cottas? Simply by employing a few Dogon villagers. At the time of the interview (which took place in 1990), the dealer said he employed sixteen villagers. He fed them for free. He instructed them systematically to search a few given areas and sneak into selected excavation sites. Thanks to the investigations of Van Beek's team, which bought an item from the Mopti dealer and later gave it to the Mali National Museum, we also have an idea of the kind of prices asked. My own subsequent investigations have enabled me to verify these prices. A beautiful terra-cotta statuette purchased for U.S. $5,000 in Mopti could easily be sold in Europe for between $100,000 and $150,000! I learned of this rate of markup with no particular surprise. Having lived in Indonesia from 1975 to 1978, I had already observed that at that time Belgian antique dealers would buy, for example, a Batak sculpture for U.S. $500 or $600 and then sell it in Belgium, after having exported it illegally, at ten times the price or more.

As a conclusion to the story of the de Grunne collection, I should add that the Belgian count sold his terra-cottas in the fall of 1990 to the Dapper Foundation in Paris for a sum estimated by some experts to have been around U.S. $10 million. To avoid questions about the origin of the items and the way in which they had been taken out of Africa, Michel Leveau, director of the Dapper Foundation, and Christiane Falgareyttes, head of the Dapper Museum, have decided to keep the collection locked in a secret place, without any exhibition planned in the foreseeable future. This contradicts Falgareyttes's 1993 announcement to directors of African museums on a visit to Europe that the de Grunne collection would be accessible to all.

I will briefly comment later on the way prices in the art market are driven up. For the moment it will suffice to point out that once the Malian terra-cottas had been, so to speak, "launched" in the eighties, a whole organization grew around their trade. Antique dealers went to meet the collectors, be they American or European. They contacted art gallery owners and the directors of the greatest museums. Some collectors, never short of ready cash, even published some glossy books, pseudo-scholarly or otherwise. Exhibitions were organized, as were sales at auctions. In other words, an entire machine was set in motion—and it has not stopped running.

Before looking into the ramifications of the illegal trade in Europe, I would like to remain a little longer in Africa to look more carefully at the clandestine methods used to obtain the works of art in the field. Their acquisition is not always as simple as the case I mentioned in Mali. First, times change. Twenty or thirty years ago dealers in ethnographic art would organize full-size expeditions into remote parts of Africa, and many of the people who were involved in the trade at that time recall light aircraft landing as close as possible to the sites, and later leaving packed full.[3] In those days, adventure was part and parcel of the endeavor. There was a kind of Indiana Jones touch to that traffic. It was not unusual to see some dealers wearing a suit and tie like prosperous businessmen when in Europe but pretending to be penniless travelers only seeking to flee city life when they were in Africa. They would ingratiate themselves with the locals, in the process laying on every flattery or favor that seemed useful. The newfound friends spent their time taking drugs together, living on the beach, getting a tan, and learning to climb the palm trees to pick coconuts and only later would the subject of antiques arise. This strategy would often result in some nocturnal rendezvous at the crossing of two roads. The young Africans who had been persuaded to steal valuable objects, often from their own families, were rewarded in cash. People in the Dogon country still remember (probably vividly) one German antique dealer who, as soon as he arrived in a village, would open his car and show a trunk full of brand-new Fr 500 bills (about U.S. $100), letting everyone know they would be exchanged for ancient artworks.

Nowadays, works of art are obtained by means that are less devious and more profitable. In Zaïre, for instance, entire groups comb the country in search of goods. They have well-defined territories and would not dare venture into a rival gang's territory for fear of reprisal. Woe betide the Western dealer who would try to acquire goods without employing their services! The hub of the central African antiques trade, at least the one centered on the Congo basin, has moved from Kinshasa to Bujumbura in Burundi because the dealers of Zaïre have become too greedy. Some European merchants have had serious problems with there Zaïrian local dealers—not with the state—and would not dare go back to Zaïre for fear of losing their lives. In some instances, the threats reached such extremes that the families of European dealers were being menaced in their own countries.

During much of my investigations, I had the initial feeling that a number of European traders were officially considered persona non grata in Zaïre. This, in fact, turned out not to be the case. They were indeed unwelcomed in the country, although not because of a March 1971 law that bans the exportation of antiquities. All one need do to take an object out of Zaïre is to go to the Ministry of Culture and pay a tax of between 5 and 10 percent of the supposed value, depending on the mood of the official in charge.

When one talks off the record with people involved in this illicit trade, they often use the word theft. The antique dealers retrench themselves behind the notion that it is chiefly the Africans themselves who pillage and sell off their own heritage. Clearly, the European and African dealers have yet to establish a relationship of warm mutual respect! However, one of the best-known dealers in Sevaré (a village located about seven miles from Mopti), Boubou Diarra, named one of his sons Emile, to honor Emile Deletaille, one of the Belgian dealers with whom he had done excellent business.

I have been told the following story by three separate off-the-record sources.[4] As I have been unable to check its authenticity, I will repeat it without vouching for its truth. Some African museums are rumored to have organized thefts from their own collections. The thief brings the stolen goods to a European antiques dealer, and a few weeks later the museum lodges a complaint with Interpol. That report is accompanied by the necessary proof of ownership as well as by the name of the antique shop that has these items in its stock. In such circumstances (when the authorities have the proof of ownership, which was not the case in the Komaland story) the intervention of the police always results in a speedy return of the stolen items to the museum, without any financial compensation to the purchaser. Thus, one can easily see that if the same operation is repeated three or four times in different European countries, substantial profits can be made.

There is no doubt that theft of cultural objects does take place in Africa (as in most other places, needless to add). The incredible appetite that European merchants demonstrated for African art obviously encouraged their counterparts in Africa to join in the adventure. On October 16, 1991, a team from the Direction Nationale des Arts et de la Culture of Bamako went to Nienou, near Bougouni, to investigate the theft of a sacred spear, the Spear of Nienou. This object, representing a horse and rider, dates from the first half of the eighteenth century. It was used each year in the context of the Komo secret-society ceremonies. Upon their arrival, the officials learned that the crime had been committed by the Odiouma

Kone gang and that the leader of this gang was the son of the very man appointed by the village to be the guardian of the spear. Without the report that resulted from this investigation (Dioura 1991), it would be difficult to understand the importance of the theft for those who were its victims. "According to the local population" wrote the chief investigator, Bouna Boukary Dioura (Dioura 1991), "the disappearance of this object will surely cause the death of the person who was appointed its guardian, and bring misfortune on his family. Because of its historical significance and its magic and religious attribute, the spear had become the symbol of the cultural identity of the village and of the union of the two communities to which it belonged." The locals affirm with great insistence that they would never have given up the Nienou spear to anyone, no matter how high the price offered for it.

If the Guimiot–Deletaille–de Grunne cartel and fellow consorts had not plunged into an unbounded and quite focused search for Malian terra-cottas, it is quite possible that the Jenne-jeno culture, for instance, would not have been plundered to near extinction. If there had not been such a craze for primitive art in the 1970s in northern Europe, the Dundo Museum in Angola, for instance (which was founded forty years earlier), would not be almost empty, as it is today (interview with Marie-Louise Bastin). In March 1992 a Luvale mask valued at about $40,000 was shown on the cover of a catalog for an auction at the Mon Steyaert Gallery in Brussels. The staff of the African Museum in Tervuren discovered that it was, in fact, an item stolen a few weeks earlier from the Livingstone Museum in Zambia (interview with Viviane Baeke). I could go on recounting numerous examples of similar robberies, but I will stop here as I believe theft is far from being the main source of supply for this traffic.

There is also talk of diplomatic pouches being used to carry things which cannot in any way be described as official documents or embassy mail. An archaeologist, who asked to remain anonymous, once told me, "You only need walk around the more affluent neighborhoods of African cities to perceive the extent of the traffic that goes on." But how can such rumor and presumption of criminality be verified? I must say I had largely discounted the rumor until a meeting with the director of the Tervuren Museum in the context of these investigations (interview with Van Den Audenaerde). With its 450,000 accessioned objects, this museum probably holds the finest collection of African art in the world. I did not even need to mention the rumor about diplomatic pouches. The director spontaneously told me that a few months earlier, a minister in the Zaïre government who claimed to be the descendant of high-ranking tribal chiefs requested an appointment with him. The minister began with a description of all the hardships of being a politician and then asked the museum director if he would be interested in buying a few antiquities that, he insisted, had been family property for generations. He swore he had not the slightest intention of siphoning out parts of his country's heritage. His sole aim was to be able to meet the costs of his frequent trips to Europe and to represent his own country, while abroad, in a dignified manner. When I asked the director if he ever bought objects in such circumstances, he said that these practices may not be frequent but they do happen, and under the bona fide principle, as it is understood in the profession, a museum director does not refuse to buy a work of art if he considers it to be a good one and if the price is right.[5] The temptation to buy an object regardless of the source will be that much greater if it is an object that will complete a collection the museum holds already.

To develop a classification of the ways in which antiquities are illegally obtained, I would like to make a few more observations. Please remember that there are no statistics on the subject. Any quantification below is only an estimate based on my inquiry, which included interviews with more than fifty persons.

The European antique dealers still go out to the field themselves to some extent to buy directly from the firsthand purveyors, but this practice seems to be less widespread now than it was ten or fifteen years ago. The figures I was given by dealers in Germany, France, and Belgium point toward the following kind of breakdown: 20 percent of their purchases are through the public auctions, 20 percent in the countries of origin, 10 percent from private African citizens who bring objects to Europe, 10 percent from fellow dealers, and 40 percent from former colonials. None of these channels can claim to be an entirely ethical method of acquiring works of art, even if some are legal, strictly speaking. Another point on which my sources seem to agree is the link that exists between the quality of an object and its present location. For one thing, truly fine African objects seem to have become quite rare. Nowadays they are more likely to be found in Europe, at a dealer's or with a collector, than in their place of origin.

Another channel of acquisition remains quite open these days: African freelancers who commute between Europe, the United States, and their own countries, bringing items on each of their trips. This trade is, of course, just as illicit as the more classical examples. Moreover, it has the reputation of being unreliable: about 50 percent of the goods are said to be fakes.[6]

Four months into my investigations, I sought to locate one of these free-lance traffickers. I knew there were several coming in and out of Brussels, and I needed an interview with one of them. I had gone to see an antique dealer in a small town in Belgium, whom the police authorities had described as a perfectly honest trader. I was sitting with him in his shop when an African man arrived with a large parcel. The shop owner later told me this was one of the regular commuters, and he gave me the name of a hotel in Brussels where these small-time traffickers stay. The place was rather disreputable: a run-down hotel near a railway station in the red-light district of town. It was only through some careful negotiations and quite a bit of caution that I managed to convince the hotel owner to let me get in touch with a few of his clients. I was, of course, posing as a potential buyer. Thus, I learned that all the major cities in Europe, mainly in Germany, Belgium, and France, are regularly visited. Each trafficker has a resident informer, also an African, in most cases a university student or a young graduate in need of pocket money. The latter contacts the city's antique dealers and art galleries but must, above all, make sure that the network remains secret and impenetrable.

I have not been able to assess the size of this network, but to provide some idea I can tell you that on each of the nine or ten occasions I went to the hotel in question I found African dealers who had goods to offer. The deals are done African style, chatting over glasses of beer, talking about anything under the sun or perhaps about the hardships of life, all in rather jolly spirits. When confidence is established, the bargaining session can begin. An object which was first offered at U.S. $4,000 might well, with a bit of bargaining, come down to $700 or $800, which indicates to me that these commuters are not really professionals.

I have mentioned earlier the way in which traffickers obtain their goods in the countries of origin. I should add that when one of these countries becomes too dangerous, for example because the bribery of customs officers no longer works in a reliable way, the traffickers merely take their goods by road to a neighboring country from which artifacts can be flown to Europe. Thus, Zaïre has acquired a reputation as being the preferred port of exit for works of art coming from a variety of other African counties—much in the same way as Belgium is the preferred port of entry into Europe. Not only do Belgium's judicial authorities point out the country's lamentable reputation: It is confirmed by eminent British experts.[7]

The illicit trade in the hands of the aforementioned African "commuters" could not take place if not for a rather large pool of customers to sustain it. However, this does not mean that the demand is purely European. In the United States, too, there are operating networks. On November 27, 1991, a cargo of art objects from Bamako was seized by the U.S. customs authorities in New Orleans; the examination of this cargo by a specialist revealed that it consisted of eighteenth-century objects of great value and that it transgressed the Mali law of 1985 forbidding the exportation of antiquities. This affair was very serious, first because it was a flagrant violation of a country's laws and because this kind of plundering was formally denounced by the United States—not a trivial state of affairs in the matter of clandestine traffic. Second, the protagonists in this transaction are well known: Samba Kamissoko, a Mali antique dealer who had already been imprisoned for illegal traffic in art objects, and Charles Davis, owner of the Davis Gallery, one of the most important commercial galleries dealing in primitive art in the United States.

Something even more unusual happened in this affair: I was able to obtain the documents[8] detailing the inventory and the estimated value of these illegally exported objects. The contents of the container were as follows: twenty-two locks at $85 apiece; five walking sticks at $680 apiece (and who can say the Nienou spear had not, in the meantime, become a single walking stick for the expediency of the customs document and that it was not among the contents of this shipment—the dates, at any rate, matched); three Bambara doors at $1,300 apiece; a Dogon door valued at $5,000; a puppet valued at $40,000; two masks at $2,500 apiece; and finally a Bambara figure in iron valued at $8,300. The invoice totaled $67,000. Two months after the interception, on January 22, 1992, a letter[9] signed by Clark W. Settles, the U.S. customs officer charged with this dossier, was sent to the Mali ambassador in Washington, Mohammed Alhoussenyi Toure. The letter informed the diplomat that, given the fact that no infraction had been perpetrated under U.S. law, the pieces could not remain much longer under seizure and that if measures were not taken rapidly by Mali to recover these objects they would have to be returned to the antique dealer in New Orleans. A few weeks later, Charles Davis and Samba Kamissoko were happy men indeed: Once again, illegally exported objects had legally entered the United States.

Davis had previously been implicated in such illegal traffic. On November 20, 1991, the celebrated auction house of Sotheby's put up for sale African art objects from the Kuhn collection in New York. This lot included ten Mali antiques, including a superb animal in baked clay, probably a sheep and probably originating from the inland delta of the Niger River. This unique piece figured on the cover of the catalog as the key piece in the sale, with the following commentary: "A highly important Inland Niger Delta zoomorphic figure, standing on apodal, thick flaring legs, with elongated waisted body, a cylindrical naval projecting on the underbelly; . . . eroded pinkish-brown patina. Length 31 inches; height 31¼ inches."[10] The catalog adds that the results of thermoluminescent analysis, carried out by the Daybreak Nuclear Company and Medical System, Inc., indicate that this ceramic is between 570 and 1000 years old. It was sold for the phenomenal sum of $275,000. Like a Dogon object and a Senufo statuette that were also part of the sale, this piece had been sold to the Kuhns by Davis and was also exported from Mali without authorization. It should also be noted that on November 20 the ambassador from Mali had been negotiating for two weeks with Marjorie Stone, the general counsel for Sotheby's, to report this sale. Affirming that the object had been illegally exported from Mali, Toure claimed that it should be withdrawn from the sale. Sotherby's staff responded—with all the hypocrisy that such an attitude implies—that there was no proof that the object of art left Mali after 1985, the year in which the law formally forbidding the exportation of antiques came into effect. And what is more, it had been imported into the United States legally.

So far, I have presented concrete case stories to give an overview of the trade, I think we should also turn to the prime factors that have created such a demand for these objects in northern Europe. I need not bring up the dominant role played by important artistic figures early this century, such as Guillaume Apollinaire, Georges Braque, and Pablo Picasso; great collectors such as the Barbier-Mullers; and galleries specializing in "Art Nègre" (to use the terminology of the time) that first opened in Paris around the beginning of this century. They all contributed to bringing tribal arts to world attention. That, in itself, was laudable, but they indirectly encouraged European expatriates in Africa during those colonial days to start collecting objects. Only in the 1970s did the market find its present structure, however. The early twentieth century was the heyday for dealers traveling to the countries of origin, combining and pillaging entire sites. Museums were then building up or completing their collections, and, of course, private collectors were buying either for their own sake, or quite often, as a form of speculative investment. For instance, in the case of the de Grunne collection of terra-cottas, because I knew at what price, on average, the Count had bought his items, I could infer that his end benefit over a twenty-year period must have been about $7 million.

Just to show how widespread the responsibility is for this plundering of African heritage, I would like to turn once more to the Tervuren Museum (interviews with Van Den Audenaerde). I must mention here that in Belgium museums are state owned and are therefore financed by the taxpayer. The Museum of Tervuren has all the outward appearances of a most venerable institution. Yet, if you look into the ways in which it has acquired African works of art in the past twenty years, links with the illicit trade become evident.

In the 1970s, the Tervuren Museum already had an extensive collection of African art, thanks to the trade links that had existed during a hundred years of historical ties between Belgium and the former Belgian Congo. But the museum lacked somewhat in its collection of West African art. To correct this gap, the directors had two options: They could buy, or they could organize expeditions to West Africa and collect in the field. They chose the first option, contacted antique dealers, art collectors, and former residents of what had been the West African colonies. The Brussels dealers saw a golden opportunity. They knew that such a prestigious museum could do much more for them than just be a good customer.

Let me describe the plot. I do not know if such is the case in the United States, but in Europe, at any rate, many museums have a kind of sister institution, a non-profit organization called friends of the museum. Its official purpose is to develop the museum's cultural activities, to promote its image, to organize temporary exhibitions, and such. In the case of the Tervuren Museum, the members of this body are art collectors, influential people from the world of politics or business, as well as antique dealers. As if by coincidence, some of the names I have mentioned earlier (in connection with the wholesale purchase of terra-cotta statuettes from Mali) were members of this organization's board until relatively recently. In addition, their organization runs a small shop within the museum buildings— mostly selling books and a number of fairly insignificant items of interest to visitors. What is significant, on the other hand, is that the so-called arrangement[11] stipulates that in exchange for the right to run the shop the organization should make gifts in kind to the museum. Herein lies the golden opportunity. The dealers and collectors, who were in a position to choose what was to be given, could pick, within their stock, items that are, so to speak, part of a series (as is often the case with African art). The rest of the series, for sale in their own galleries, could then be valued at a much higher level. That parts of the series were in one of the world's most prestigious museums could be considered proof of the high quality of these objects.

That this cozy arrangement has worked for twenty-odd years is largely thanks to the approval of the head of the museum's ethnography department, Huguette Van Geluwe. She, among others, convinced the director to opt for buying rather than collecting in the field. Thanks to her, a privileged dealer, Emile Deletaille, became the museum's main supplier. Van Geluwe gave her approval to the choice of gifts in the arrangement I have described. In a similar arrangement, she ensured that the museum took on loan a number of items belonging to her merchant friend—also to increase their value. This story demonstrates that the head of a department in the world's largest museum of African art deliberately closed her eyes as to whether or not the objects she received had been obtained in a legitimate manner. What her share of responsibility is in the plundering of Africa, I leave for you to judge. When I interviewed the museum's director in 1992, he confirmed that whenever Van Geluwe would show him a new object on offer, it was difficult for him to tell if there was already a similar one among the museum's 450,000 objects. He also told me that he decided two years ago that, as a matter of policy, the

museum should no longer buy any objects that lacked a legal certificate of exportation. But this paperwork presumably was not demanded in the case of the Zaïre
politician I mentioned earlier, who was selling what he described as family goods.

It may sound like I am critical of the very existence of museums, but this is not
my purpose. I am well aware they should not be tarred with the same brush that
some private dealers and collectors deserve. What goes into a museum becomes
accessible to the public and is available for research, while inclusion in a private
collection is quite often equivalent to consigning works of art to oblivion. But the
unfortunate fact remains that, to some extent, the museums themselves have contributed to the expansion of this illicit trade. For in fact the traders have made use
of a kind of organic link with these institutions to give their trade an aura of re-
spectability and renown which was essential in its development.

During the course of my inquiries, I spoke with Sylvia Williams, director of the
National Museum of African Art, to check on information concerning the sale, in
the mid-1970s, of a batch of African objects that had until then been in the hands
of a Brussels antique dealer of dubious reputation. Williams was at first extremely
guarded and asked repeatedly why I needed to have this information. (I have
often noticed, during this investigation, a kind of secret-society behavior whenever the conversation touches on the illicit side of the trade.) Eventually, when
she understood that I already had key pieces of information, she admitted that
the Smithsonian had bought "a few" items from the Belgian dealer. Once more,
the dealer involved was one of the members of the group I have mentioned
before, so there is little doubt that the objects purchased from him had been exported illegally. In other words, the Smithsonian does not always check whether
the objects it buys have a legal certificate of exportation, in spite of the U.S. Information Agency's efforts to encourage American museums not to import looted
objects.[12] I have already mentioned a similar example of moral laxity in the case of
the Tervuren Museum. In spite of a code of ethics published by the International
Council of Museums in 1990, I believe such practices may still be widespread in
all domains of art and in museums around the world.

Before summing up, I would like to consider recent trends in Europe that have
appeared as a result of this illicit trade and that are causing archaeologists serious
concern. Knowing that the patterns of the trade are bound to change with time
(because of the exposure of some networks or because of the decreasing availability of new objects), the traders of today are planning ahead for years to come.
In this respect, their best investment is to establish and maintain good contacts
with the people who in the future will have influence within the field—art history
students, future archaeologists, and ethnologists.

The antique dealers know very well that it is the ambition of most students in
these fields to go out in the field as soon as possible and develop a subject for their
thesis. They also know that scholarships do not abound, and that many parents
are reluctant or unable to finance a stay of a few months in the bush for a son
or daughter who has chosen what is not, after all, a very lucrative profession. Traders can therefore take on the guise of providential patrons, sometimes through
pseudocultural foundations created for that purpose. But the grants are not, as you

may guess, without strings attached. The donor asks to be rewarded in objects or with photographs and information about sites where it still is possible to find objects. There was a time when the dealers, some of whom had become persona non grata in Africa, would send their restorers or an employee to do the dirty work. Now they have turned to buying the services of young scientists and scholars, which is less risky and less costly. Sadly, when I interviewed a few such students and asked them if they feared the possibility of being sucked into a corrupt spiral, they told me, in very down-to-earth manner, that the illegal aspect of the trade was not their problem.

Another trend that seems to be growing is that some merchants now behave as if they were scholars of art. They publish articles, magazines, and books about a given tribe or about a given aspect of African art. Why have so many books about the arts of Tanzania appeared on the market in recent years? Traders have recently found a new source of objects in that country, and publication proves to be the best way of advertising their wares and pushing up their value. All this occurs, of course, very much to the indignation of the real scientists. They see such practices as a danger to their profession as well as a quite unacceptable usurpation and distortion of scientific methods.

What I have discussed here amounts to only a few snapshots illustrating the nature of this trade. There are many more very real questions to be addressed. Why, for instance, are 99 percent of the countries that have ratified the UNESCO convention of 1970 non-European? Why is it that in twenty-fives years of this convention's existence only two countries in the industrialized Northern Hemisphere—the United States and Canada—have confirmed their ratification with a set of specific laws? There is no doubt that if this illicit trade continues on the European side of the Atlantic without being disturbed, it is largely thanks to a kind a legal black hole. The exportation of works of art may be forbidden in Africa, but their importation into Europe is not forbidden. Add to this the fact that in Belgium the possession of a stolen object can be redressed by law only if a complaint is lodged within three years of the date of the theft and you will understand why the country has become—with Switzerland—the hub of the illicit trade in African objects as well as many other classes of art. Legislation would perhaps not halt the traffic, but there is little doubt it would do much toward diminishing it.

It has to be said, however, that police authorities in northern countries make genuine efforts in connection with their African counterparts. Let me recall the impounding by New Orleans customs of a shipment of items that Charles Davis had bought from Samba Kamissoko. Recently, an Italian dealer was arrested in Las Palmas, Canary Islands: He had with him a large batch of Dogon items, all of them ancient and illegally exported from Mali. He was transferred to Madrid for questioning and was released a few hours later, but his loot was confiscated. And in September 1993 a general meeting of police authorities from around the world took place in Lyons, France, under great secrecy, with the illegal trade in works of art as its sole theme.

As for other questions that can be raised, one should only do so with the greatest care because this situation is both complex and ambiguous. To what extent, for instance, can we say that the thermoluminescence dating by the archaeology laboratory at Oxford University has held out a helping hand to the traffickers (McIntosh 1992)? For years, merchants of art have relied on this process to date their terra-cotta objects. When asked about this, the director of the lab said he knew perfectly well that most of the objects had been obtained illegally but that he had to run his lab as a business concern in order to finance his other research.[13] What are we to think of such an attitude? It just goes to show that we all stand on shaky ethical ground as long as we allow such practices and attitudes to go on unchallenged.

Here, then, is the dilemma: Is there a strong ethical reason for preventing an African family or ethnic group from selling things that are their own property if they wish to do so? Should we feel indignant that museums go on buying objects that lack the proper export authorization? Or should we, on the contrary, be thankful that these objects do not end up hidden away in private collections or in bank vaults? How should we define a cultural heritage, and how exclusive should that definition be? Should it include every single small object from the past?

These questions and many others are pertinent to the ongoing controversy about the restitution of museum pieces demanded by some countries. But is it reasonable to imagine that museums the world over should begin shipping back their entire contents to the countries of origin? To raise one question on ethical grounds means having to raise another connected question. But one clear observation remains: A small but powerful section of European society has focused its attention on African art and put into action every means at its disposal, in terms of both influence and money, to take possession of it. Their greed-driven definition of ownership is generated more by status and financial gain than by sincere admiration for art itself. Thus, we arrive at such ironic junctures as this one: The great-grandsons of great African artists whose creations are now selling for hundreds of thousands of dollars and enriching the elites of distant lands are today living in dire poverty. Is it not frightening for so-called civilized people to witness that it is precisely at the moment when the African peoples have begun to acquire their independence—during the 1960s and 1970s—and thus begun to hold their heads high, to hope in the future, that this clandestine traffic of antique objects developed and took on such huge proportions? And is it not also terrible to realize that after having stripped Africa of every culturally significant artifact to be found on its surface we are now stripping that continent of the patrimony that lies buried underground? But the greatest damage that comes out of all this is that entire cultures are being sucked into oblivion. Entire chapters of humanity's history may disappear or be out of reach for future research. And how long will it be before the nations of Europe understand that Africa faces not just a troubled present and an uncertain future but also the disappearance of its past?

ACKNOWLEDGMENT

I would like to take this opportunity, both in my own name and on behalf of all those in Europe who are preoccupied with this problem, to thank the organizers and sponsors of the 1993 Carter Lecture Series entitled "Africa's Disappearing Past: The Erasure of Cultural Heritage" for the opportunity to bring the results of my investigation before an academic audience. Wide distribution of such knowledge is the best way to raise the awareness of African and Western governments, to encourage the international community to take action to eradicate a despicable trade, and to restore the dignity of our African friends that this traffic has so badly damaged.

NOTES

1. At the 1993 Carter Lecture Series, Merrick Posnansky told the audience that during a trip through Mopti in 1973 he met dealers buying looted terra-cottas for major European collectors.

2. For more on this film and its impact on the trade in Mali on terra-cottas, see the chapter by Roderick J. McIntosh in this volume.

3. In this type of investigation, it is obvious that some informers only agree to talk to a journalist on the condition that the source will remain anonymous. This information was given to me by sources who all requested not to be named.

4. For more details about some famous thefts, and notably that of the *Afo-a-Kom* figure, see Paul Nkwi's chapter in this volume.

5. The bona fide principle on which European laws are based is as follows: If an owner who sells a work of art declares that he originally purchased it from a trustworthy source, without suspicion of theft or illegal importation, the courts will usually consider that he is the rightful owner of the item. As can be seen, this principle is vague and full of potential loopholes. See Prott, this volume.

6. This figure is given by a number of African art dealers established in the Sablon quarter, Brussels.

7. Malcolm Billings of the British Broadcasting Corporation and Philip Saunders of *Trace* magazine interviewed in December 1992 by Valerie Colin, my colleague at *Le Vif/L'Express*, who investigated with me the illicit art trade worldwide.

8. Shipping document: Air Cargo Manifest, #142-95704803, dated November 24, 1991.

9. The list of objects was attached to a letter of January 27, 1992 (Reference: ENF-1-V:E:S:NO ST No08PR2No011), sent by Clark W. Settles, Special Agent in charge of Department of the Treasury, U.S. Customs Service, New Orleans to Mohammed Alhoussenyi Toure, Mali's ambassador to the United States.

10. Catalog: The Kuhn Collection of African Art, Auction, Wednesday, November 20, 1991 (at 10:15 A.M.), Sotheby's.

11. This is an unwritten contract for gifts in kind given by the friends that make up for the lack of proper rent for the shop.

12. For more details about these efforts, see the chapter by Maria Papageorge Kouroupas in this volume.

13. Interview with Michael Tite, by W. Van Beek, recorded in the film *The African King*.

REFERENCES

Brent, Michel. "Afrique, le Pillage Continue." *Le Vif/L'Express* 2167 (January 1993):34–37.

Dioura, Bouna Boukary. "Ordre de mission no. 00730/DNAC." Direction Nationale des Arts et de la Culture. Ministère de la Communication et de la Culture: Mali, 1991.

International Council of Museums. *Code of Ethics.* 1990.

McIntosh, Roderick. "New Oxford University Policy on TL Authentication Services." *African Arts* 25, no. 4 (1992):103.

Veillard, G. "Sur quelques objets en terre cuite de Djenne." *Bulletin de l'Institut Fondamental d'Afrique Noire (B)* 3 (1940):347–50.

INTERVIEWS

Robert Badu, November 13, 1992.

Viviane Baeke, September 16, 1992.

Marie-Louise Bastin, December 15, 1992.

Samuel Sidibé, December 16, 1992, January 7, 1993.

Dirk Thys Van Den Audenaerde, June 23, 1992, December 18, 1992.

Sylvia Williams, December, 1992.

6

THE FIGHT AGAINST THE PLUNDERING OF MALIAN CULTURAL HERITAGE AND ILLICIT EXPORTATION

NATIONAL EFFORTS AND INTERNATIONAL COOPERATION

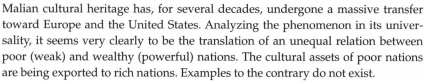

Sᴀᴍᴜᴇʟ Sɪᴅɪʙᴇ́

Malian cultural heritage has, for several decades, undergone a massive transfer toward Europe and the United States. Analyzing the phenomenon in its universality, it seems very clearly to be the translation of an unequal relation between poor (weak) and wealthy (powerful) nations. The cultural assets of poor nations are being exported to rich nations. Examples to the contrary do not exist.

The conditions under which this transfer occurs pose problems of legitimacy, of law, and of ethics. Many of the nations of the world have enacted laws protecting their heritage from illicit exportation. Moreover, the international community has, through the 1970 UNESCO convention, of which Mali is a signatory, been mobilized against the illicit transfer or exportation of cultural heritage. In spite of national and international efforts, the plundering of the cultural heritage of the Third World still continues, justifying the fact that the scientific and international communities are mobilized anew to research means adequate to deal with the situation of persistent plundering.

MALIAN CULTURAL EXPLOITATION: FROM COLONIAL EXPROPRIATION TO THE INTERNATIONAL MARKET

The transfer of Malian cultural heritage to Europe—to France in particular—goes back to the colonial era: it first took place in the shadow of conquest. The treasures of conquered monarchs were seized and exported to the colonizing country. So it was during the conquest of Ségou. It was also the case with Amadou Tall, the Tukulor monarch, and Babemba Traoré, king of Kénédougou at the time of the conquest of Sikasso in May 1898.

On the other hand, the needs of colonial policy, the development of ethnology (how does one separate the ethnographic practice of that time from its colonial context?), a taste for exoticism led the colonial administration to engage in object-collection campaigns. Several missions were organized across the continent. For the Western Sudan, one can cite the Gauthier and Chudeau mission of 1904–05, the missions of Frobenius in 1910, and Gironcourt's mission of 1914–18. The Dakar to Djibouti mission led by Marcel Griaule from May 1931 to February 1933 is, however, the most important, because of the number of objects collected as well as because of the methods used by the ethnographer. Patronized by French public instruction ministers, ministers of colonies, of agriculture, of the French Institute, of the University of Paris, and of the natural history museum, the mission went from West to East Africa, from Dakar to Djibouti, passing through fifteen countries. Michel Leiris, the mission's archive secretary, recounts in *L'Afrique Fantôme* (1981:104) how in 1931 Griaule and other mission members took away the *kono* of a Bamanan village by trickery and by betraying the trust of the village and its inhabitants, committing a sacrilegious act. Leiris concludes, "The 10 francs are given to the chief and we leave in haste, in the midst of general astonishment, adorned with an aura of demons, of particularly powerful and daring bastards." Leiris's book is full of recollections of such behavior: violation of sanctuaries, requisitions, thefts, and so forth. The essential collections by this mission went to the Musée de l'Homme.

Parallel to these missions organized from France, administrators serving in Sudan organized archaeological excavations whose results were exported. Such is the case with Théodore Monod, Lieutenant Desplagnes, who excavated certain tumuli at Killi, especially that of El Oualadji in 1903–07, and with Henri Clérise, the journalist who ultimately mutilated the megalithic site of Tondidaru. The excavated materials of Desplagnes and some megaliths of Tondidaru are preserved at the Musée de l'Homme.

The creation of the French Institute of Black Africa (IFAN) in Dakar in 1936 did not considerably modify the policy of bleeding cultural heritage. Although a section of the Institut Français d'Afrique Noire existed in Mali, at Bamako (this section was the origin of today's national museum), the collections and results of archaeological researches conducted by IFAN were dispatched to Dakar or to France. IFAN collections are thus rich in the steles of Gao Sané, the results of excavations done by Théodore Monod, founder of IFAN, of Raymond Mauny, and of many others. Only with the coming of independence did colonial expropriation come substantially to an end.

AFRICAN ART AND THE INTERNATIONAL MARKET

From the beginning of the twentieth century, with the help of the cubist movement and of Pablo Picasso in particular, certain objects acquired the status of works of art. African sculpture did not become widely recognized by the art lovers in the general public until the second half of the century, at which time African art found its place in art museums beside works of European or Asian tradition. This success reduced African art to the status of merchandise, thus leading to the development of one of the most scandalous forms of international trade in our time.

In 1957 Gérard Brasseur, the director of the Western Sudanese museum, expressed his anguish in the face of the considerable leakage of Malian objects of art: "With the development of air transport, many Dioulas got involved in the international trade of these objects, not only with Paris and Europe, but also with the United States." Despite attempts to arrest this trafficking of Malian cultural heritage (establishment of export authorization, adoption of a decree that dates back to January 25, 1944, that extended to the L'Afrique Occidentale Française the law of December 31, 1913, concerning the protection of historical monuments and provided, among other things, for the regulation of excavations and forbade the exportation of classified objects), the exportation of heritage continued.

During this period, trade occurred primarily in wooden objects, masks, and statues. Antique dealers traveled all over the country to buy or steal such objects or plunder places of worship. The caves in the cliffs of Bandiagara were largely emptied. A dealer in antiques with whom we met remembered the time when entire containers were filled up and exported to Europe and the United States. The discovery of terra-cotta statuettes at archaeological sites of the interior delta of the Niger redirected the market toward this type of object. The phenomenon of plundering was henceforth extended to archaeological sites.

THE PLUNDERING OF ARCHAEOLOGICAL SITES

For many years, the plundering of archaeological sites had affected the regions where budding archaeology had brought terra-cotta statuettes into the limelight. Plundering occurs primarily in the Inland Niger Delta, the region of Djenné in particular, where in 1941 the first statue was discovered. Next, plundering affected the south of Mali, following the discovery of the statues known on commercial markets as Bankoni style. Timid at first, the plundering of archaeological sites has increased brutally in the last two decades, partially because of the degradation of the living conditions of rural populations following severe periods of drought experienced in West Africa since 1974. But it has also escalated because of an increasing interest by museums and galleries for such objects as well as the demand of European, French, Belgian, and American collectors for ancient Malian arts.

This increase was characterized by a geographical extension of the plundering, by a greater diversification of choice objects, and by a systematization in how pillage was conducted. Today, all the areas where commercially valued objects can be found have been altered by looting. The phenomenon has become so dramatic that our knowledge of ancient artifacts is more strongly linked to pillage than to archaeological research. Archaeologists trail behind the looters.

Beyond its increased geographical scope, plundering is characterized by its systematic execution. In the Inland Niger Delta, for example, or in the lacustrine zone where an inventory of sites has been carried out in the last five decades by the Institut des Sciences Humaines (Institute of Human Sciences), it seems that 80 to 90 percent of the sites have been affected by pillage. This systematization is accompanied by a more destructive pillage: from area collection to the superficial erasure characteristic of individual peasant pillage is added an organized (or acting partner) pillage that disturbs sites on a large scale.

Mamadi Dembélé and J. Diderik van de Waals (1991) describe the organization of this looting in the Inland Niger Delta by distinguishing two forms: an independent pillage, in which groups organized in local teams operating by themselves designate one of their members as the leader, responsible for selling the result of their looting to antique dealers on the weekly market days at Sofara, Djenné, and Mopti; an acting partner pillage, in which groups are recruited and supported by an antique dealer who supplies the tools for the pillage and food for the campaign. The fruit of the pillage belongs to the investor, who compensates the workers in proportion to the harvest.

According to evidence revealed from research in the Djenné region within the framework of the Toguè project financed by the Netherlands international aid program, 17 percent of 834 inventoried sites have been affected by large-scale pillage, and 2 percent are totally disfigured by large and deep trenches covering the site. Some examples: In 1989, the Toguéré of Kaney Boro, near Djenné, was disemboweled by a large trench thirty meters long, six meters wide, and eighty centimeters deep. The area plundered was about six hundred square meters. In 1990, the Toguéré Hana Djam, near Sofara, was totally disfigured by several teams of looters that came to settle the sites during the rainy season. That same year, the Natamatao site near Thial village in the Tenenkou circle was plundered by the inhabitants of the surrounding villages following the accidental discovery of a terra-cotta statuette. About ten contiguous wells between two and four meters deep transformed the site into a veritable pit. The looters are generally Bozo and Dogon farmers, riverine populations of the Inland Niger Delta who traditionally emigrate seasonally in the flood-prone zone, where they serve as laborers for rice harvesting. Taking climatic pejoration into account (due to the weakness of the annual flood, rice production has decreased significantly), these populations seem to have found a new source of revenue in plundering.

In the northern region of Mali, intensive plundering is above all the work of the Moorish populations. The Gao Sané site has been for more than six years the object of a systematic pillage by Moorish groups living on the site. In 1990, we were able to visit this site, which looks rather like a gigantic Swiss cheese. Hundreds of methodically placed wells (holes) are dug into the natural soil with galleries linking them together. This site, which dates to the ancient Songhai empire, can be considered irreparably lost. It is certainly not the only plundered site in this region.

One could multiply examples from other areas where one encounters evidence of ancient civilization. Although terra-cotta statuettes are still the most valued objects, the market has also integrated beads, vases, beautiful coated bottles from the Timbuktoo and Gao regions, and bronze figurines. Arrowheads and other Neolithic tools of the Sahara also appear on the market.

ILLICIT TRADE

I will not belabor the negative impact of pillage on the knowledge of the history of ancient cultures and societies. It is more important for us to understand the mechanisms of trafficking so that we can wage war on this plague.

Who are the protagonists? Our knowledge of the network enables us to advance the following points:

1) At the top of the process of revitalization of the market is a multitude of contributors: local farmers, individual plunderers, or a network of pillagers organized by antique dealers or operating on their own. In Northern Mali, where the pillaging is carried out by Moors coming generally from Mauritania, the network appears to be less structured, at least in relation to the international market. Looters look mainly for beads, which are sold in the Mauritanian market. Léré was in times past considered the center of this trafficking.

2) At the intermediary level are the antique dealers. They are located in the important suburbs at Bamako, at Mopti, and at Djenné. These antique dealers sometimes have collectors settled in secondary suburbs. These collectors rarely have access to the international market, although they sometimes run basic shops. An investigation carried out by the Bougouni police showed that these intermediaries can be implicated in other illicit activities. For the antique dealers of Bamako, Mopti, or Djenné to have access to the international market depends on financial capability and the existence of a network of "friends" in Europe, the United States, and perhaps in Mali.

No matter how powerful they are in the network, the antique dealers maintain a local market in Mali, frequented mainly by tourists and European and American expatriates, officials, and diplomats. This market presents secondary and false pieces (copies, one might say), whereas the major pieces are hidden in the backyards or in the back of bedrooms, to be sold to collectors who can buy them at exorbitant prices. We have acquired for the National Museum of Mali a piece of this kind by posing as American collectors living in France. We quickly convinced the antique dealers of our interest by making a distinction between copies and old pieces with assurance. By so doing we were led by the antique dealer to his house and shown the pieces "which he dared not display at the market because the National Museum could make trouble for them."

3) At the third level are the European and American markets: sales galleries, collectors, and museums. The relationships between African antique dealers and the international market are not well known. It seems, if one is inclined to believe a survey carried out by one of the antique dealers from Mopti, that the market functions on the basis of a network of correspondents, which explains the relative specialization of antique dealers as to the destination of their consignment. Some are more oriented toward the United States, others toward Belgium or France. The illicit trade in art implies trust.

Taking into consideration the risks that the European traders could run, it seems that they are making fewer and fewer trips to Mali. More and more Malian antique dealers undertake the journey to Europe.

Besides moving by air routes, a significant portion of the objects is illicitly exported by road or by rail to the Côte d'Ivoire and Senegal. These two neighboring countries have sales galleries operated by internationally recognized Lebanese dealers. In these galleries one can see archaeological objects from Malian archaeological sites. It is certain that these antique dealers play an important role in the illicit trafficking to Europe and the United States.

The level of demand has led to the creation of an industry to produce fakes. A number of antique dealers specialize in this industry, although this does not prevent them from engaging in plundering. The counterfeit industry, moreover, serves as a cover for illicit activities. The techniques to produce fakes have been refined considerably in the last few years. The results are sometimes so remarkable that it is difficult to distinguish between genuine and fake ancient objects. It is at this juncture where the role of some scientists, archaeologists, art historians, archaeometric laboratories, editors, and museums stands out clearly in the support that they give the illicit trafficking. By authenticating the works of art of collectors or traders without giving any thought to the legitimacy of exportation of the work, laboratories make a major contribution to the pillaging of sites. "Business is business," proudly said an Oxford thermoluminescence laboratory analyst several years ago. Some museums justify purchase of dubious objects by saying that if they do not buy the object, other museums will do so.

By posing the problem in these terms, there is no doubt that museum professionals do not put themselves in a position to contribute to the battle against plundering and to conserving knowledge of ancient cultures. As we know, objects from pillaging are without origin or known context. Exhibiting them in museums uniquely enhances their aesthetic and market value. I will not dwell on this question, which has been developed considerably by Roderick J. McIntosh and Susan Keech McIntosh (1986). It will suffice to affirm that the battle against pillage has not addressed the elaboration of an adequate code of ethics acceptable to all scientists.

Some voices are arising to suggest that the commercialization of objects could help finance research. It is important to note that those who make this suggestion are not archaeologists but rather are people whose prime aim is to acquire objects. It is evident that it is better to acquire them when one has minimum information. But must archaeology feed the market? Archaeologists know that is not their objective.

FIGHTING THE ILLICIT TRADE

I will turn from the analysis of pillaging and of illicit trafficking to examine what Mali is doing to fight this phenomenon and to suggest how new actions can be developed on both internal and international levels.

At the national level, there has been recent adoption of legislation aimed to meet the needs of the battle:

Law no. 85-40/AN—RM of July 26, 1985, relating to the protection and the promotion of national cultural heritage;

Decree no. 275/PG—RM of November 4, 1985, regulating archaeological excavations;

Law no. 86-61/AN—RM of July 26, 1986, relating to the profession of the traders in cultural possessions;

Decree no. 999/PG—RM of September 19, 1986, relating to the commercialization of cultural possessions.

This legislation constitutes an appreciable link in an action-designed policy to challenge pillaging and illicit exportation. The measures contained in these texts concern the battle against illicit transfer, by controls on exportation; against clandestine excavations, through regulating archaeological excavations; and against the commercialization of cultural possessions, through the organization of the profession of traders in cultural objects.

The adoption of laws has provided a framework of regulation concerning protection, but the application of these measures encounters important difficulties. Regarding the protection of sites and the war against looting, it is very difficult to implicate populations in processes of protection. Despite the creation by the state of local commissions to safeguard heritage, there is no real mobilization around the objectives of the battle against plundering.

Two kinds of exploration can be proffered for this situation: First, the texts of the laws are not sufficiently disseminated; second, the notion of heritage as it is developed around archaeological sites does not correspond to a reality experienced by the population. People do not seem to understand the ban placed on pillaging or exploitation of sites to remove marketable products, especially since the economic situation is dire at present. Prohibition is perceived as the state's will to have a monopoly. In this context, archaeology is seen as exploitation of treasures.

Administrative authorities responsible for control and repression of pillaging and trafficking are not sufficiently sensitive or technically competent to assume their mission. As we fight for efficacy against pillaging and illicit trafficking, we must also define methods of action that will enhance common values. In this perspective, it is necessary to develop educational policies on heritage through exhibitions, popular publications, conferences, films on archaeology. Thus, the meaning of this discipline and the interest in archaeological sites will be understood. For example, in 1993 the Malian government installed, on an experimental basis, cultural missions on three sites classified as having national and world patrimony (Timbuktu, Djenné, and Bandiagara) with the objective of sensitizing populations to the protection of their heritage. People's attitudes are appreciably different when it comes to living patrimony. Groups still practicing traditional religions fiercely defend their objects of worship against robbers.

The creation of local museums and eco-museums can also help to involve populations in the management of their heritage. Alas, the still extant tendency to preserve everything at the capital constitutes a handicap for the development of a real safeguard policy of heritage. It is essential today to integrate into curricula an education on heritage and the history of populations. The efforts of the National Museum of Mali through its educational programs could find here a decisive support.

To put such a policy to work supposes the development of the knowledge of the past. Archaeological research remains timid and always oriented toward academic perspectives, whereas the extension of pillaging ought to push toward the development of an archaeology of rescue. The battle against pillaging and illicit trafficking also necessitates the formulation of policies of inventory both within and outside the country. Museum professionals from Europe and America could help with this inventory, which, furthermore, can serve as the basis of an international and fruitful cooperation.

At the international and regional levels Mali is a signatory of the 1970 UNESCO convention. With this status and scope, the government of Mali submitted to the U.S. government a request to fight pillaging and illicit trafficking. That request resulted, in September of 1993, in the first ever bilateral agreement to ban the import of broadly inclusive classes of antiquities (see McIntosh, this volume). The international partnership represented by this agreement marks a substantial contribution to the battle against the pillaging of Malian heritage and has helped Mali in its efforts at the national level.

The extension of the trafficking network to neighboring countries in West Africa should inspire us also to seek an efficacious collaboration at the regional level. A regional workshop on illicit exportation, planned by UNESCO and held in Bamako in October 1994, had as its objectives, among other things, to harmonize legislation and to put in place a regional mechanism capable of checking pillaging and illicit trafficking. The degree of goodwill shared by the delegates—museum and antiquities service professionals, heads of national Interpol bureaus, archaeologists, and UNESCO representatives—and their dedication to stopping the illicit trade in art and antiquities out of Africa were truly inspiring. We now begin to have reason to hope for a new day of international cooperation in the fight against the plundering of Malian cultural heritage.

REFERENCES

Dembelé, Mamadi, and J. Diderik Van der Waals. "Looting the Antiquities of Mali." *Antiquity* 65, 249 (1991): 904–05.

Leiris, M. *L'Afrique Fantôme*. Paris: Gallimard, (1934) 1981.

McIntosh, R. J., and S. K. McIntosh. "Dilettantism and Plunder: Dimensions of Illicit Traffic in Ancient Malian Art." UNESCO *Museum* 149 (1986), 49–57.

Togola, Téréba, and Michel Rainbault. "A National Plague: The Pillaging of Malian Archaeological Sites." *Jamana* 23 (September 1989): 19–21.

7

U.S. EFFORTS IN THE PROTECTION OF CULTURAL PROPERTY

IMPLEMENTATION OF THE 1970 UNESCO CONVENTION

Maria Papageorge Kouroupas

Eight-one countries have become party to the Convention on the Means of Prohibiting and Preventing the Illicit Import, Export, and Transfer of Ownership of Cultural Property since its adoption by UNESCO in 1970. The convention establishes a framework for international cooperation to reduce the incentive for pillaging by restricting the illicit movement of archaeological and ethnographic material. With U.S. implementation of the convention, which began in 1983, this framework has become operational—operational, that is, from the point of view of art-rich nations that have suffered vast losses to their national cultural patrimony through looting and unauthorized trade.

The United States remains the only major art-importing country to ratify the convention. Its enabling legislation, the Convention on Cultural Property Implementation Act, authorizes the president to receive requests from other parties to the convention seeking U.S. import controls on certain archaeological or ethnographic material. These requests include documentation that the national cultural patrimony is in jeopardy from the pillage of this material; that internal protective measures are in place; that the United States is a market for the material; that U.S. action would be in the interest of the general public for educational, scientific, and cultural purposes; and, if applicable, that certain emergency conditions obtain.

Each request is evaluated through an advisory and decision-making process that addresses the matter of looting and illicit trade on a country-by-country basis. Except in instances of the theft of articles of cultural property that are accounted for in museum inventories or other records, the U.S. enabling legislation offers no automatic protection to other countries. It is therefore incumbent on an individual state party to the convention to submit a request seeking the protection of U.S. import controls on archaeological material that may yet be unearthed or ethnographic material that remains in its societal context. Enforcement of such controls by the United States is significant, for it essentially removes a major art-consuming nation from the marketplace for specific material and has the effect of enforcing the export controls of the requesting country.

Protection under the act is prospective; U.S. implementation of the convention emphasizes not the recovery of past losses but rather the protection of cultural property that remains in situ in the country of origin, the undocumented material that, stripped of its provenance, feeds a large clandestine trade bringing high yield with little risk to the participants in this trade. Most vulnerable are those countries where there is a large universe of unexcavated sites, where the cultural patrimony is provided little in the way of financial resources and skilled personnel to preserve it, and where protective measures may be inadequate, not enforced, or unenforceable. Since U.S. protection under the act is prospective, it is in the best interest of an art-losing country to be expeditious in submitting a request for U.S. sanctions.

The United States is also prepared to implement the 1970 UNESCO convention where applicable by working with other signatories to the convention to minimize the problems of pillage and illicit export. This readiness is underpinned in a statement issued by the U.S. Department of State at the time of ratification of the convention:

> U.S. foreign policy supports the restoration of stolen cultural objects to their countries of origin. There has been an expanding trade in archaeological and [ethnographic] artifacts deriving from clandestine activities and excavations that result in the mutilation of ancient centers of civilization. The appearance in the U.S. of important art objects of suspicious origin has often given rise to outcries and urgent requests for return. The U.S. considers that on grounds of good foreign relations it should render assistance. In following this policy, we are motivated also by ethical and moral principles . . . [that] the U.S. should not become a thieves' haven.

U.S. ACTION UNDER THE CULTURAL PROPERTY IMPLEMENTATION ACT

The U.S. Information Agency (USIA) has the lion's share of the responsibility for implementing U.S. participation in the 1970 UNESCO convention. It not only administers the Cultural Property Advisory Committee but also carries out most of the president's executive responsibilities under the Cultural Property Act. By late 1995, the director of the agency, on behalf of the president, had received seven state party requests for import controls—from Canada, El Salvador, Bolivia, Peru, Guatemala, and Mali.[1] Mali has the distinction of being the first African country to submit a cultural property request under the convention and the first outside the Western Hemisphere to do so.[2]

All of these requests were reviewed by the Cultural Property Advisory Committee, comprised of eleven members, including archaeologists, anthropologists, ethnologists, experts in the international sale of art, representatives of museums, and the general public. The committee's recommendations on these requests were submitted to the president's designee, who, in turn, rendered favorable decisions with respect to the Salvadoran, Bolivian, Peruvian, Guatemalan, and Malian requests. A decision on the Canadian request has yet to be announced.

Most of these requests have been treated under the emergency provision of the Cultural Property Act, which enables a U.S. response to clearly circumscribed situations of pillage. El Salvador, for example, needed protection of pre-Hispanic material originating in a well-defined archaeological zone where an estimated five thousand looters' pits had already been dug, posing a serious threat to any scientific archaeology. This material is prohibited from entry into the United States unless accompanied by a Salvadoran export permit. In 1995, the U.S.–El Salvador agreement was revised to confer renewable, five-year protection to all classes of pre-Columbian antiquities from the entire country.

Bolivia needed U.S. import protection on unique antique textiles belonging to Coroma, a small Andean community visited by art dealers and middle-men who, it is alleged, arranged for the systematic removal of the textiles from their ceremonial bundles. The textiles subsequently began to appear on the U.S. commercial market, and some were mounted in a traveling exhibition sponsored by a major American museum, a move that likely enhanced their value as commodities. These textiles are not considered commodities by the villagers of Coroma, however, because they are integral for political, social, and religious practices. Handed down through generations, the textiles are the single most vital link in the past, present, and future of Coromans. But their unique stylistic characteristics made them a desirable commodity on the art market. It is now illegal to transport this material into the U.S. without an export license issued by Bolivia.

Peru sought protection of newly discovered Moche material—mostly gold, silver, and copper objects—found on its northern coast at the site of Sipan. It is claimed that this site has yielded the richest intact tomb yet found in the Western Hemisphere. The site had already been partially looted before armed guards were brought in to protect it, and some of the looted material had quickly made its way to California, England, and supposedly elsewhere in Europe as well. It is now illegal to bring this material into the United States without a Peruvian export certificate. Guatemala, too, petitioned the United States for an emergency import ban on all Mayan artifacts originating in the Peten region. Guatemala's petition explained how "this magnificent cultural legacy, in which all Guatemalans take pride, and which foreigners admire, has been greatly damaged and diminished by pillage and theft." Effective April 15, 1991, this material may not be imported into the United States. Of the actions taken to date, this is the one that may affect the greatest number of American museums. The Canadian request seeks an agreement with the United States that imposes import controls on both archaeological and ethnographic material, making it broader in scope than most other requests.

A distinguishing feature of Canada's request is that it comes from a Western industrialized country with which the U.S. shares a long border and a common heritage. It demonstrates that even a country with sufficient resources to protect, conserve, house, and exhibit its cultural and artistic heritage may itself be a victim of pillage. In the United States, knowledgeable sources frequently report the loss of vast amounts of Native American artifacts to the international art market. Foreign financing, it is said, supports much of the clandestine looting of Indian sites in the Southwest.

THE AFRICAN REGION

Of the eighty-one countries that have become state parties to the 1970 convention, twenty are in Africa: Algeria, Angola, Burkina Faso, Cameroon, Central African Republic, Côte d'Ivoire, Egypt, Guinea, Libya, Madagascar, Mali, Mauritania, Mauritius, Niger, Nigeria, Senegal, Tanzania, Tunisia, Zaïre, and Zambia. Africans and Africanists know intimately the extent to which the cultural resources of sub-Saharan countries in particular are being exploited to satisfy market demands outside the continent. But of the African countries that are party to the UNESCO convention, Mali is the first and only one to submit an official request to the U.S. government for protection of its cultural patrimony.

Perhaps others will follow suit. Perhaps a country such as Ghana, which is not a signatory to the convention, would find it advantageous to ratify it, thus becoming eligible to request U.S. import controls on the gold regalia of the Akan peoples. Similar to the Coroma textiles of Bolivia, these regalia are used for ceremonial purposes and are passed on to subsequent generations. Although purportedly held in common trust, like the textiles, these pieces too are finding their way to the international art market.

"Lost Heritage: The Destruction of African Art," an article by Andrew Decker that appeared in the September 1990 issue of *Artnews*, exposes the extent of depredation and neglect suffered by the cultural heritage of West African nations: "Hundreds of thousands of objects in African museums, many of them undocumented, are disappearing—rotting or being eaten away. The magnitude of the destruction is immense," wrote Decker, who visited Africa and interviewed numerous cultural officers there. Added to the catastrophic effects of the environment and the general lack of basic conservation skills and equipment is an ineffectual law enforcement apparatus. It seems that the cultural heritage of Africa, if not in a state of irreversible decay, is subject to theft or illegal export. These problems are by no means unique to the African continent.

A further complicating factor is the inherent African view that such objects are more important for their functional attributes than for their aesthetic qualities. Reconciling this view with the need for effective national cultural policies and adequate museum infrastructures is not a small task for the few but an undertaking for dedicated professionals within the African cultural community.

AMELIORATIVE TRENDS

Decker wrote that "the problems are so vast and so widespread that the African cultural heritage is in danger of being lost entirely." This bleak forecast is not without some hope, however. One of the most promising developments involves the International Centre for the Study of the Preservation and the Restoration of Cultural Property in Rome (ICCROM), which has launched a long-term conservation training program for African museum personnel. Basic principles of preventive conservation are taught in an annual eleven-month course in Rome that is augmented with on-site training seminars in Africa. One such seminar was partially supported by the USIA. A major goal of the ICCROM program is to build a cadre of trained Africans so that in a few years 90 percent of the teaching staff in the Rome course is African.

The West African Museums Project based in Dakar is another positive sign. Founded in 1982, this program, supported primarily by the Ford Foundation, offers grants and professional assistance to museums in West Africa.

There are many Western anthropologists and archaeologists working throughout the continent who are struggling to find ways to support their African colleagues and cultural officials, who continue to make small but steady gains in implementing the policies that will sustain those institutions necessary to protect and manage what remains of Africa's cultural resources. A proactive stance was taken by members of the Society of Africanist Archaeologists, who, in their biennial meeting in 1990, endorsed a resolution condemning the illicit market in African antiquities and pledging the society's efforts to undermine this trade through ethical practices and by searching for reasonable alternatives to the trade.

Other developments deserve mention. For example, in 1987 the International Council of Museums (ICOM) adopted a code of professional ethics (translated into eighteen languages) urging museums to "recognize the relationship between the marketplace and the initial and often destructive taking of an object for the commercial market, and recognize that it is highly unethical for a museum to support in any way, whether directly or indirectly, that illicit market." In addition, in recent years curator and conservator groups have taken steps to modify their own codes of ethics to offer guiding principles in handling objects without provenance, objects that may have been acquired outside prevailing legal and ethical parameters.

Numerous museums in the United States have adopted stricter acquisitions policies. For example, the acquisitions policy of the University of Pennsylvania Museum takes a very high road, indeed. It states that the museum's board and staff "will not knowingly acquire, . . . any materials known or suspected to have been exported from their countries of origin since 1970 in contravention of the UNESCO Convention of that year," to which the museum fully subscribes. The museum will not knowingly support this illegal trade by authenticating or offering opinions concerning such material. "Objects offered to the museum in the United States prior to the adoption of the UNESCO Convention of 1970 will be considered in the light of the laws in place in their countries of origin at the time of their documented appearance in the United States."

In May 1973, the Smithsonian Institution adopted a policy that prohibits the acquisition and/or display of material that has been unethically acquired, unscientifically excavated, or illegally removed from its country of origin after the date on which the policy went into force (see Brent, this volume).

Yet another interesting development, albeit subtle, is illustrated in the March-April 1990 issue of *Museum News* in an article by Stephen E. Weil, deputy director of the Hirshhorn Museum and Sculpture Garden. Weil writes about a new set of basic museum functions that emerges from the paradigm of five tasks that has served museum operations over the past twenty years or so. The original five essential functions (to collect, to conserve, to study, to interpret, and to exhibit) are evolving into three (to preserve, to study, and to communicate). Perhaps it is no accident that, in an atmosphere of growing sensitivity to cultural property issues and to the relationship of museums to those issues, the collecting function is being subsumed by the preservation function. This emphasis on preservation also strengthens the responsibilities of museum stewardship by urging museums to preserve humanity's artistic and cultural heritage through more prudent collecting practices consistent with international standards and regulations affecting the movement of cultural property.

These changes suggest a developing dynamic that, in time, could foreclose on the collecting practices of old and encourage the pursuit of new avenues of access to protected material. The U.S. Cultural Property Act seeks to ensure such access and explicitly provides "that the application of import restrictions . . . is consistent with the general interest of the international community in the interchange of cultural property among nations for scientific, cultural, and educational purposes" [(Section 303(a)(1)(D)].

CONCLUSION

The lion's share of responsibility under the Cultural Property Implementation Act rests with the USIA, an independent agency of the executive branch that is responsible for the overseas information and cultural programs of the U.S. government. The agency's foreign service officers work alongside their state department colleagues in U.S. embassies and consulates throughout the world—there are more than two hundred such posts in one hundred thirty countries. These officers, a vital link with leading citizens of their host country, utilize the agency's programs and services in advancing the agency's overall mission to "increase mutual understanding between the people of the United States and the people of other countries." The USIA is the major source for servicing the program needs of our posts abroad. It is the agency that supports the academic exchanges of the Fulbright program, sponsors hundreds of international professional exchange programs, and supports United States Information Service library services abroad.

These officers are also the information link between the USIA's cultural property staff and cultural officials in UNESCO signatory countries that are eligible to submit requests for U.S. protection. As a result of the efforts of these officers, the United States expects to receive requests from art-losing countries in Asia and Europe as well as from Latin American countries.

The USIA recently undertook an initiative to sponsor a regional symposium on cultural heritage preservation—policy development and implementation—in South Asia and the Pacific. The symposium examined how land use, tourist development, the environments, and other factors such as looting combine to threaten both movable and immovable cultural heritage and how efforts to deal with these threats must be integrated for coherence and maximum effectiveness. A similar symposium on the protection of cultural property for Arabic-speaking countries in the Middle East and North Africa was held in Cairo in November 1993.

It becomes increasingly clear that laws, while of absolute importance, represent neither the only nor the ultimate answer to the problem of pillage and illicit trade. Although they must have a prominent and enforceable presence, laws are most effective in an integrated partnership with the policies and infrastructures that support the viability of museums and other cultural institutions in achieving the effective management of cultural resources. The USIA supports programs concerned with worldwide conservation and preservation needs, museum training needs, inventories of cultural and artistic resources, systematic archaeology, site management, collections management, and so forth. Such program opportunities, combined with the USIA's statutory responsibilities under the Cultural Property Act, not only place the agency at the forefront of international legal efforts to curb illicit trade, but also define the agency as an important catalyst in advancing worldwide efforts to mitigate the loss of our irreplaceable cultural heritage.

NOTES

1. Of the seven state party requests received by the United States through mid 1995, the seventh, from El Salvador, sought a bilateral agreement with the United States for protection of all its pre-Hispanic cultural resources. The bilateral agreement, the first ever under the Cultural Property Implementation Act, was signed on March 8, 1995.

2. Effective September 23, 1993, archaeological material from the region of the Niger River Valley and Bandiagara Escarpment of Mali is restricted from importation into the United States. This emergency action is taken under article 9 of the 1970 UNESCO convention as implemented by the U.S. Convention on Cultural Property Implementation Act. USIA arranged two international television interactives as follow-up to this action. One was between Washington, Mali, and other West African countries; the other, between Washington, Bamaka, and Paris. The Paris-based audience and participants included French government officials, media representatives, and representatives of international organizations. The *Art Newspaper* and other publications and radio broadcasts in Europe carried news of U.S. action to protect Mali's cultural heritage.

8

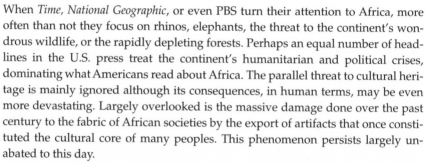

AFRICA'S VANISHING CULTURAL HERITAGE

REFLECTIONS OF AN AMERICAN CULTURAL DIPLOMAT

ROBERT R. LAGAMMA

When *Time, National Geographic,* or even PBS turn their attention to Africa, more often than not they focus on rhinos, elephants, the threat to the continent's wondrous wildlife, or the rapidly depleting forests. Perhaps an equal number of headlines in the U.S. press treat the continent's humanitarian and political crises, dominating what Americans read about Africa. The parallel threat to cultural heritage is mainly ignored although its consequences, in human terms, may be even more devastating. Largely overlooked is the massive damage done over the past century to the fabric of African societies by the export of artifacts that once constituted the cultural core of many peoples. This phenomenon persists largely unabated to this day.

Here, I will address my own perspective, which I believe reflects the experience of many of my United States Information Service and other foreign-service colleagues in Africa over the past three decades. I must begin by candidly noting that those of us who are U.S. representatives in Africa have only recently begun to realize the seriousness of this issue. My own rather dramatic awakening to the vulnerability and fragility of Africa's cultural heritage occurred in 1965, when I sought to visit the Elisabethville museum in the Congo, which had been ravaged by civil war. I was told that the museum was empty, allegedly pillaged by the Ethiopian contingent of United Nations peacekeeping forces, who had then proceeded to the town square to peddle artifacts to the highest bidders.

Who among us that has lived in Africa has not been frequently accosted by the gnarled old men proffering what they claim are art treasures? The old man is no African Santa Claus. The objects in the sack are usually said to be very old indeed, but most have been subjected to clever aging techniques in the old man's backyard. These peddlers seek to convince buyers that they can purchase genuine art treasures ripped from villages where they had been used in sacred ceremonies for generations. Sometimes they are. But if, as is more often the case, the objects are not sufficiently convincing to prospective buyers, sellers will often hold out hope that, for an appropriate price, authentic originals can be procured.

The most enterprising of those old men now have a fair notion of the value of genuine artifacts in the auction houses of New York, London, and Zurich. Many of these vendors are connected to agents in their own capitals or in the West. The old men sometimes have superb networks of contacts among merchants who travel widely through the interior with an eye open to the availability of a particularly fine old mask. Their cousins may know an underpaid guard at a poorly secured national museum. They are likely to be alert to newspaper headlines reporting drought or natural calamity in an area possessing a rich cultural heritage. If insurrection strikes areas with repositories of cultural artifacts, plunderers will have little difficulty in finding their way to the old men's places of business.

So who is at fault? Should African governments throw the old men into dungeons? Should they arrest Western clients with a lust for art treasure? What about the corrupt museum official or the village chief or farmer afflicted by grinding poverty who may be tempted to peddle the village ceremonial objects, which may, in their eyes, have lost some of their sway in the face of dwindling adherence to traditional religious beliefs? Who is to blame? The answer is probably everybody and nobody.

Laws are usually unclear, often unenforced, and sometimes unenforceable. The ethical terrain is murky. Greed is pervasive and corruption rampant on both sides. The economic power of the West has combined with the enormous temptations that Africans find so difficult to resist to make Africa a cultural sieve, a colander with a thousand orifices through which artifacts flow ineluctably.

USIS offices overseas often enjoy close relations with cultural ministries and museums. U.S. exchange programs frequently seek to assist African museums with the preservation of cultural heritage by arranging to bring U.S. specialists to Africa and African museum officials to the United States for professional contacts. USIS representatives sometimes arrange museum affiliations or loans or assist in identifying artists who might be included in exhibitions in the United States. But there is a frustration that this may address merely the tip of the iceberg.

As the official cultural representatives of the United States, USIS officers over the years have been contacted by museums and cultural ministries seeking to recover objects of cultural or historical importance. Given the seriousness and urgency of the problem, such contacts have been surprisingly infrequent. In the face of so many other problems, the issue of the loss of cultural heritage has only gained prominence in a handful of countries. While there may be a growing consciousness of the importance of giving priority attention to that issue, for many African governments it may be a matter of locking the barn door after the cows have escaped.

In 1991 as USIS director in Nigeria I was involved in the recovery of a stolen art treasure, a Benin bronze head. This experience provided me with some insights into the complexity of recovering cultural property. The case was unusual in that it involved the importation of the stolen artifact not into the United States but rather into Switzerland. The drama began to unfold on the evening of November 25, 1990, with a phone call from Zurich art collector Peter Schnell to an authority on Nigerian art, John Pemberton III, Crosby Professor of Religion at Amherst College. The collector had been offered and had declined to purchase a Benin bronze that he believed bore a striking resemblance to one depicted in a Nigerian

National Museum catalogue. He wondered if Nigeria was selling off its antiquities, or if this was a fake or perhaps a second, almost identical, original. To complicate matters, the Zurich dealer who had presented the work for sale apparently provided documentation alleging that the work had been acquired prior to the theft of the one in the museum.

Pemberton referred the matter to Kate Ezra, the Metropolitan Museum of Art's African art curator, and to Constance Lowenthal of the International Federation of Art Research. Ezra and Lowenthal were able to determine that the Benin head appeared to be one of ten art treasures stolen from the National Museum at Jos on January 14, 1987. The bronze had spent four years in what appears to be a vast underworld of art treasures. Its abduction, however, was duly recorded and circulated to individuals and institutions around the world and to Interpol through UNESCO's International Council of Museums *News* in accordance with its 1970 Convention on the Means of Prohibiting the Illicit Import, Export, and Transfer of Ownership of Cultural Property.

Accordingly, Pemberton contacted the prospective buyer to warn him that the bronze was stolen property. Lowenthal contacted the Zurich police specialist responsible for art and antiquities, Karl Fiechter. From these contacts it was learned that the art dealer who held the work planned to put it up for sale at the Mangisch auction house in Zurich. Under Swiss law, however, a work of art sold at auction cannot be returned to the original owner, even if it is determined to have been stolen, unless the original owner reimburses the buyer the amount paid within five years. It was further learned that the bronze would be auctioned on December 7, just two weeks from the time Pemberton had been initially contacted.

While the U.S. experts and the Swiss authorities had been activated, it remained for Nigerian authorities to formally claim the stolen work and to present the appropriate proof to document their claim. Nigerian embassy officials in Bern and at the London High Commission were contacted, but both offices responded that they could not act without instructions from Lagos. Therein lay a seemingly trivial but nonetheless formidable problem: notification of museum officials through Nigeria's impenetrable telephone system. After a number of failed efforts to contact Nigerian authorities directly, Pemberton tried another route. He phoned the USIS office in Lagos and spoke to me about the need to brief Nigerian authorities and urge them to act quickly to register their claim to the bronze before the auction gavel could fall.

USIS then set up a channel of communication between the National Museum's Ade Obayemi, director of Nigeria's National Commission for Museums and Monuments, and Pemberton. Obayemi immediately assigned his chief curator and head of museums, Helen Kerri, and her colleague, David Akinpelu, who was in charge of documentation, to prepare Nigeria's claim, and they arranged to have Akinpelu travel to Zurich to work with Nigeria's embassy in Switzerland. Despite the urgency of the task, Nigerian museum officials confronted the excruciatingly painful need to work through their labyrinthine bureaucracies. As time ran out, senior officials could not be found or motivated to act quickly enough and the connections between cultural and foreign ministries necessary to issue instructions to Nigeria's diplomats and authorize and fund overseas travel were not forthcoming.

To break the logjam, a Nigerian patron of the arts with good political connections was contacted and asked to appeal the matter to Nigeria's vice president, Augustus Aikhoumu, who just happened to be from Benin City. High-level intervention just two days before the deadline produced travel orders and an airline ticket for Akinpelu. With the evidence he provided and with the help of Eberhard Fischer of Zurich's Reitberg Museum, conclusive proof was provided to Swiss authorities establishing that the bronze in question was indeed the work stolen from the Jos museum.

Two weeks later the Benin bronze was back in Nigeria at the National Museum, which welcomed it back with a gracious ceremony presided over by the minister of culture and social affairs, Y. Y. Kure. In his remarks to the large audience, including the national media assembled in the courtyard of the museum, the minister offered Nigeria's appreciation to all those in the international community, especially Pemberton, who contributed to the return of the priceless art treasure. Kure also noted the importance of the cultural agreements into which Nigeria entered making possible the return of a priceless, irreplaceable, stolen artifact.

The difficulties encountered in the recovery of the Benin bronze are typical of the challenges faced by African countries in retaining and recovering art treasures. First and foremost, there is the laxity of security at museums charged with protecting art treasures. Second, priceless works in insecure environments are vulnerable because they can fetch a king's ransom in Western markets. In fact, only the scrupulousness and integrity of a potential buyer kept this work from disappearing without a trace. Third, there is the matter of poor channels of communication between African countries, the art markets where works are sold, and potential allies in the United States and Europe. Fourth, the bureaucratic tangles in African governments can be daunting. Finally, there is the dearth of political will, the absence of resources, and the relatively low priority given to cultural matters.

Increasingly, as in the case of the Nigerian recovery, USIS officers in thirty-seven African countries are being sensitized to their role in facilitating cooperation in this realm. The U.S. Congress assigned this mandate to the agency in 1983, in the wake of the U.S. acquiescence to the UNESCO convention on cultural property. But many USIS agents in the field are naturally inclined to collaborate closely with museums to demonstrate the U.S. government's sympathy and support for Africans interested in preserving their heritage.

One notable case is that of the USIS agent in Bamako, public affairs officer William Crowell, who worked closely with museum authorities and high Malian government officials to craft and advance a proposal that would lead to the imposition of a ban on the importation of certain Malian art treasures into the United States. This ban, now in effect, is in accordance with the UNESCO convention and represents the first of its kind between the United States and an African country.

It is important to the success of such an accord that as many loopholes as possible be closed. Especially important is the enhancement of Mali's ability to enforce measures designed to prevent the export of its art treasures. The first and most important guard against the flight of cultural artifacts has to be positioned by the country concerned. Equally important is the need to launch cooperative efforts with other major destinations. It serves little purpose for the United States to ban importation of African art heritage if the doors of France, Switzerland, and Japan, for example, remain wide open.

Also important is the need to launch educational campaigns to assist Africans in better appreciating the need for conservation of their heritage and to educate potential buyers about the ethical standards that should condition their behavior. On a very modest level, the USIS has decided that a basic orientation on respect for cultural heritage should be an integral part of the training not only of new USIS officers but also of incoming State Department officers. For too long diplomats of First World countries have been part of the problem.

I conclude this personal reflection on a pessimistic note. So much has already been lost, and mechanisms to halt the flow of art treasures still remaining in Africa are so ineffectual, that in the face of the enormity of the task those interested in addressing this conundrum may need miracles. More coordination is certainly needed among scholars, museums, and governments. More resources are required to assist African countries in providing adequate museum security. Expanded exchange programs are required to train personnel, including the "art police" of many African countries. Educational programs within Africa must be designed within existing school curricula. Realistic ethical standards must be refined and promulgated in the West.

The USIS, which has an on-the-ground presence in Africa, hopes to continue working with scholars and museums to achieve an objective that may seem beyond realization today but that someday, with imaginative, collaborative efforts, we may obtain.

9

A CONSERVATION DILEMMA OVER AFRICAN ROYAL ART IN CAMEROON

PAUL NCHOJI NKWI

More than twenty years ago, I took part in an emotional celebration for an event that took national proportions and projected a small unknown kingdom into the national and international scene. On December 11, 1973, the stolen symbol of Kom royalty, the *Afo-a-Kom* (the Kom thing) was restored to its original owners, the Kom people. Thieves had stolen the royal life-size figure from the Kom palace using a highly sophisticated system including land rovers, trucks, airplanes, and a host of interested African art dealers. When the *Afo-a-Kom* was discovered in the possession of an American art dealer named Furman, political and diplomatic confrontation was vital for its retrieval. Because of its symbolism and significance to the people of Kom, its return after seven years of sojourn in foreign lands was an emotional and a memorable occasion.

The *Afo-a-Kom* is chiseled out of a block of iroko, a hard and heavy wood. It forms a throne figure—an upright man, crowned and holding a scepter. It is a primary symbol of kingship and has the paramount significance of the undisputed symbol of Kom kingship. Each foot has three toes: The ruler (*foyn*) is the guarantor of the fruitful outcome of rituals, and Kom rituals are performed always to guarantee the three Kom hands (children)—lineage continuity (*wain*); food (*afo-anyina*, agricultural production); prosperity (*nyamngvin*). The *foyn*'s main functions are to guarantee these basic values. The throne figure tries to capture this concept.

The Kom chauffeur given the honor of driving the delegation that returned the figure summarized the sentiments of the people: "You must wonder why there are so many of our people out to greet us, why they are so happy. And I will tell you that the homecoming of the statue is like the return of the crown jewels to England. Yes, that's it, the return of the crown jewels to England if they'd been stolen and kept in hiding for seven years" (Ellis 1974:142).

The dramatic discovery and return of the *Afo-a-Kom* reveals just the tip of the iceberg of the black market and trafficking in African art. Thousands of Africa's finest art pieces have been stolen or sold for little or no money. A majority of these objects are locked in private collections and will never return to their original owners, the people whose culture these objects embody.

This incident illuminates the problems involved in the conservation of Africa's cultural heritage, showing how poverty and avarice meet at crossroads of desperate necessities. The theft of the Kom royal throne figure was organized by those who can easily afford their daily bread. They exploited those who can barely subsist and who would thus even compromise their cultural heritage. For several centuries, Europeans have pillaged the rich cultural heritages of discovered cultures, as European museums today attest.

FOYN YUH: THE CARVER, THE TEACHER

The kingdom of Kom is situated on a plateau about five thousand feet above sea level and located in the mountainous district of the Bamenda western grassfields. The founding dynastic clans came here more than 350 years ago. The tradition arose that each ruler would replenish the royal treasury with some institutions or art objects that commemorated his reign. Today there are hundreds of pieces that date back to the eighteenth century in the royal storage hut. Ethnographic evidence shows that the seventh king, Yuh, was not only associated with the expansion of the kingdom to its present size, but also was loosely linked to the carving of one of the finest pieces of African art. What is now known as the kom style dates from his reign (Northern 1973).

King Yuh was bold, enterprising, astute, and innovative, traits that earned him a two-year exile during which he mastered his carving techniques (Nkwi 1975:122). When his mother's brother, Kimeng, died in 1865, Yuh returned from exile and became king. He consolidated his kingdom by revitalizing the palace and village war lodges and he conducted several wars of expansion. He stands out in Kom history as the man who withstood the German onslaught for six months. The German punitive expedition finally ended in August 1905 with the signing of a treaty accompanied by an exchange of gifts.

From 1865 to 1912, Yuh dedicated his leisure time to the promotion of arts for pleasure and entertainment. Although he invited blacksmiths to produce what has become known as the *kwifoyn* things (*ufo-kwifoyn*) or *kwifoyn* sacra, he is said to have personally enjoyed producing masks, stools, door posts, and other such objects. To do so effectively, he established a school. Ethnographic data gathered in 1973 shows that Yuh's sister's son, Rudolph Chah, and Nguo Fang of Acha were the most well-known students of King Yuh's school. Chah became known as *bomukum* (the father of masks) for his production of beautiful masks and door posts. Nguo Fang is said to have assisted Yuh in the production of the life-size figures that are now so well-known in the art world.

Under Yuh's supervision, the school produced four pairs of life-size male and female figures. Today, two pairs are found in Germany and the United States. The pair in the Berlin Museum Für Voelkerkunde was brought to Germany by Captain von Putlitz in 1905. How he obtained the figures is not known. Were they a gift? Were they part of the surrender terms after Kom signed a treaty in August 1905 that ended the punitive expeditions? The latter seems likely. Another pair was acquired by R. Rohde, a German who visited Laikom, the capital of Kom. In addition to the figures, he took two royal clay-and-brass pipes, all of which were acquired by the Museum Für Voelkerkunde, Frankfurt, in 1904. In 1934 the female of this pair left Frankfurt for Berlin, becoming part of the Speyer collection. Charles Ratton acquired it and later sold it to Katherine White Reswick in the mid-1960s (Northern 1973:11–12). This female piece appeared in international exhibitions and became an African masterpiece. These two pairs were not beaded as were the three figures that did not leave Kom until 1966.

THE DISAPPEARANCE AND RECOVERY

Collectors in Europe and the United States did not know the existence of the beaded versions in Kom. The Reswick acquisition traveled through Berlin, Paris, and then to Los Angeles, probably enhancing the value of the three beaded versions still in the hands of their original owner in Kom. Were people interested in acquiring them? One can confidently assert that the market in African art was rather lucrative in the 1960s and 1970s and remains so today. In Cameroon, the network was closely controlled by Muslim dealers whose religious convictions galvanized their thoughts and actions, often leading to unscrupulous trafficking in African art objects. These dealers do not hesitate to buy and sell objects that may be considered religious and symbolic to tribal groups. The network through which the beaded *Afo-a-Kom* left Cameroon included Muslim dealers in Foumban, French dealers in Douala, and stopping points in France on the way to the most lucrative market—the United States.

Barna was a bus driver on Kom-Bamenda road. In July 1966 he drove to Fundong with a bus filled with passengers. It was not business as usual. He dropped off his clients and disappeared into a nearby village, where he met a middleman who had taken the *Afo-a-Kom* out of its storage house. And so the most revered art piece of Kom left its sanctuary under very suspicious circumstances. From Bambui, the male figure reached Foumban, and from there it went to Douala. The *Afo-a-Kom* reached its final U.S. destination after a brief stay in France. A few days later it was reported missing. Rumors had it that one of the princes had sold it without the ruler's consent. The regulatory society began a search. Government authorities were informed, and measures were taken to recover it.

The government of Cameroon, whose prime minister was a native of Kom, knew the figure's importance to the Kom nation and ordered an investigation. With little jurisdiction over the French administration in east Cameroon, the investigation ended where it started. When the male figure resurfaced and finally returned to Cameroon in 1973, a government insensitive to the initial recovery efforts in 1966 now claimed the *Afo-a-Kom* as a symbol of national cultural heritage. At a ceremony organized to receive the object and the accompanying U.S. delegation, the minister of information and culture tried but failed to give the statue a national identity when he said: "It belongs to all of the people of Cameroon. . . . The statue . . . is a national treasure, not just a Kom one" (Ellis 1974:142). Although the government maximized the value of the stolen object, there was no policy to protect such an object before the theft, and there is still none today.

Three factors explain why the theft occurred and why it will happen again: the breakdown of the sociocultural institutions; the lack of a policy to protect such cultural objects; and the high value of such objects in the international market or community. The theft resulted from a wide-ranging conspiracy rather than from politics within the royal household, as some authors have insinuated (Ellis 1974:143–45).

Tamara Northern must receive credit for her contribution to the discovery of the *Afo-a-Kom*. When she mounted an exhibition at Dartmouth College in 1973, she borrowed the object from Furman without knowing it had been stolen and sold to him. The exhibition, entitled "The Royal Art of Cameroon," highlighted what she called the kom style. The *Afo-a-Kom* appeared on the cover of the catalog, marking the first time it had been seen since 1966. Diplomatic and political discussions began in Washington and Cameroon and successfully ended with the return of the statue of the Kom royal treasury.

THE ROYAL TREASURY

The kingdom of Kom has a centralized political organization whose ruler (*foyn*) is the sacred representative of the founding dynasty. He controls more than forty-five villages, each with its own hereditary head who is responsible to the *foyn*. As the political leader of his people, the *foyn* is the embodiment of traditions and values. He also provides priestly leadership and is the cultural guardian and principal actor in state ceremonies, rituals, and secular affairs. The *foyn* takes an active interest in the promotion of artistic production. His palace is the center of the kingdom's art. The regulatory society (*kwifoyn*) acts on behalf of the ruler and his people as the custodians of ceremonial and ritual art preserved in the treasury within the palace precinct and guarded by the retainers of the *kwifoyn*. Northern describes the royal treasury more vividly:

> The royal treasury comprises the full and splendid panoply of artistic manifestation, consisting of insignia that invest the *foyn* with total representation of privilege and royal prestige: architectural sculpture, ancestor figures, masks, stools, caps, drinking horns, pipes, loincloth, gowns, necklaces, armlets, anklets, whisks, staffs, standard swords, ivory tusks, calabashes, ceremonial and food vessels, display cloths, drums, beds, bags. Several of these regalia share the aegis of the palace and the regulatory society. (1984:31)

In 1989 I had the privilege of inspecting the treasury. Admitted into the most respected lodge of the regulatory society (*kwifoyn* of the night), I found valuable pieces stored in terrible conditions, placed in no order in different parts of the lodge. The various insignia and sacra that enhance the wealth and vitality of the ruler and his kingdom and record the people's past were preserved in such poor conditions that their survival is doubtful.

Missing from among these insignia and sacra were in *Afo-a-Kom* and the two other figures. Their international importance raised the awareness of Kom rulers; consequently these pieces are maintained in the royal sleeping chamber. Hundreds of other objects are preserved in two storage houses in the *kwifoyn* compound. Several decades ago the houses in the compound served as storage facilities and were constantly guarded by retainers recruited and trained for the purpose. All sacred objects and insignia were placed under the guardianship and custody of *kwifoyn* members (*chisendo*), who guarded the sanctuary on a permanent basis. The main storage house where the *kwifoyn* holds its weekly meetings is never closed, even when its members are not physically present. This situation prevailed in 1966 when the *Afo-a-Kom* was stolen, and it remains the case today for hundreds of precious royal art objects. The disintegration of the regulatory society exposed the royal objects to serious conservation problems. The recruitment of retainers for palace services, including the guarding of the royal treasury, is a major problem. Today, parents prefer to send their children to modern schools rather than giving them to the service of the ruler.

CONSERVATION OF THE ROYAL TREASURY

Throughout the western grassfields of Cameroon, the regulatory society—known variously as *kwifoyn, ngumba, tifoa, ngwerong,* and *kwifo*—is the royal agency of social control and law enforcement. It ensures that traditional mores and values of ancestral origin are respected and maintained by all, including the ruler. It implements and enforces the beliefs and values of the kingdom. As an executive arm of government it enforces normative behavior, especially in the areas of civil and criminal justice. The *kwifoyn* controls the ostentatious use of food for death celebrations and guarantees the careful management of resources (Northern 1984:62).

Membership in the society is restricted to men, who are recruited while they are between the ages of ten and fifteen years. These young men are drilled in the skills of state diplomacy, the management of the royal household economy, the maintenance of state security, and the organization of major rituals and state ceremonies. They also have the special duty of guarding the royal treasury (the masks of the different lodges) and other state sacra.

In Kom art, retainers are often depicted on stools, beds, and vessels as caryatids in the posture of support. They were the mainstay of the palace and state apparatus. The smart and intelligent ones often gained the confidence of the ruler and rose to diplomatic ranks and became great negotiators in times of interstate quarrels. They also received accoutrements of prestige from the ruler. In Bamum the three famous thrones represented the male and female retainers commemorating the ruler's reliance on them in the political power structure of the palace (Northern 1984:39).

The *kwifoyn* had a series of lodges into which the retainers were recruited on payment of specific fees. The sacra of the lodges were under permanent surveillance by *chisendo*. At no time could the sacra objects be left unguarded. Each retainer provided at least ten years of service to the state. Those who had served the ruler conscientiously were rewarded with wives and other gifts on the day of their graduation.

Retainers were recruited throughout the kingdom; former retainers were required to send sons to the palace to serve. *Chisendo* were also forcibly recruited from among the brightest young men of the kingdom. Up to the 1940s and 1950s, modern education did not constitute the fastest way of gaining social recognition in society; the regulatory society was the most appropriate instrument for attaining status, and it was easy to recruit members. *Kwifoyn* retainers enjoyed a considerable amount of prestige and power, and it was a source of pride for a family to have one of its sons join. The enhanced prestige was reflected during one's lifetime as well as in death ceremonies. The palace art treasury that housed the masks of the different lodges (*nko, mabu, menang*, and others) had sufficient curators.

By the 1960s, most parents saw formal education as a greater mechanism of social mobility, and recruitment into the *kwifoyn* ranks did not produce high social status. The remuneration of retainers through an irregular gift process did not attract many young men to the service of the king. The number of retainers recruited did not suffice to perform the variety of duties that the *chisendo* once performed. The royal art treasury became exposed to theft more than ever before. The loosely guarded treasury contained objects whose high monetary value outweighed the social and ritual importance of such sacred objects, leading to the frequent disappearance of art pieces. Today, there are five retainers in the palace at any one time, compared to a hundred young retainers in the late 1940s.

Is the *Afo-a-Kom* also exposed to this insecure situation? Could it be stolen again? What measures has the state taken to protect it and other objects? The *Afo-a-Kom* certainly has no legal protection, and the ritual and ceremonial functions among the Kom remain the only guarantee against future theft.

AFO-A-KOM: ITS RISE TO GLORY AND ITS FORGOTTEN PAST

On its homeward journey after its discovery in the United States, the crated *Afo-a-Kom* flew to Cameroon as a passenger. It was not stacked away in the plane's luggage compartment, but instead it sat next to the director of the Washington, D.C., Museum of African Art and to Lawrence Gussman of Scarsdale, New York, a philanthropist who provided part of the money for the figure's retrieval from Furman. It was received officially by the Cameroon government, and a cocktail party was thrown at the five-star Mont Febe Novotel in its honor. On December 11, 1973, the minister of information and culture flew to Bamenda with the U.S. delegation to return the royal art piece to the Kom people.

From the borders of Kom and Babanki, the road was lined with men, women, and children. As women cried out in joy and men dressed in traditional attire fired guns skyward, the *Afo-a-Kom* made its triumphant return. *Kwifoyn* members were particularly relieved and happy. From now on, the statue would take its rightful place among the other royal sacra. Three days later the crate in which the *Afo-a-Kom* made its return journey was ceremonially buried. Looking like a coffin, its image haunted many people in the palace. The *Afo-a-Kom* was then stored away in the royal sleeping chamber of the *foyn* rather than in the *kwifoyn* sanctuary, which was now deserted.

When the Smithsonian Institution decided to mount an exhibition of art from Cameroon in 1984, the curator, Tamara Northern, brought back the entire *Afo-a-Kom* ensemble as part of the Smithsonian Institution Traveling Exhibition Ser-

vice. The *Afo-a-Kom* had suffered immense damage over the ten years following its return to Kom. Some of the beads on the arms, neck, and legs were falling
off. How can local communities be assisted in preserving their valuable ritual
objects?

When the *foyn* of Kom, in consultation with the *kwifoyn* and the queen mother,
decided that the *Afo-a-Kom* could return to the United States, they believed that
the ensemble would attract fees from those who would visit it during its sojourn.
When the pieces returned to Kom in 1989, the Smithsonian Institution representative, Matou Godwin, gave the *foyn* a gift equivalent to three hundred dollars. I accompanied her when she returned the objects, and we spent a night in Bamenda.
As we were leaving for Douala, we were stopped by the police and asked to
attend a meeting at the Delegation of Information and Culture. The participants
in that meeting included the government delegate for information and culture,
the secret police, gendarmes, officials in charge of the Bamenda museum, and the
foyn's representatives.

At that meeting I was accused of withholding funds accrued during the *Afo-a-
Kom's* U.S. visit. Godwin told the government and the ruler's representatives that
I had not received a penny from her organization. She went on to explain that the
presence of the *Afo-a-kom* ensemble in that exhibition had actually raised the
object's value and prestige. We tried to explain the whole philosophy of international exhibitions, but it seemed that nobody was prepared to understand the
rationale. To their way of thinking, the person who borrowed the *Afo-a-Kom* ensemble had profited from the exhibition and the owner of the objects deserved
part of the proceeds.

I perceive more pressing problems than the quarrel over proceeds from an exhibition, however, including better preservation of these sacred objects, the purchase of beads, and the restoration of the statue. How can international agencies
and institutions assist in the conservation or preservation endeavor of African
living cultural heritage? Can the present storage facilities in Kom be improved?
How can we guarantee the safety of the *Afo-a-Kom* and other pieces? The threat of
theft still exists. Five years ago, some masks were stolen from the *kwifoyn* storage
house, and someone is currently serving a prison sentence for the theft. Recent
mob justice resulting from a newly discovered democratic freedom led to the discovery of the masks in the house of a respected prince.

LEGAL PROVISIONS

Most African nations have not signed the 1970 UNESCO convention protecting
antiquities and objects of cultural and historical importance. The right to a cultural heritage has been violated again and again on the continent. The participation in the cultural life of a community is codified in article seven of the Universal
Declaration of Human Rights, but many African countries have not taken this
document seriously either.

Cameroon does not have precise laws and regulations that protect cultural
heritage. Even the statehouse, left behind by Ahidjo and his colonial predecessors,

was looted of its historical objects by officials who did not care about the importance of such objects. Although the statehouse was turned into a museum, the
government has taken no significant measures to protect what was left after the
looting.

We cannot underestimate the "power of the object to communicate, encapsu-
late, and evoke history. Objects in museums bear witness to knowledge that has
been historically constituted" (Ravenhill 1992:274–75). When Yuh produced the
Afo-a-Kom ensemble, he not only commemorated his reign and the royal family of
which he was the living symbol, but he also enriched the social history of the
people's artistic performance. Twenty years ago the government of Cameroon
wanted to give the object its new significance and symbolism when it declared on
its return that the object was a national symbol. Despite the emotionally charged
receptions and the wide publicity the object provided to Cameroon, little was
done to protect it or to provide it with dignified storage facilities.

The pillage of Cameroon art has continued. In 1984 I visited an African art
dealer in San Francisco and found pieces that seemed familiar. When I told him I
was from Cameroon, he took me into another room, where he showed me pieces
he had recently acquired on a trip to Cameroon. Having visited a number of such
collections, I believe that hundreds of very good pieces leave Cameroon every
year. Dealers use a network that is highly specialized and skillful in avoiding
whatever scant legal protection does exist for such objects. Foreign researchers
(archaeologists and anthropologists) take some of these pieces in the name of science. About fifteen years ago an anthropologist made several visits to Cameroon
on the pretext of studying the religion of a chiefdom known for its masks, stools,
and other material objects. He collected very good pieces from that chiefdom and
from its neighbors, and while in the United States described to students of African
art how anyone can buy museum pieces in Cameroon for less than ten dollars.
Someone who knew the importance of such objects for local museums was telling
others to deplete Cameroon of its art objects.

Although the permit given to foreign researchers stipulates that they can take
out specimens for scientific analysis only when there is due authorization, many
researchers leave the country with numerous cultural artifacts without receiving
permission, and there are few sanctions for such unprofessional behavior. The
best that officials do is to reject future applications for research permits. It is expected that the new Ministry of Culture will develop rules and regulations protecting Cameroon's cultural heritage, thereby empowering people and giving
them the means to act as curators of local living museums.

PEOPLE AS CURATORS OF THEIR OWN OBJECTS

The role of museums in using collections, research findings, and data to inform,
educate, and entertain or engage their different publics (Ardouin 1992:240) is usually compromised by the lack of government measures that reinforce such roles.
Ardouin asserts that the future lies in the development of regional and local mu-

seums, which will permit interaction among community members as the museum becomes part of their lives.

When the *Afo-a-Kom* returned to Cameroon, the government wanted to keep it in the capital as a national symbol, but there was no justification for such a move. The national museum at the time was without adequate resources. Funds for annual acquisition were barely above two thousand dollars. The *Afo-a-Kom*, retrieved at the cost of sixty thousand dollars, could not receive government financial support for the construction of its sanctuary. Although the provincial delegation for information and culture provided one thousand dollars for the construction of a small museum in which the *Afo-a-Kom* was to be preserved on permanent exhibition, the amount was so small that efforts were wasted and the *kwifoyn* had to adopt its own strategy to conserve the ensemble. The *foyn* became the curator and principal guard.

In the western grassfields of Cameroon, all palaces have their ritual and entertainment art. The responsibility of protecting, repairing, and using it falls on the people to whom the rulers look for material support. As Marc says, "Conserving a cultural heritage is always difficult. In Africa weak institutional capacities, lack of appropriate resources, and isolation of many culturally essential sites are compounded by a general lack of awareness of the value of cultural heritage conservation" (1992:259). Most officials think that spending money on cultural conservation is a waste, although a few do realize the role of museums and the need to provide both the legal and material support to sustain them.

Local communities are far more aware of the symbolism and ritual significance of these objects. If these objects have lived through history, it is because of their dynamic dimension. Marc is correct in saying that "the dynamics of local initiatives and community solidarity systems which are among the strongest in the world, are impressive assets. These indigenous forces should be enlisted, enlarged, and empowered to preserve and protect a heritage unique to the continent and of inestimable value to a wider realization of the development goals of the continent" (1992:259).

The enhancement of this inner potential in local communities is left to Africans who have made it their business by giving their cultural heritage the protection it deserves. The whole process of conservation is central to the concept of ownership and the symbolic nature of the objects. If people are given a greater sense and awareness that cultural heritage is their property and deserves conservation for future generations, they may respond positively to conservation efforts. The empowerment of people becomes a central concept. Their ownership must be reflected in the living character of the objects. For most Africans, masks and figures have meaning when they become alive in ritual or ceremonial occasions rather than sitting in a box or an enclosure in a museum. The banalization of ritual art or the deritualization of African art renders it devoid of the meaning intended by the creators. Giving these objects a casual and nonritual image demystifies the creative meaning and symbolism that have sustained the existence of African art through the years. Placing art within its ritual and ceremonial context may constitute another strategy in encouraging communities to conserve art, using it on specific occasions.

In Kom the annual dance organized by *foyn* and *kwifoyn* displays the various masks' societies. The dance usually occurs on the day new pieces of palace art are displayed. Some of the symbolic pieces are presented to the public. One would agree with Marc (1992:259) that participating in decision making can become effective if it affects the lives of people. Symbolism captures their minds and maintains their interest.

The *Afo-a-Kom* was received twenty years ago with great pomp by the people of Kom. The ensemble, displayed occasionally, was deeply revered for its meaning. One of the strong justifications for the purchase and return of the *Afo-a-Kom* was the fact that it was a ritual symbol of the people and the incarnation of their values. This symbolism and the cultural revival movement among the modern elite have revealed the problems of conservation of cultural heritage. In 1984 the local village association of elites, Njinikom Area Development Association, embarked on a palace restoration program. The program had as its priority the provision of adequate quarters for the *foyn* and for the royal art pieces. Some houses in the palace were rebuilt and more houses in the *kwifoyn* compound were also built.

Since 1975 there have been enormous efforts to give the *kwifoyn* institution a new look. King Jina Bo II (1975–1989) started a program of recruiting retainers from among the Cameroon civil service. For him the protection and conservation of Kom cultural heritage could only be effectively done with men of new thinking and vision. Today, the *kwifoyn*, once composed of nonliterates, has highly skilled and learned people such as teachers, lawyers, civil administrators, police, soldiers, and many other modern professionals. They have enhanced an organization whose disappearance was imminent with the rapid change of things.

Empowering people to run their own museum requires at least minimum support from public authorities. It is not sufficient to have the good will of the people; it is absolutely essential to develop a program of capacity building for these living museums. African governments will succeed if local people are trained in conservation techniques. Because community museums are the way of the future, the training of such persons would prepare them and enhance the whole process of conservation. The establishment of trust funds or endowments managed by local communities may lead to greater sustainability of local efforts.

REFERENCES

Ardouin, C. D. "What Models for African Museums: West African Perspectives." In *Culture and Development in Africa*, eds. I. Serageldin and J. Taboroff, 233–43. Washington, D.C: World Bank, 1992.

Ellis, W. S. "A Sacred Symbol Comes Home." *National Geographic* (July 1974): 141–48.

Marc, O. A. "Community Participation in the Conservation of Cultural Heritage." In *Culture and Development in Africa*, eds. I. Serageldin and J. Taboroff, 250–71. Washington, D.C.: World Bank, 1992.

Nkwi, Paul N. "The Return of a Stolen God." *Abbia* (1975):121–28.

Northern, T. *Royal Art of Cameroon: The Art of the Bamenda-Tikar*. Hanover, N. H.: Hopkins Center Art Galleries, Dartmouth College, 1973.

———. *The Art of Cameroon*. Washington, D.C.: Smithsonian Institution, 1984.

Ravenhill, P. "Public Education, National Collection and Museum Scholarship in Africa." In *Culture and Development in Africa*, eds. I. Serageldin and J. Taboroff, 272–85. Washington, D.C.: World Bank, 1992.

10

PAST AS PROLOGUES

EMPOWERING AFRICA'S CULTURAL INSTITUTIONS

Henry John Drewal

The past is continually shaped by the present. Examining the interests, attitudes, and actions of those concerned with Africa's "disappearing past," whether outside or within the continent, suggests the need for certain fundamental reorientations in our ways of thinking and operating. This chapter speaks of two distinct yet very much interrelated mutually dependent groups: Africanists and African colleagues. I begin by addressing certain basic conditions, attitudes, and actions—first, among those of us outside Africa and then among those within—that have, I believe, in many ways brought us to the present crisis concerning Africa's disappearing past. Next I suggest certain changes to deal with this situation. Finally, I outline a proposal in progress that offers several strategies to meet our present challenges, and I close with some advice on taking action.

POSTCOLONIAL, POSTMODERN REFLEXIVITY AND SYMMETRY

We are said to live in a postcolonial and postmodern era. Let us reflect on the rhetoric of such a concept. If it were true, what would it mean? Such "post" constructions proclaim a certain importance for what we are doing as somehow distinct from and, by implication, more advanced and progressive than what our predecessors the colonial-modernists did. Yet at the same time, such terms reveal deep-seated insecurities and uncertainties about where we position ourselves in relation to the past, the present, and the future. Such consciousness is double-edged. It should be helpful in forcing us to question and reevaluate our assumptions, to continually reflect upon our ways of thinking and acting. It could move us to different levels of awareness, sensitivity, and understanding, not just of ourselves, but also of others and their cultural practices and products. For, whether in our research or in our assessment of the present loss of cultural heritage in Africa, the questions we ask ourselves (and others) are as important as, if not more important than, the answers we propose (see Drewal 1990). Yet the questions remain: Has such awareness begun, and has it been productive?

I would suggest that in many significant ways a postcolonial, postmodern consciousness has not yet emerged, either outside or within Africa. Rather, what I see are essentially neocolonist, hegemonic attitudes and actions—and neocolonized reactions/responses.

A recent and scathing critique by Olu Oguibe of the contemporary African art exhibit called *Africa Explores* makes the point eloquently when he asks us (Africanists) if we can ever learn to depart from the "frames and prejudices of orthodox 'Africanist' traditions" that continue to insinuate "the same old binary of the Self and the Other. The Self, which is America and the West, is again universalized and hegemonized, and endowed with the monopoly of cognition/ sanction. That which it does not know is unknown. That which it does not present is not represented, and that which it does not speak for cannot speak" (Oguibe 1993:18). I believe Oguibe is essentially correct in his assessment.

One aspect of a so-called postmodern condition would be reflexivity, that is, consciousness of being conscious. The double sight provided by being reflexive is meant to be beneficial because it does not end in self-indulgence. Instead, reflexivity demands that we move beyond to consider our own positionality— our own motives and intentions—in intercultural exchanges. Such a perspective should sensitize us to the ways in which we shape and manipulate situations for our own purposes and to the ways we construct, translate, and understand those situations—to learn how to operate differently.

One of the things that ought to emerge from such reflexivity is a rethinking of our relationship to our subject. Rather than claim to distance ourselves in order to attain an illusory objectivity- -an impossible and arrogant posture that connotes superiority—we should question the usefulness of such objectivity and recognize the inevitable and enlightening importance of interaction, involvement, engagement, and shared experience as sources of important insights into multiple ways of living and creating and, for our purposes here, different ways of conceiving, understanding, appreciating, preserving, and representing the past.

Yet this process of dialogue, debate, and discussion requires an important precondition: a coequal relationship between researchers and researched, friends and befriended, supporters and initiators/actors—symmetrical exchanges of questions, ideas, answers, and actions. We still need to move beyond the kinds of asymmetry embodied in evolutionary, colonial, and neocolonial thinking.

TRADING PLACES

If anything would characterize this long-awaited, still-anticipated postcolonial, postmodern era, it would be a fundamental reorientation of power centers in the world that shape significantly the direction and flow of people, ideas, services, technologies, products, wealth, and cultural heritages. For what we today label first, second, third, and fourth worlds are changing as we speak—and we should reflect on the consequences. Consider the following hypothetical country case study: significant portions of its industries and most valued real estate are owned or controlled by foreigners; its citizens often prefer and purchase imported goods, leading to increased unemployment in domestic industries and a widening gap

between the rich and a growing underclass; its infrastructure is outdated; its technologies are becoming obsolete, so that existing ones compete with difficulty in
domestic and world markets; major technological innovations take place elsewhere and determine market flow; it becomes one of the largest debtor nations;
and, extending this hypothetical case more specifically to issues of this nation's
cultural heritage, some of its most prized national treasures—major architectural
sites symbolic of the nation's wealth, power, and identity and famous works of
art, etc.—are sold to foreigners, and some of these treasures leave the country. Increasing numbers of citizens or public institutions may have to auction their collections (some of which contain what are called national treasures) to cover their
losses. Such a situation creates the need for policies and mechanisms to protect
cultural properties. Who would support such moves? Who would oppose them?
How would such campaigns be organized and waged? What outcomes might we
expect? How and in what ways would we react and act?

Of course what I have described is not hypothetical at all—it is us—that is, the
United States. My point: Only if we begin by reflecting on and being reflexive
about our own positionality, our motives, our actions with regard to the erasure of
our cultural heritage can we ever hope to contribute insights that might be useful
to African peoples.

HISTORY IS THE PAST WE CHOOSE TO REMEMBER

I begin with the view that the past is an invention of (and for) the present—that
we continually make the past in terms of our image of ourselves in the present. As
Hayden White (1987) has suggested, history, which in its earliest usage meant a
narrative account of events, continues today to be the result of "narrative capacities that transform the present into a fulfillment of a past from which we would
wish to have descended." Pasts are indeed prologues.

Thinking reflexively, consider first the refashioning of our own (American)
past—the Vietnam era. For many years after this disastrous period, it was erased
from view, seldom invoked because this was not a past from which we would wish
to have descended. But then the creation of the Vietnam memorial (and the counter memorial of traditional bronze statuary it provoked), together with a host of
books, films, analyses, political campaigns, and so forth, reasserted it in our collective conscience, forcing us to deal with it. The process of re-visioning the past is
continuous. An African proverb makes the point succinctly: "The white man who
invented the pencil also invented the eraser!"

What about African makings and remakings of the past? One example might be
Nigeria's ongoing process of creating states that attempt to more closely reflect
self-identities linked with precolonial sociopolitical–religious–ethnic entities rather
than those imposed by colonial outsiders. A second example might be the survival
and reassertion of forms of government that continue indigenous principles and
procedures because, despite the almost total disempowerment of traditional rulers
by colonial regimes, they still possess significant prestige and authority for local
(and sometimes regional) populations. And what about such imported religions as

Islam or Christianity, which thrive best when they incorporate thoroughly indigenous forms of worship? Such constructions of present realities are composed of contestations, celebrations, and/or denials of certain versions of the past—some to be preserved, others not.

If this is so, and it holds for written as well as oral histories both within and outside of Africa (as I believe it does), then we need to ask the fundamental questions of for whom, how, why, and when do Africans concern themselves with the preservation of cultural heritage? And are African answers and actions (strategies, tactics, products) with regard to such questions the same as ours? Even if we ask such questions, which I think is rarely the case, do we really listen to African voices, opinions, and actions?

I think that generally we do not. Why? Because we have been trained in colonialist, hegemonic thinking and, at least for now (though I perceive changes coming, as discussed above), we have the financial and technological resources to impose our own views. Our (outsiders') relationship with Africa has been for almost five hundred years a starkly asymmetrical one—one in which we called the shots, because we had the power (defined as the will and the means to dominate) to literally shoot the shots from our so-called superior weapons of destruction. Guns joined by money—a worldwide system of capitalism—have perpetuated this situation of unequal capacities in what must be recognized as a neocolonial world struggling to become, somehow, postcolonial. One critic, Gayatri Spivak, speaking about Western (and male) hegemonic practices, has said that we must "learn our privilege as our loss"—in other words, our privileged position has limited and circumscribed our capacity to learn from others, making us think we have authority to do what we wish, to impose our will on others. This has made us deaf and blind, ignorant of or insensitive to the voices and ways and means of others.

I think it is instructive that the Yoruba word for educability, the capacity to learn, is *iluti*, which refers to the ear (*eti*) and literally means "the ability to listen well," and thus to learn. One of the preconditions for listening is not talking! As a drummer once told me, "Music is as much about silence as sound." My advice to Africanists is that we speak less, listen more, and learn from our African colleagues.

Let me turn such general remarks to the specifics of our concerns with Africa's disappearing past—the erasure of its cultural heritage. If we agree that peoples have always created and shaped their sense of self and group identity, and that artificially, externally imposed identities will sooner or later be contested and displaced (as we are witnessing in Europe today), then we must recognize that one such colonial imposition was and still is the museum. Both as concept and as institution, it is a decidedly Western reality. Based on royal and aristocratic *cabinets de curiosités* for the collection of exotica from around the world, the museum houses a world that could be simply bought or taken by force. Such museums served, and still to a large degree continue to serve, non-African audiences—resident expatriates, visitors, international corporations, diplomats, and tourists—not local populations.

But the colonial period was but a brief moment (less than seventy years) in Africa's long history. What we need to examine closely and understand well are precolonial, indigenous ways and means taken by African peoples to recall their past, and those projects that anticipate a truly postcolonial future. We need to appreciate and to support these phenomena, helping them to serve present and future African interests, not ours. Such African ways and means exist—they did in the past, and they do in the present. Perhaps some of them can serve in the future. They are indigenous sites and situations for the preservation of cultural heritage, for recollections of the past.

Let us consider a few telling examples, if only we are prepared to listen and learn: 1) Treasure houses (*aban*) at Kumasi where the rulers of the Asante Confederation developed over several centuries collections and displays of goods from around the world—the cultural properties of their trading partners—including Dutch and English porcelains, German crystal, Islamic brass basins, etc.—as evidence of their wealth, power, and internationality (McCaskie 1989); 2) The regular display of family/lineage/community regalia at festivals in many realms; 3) Palace collections that preserve and celebrate the past as they enhance the prestige of present rulers; and 4) Domestic and communal altars containing and displaying religious works of art (although much of this is being erased—either destroyed or dispersed—because certain groups or governments regard such primitive, pagan, backward evidence to be part of pasts from which they do not want to be descended).

We need to know what works now, ask why, and recognize how we can learn from these cases. For example, one very successful recent exhibit in Burkina Faso dealt with the history of the bicycle, partly because almost everyone could relate to it in very personal ways (Ravenhill 1992:280). Another example is the enthusiasm (in certain areas, at least) surrounding the creation of a Biafran war museum; and in Lagos, Nigeria, one of the most popular museum displays is the bullet-riddled limousine in which the much-admired reformist head of state, Murtala Mohammed, was assassinated (Ravenhill 1992:280). Crowds came to see the desk of the first district officer at the Museum of Colonial History in Aba, Nigeria (Akata, cited in Ravenhill 1992:279). Family members have put loving care into the preservation of the mansion and furnishings of Balogun Kuku at Ijebu Ode, Nigeria—a building designed and built by an Afro-Brazilian (and Muslim) architect named Balthazar Reis in the 1890s and filled with English Victoriana (M. Drewal 1992: 139–43). Consider also the pan-African importance given to orality and the performed preservation of cultural heritage; the sagas, epics, myths, and cultural sites and situations that foster it—marketplaces, palace display areas, initiation and graduation/coming-out ceremonies, festivals, and so forth. Perhaps the regional masking festivals/competitions, like that at Enugu, Nigeria, might become important vehicles for cultural expression and preservation. Too, there are the armies of videographers who have begun to replace photographers as the major conservators of important family and community histories in the form of important cultural performances.

What do these tell us? That African peoples have a clear sense of their pasts and ways of preserving them. But have we supported the survival of that limousine? Those bicycles? District officers' desks? Masking festivals? Or videographers?

SPEAKING UP, TAKING ACTION

While Oguibe concentrated his scathing critique on the exhibit *Africa Explores* as an outsider's self-serving and distorted view of what constitutes contemporary African art, he did not spare his African compatriots either. Chiding them, he cited Chinua Achebe writing on colonialist criticism: "The man who does not lick his lips must not complain should the Harmattan do it for him." In other words, if people don't speak out for themselves, others will do it for them and they have no one to blame but themselves. Oguibe's and Archebe's critiques were thus double-edged, double-directed, toward outsiders who claim to speak authoritatively for Africa and Africans and toward Africans who, by their silence, appear to accept such views. I think there is a central question and issue for all of us in this as well: Whose interests are served by preservation, whether past, present, or future? During the colonial moment, preservation served the masters—colonial regimes that often patronizingly imposed their version of the past for their own honor and glorification as beneficent rulers of protectorates. Colonial museums' very limited audiences were almost entirely non-African or sometimes included another very small, privileged group— Western-educated African elite. No wonder then that preservation of cultural heritage was not, during this period, a major issue.

But since 1960, it must be recognized that preservation still serves the interests of very limited audiences. Outside Africa, those audiences are non-African scholars, students, museologues, international corporations, and nonprofit foundations. Within Africa, preservation has an even smaller constituency—minuscule in fact—consisting of university and museum personnel, some students, and fewer government bureaucrats, all constituents with limited monetary resources and even lesser sociopolitical clout. My point here is not simply to describe the dire situation in which we find ourselves but rather to suggest this: Until broadly based African interests—large percentages of local, regional, and national populations—are served by preservation, we can never hope to reverse the present erasure of the past. Otherwise how can one explain and rationalize why (as of 1990) not a single African country had petitioned the U.S. government to take action to implement and enforce the 1983 Convention on Cultural Property Implementation Act? The act "authorizes the U.S. government to join with other countries in curbing the illicit trade in cultural property" (USIA 1989). Mali has been the first to do so, and a Mali-U.S. emergency antiquities ban was enacted in 1993. Why in twenty-five years had only fifteen sub-Saharan African countries signed the UNESCO 1970 convention? Why are even fewer actively encouraging other countries to sign and to act?

Now while these questions are directed to my African colleagues and their governments, let us remember that, except for the United States, none of the major European or Asian importers of illegal cultural property has signed the UNESCO convention. Whose voices are raised? What campaigns are being waged to alter this situation? Both victimizers (trying to become postvictimizers!) and victims (trying to be postcolonials!) must speak out, or else a storm, a Harmattan, of runners, art dealers, and collectors will create a landscape barren of cultural heritage.

What follows are excerpts from a proposal recently drafted by me and a group of Africans and Africanists hoping to establish the Foundation for African Archaeology/Fonds pour l'Archéologie Africaine (FAA).[1] I present it here as an example of one possible strategy of action that responds to some of the issues I have raised above. Its success and effectiveness remain to be proven.

EXCERPTS FROM THE FAA PROPOSAL

Objective

Concerned about the widespread destruction of archaeological sites and the consequent loss of data essential for the reconstruction of the artistic and cultural history of (sub-Saharan) African civilizations, we intend to establish an international, nongovernmental, nonprofit organization composed of African and Africanist (American, European, Asian) colleagues in a variety of relevant disciplines (archaeology, art history, anthropology, history, museology, etc.) to work together in assisting African cultural institutions and archaeologists. We will provide financial, material, and personnel support for emergency, in-progress, and long-term archaeological projects, especially (but not exclusively) those focused on the last two to three millennia—a period in which the processes of urbanization and nation-state formation produced rich, sophisticated artistic traditions comparable to any created anywhere in the world—and which, as a result, are in the highest demand in the illegal international art market. . . .

Rationale

The history of archaeological work on the last two to three millennia in Africa (except for Egypt) is remarkably brief and sporadic, and yet in that brief time it has revolutionized our views of the origins and growth of African civilizations (Connah 1975, 1987; Phillipson 1985; Robertshaw 1990; Shaw 1978). The discoveries of Nok, Igbo Ukwu, Jenne, Ife, Koma, Sanga, Mapungubwe, and Lydenburg—most of them accidental finds and all with an archaeological richness largely unpredicted by local histories—have proved that extraordinary cultural and artistic histories await only serious, systematic archaeological surveys and excavations. It is precisely during this era of the last two millennia that we have growing evidence of major cultural developments—animal husbandry, sedentary agricultural technologies and practices, metalworking technologies, trading networks, urbanization, craft specialization, centralized governments and city-state, nation, and empire formation in Africa—and rich attendant material cultural production, including some of the world's finest artistic achievements (Connah 1975, 1987; Eyo and Willett 1980; Garlake 1974, 1977; Hall 1990; McIntosh 1980, 1989; McIntosh and McIntosh 1979; Shaw 1970; Shinnie 1967).[2]

The reconstruction of Africa's past and archaeology's role in this have had to confront numerous challenges, among them the following:

1) *Research Practicalities*: Traditions of material and artistic production in perishable media such as wood, fiber, or sun-dried clay, which disintegrate after one or two hundred years, thus greatly increasing the importance of archaeological research on works in more permanent media such as terra-cotta, stone, and metal; uneven and unsystematic surveys of potentially important sites; difficulties and high costs of archaeological work in often remote and inhospitable locations; difficulties posed by African poverty and bureaucracy, which have contributed to a serious lack of local funds for archaeological research and inadequate cultural heritage policies; lack of written sources predating Arabic travelers' accounts of the ninth and tenth centuries; and, colonial priorities, neocolonial disinterest, Eurocentrism, and racist policies, especially in parts of southern and eastern Africa.

2) *Effect of the Illicit Market*: The widespread and dramatically increased looting and destruction of archaeological sites and the consequent loss of information about material/expressive culture for the reconstruction of Africa's past. As with pre-Columbian, Cambodian, Indian art, and so forth, the artistic/cultural heritage of African countries has been and continues to be looted, dispersed, and commodified in the world's art market without being properly researched and documented in systematic archaeological excavations. Before 1950, early African art was much less known. It was generally spared because the prices for works were relatively low compared to other, better-known and appreciated traditions. All that has now changed. African artworks, especially archaeological works, now command enormous prices on the world art market. In some cases, they may even have become a country's major source of export income! As a result, sites are being looted at an unprecedented rate and action to stop this must be taken as soon as possible (Ekechukwu 1990). The countries affected are not only losing unique, irreplaceable objects that are part of a global human heritage, they are losing objects and cultural histories that are extremely important for national cultural heritage, education, and identity.

3) *Financial Concerns*: Limited funds and personnel for proper (long-term, comprehensive) archaeological investigation of sites. In some cases, sites became widely known and were looted before thorough and systematic excavations could be carried out, such as at Jenne, Mali and Komaland, Ghana. As a consequence, the destroyed sites and dispersed objects have become orphans in history, and the data that might have placed them in a precise cultural/historical context are irretrievably lost. In other instances, important sites have had to be kept secret for fear of looting before investigation (Gaddo 1989).

4) *Archaeology as Source Material*: Minimal use of archaeological research in the writing of Africa's past (Vansina 1984). Extending its sense of history through archaeology, Africa will be able to attract attention and respect on a par with other regions of the world. The West has tended to value most what it perceives to be its own ancient roots—Egypt, Mesopotamia, Greece, and Rome—and to generally confer greater importance on cultural traditions based on writing, such as those of China and India. Without being able to document their own early artistic and cultural contributions—their unwritten history through archaeology—African civilizations will never receive proper recognition or appreciation for their contributions to human history.

What we propose to do is to respond to the priorities identified by our African colleagues and to develop comprehensive, holistic solutions to problems. The needs are urgent and extensive.

Guiding Principles

Our basic philosophy and fundamental operating principle will be to develop and maintain true partnerships for all projects—that is, symmetrical relationships based on mutual dialogue. Prior to creating such partnerships, however, we would expect to 1) listen and respond to the priorities, initiatives, and proposals put forward by African institutions and colleagues (Dewey 1992), and 2) consider only those proposals from non-African Africanists that demonstrate clearly articulated, cooperative partnerships that respond to the needs of African participants (cf. Andah 1990).

We believe that the current state of archaeological work in Africa—a complex web of social, historical, political, religious, economic, and scholarly problems, forces, and issues—requires flexible, multifaceted responses and actions to find solutions. Such a holistic perspective would be a guiding principle. Where possible, specific, well-defined projects would be supported from beginning to end products and programs: site identification, survey, excavation, collection, documentation, conservation, exhibition, publication, dissemination through education, outreach programs, mass media, and exchanges with research partners. Alternatively, we would support one or more specific aspects (for example, conservation, including survey, treatment, training) of multidimensional projects that were already well conceived and well underway.

We also believe a clear sense of economy of scale is needed, that is, the scope and nature of support must meet local needs, means, and aspirations. Many so-called development projects in Africa (and elsewhere) have failed precisely because they ignored local conditions and capacities and instead imported and imposed concepts, methods, and equipment that were completely inappropriate to the situation. The approach elaborated in *Small Is Beautiful: Economics as if People Mattered* (Schumacher 1973), where projects were identified and prioritized from within, is one we would accept.

Proposed Programs

Of the various types of programs that would be supported and carried out, some might be short-term, others long-term. They are not in any order of priority, since this would be determined by the African proposers or Africanist partners involved: A) Practice, B) Training, C) Publication and/or Dissemination of Information, D) Public Education, E) Advocacy.[3]

A) Practice—Archaeology projects would be identified and prioritized by African institutions and scholars. They would then develop proposals for submission to and consideration by FAA. We will respond to the needs and priorities identified by such African institutions and colleagues, not impose priorities from outside. Projects must be African-identified and African-defined and have the full approval and support of both the appropriate African institutional and governmental agency(ies), or they must be joint ventures between African and Africanist scholars/institutions with full African approval and support.

All data collected as a result of such projects would be the property of the country in which the work was carried out. Photo documentation and analysis data of material would be duplicated for use among research partners. Agreements regarding the loan or exchange of artifacts and/or data for exhibitions, and so forth, would be shaped by African national regulations and the nature of collaboration established in specific projects. All costs for the temporary removal of artifacts/data for the purposes of high-tech laboratory analysis must be budgeted in advance to guarantee the expeditious repatriation of all artifacts/data (Gaddo 1989).

Where useful, we would provide data to our African colleagues from recent (and very expensive) technologies that might assist them in their research efforts—such as Landsat/Spot satellite data, aerial photos, geographical information systems (GIS), and automatic computerized data entry systems. For example, satellite photographs of ancient camel trails led to the discovery of an ancient metropolitan center (Umar) in the eastern Arabian peninsula, thus confirming local traditions. In another case, GIS surveys of dam construction and urban spread in West Africa aided in investigations of ancient cities and trading networks that produced exquisite sculpture in terra-cotta from the Inland Niger River Delta dating to about A.D. 1000 (McIntosh and McIntosh 1979).

Types of projects that might be supported include: 1) surveys and inventories of actual and potential archaeological sites (Kiéthéga 1983); 2) rescue operations—controlled excavations of sites that are in immediate danger of destruction, whether from looting or impending development projects; 3) site excavations—anticipated projects identified by local scholars and needing international cooperation and assistance (funds, equipment, personnel, etc.); 4) specialized expertise projects such as advice on conservation matters of unusual media; or a team of African student/technicians to use archaeomagnetism sample-taking for specific sites; and 5) documentation and conservation projects—in some projects, the highest priority might be the labor-intensive cataloging/labeling, cleaning, reconstruction, etc. and conservation of artifacts from excavations.

B) Training—Projects for the training of African professionals in fields related to archaeology would be supported by the FAA. The FAA would work actively to foster communication and cooperation between African universities and museums. This would include training at all levels, with special emphasis being given to lower and middle levels: postgraduate students—fieldworkers, supervisors, etc.; technicians; conservators; archivists (photo, library, and others); educators; and outreach organizers. . . .

C) Publication/Dissemination of Information—Frequently, the costs of publishing the results of archaeological projects are prohibitive, especially when such publication requires extensive photographic documentation, as anticipated for projects to be supported by FAA. Funds for publication often are not included in initial proposals, with the result that much archaeological information never reaches a wider audience or is greatly delayed. As part of our holistic, multifaceted approach, we would expect this aspect of any project to be anticipated and supported vigorously. We seek projects that will produce concrete results/products, whether in the form of a public display/exhibition, extension programs, catalog, video/film, publication, local TV program, etc. We would actively encourage and support the publication of results in Africa by African publishers, for local audiences that want and need to know more about local histories. We might also support, for example, such archaeology periodicals as the *West African Journal of Archaeology* and provide funds for the production of high-quality plates and textual illustrations which are often very expensive. We would also assist and encourage bilingual summaries of all publications to facilitate intra-African communication and cooperation. Indigenous African publishing is at present one of the program priorities of the Rockefeller Foundation. The FAA would cooperate with this effort, encouraging and identifying appropriate projects for support. We might want to consider the development of a publishing operation using PCs (low-tech) that could produce quick, desktop publications at minimal costs. Since the maintenance of such equipment is frequently a problem, training programs for museum/university technicians would also be considered.

We are sensitive to the problem of publications that endanger the security of sites and objects. However, we feel that one of the best ways to safeguard such objects is precisely by publishing them so that a country can document their presence and ownership for any future litigations regarding repatriation. The widespread publication of objects can then serve as a deterrent to those who might contemplate stealing, trading, or buying them.

D) Public Education—Efforts to preserve Africa's artistic/cultural heritage will fail if the citizens of the countries involved do not understand or share this concern. Therefore, all projects must be designed to develop public awareness and support for archaeology and its role in the preservation of art historical, historical, and cultural heritage. Projects will be accompanied by extensive and effective educational programs aimed at various segments of populations, from those most personally and immediately affected by an archaeological project (community people at the site), to students (in Koranic, Christian, and government schools and universities), to community leaders, to the general public (via newspapers, radio, and television), to government officials responsible for cultural policies, and to the nation's diplomats in the international arena. For example, in Ghana (and elsewhere), national television authorities are beginning to mandate and develop more and more locally-produced programming. Programs aimed at popularizing archaeology as a profession and documenting the history and glory of artistic/cultural achievements within the nation would be produced. These might also include the important role to be played by archaeology, programs on the nation's laws protecting cultural properties and so forth, and on who should be notified if archaeological material comes to light accidentally, etc. International and interdisciplinary teams (archaeologists, museum educators, television communications personnel, and others) would work with their African counterparts on such projects (Posnansky 1989).

A second example comes from the Togolese archaeologist Angele Aquigah, who has proposed a teaching program for women in pottery techniques as part of her archaeological investigations. This would not only revive and valorize an ancient tradition of domestic pottery; it might also offer some economic stability for women potters in providing an affordable alternative to imported cooking equipment (Ezra and Aquigah 1992).

A third example of a public education project would be the establishment of site museums. An example of such a local site museum, one that has worked well to raise local public awareness and commitment, is the Otunba Suna Museum at Imodi, Ijebu, Nigeria. The excavation was carried out by archaeologists David Calvocoressi and Nicholas David of the Department of Archaeology, University of Ibadan and Omotesho Eluyemi and Opeoluwa Onabajo of Obafemi Awolowo University. A small pamphlet in Yoruba and English was published (Calvocoressi 1977) and serves as the guide to the museum and collection for both local and foreign visitors. Other examples might include mobile exhibits, adult education and extension services, and integration of archaeological knowledge into school curricula (Ardouin 1992, 1993; Posnansky 1989). . . .

E) Advocacy—The FAA would work to encourage the support and implementation of the UNESCO accords regarding the preservation of cultural properties in Africa. We would include all constituencies in this effort. At the local level, we would help educate local governments about the importance of projects and of protecting antiquities.

In Europe, America, and Asia, we would work with and encourage art dealers and collectors to understand and support our concerns and efforts in concrete ways, for example in contributing information (photos, field notes, etc.) on sites and objects that can help in the identification and reconstruction of specific traditions. We would also work with our scholar colleagues (in museums and universities) to develop professional ethical guidelines concerning the dating, acquisition, publication, repatriation, and display of archaeological materials.

We would facilitate workshops/training for upper-level personnel (curators, museum administrators/directors, university scholars/professors, law school faculty) to assist in their efforts to lobby politicians (at all levels), government officials (all levels), and national diplomatic corps to develop supportive and effective legislation and controls concerning the illegal traffic in cultural patrimony. We would also work with the World Bank, USAID, the EEC, and the development agencies of various countries to ensure proper site surveys to protect cultural properties in the face of development projects.

Empowerment must come from within—but also with, as the song goes, "a little help from our friends." I am sure there are many African theories of empowerment and agency, but the one I learned from Yoruba people is known as *ase*—performative power, the power to get something done, to accomplish a task, to make things happen. *Ase* encompasses both the will and the means, the know-how to get results. So my advice is this: If we want the present erasure of Africa's past to stop, and remembering my drummer friend's image of sweet music created with both silences and sounds, then we Africanists need to talk less, listen more, and help when asked, and Africans should speak out, demand that we listen, and take action—ASE!

NOTES

1. These excerpts come from a proposal drafted by me that incorporates ideas of the FAA Proposal Working Group (Claude Ardouin, William Dewey, Henry Drewal, Kate Ezra, Roderick McIntosh, Merrick Posnansky, Philip Ravenhill, and Doran Ross) and African archaeologists and museum personnel (Joseph and Alexis Adande, Dola Aguigah, Emanuel Arinze, Raymond Asombang, Hounsinou Aubin, T. K. Biaya, Boureima Diamitani, Joseph-Marie Essomba, Antonia Fatunsin, Boube Gaddo, Colette Gounou, dele jegede, Abdu Juma, Iphrahim Kamuhangire, J. B. Kiethega, Haladou Maman, Manyando Mukela, and others) at the following meetings: Eighth Triennial Symposium on African Art, 1989; the Workshop on Archaeology, Art, and the Art Market at the 1989 ASA Conference; the 1990 panel and workshop on Archaeology, Art, and the Art Market in Africa at the Society of Africanist Archaeologists (SAfA) Conference; the 1991 meeting on "Museums in West Africa" at the Rockefeller Foundation; the 1992 Biennial Conference of SAfA and the conference on Cultural Preservation: Art and Archaeology in Africa at the University of Iowa; and an FAA Working Group meeting, September 1992, which included John Mack.

2. An anonymous reviewer of this essay has suggested that the tone of my opening critique seems "inconsistent" with that in excerpts from the FAA proposal. I would certainly agree that there is a shift in rhetorical style, from my more theoretical and critical introductory remarks to the more practical and concrete aspects of the funding proposal, a shift that reflects in part the geopolitical and economic realities of grantsmanship. The proposal is a document of specifics meant to persuade funding agencies in the so-called First World. Being a collaborative effort of all those mentioned in note 1, the rhetoric of the proposal attempts to bridge worlds in order to achieve results.

3. Editors' note: The FAA amplifies the mission of a similar but older institution, the Foundation for African Prehistory and Archaeology (FAPA), which was founded in 1982 by African and Africanist archaeologists. Dedicated to cultural resource management, training, and development of increased capacity to protect Africa's past, FAPA has participated in projects such as archaeological impact assessment studies in Somalia, the creation of a new academic unit for archaeology at the University of Dar es Salaam, the training of many Africans at the higher degree level in archaeology, the sponsorship of research in Africa, the making of documentary films. It is based in the Center for African Studies at the University of Florida, 427 Grinter Hall.

REFERENCES

Andah, Bassey, ed. *Cultural Resource Management. An African Dimension.* Special volume 20 of the *West African Journal of Archaeology.* Ibadan: Wisdom Publishers Limited, 1990.

Ardouin, Claude. "West African Museums Project: Brief Introduction." *Bulletin, West African Museums Project, Dakar* no. 1 (1990):4–5.

———. Letter to author, May 1992.

———. Letter to author, 19 January 1993.

Calvocoressi, David. *Rescue Excavations of the First Otunba Suna at Imodi, Ijebu-Ode.* Ibadan: Department of Archaeology, University of Ibadan, Nigeria, 1977.

Connah, Graham. *The Archaeology of Benin.* Oxford: Clarendon Press, 1975.

———. *African Civilizations: Precolonial Cities and States in Tropical Africa: An Archaeological Perspective.* Cambridge: Cambridge University Press, 1987.

Dewey, W., ed. "Prospects for Collaboration between African and American Institutions." Proposals prepared by African participants at the SAfA Biennial Conference, UCLA and the Ninth Triennial Symposium on African Art, University of Iowa, 1992.

Drewal, Henry J. "African Art Studies Today." In *African Art Studies: The State of the Discipline*, ed. E. Lipschitz, 29–62. Washington, D.C.: Smithsonian Institution Press, 1990.

Drewal, Margaret T. *Yoruba Ritual: Performers, Play, Agency*. Bloomington: Indiana University Press, 1992.

Ekechukwu, L. C. "Disappearance of Nigeria's Cultural Property: Need for Increased Security." *West African Journal of Archaeology* 20 (1990): 179–87.

Eyo, Ekpo, and Frank Willett. *Treasures of Ancient Nigeria*. New York: Knopf, 1980.

Ezra, Kate, and Angele Aquigah. Letter to the author, May 1992.

Gaddo, Boube. Paper presented at the Eighth Triennial Symposium on African Art, Washington, D.C., April 1989.

Garlake, Peter. "Excavations at Obalara's Land, Ife: An Interim Report." *West African Journal of Archaeology* 4 (1974): 111–48.

———. "Excavations on the Woye Asiri Family Land in Ife, Western Nigeria." *West African Journal of Archaeology* 7 (1977): 57–95.

Hall, Martin. *Farmers, Kings and Traders: The People of Southern Africa 200–1860*. Chicago: The University of Chicago Press, 1990.

Kiéthéga, Jean-Baptiste. *L'or de la Volta Noire: Archéologie et histoire de l'exploitation tradition-nelle (Région de Poura, Haute-Volta)*. Paris: Editions Karthala, Centre de Recherches Africaines, 1983.

McCaskie, T. C. "Asantesem: Reflections on Discourse and Text in Africa." In *Discourse and Its Disguises*, ed. Karin Barber and P. F. de Moraes Farias, 70-86. Birmingham: Centre for West African Studies, 1989.

McIntosh, Roderick, "Jenné-Jeno: An Ancient African City." *Archaeology* 33, no. 1 (January/February 1980): 8–14.

———. "Middle Niger Terracottas Before the Symplegades Gateway." *African Arts* 22, no. 2 (February 1989): 74–83.

———. "Resolved: To Act for Africa's Historical and Cultural Patrimony." *African Arts* 24, no. 1 (January 1991): 18.

McIntosh, Roderick, and Susan McIntosh. "Terracotta Statuettes from Mali." *African Arts* 12, no. 2 (February 1979): 51–53.

Oguibe, Olu. "Review of Africa Explores: Twentieth Century African Art." *African Arts* 26, 1 (January 1993): 16–22.

Phillipson, David. *African Archaeology*. Cambridge: Cambridge University Press, 1985.

Posnansky, Merrick. Letter to the author, 24 March 1989.

———. Letter to the author, 12 January 1993.

Ravenhill, Philip. "Public Education, National Collections, and Museum Scholarship in Africa." In *Culture and Development in Africa*, ed. I. Serageldin and J. Taboroff, 272–85. Proceedings of an international conference held at the World Bank, Washington, D.C., 1992.

Robertshaw, Peter, ed. A History of African Archaeology. London: James Currey, Ltd., 1990.

Schumacher, E. F. *Small Is Beautiful: Economics as if People Mattered*. New York: Harper and Row, 1973.

Shaw, Thurstan. *Igbo-Ukwu: An Account of Archaeological Discoveries in Eastern Nigeria*. 2 vols. Evanston, Ill.: Northwestern University Press, 1970.

————. *Nigeria: Its Archaeology and Early History*. London: Thames and Hudson, 1978.

Shinnie, Peter. *Meroë: A Civilization of the Sudan*. New York: Praeger, 1967.

USIA, Cultural Property Committee. *Curbing Illicit Trade in Cultural Property: U.S. Assistance under the Convention on Cultural Property Implementation Act*. Washington, D.C.: United States Information Agency, 1989.

Vansina, Jan. *Art History in Africa*. New York: Longman, 1984.

White, Hayden. *The Content of the Form*. Baltimore: Johns Hopkins University Press, 1987.

11

NIGERIAN ART AS ENDANGERED SPECIES

DELE JEGEDE

On the night of January 14, 1987, thieves broke into Nigeria's national museum in Jos. A total of nine artworks—four ninth-century Igbo-Ukwu items, two heads from Ife, and three Benin pieces—were stolen.[1] Almost a century earlier, in January 1897, a chain of events had occurred that resulted in an equally—if not more—disastrous consequence for Nigeria. A British consul, James Philip, had insisted on meeting with the *oba* of Benin, Ovonramwen. The *oba*'s aide, Chief Ologbosere, told the consul that since the *oba* was deeply involved in the annual Igue festival, during which he would not meet nor be met by any foreign subject, the request could not be granted. Philip remained adamant, and in the ensuing confrontation seven members of his nine-man team unfortunately lost their lives. Soon after this, a British expedition descended upon Benin City and sacked it. The *oba* was sent into exile and thousands of artworks were plundered.

Although separated by a time span of almost a century, these two incidents are undoubtedly connected by one factor: robbery. While the Jos incident exemplifies a growing audacity on the part of those who have continuously masterminded the illegal stripping of the cultural property of a sovereign state, the Benin pillage of 1897 epitomizes an aspect of cultural imperialism. Until the second half of this century, when most African nations intensified the struggle for political independence, imperialist overlords were convinced that their claim on the soul, resources, land, and cultural property of their African colonies was inalienable.

In this essay, I will examine the illicit trade in cultural property in Africa, with specific reference to Nigeria. What legislative mechanisms have been designed to confront and combat this monstrous threat to a people's pride and history, and how effective are they? What are the attitudinal, economic, and sociopolitical variables at play, and who are the dramatis personae in this obnoxious trade? These and related questions will be addressed against a background that situates the problem within a continental framework: A panoramic view of the impact of this malaise on Africa becomes our point of departure.

WESTERN INTERESTS, ILLICIT TRADE, AND AFRICA

From slavery through colonization and the postindependence era, Africa, it would seem, has remained a pawn on the chessboard of Western economic interests. The disturbing prevalence of the illicit trade in African art today and the economic, psychological, and sociocultural implications of this trade for Africa argue eloquently in support of this assertion. One can contend that without the West's overwhelming interest in African art, illicit trade in cultural property on the continent would not have assumed the alarming dimensions that it has reached, especially in the last three decades. As Peter Schmidt argues elsewhere in this volume, the erasure of Africa's cultural past is a second stage in the process of denigration of the African past by the West; the first was colonization. Indeed, the story of the illicit trade in African art is, in large measure, the story of the unscrupulous Western exploitation of loopholes, perceived or created, within the organizational and social structure in Africa for personal gratification or for corporate, institutional, or national aggrandizement.

This dilemma, in which Africa continues to lose not only monetary benefits but, more devastatingly, its past, pride, and creative virility, is rooted in the difficult and often unintended path that the appreciation of African art and culture has taken in the nine decades since a group of avant-garde artists in Paris extricated this art, once considered heathenish and opprobrious by Eurocentric apologists, and placed it at the center of international aesthetics. Prior to this event, art history as a field of study had no serious room for African art: Roy Sieber, who pioneered it in the United States, was at least four decades away. Following the mood then prevalent—of extolling racial pride and celebrating mechanistic achievement—European ethnologists and anthropologists were influenced in their study of African art by ethnographic and ethnocentric considerations; aesthetic and historic significance of the items collected were only of secondary importance. In the ecstasy that the Industrial Revolution brought and the negative mystification of the continent in classical literature, Africa became a dark continent waiting, in the estimation of the patriotic European missionary and trader, to be discovered. Its cultural property was collected with condescension, to be exhibited as evidence of the supremacy of European civilization and the barbarism of the exotic cultures of Africa. European imperialism had at last established an impeccable justification for colonization. The advent of the white man in Africa produced cultural tension, as pious missionaries insisted that the work of God could not go apace until heathenish fetishes and idols had been destroyed.

All this has become part of the history of a continent that, since its contact with the West, has remained in the throes of convulsive, externally induced changes. Africa has always reacted to these events, rather than containing them. Illicit activity in the cultural domain represents fallout from European contact. Such activity has thrived because of Western interests—interests fueled by the opposing forces of preservation, contextualization, and appreciation on the one hand and those of vandalization, expropriation, and commercialization on the other. As the 1993 Carter Lecture Series has amply revealed, if there is any part of Africa that has not been touched by the destructive activities of antiquarians, it is not because attempts have not been made; rather, it is probably because there is nothing worthwhile to harvest.

We also must not forget the inability or unwillingness of African nations to pursue legal options for safeguarding their cultural heritage and for the retrieval of those objects that may have been illegally taken from them. According to Lyndel Prott (this volume), as of late 1995 twenty-five African nations had not ratified the 1970 UNESCO convention. And only two countries—Nigeria and Senegal—are members of UNIDROIT, the International Institute for the Unification of Private Law, based in Rome. With the exception of Mali, no African nation has placed before the United States a request for official protection of its stolen art.

THE ANTIQUITIES TRADE IN NIGERIA

With this brief background, we may now look at the Nigerian situation. It is appropriate to begin with an examination of the nature and structure of the art and antiquities trade. The first attempt by the colonial government in Nigeria to regulate the illicit trade in the exportation of cultural property came with the Antiquities Ordinance of 1953. It defines antiquities as, among other things, objects of archaeological interest, including the land in which the object was discovered, and any work of art made before 1918, deemed to be of historical, scientific, or artistic interest, and currently or previously used in ceremonial or traditional context. The 1953 antiquities ordinance gave antiquities an elastic definition temporally and spatially. The temporal dimension becomes, by virtue of being tied to performance and traditional ceremony, an active present. While 1918 would appear to have no historical significance other than that it gave a minimum time buffer of thirty-five years from the date the ordinance was issued, the recognition of performance as an index in the definition of antiquities accorded necessary legal protection to Nigeria's cultural heritage. This measure becomes particularly important once it is recognized that other than archaeologically excavated objects, which can be scientifically dated, dating cultural objects remains a frustrating exercise. Information regarding manufacture and, in particular, information regarding the name of the maker and the year the work was made cannot easily be extracted from the object. Unlike the practice in the West, artists do not sign their works, although this does not mean that such works are not identifiable.

As time went by, the Antiquities Ordinance of 1953 became an ineffective instrument in the efforts to make illicit trade in antiquities an unprofitable enterprise. By 1970, a decade after Nigeria attained independence, major inroads had been made by organized groups, masterminded by Euro-American interests that specialized in the stealing and illegal exportation of Nigerian antiquities to the international market. Under the law then in existence, trading in antiquities was not a regulated business—anyone could buy or sell them. And where outright purchase of objects was not possible, they were stolen. Such activities were not confined to any single institution or any particular part of the country. The problem was compounded by Nigeria's vast coastline of more than seven hundred miles and a land boundary of two thousand miles, all of which placed considerable strain on the resources of law enforcement agencies that often did not have the means to counter the ingenuity of the smugglers.

In 1970, unbridled activities in the illicit exportation of cultural objects across Nigeria became a source of concern for perceptive Nigerians, the mass media, and some educational institutions. For example, the Institute of African Studies of the University of Ibadan reported two major losses of antiquities for the months of August and September; one, in the Osun shrine in Osogbo, involved sacred carvings; the other, in Ibadan, involved the removal of the altar screen of a Sango shrine and its replacement with inferior pieces (see jegede 1970–71:5). Subsequently, the institute organized a symposium on Nigerian antiquities in April 1972. At the end of the exercise, the symposium recommended, among other things, that museum work be made professional, that willful destruction and mutilation of cultural objects be legally discouraged, that illegal possession and exportation of antiquities be made a punishable offense, and that trade in antiquities be regulated, with dealers having to obtain valid permits to transact business.[2]

This setting provides the background against which the National Commission for Museums and Monuments Decree no. 77 of 1979 was established. The decree retains the definition of antiquity as contained in the 1953 ordinance, with appropriate elaboration. It establishes the National Commission for Museums and Monuments as a body upon which the responsibility of coordinating the implementation of the decree devolves. The decree provides for the registration of an antiquity by its possessor and for any endangered pieces to be taken into custody by the national commission, either through purchase or by loan. The commission is empowered to declare any cultural property a national monument and to ensure its preservation and protection. An important dimension of the legislation is the regulation of trade in antiquities and the prohibition of transfers. The decree makes it a punishable offense for anybody other than an accredited agent to buy or sell antiquities. It forbids the exportation of antiquities from Nigeria without a permit and empowers the Department of Customs and Excise to search and seize without warrant anything meant for exportation from Nigeria. Fortuitous archaeological discoveries are to be reported within seven days, and no excavations are to be carried out except with permit. The decree forbids willful destruction, alteration, or defacement of cultural property.

Undoubtedly, the decree benefited not only from the insights offered by the Ibadan symposium but equally from the 1970 UNESCO convention. The preamble to the UNESCO convention (1984:357) acknowledges that "cultural property constitutes one of the basic elements of civilization and national culture, and that its true value can be appreciated only in relation to the fullest possible information regarding its origin, history and traditional setting," stressing that it is "incumbent upon every State to protect the cultural property existing within its territory against the dangers of theft, clandestine excavation and illicit export." Adequate provisions are made for these declarations in Decree no. 77 of 1979.

Nigeria realized that it is not only desirable but also beneficial to accede to the 1970 UNESCO convention. Having decided to support the measure, it is natural for Nigeria to hope that all nations—especially Western countries—would ratify the convention. This enthusiasm is borne out by the fact that the country's museum was founded on the principles extolled by the UNESCO convention: the realizations that artworks and cultural objects embody precious information about a people, that they telescope history and reify societal values, that they enrich a people's cultural life and promote mutual respect among races, that their worth can be appreciated best when they are not violated, decapitated, and callously de-contextualized, and that, being so priceless, they should be protected by the state.

The groundwork for the establishment of the National Museum in Nigeria was laid by E. H. Duckworth, an educational officer and editor of *Nigeria Magazine* from 1933 to 1953, and Kenneth Crosswaithe Murray, an astute Africanist who arrived in Nigeria in 1927 as an art teacher and retired thirty years later as the first surveyor of antiquities, a post to which he was appointed in 1943. Murray's travels in Nigeria strengthened his conviction that the establishment of a museum in Nigeria was a cultural imperative. His argument was brilliant and his reasoning lucid. "In a Museum can be gathered together the evidence of past civilizations and achievements in art that will help the Nigerian to have pride and confidence in himself" (Murray 1942:247). He recognized the irreparable loss that Nigeria would suffer if urgent steps were not taken to stem the disappearance of invaluable objects through natural elements or human agents. In conclusion, Murray provided a moral and intellectual underpinning for his advocacy: "The need, indeed, for a collection of Nigerian art in Europe cannot be as vital as the need for one in Nigeria. In Europe, it would chiefly have an academic purpose, but in Nigeria it is wanted for the cultural life of the country itself. A collection, therefore, must contain first rate works, not those which remain after the cream has been taken for foreign Museums" (1942:247).

Bernard Fagg succeeded Murray at the National Museum, and Fagg, in turn, was succeeded by Ekpo Eyo in 1968. Eyo became director-general in 1974, a post he held until 1986, when he retired. A respected archaeologist and experienced museum administrator, Eyo will be noted for the passion with which he advocated an African perspective at international forums for the restitution of cultural objects. That Nigeria has demonstrated a keen sensitivity to the issues of preserving its past and preventing the desecration of its cultural property is not in question. Perhaps no further proof of this is needed than the fact that Nigeria was the third country to ratify the 1970 convention (after Bulgaria and Ecuador) and the first African country to do so.[3]

As an institution, the museum in Nigeria has great potential for integrating itself into the social fabric. Unfortunately, it has not been able to maximize such potential. In several quarters and for a variety of reasons, the museum is still perceived as a government institution, a paradoxical misconception. Such misconceptions about the essence of museums and their role in the community harden, over time, into a psychological barrier for prospective patrons, especially in the absence of an educational and integrative approach that seeks to make the museum a user-friendly institution. This paralysis isolates museums from the public and assigns to them a dreadful profile comparable to that of a mortuary, which one does not visit unless it is absolutely necessary. Furthermore, such paralysis engenders, in some instances, antagonism in those segments of the society whose support is needed in the battle against the incessant rape of the nation.

For the majority of Nigerians, particularly those in the rural areas, cultural and religious factors promote inhibitory attitudes toward the museum. For them, the museum is a government shrine, government property that is nobody's property. This is antithetical to the popular conception of shrine, which, as a metaphor, conjures intimacy, privacy, and sanctitude; it invokes reverence and possessive-ness. Be it a personal or community shrine, an expectancy pattern is evoked. There is familiarity not only with the objects but also with the sequence of events, with causes and effects and probable resolution through rituals and performances. Un-fortunately, the museum does not offer any of these privileges. What is more, it has hours of business and contains objects from everywhere, objects that are per-petually exposed for all to see, objects to which no sacrifices are offered and no appeasement is made. From this standpoint, the museum is an inactive institu-tion. For latter-day converts, the metaphor of the museum as a shrine is a sacri-legious concept that is as odious as it is repulsive. It invokes idol worshiping and impiety, both of which are seen as damning acts against Christendom and Islam.

This brings us to the nature and structure of the antiquities trade in Nigeria. The question is: Does the market—as proscribed by the law—exist? Decree no. 77 of 1979 presupposes the existence of such a trade and proceeds to regulate it. Part III, section 21, states: "(1) No person shall (a) buy any antiquity unless he is an accred-ited agent; or (b) sell any antiquity to any person other than an accredited agent." The Nigerian economy is characterized largely by trading. This penchant has become even more pronounced in the last ten years as a result of fiscal policies that have tightened the grip on the manufacturing sector, where the business of manu-facturing has taken a backseat to that of chasing the elusive foreign exchange. A drive on the ever-congested streets of Lagos will confirm the ingenuity of Nigerian traders. The range of articles that one can buy on Lagos streets while driving in the stop-and-go traffic is truly amazing: from beautifully framed prints of Frank Lloyd Wright's "Falling Water" to lingerie; from *Time* magazine to tourist-inspired ebony carvings of female busts. An observable pattern in trading activities in Nigeria suggests the emergence of a loose specialization along ethnic lines. For example, trading in automobile parts is dominated throughout the country by the Igbo, while the Yoruba are noted for trading in woven textiles (*aso oke*) and tie-dye (*adire*). The arts and crafts trade and, by extension, the trade in antiquities, is domi-nated by the Hausa, who are often found in the crafts section of any respectable market, especially in large cities and in most hotel foyers in Nigeria.

But why would anyone want to trade in antiquities in Nigeria? How good are Nigerians as consumers of antiquities? In the first place, the development of museums in Nigeria remains largely within the public domain. One longs to see the development of a mutually reciprocal relationship between Nigerian mu-seums and Nigeria's educational institutions. However, educational institutions and nongovernmental organizations are not yet willing to make annual budget appropriations to build up distinguished collections. The collections that remain within some universities are modest, to put it flatteringly. Most do not represent the country's artistic diversity and none, to my knowledge, has any impressive collections of cultural property from other African countries. Moreover, such col-lections as exist in Nigerian universities have remained stagnant in the last few years for a variety of reasons, including theft and poverty. Drastic cuts in the subventions to universities have become a predictable norm since the introduc-tion of the Structural Adjustment Program, affecting budgetary allocations to all departments.

For example, the small but exquisite collection of cultural property owned by the Centre for Cultural Studies of the University of Lagos has remained frozen for the last ten years. The last time the collection enjoyed public viewing was in 1977, when objects drawn from it were augmented by some that were obtained on loan from expatriate staff members. The show recorded a loss: a precious item disappeared. In the last five years, the University of Lagos's annual budget for the acquisition of cultural property has not exceeded the equivalent of eighty-three dollars. Nigerian universities are enmeshed in such financial straits that funding an institutional collection is often considered an avoidable cosmetic expenditure. Between June 1992 and February 1993, for instance, a series of crises occurred involving academic, administrative, and technical staff of all universities in Nigeria. A wave of strikes followed in which all three segments of the workforce took turns. Many universities remained completely closed or, at best, critically paralyzed. The Academic Staff Union of Universities, the umbrella for all members of the faculty, was proscribed by the military government. The situation deteriorated in 1993 as all thirty-one universities in Nigeria came to a complete standstill. Students, too, often went on sympathy boycott of classes in support of their teachers, who were asking for a reversal of the general deterioration experienced by universities and for higher wages.

Second, a tradition of collecting antiquities for pleasure, fun, or even profit must be in its infancy in Nigeria, if it ever existed at all. Of course, among the literati and some discerning members of the middle class it is possible to see what may be called collections, a good part of which may be indicative more of desire than taste. In fact, the trend in Nigeria today favors collecting contemporary Nigerian art, a field that has developed vigorously, especially in the last ten years. Certainly, the prospective trader in antiquities would not count on those in the low-income stratum for patronage. Within the upper income group, there are those who do not feel comfortable with cultural objects in their living room, for associative, religious, or even aesthetic reasons. The point here, therefore, is that traders in antiquities in Nigeria do not cater to the needs of the Nigerian patron since patronage of this genre by Nigerians is indeed insignificant. Traders' clientele consists primarily of tourists and expatriate visitors or workers in the country. Of course, the biggest market is in Europe and the United States of America.

Are there dealers who are accredited according to the provisions of the law? The simple answer is no. No one outside of the government establishment is accredited to buy or sell antiquities. The National Commission for Museums and Monuments occasionally invokes the power vested in it by the law to authorize certain persons to act on its behalf and collect cultural property for the museum from various parts of the country. This raises a second question: Do people sell antiquities to those not accredited by law? Yes, although such practices are illegal. But this aspect of the law is not readily enforceable. For the law to require that antiquities shall be sold only to accredited agents presumes that such agents shall be available in sufficient numbers and that they shall carry on them at all times enough money to buy antiquities. This, of course, is not always so: Museum agents do not often have the money at hand to pay those who, because they are economically handicapped or are no longer interested in their property, are ready to dispose of it.

WHAT IS ANTIQUITY?

What, then, is antiquity to the Nigerian people? How different is their perception of antiquity from that of the government? What is their own conception of museums and of the preservation of venerated cultural objects, and what is their reaction to illicit trade in cultural objects? To many Nigerians—and here emphasis is on the majority of those who are not literate—antiquity may connote a different spectrum of meanings, depending on the way the subject is presented. If one accepts the Western definition of an antiquity—cultural property that is to be extracted and divorced from its possessor, property that is to be excavated, analyzed, deciphered, decoded, methodically documented, dated, attributed, and, in some instances, finally displayed in the sedate and sanitized environment of a museum for others to view but not touch—perhaps Nigeria and, indeed, many African countries south of the Sahara may rightly claim that there is nothing called antiquity. In the sense, however, that cultural property is living culture, regardless of whether it is buried deep in the soil and separated by several generations, or tied to the rafters waiting to be summoned for yet another ritual or festival, or erected, hung, or casually tossed in the sacred environment of the shrine, a substantial part of the continent may indeed qualify to be declared as antiquity. Cultural apparatus and historical monuments, be they buried in the soil, abandoned, or excavated, evoke a strong sense of association and a passionate reverence and commitment in the people within whose territory the objects or edifices may now be located.

For example, let us examine the approximately eight hundred Esie soapstone figures, the origin of which remains steeped in mystery. Esie people have, however, reconstructed a matrix of relationships within which the figures, now conceived as ancestral images, are venerated. Eyo's experience during an excavation exercise in Ile Ife provides a second example. In 1963, according to Eyo (Eyo and Willett 1980:13–14), the late Ooni of Ife, Sir Adesoji Aderemi, visibly agitated upon being shown what appeared to be a burial site of Ooni Lafogido, promptly ordered that further excavation be stopped because he "did not wish the bones of his ancestors to be disturbed."

Clearly, owners of cultural objects not only appreciate them but are also possessively protective of them. The reasons for this are not difficult to understand. Many of the objects connote levels of meanings of life because they communicate visions of art. The objects are often inextricably interwoven with the existence and wellness of the owner, remotely or directly influencing modes of performance, occasionally dictating courses of action and affecting the spiritual spectrum. Thus, in the domain of aesthetics and appreciation, the spirituality of the object and the role it plays in the life of the individual are, more often than not, considered over and above its form. At issue here is the recognition that birth and death and growth and decay are important elements in the aesthetic construct. This appears to be a key element in understanding the attitude to the issue of preservation of cultural objects of some Nigerians, who still cling to and respect certain aspects of traditional rites and religious observances.

In Nigeria social, religious, educational, economic, and political factors, separately and in combination, influence the perception of cultural property and the attitude toward its preservation. On the social-political platform, a succession of civilian and military governments has, since 1960, continuously tinkered with the structure of society through bills, edicts, and decrees that were no doubt aimed at promoting good governance but that have had a deleterious effect on the cultural sector. Since May 1967, when the three former regions of Nigeria were split into twelve states, a move considered a masterstroke for winning the Biafran war, which eventually lasted for thirty months, many more states have been created through military fiat—seven in 1976, two in 1987, and nine in 1991. In addition to the Abuja Federal Capital Territory, there were thirty states in Nigeria in 1993. Predictably, a corresponding increase in the number of local governments also occurred. There were 593 local governments in 1993, and there is a strong possibility that many more may be created. As a result of this phenomenon, the authority of traditional rulers, local chieftains, and chief priests—the custodians of cultural property—has dissipated.

In many respects, the creation of states and local governments was accompanied by what was termed development. With respect to the culture sector, development often meant ad hoc decisions and poorly planned projects that were executed in an equally shoddy manner. Roads were constructed, buildings torn down, and townships planned with very little thought for edifices or monuments that have served as a source of spiritual bonding for the community. Among the Yoruba, traditional rulers who invariably became the statutory chairmen of the newly created local government councils saw the acquisition of new cars—preferably Mercedes Benzes—and the construction of new palaces as elements of the new social order. Consequently, vast segments of an older palace may be abandoned to rust and decay while considerable time is devoted to the acquisition of building funds for the new palace, usually an architecturally barren and culturally alien edifice that is often referred to as ultra-modern.

Perhaps it is in the religious sphere that some of the most fundamental shifts in values and attitudes have occurred. Although the advent of Islamic religion preceded that of Christianity in Nigeria, and in spite of the fact that Islam is averse to representational art, it was the introduction of Christianity to Nigeria in the 1840s that made the desecration of traditional shrines, the vandalizing of cultural objects, and the systematic burning of artworks a pivotal part of proselytization. Perceived then as symbols of a degenerate culture of "native pagans," cultural property became the target of religious zealots. This act has since remained a feature of Christian conversion, although its observances are now much less frequent than in the past. Ulli Beier (1972:33) reported as recently as 1970 that among the Yoruba some churches continued to collect and destroy art objects that they referred to as idols.[4]

Directly related to the transplant of the new religious order is education—Western education. Translated into the vernacular, Western education meant the inculcation of Western values in Nigerian youths, the promotion of Western affectation, and the disregard, neglect, and, in some instances, denouncement of cultural heritage. Such heritage is seen not only as antiquated and not modern but also as idols, voodoos, and fetishes, all of which are unbecoming of the modern Nigerian. Western education effected a slow but certain alteration in the source of artistic enterprise. It replaced existing artistic philosophy and the raison d'être, thereby altering the outlook and role of art in the new society. A new pattern of patronage emerged in which art was moved to the upper stratum of society and the artist-priest became an extinct group. Priests, carvers, and other specialists are being replaced by a new breed of bishops, sculptors, and academics. Children are no longer sent to learn art through the apprenticeship system. Instead, they study the subject in the art departments of colleges of education, in polytechnics, and in universities throughout the land. The construction and reconstitution of society have gradually but certainly imperiled the old cultural order; with the relentless efforts to illegally buy, steal, plunder, and export those artworks that are firmly rooted in Nigerian history, the erasure of cultural heritage becomes a frightening reality. Nigerian art, defined within this context, becomes an endangered species.

THE DRAMATIS PERSONAE

This brings us to the field, where two distinct groups are identifiable in the illegal disposal of cultural property. The first consists of iconoclasts who, mostly for religious reasons, so loathe artworks and are so full of self-serving righteousness as to make the destruction rather than the commercialization of cultural property an overriding preoccupation. Associated with this group are those who sell cultural property either because they have no particular attachment to it or because such property is not theirs, is no longer cared for, or is part of an inheritance that now holds little value for them in a rapidly changing age. Perhaps the strongest impulse to dispose of cultural property is precipitated by economic hardship. For instance, J. O. Odu, a senior officer in the Nigerian police, recalls the theft of the entrance doors to the palace of the *owa* of Idanre (1972:38). The doors were so heavy that it would take four able-bodied men to carry them, yet no one claimed knowledge of the theft. This situation is curious because the palace of the *owa* is located atop the rocky hills of ancient Idanre, accessible only through scores of steps hewn out of rocks. In the same article, Odu tells the story of an Ibadan family that sold its antiquities for six hundred pounds (sterling) and received a replica of the carvings in the bargain. In these two instances, which may be considered prototypical, poverty and disinterest become strong reasons for the disposal or removal of cultural property or for becoming an accessory to its disappearance.

But it should be emphasized that for every Ibadan family willing to be divested of property, there are probably three others who have taken steps to prevent loss or illegal transfer of heritage. In Cross River State, according to Keith Nicklin (1981), the head of Alok, Robert Ntool, foiled a bold attempt by thieves to steal some of the huge monoliths for which this area is known. The thieves would probably have stopped at nothing to remove the objects—including smashing the heavy monoliths to small pieces. Large, decorated, freestanding carvings of the Mbembe, Bahumuno, Yako, and Biase people have been reduced to stumps by thieves, the upper part amputated and carted away. Some of the remaining stumps have now either been cemented into the ground by the people or had protective shelters built over them, clearly an indication of desperation by an embarrassed people.

The foregoing cases not only exemplify the epidemic nature of this affliction but also confirm a disturbing pattern of desperation and boldness on the part of the thieves. No cultural object is too large or too sacred for them to plunder. Indeed, the more sacred an object is, the better. In Ikere-Ekiti in 1985, for example, five precious beaded crowns belonging to the chief priest, the *olukere*, were plucked from the innermost recesses of his chamber on the eve of the annual Olosunta festival. Some of these crowns had been left by the town's founder as a heritage for the people. Others were made by a succession of *olukeres*. In other words, it was not just crowns that were stolen; significant chunks of the cultural history of the town disappeared with the crowns. For a people who place so much importance on oral history, cultural property becomes a living vessel through which history is actualized. Crowns are among those cultural properties that assume, within this context, monumental importance.

A preliminary ethnographic survey of Ondo State that this author conducted in Nigeria in 1977 revealed that thieves had successfully penetrated shrines and palaces, as well as other sites. A particular case deserves mention here. In Ise Ekiti, the hometown of Olowe, who has been acknowledged as one of the greatest Yoruba carvers of this century, the regent became apprehensive about the mission and hesitated before granting me an audience. It turned out that only a few days earlier the courtyard of the palace had been relieved of some beautiful house posts, many of which were carved by Aoyo and Olowe, two competing carvers. The regent's position was precarious. Because of the temporary nature of her reign—she was appointed, not elected, to rule pending the installation of a male *oba*—she was anxious that history would not note her as the one who presided over the disappearance of her people's heritage. She had consulted with the elders-in-council and ordered that all carved items in the palace, including doors, be retrieved and retired. A curse—*ase*—was then placed on the thieves who had removed the house posts, with firm assurances by the chief priest who administered the curse that the thieves would not survive the week. Unfortunately, the thieves returned the following day and promptly stole more house posts.

Does the Nigerian National Museum leak? Not only does the museum leak, Nigeria as a country is a cultural sieve. For as the repository for national treasure, any leakage from the museum becomes a national disaster. There is abundant documentation of the profuse and perennial leakage that Nigeria has been experiencing. Arnold Rubin (1971) expressed dismay at the incredible amount of Adamawa art unlawfully brought to the United States, in addition to the huge quantity of Yoruba and Igbo sculpture now residing in this country illegally. We may never know the number of artworks that disappeared during and shortly after the Nigerian civil war.

A pattern of operation now seems to emerge. By the 1970s, a sizable amount of what was available through public shrines, palaces, and private domains had been illegally removed from Nigeria. During the seventies the activities of an army of looters from the West intensified. They recruited the gullible poor and charmed the traders. The alarming rate of looting during this period found echoes in the reports and editorials that appeared in the local media. By the 1980s, the cumulative impact of certain factors made illegal operations in antiquities a tougher enterprise. First, through a series of publicity campaigns mounted by the National Museum, the mass media, and some cultural institutions, the public had become sensitized to the need to take closer custody of their cultural property. Those who may have missed the repeated radio and television messages on this matter would have been told either by local chieftains or by their neighbors. Second, a shift in the production of art had become more pronounced as the effects of Westernization took hold, resulting in the emergence of contemporary art. The generation of carver-priests who put their art in the service of the community was replaced by a new set of those who received their training in art colleges. This meant, for the antiquarian, lean harvests from the field. This situation appeared to have emboldened rather than deterred poachers, who then focused their attention on the richest of all the shrines, the National Museum.

Beginning in the 1980s, reports of the disappearance of museum objects became a regular feature in the literature. For example, *Primitive Art Newsletter* notes in its November 1982 edition that a variety of rare and exquisite museum objects, including Nok, Ife, and Benin heads, fragments, plaques, pectorals, wooden objects, and bronze pieces, had appeared on the market in Togo, Switzerland, and the United States. *Primitive Art Newsletter* cites *Stolen Alert* for the information that three of the items—a bronze plaque, a three-figure pectoral ornament, and an Oduduwa bronze head—had been purchased in and shipped out of Nigeria by an American businessman. The American businessman claimed that he had obtained official permits, yet it is interesting that attempts were made to tamper with the museum numbers on the objects, which were always purportedly offered at ridiculous prices. Ava Plakin's short article in *The Connoisseur* (1983) puts the value of the three stolen Benin bronzes at £600,000. Eyo (1986:207–209), who at the time of these thefts served as the director-general of the National Commission for Museums and Monuments, gives a vivid account of the American businessman's adventure and of the roles played by the Nigerian government and a dealer in New York in effecting the return of the objects.

In 1980, according to Eyo, the Pace Gallery in New York asked whether the National Museum in Lagos had lost three Benin objects. Eyo immediately acted and, with the cooperation of diplomatic and law-enforcement agencies, the pieces were taken into custody while the FBI arrested the vendor. To identify the source of the theft, which was believed to have been masterminded by some personnel of the museum, Eyo chose not to prosecute the dealer. Instead, he invited him to Lagos for a week at government expense on the understanding that he would help to identify the collaborator. The businessman spent a week in Lagos but refused to assist the museum. Furthermore, he demanded, upon his return to the United States, a refund of $25,000 before he would release the objects. On his next trip to Lagos, he was promptly arrested and made to authorize the return of the objects.

There is yet another case which demonstrates that even with cooperation among countries that have signed the 1970 UNESCO convention, legal technicalities may thwart what may initially appear to be a simple and direct case. A dealer, Issaka Zango, and his associate were arrested at Calgary International Airport on December 2, 1981, for illegally importing a Nok terra-cotta into the country. (Canada ratified the UNESCO convention in June 1978.) The case went to court and was appealed twice. Finally, on March 11, 1985, it was formally discontinued on the technical ground that there was insufficient evidence to obtain a conviction since Nigeria was unable to supply sufficient proof that the object was illegally exported from the country. In his own note, Issaka Zango claims that although he purchased the object in France in 1979, it had been taken out of Nigeria in the 1950s. At the time Zango was arrested, he was on his way to show the piece to officials of the Glenbow Museum in Calgary in an effort to get Mobil to purchase it for $650,000 (Clark and Levy 1986:227–29).

From available evidence, it is apparent that illicit trade in cultural property is an act perpetrated by organized groups in the West who explore obvious weaknesses in the museum system to blackmail and exploit. According to Eyo (1986:209), the Pace Gallery once informed him that a bronze item was about to disappear from the National Museum. The item was eventually stolen. The gallery then demanded that a refund of $35,000 be paid to the buyer before the bronze plaque, valued at about $500,000 was returned. The Nigerian government had to provide the money because it was anxious to avoid the dilemma in which it once found itself with regard to an Ife terra-cotta head, whose sale by Sotheby's Eyo had discouraged. Should a government enthusiastically repurchase objects that have been stolen from its collection? Should a government pay a relatively small amount to buy back such objects and remain silent about the ethical and moral dimensions of such a deal? Can such a government survive the wave of exploitation and blackmail that is likely to follow?

It is clear that the museum system in Nigeria is infested. In an article in the September 2, 1991, *Newswatch*, Mercy Ette confirms that museum personnel are deeply involved in the theft of objects. For example, on May 3, 1990, Ajayi Odion caught Olufemi Ayeni with two objects in his possession. Both Odion and Ayeni were staff members of the National Museum. Previously, Ayeni had sold four *sango* staffs and two pairs of *ere ibeji* to some Hausa traders. Although Ayeni gave a written undertaking, he failed to return the objects. Instead, he stole more objects. In August 1991, he was caught again with another object. In the same article, Ette reports that two archaeologists from the Jos Museum had been charged in court with the disappearance of a terra-cotta piece that was discovered in Fai, Plateau State. According to Eyo (1986:209–10), when an inventory of the Lagos museum collection was taken in the early eighties, two carefully camouflaged holes were discovered in the ceiling of the storeroom. Police investigations revealed that the holes led directly to the office of a senior member of the museum who had been with the traveling exhibit *Treasures of Ancient Nigeria*.

Robert LaGamma's experience (as former director of the United States Information Service in Lagos) in the successful retrieval in 1991 of a Benin bronze head, one of those stolen from the Jos Museum on January 14, 1987, highlights the immense benefits offered by the 1970 UNESCO convention, but also illustrates the continued necessity of personal interventions when countries such as Nigeria are not state parties to the convention (LaGamma, this volume). At the same time, it also demonstrates the excruciating difficulties African countries experience in the preservation and retrieval of their cultural property. In this connection, LaGamma identifies five major impediments: a) inadequate security at the museums; b) vulnerability of museum objects; c) absence of good communication networks at intra-African and international levels; d) cumbersome bureaucratic red tape; and e) the low priority African governments accord to the culture sector (LaGamma, this volume).

Current developments indicate that at no time in its history has the museum system in Nigeria been under greater stress than now. Dependence on the government for all of its budgetary needs certainly has its own disadvantages. In the last quarter of 1992, museum staff who had gone on strike to demand salary increases and improved conditions of service were ordered locked out by the minister of culture. In the volatile political climate of Nigeria, ministerial and other major government appointments are characteristically made on radio and television broadcasts. Predictably, too, such appointees often learn through the same source when they are relieved of their appointments. Although the Nigerian museum is one of the most professionally administered museums in Africa, its efficiency is severely compromised by bureaucracy. Since the mid-1980s, a steady corrosion has set in. It culminated, in 1991, in the forced retirement of two of the National Museum's competent hands, the dissolution of the governing board of directors, and the termination of the appointment of the director-general, Ade Obayemi. Earlier, a succession of deaths had robbed the museum of the expertise of three of its experienced professionals. Since 1985, when General Ibrahim Babangida seized power, no less than seven ministers of culture have been appointed, a situation that does not promote continuity in government policy.

In a situation such as this, the debate should not center on whether the National Museum leaks. Rather, we should be concerned with the extent and volume of such leaks. As has been shown in the foregoing, illicit trade in cultural property on the African continent is sustained by the West, by default at times but also by design at other times. Clearly, looting and illicit exportation of cultural property in Africa is a one-way traffic—from Africa to the Euro-American metropolis. Multinational companies with the wherewithal to bypass legal channels could ship a couple of seemingly innocuous cultural items as part of an executive's personal effects—several items have left Nigeria in comfortable packages protected by diplomatic immunity. In addition, some scholars doing fieldwork frequently find objects too irresistible to be left behind, and missionaries for whom the robe is a protective armor, expatriate workers who are familiar with the system, tourists, and ubiquitous Hausa traders are all accessories to the illicit trade. In the Nigerian context, the efficiency of the police and the customs officials depends on certain variables, including the status of their clients (or victims, as the case may be) and the perceived potentials for instant remuneration. It can be said that where there is money, there are no customs. Secrecy and privacy, once considered attributes of bribery, have since been replaced by brazenness and extortion; bribery has been elevated to an art that is now practiced in the open, as most perceptive observers of events at the Murtala Muhammed International Airport in Lagos would confirm. Indeed, Nigeria leaks.

But such leaks, it bears emphasis, are induced by the West—by the insatiable lust of public-trust museums, dealers, and collectors of cultural property for which no production line exists, property whose export is controlled by the state because culturally, historically, and emotionally it defines the character of a people. Such leaks are funded by Euro-American dealers who realize sumptuous yields from such polluted investment. From the vast quantity of fakes and hybrids that have now flooded the market, from the deliberate aging of poorly manufactured pieces to the staging of ceremonies to authenticate newly produced objects in the field, the message is unmistakable: The antiquity market holds such allure for its operators that mere rhetoric and verbal punches have little effect.

CONCLUSION

What is called for by the international community, but more especially by African governments, is a concerted agenda that will address the multifarious ramifications of this phenomenon and propose workable solutions to them. A look at the situation reveals startling paradoxes. Today, it is much easier to study African art in the West than it is to do so in African institutions. In terms of scholarship, there are more American experts in the field of African art, for instance, than one would find in all of Africa. In any single year, more research on African art and culture is probably undertaken, more publications released, in Europe and the United States than would be possible in any fertile decade within the African continent. Africa's loss becomes the West's gain. While African museums are stripped of what rightly belongs to them, while villages and communities are being deprived of their property, galleries, museums, and private collections in the West are growing richer. In a sense, what we are witnessing is the confirmation of Merrick Posnansky's fears (1975:89): The second half of the twentieth century has indeed become the art equivalent of the slave era. Thurstan Shaw puts it succinctly: "The denudation of the art of these countries is still going on, largely through stealing, smuggling and illegal export. 'By right of wealth' has now replaced 'By right of conquest': 'Send a gunboat' has been superseded by 'Send a cheque'" (1986:46–47).

The first obstacle that African nations must tackle is the disorder in their own homes. They must create a system that will considerably curtail, if not totally eliminate, the spate of leaks within their own institutions—a system that will sanitize the institutions and make professionalism the cornerstone of their operations. To succeed in this direction, the ratification of the 1970 UNESCO convention by those African countries which have not done so should be seen as a sine qua non. It is imperative that African nations should avail themselves of the advantages UNESCO channels provide and of instruments for the protection of cultural heritage. The excellent example of Mali should be followed by those who are serious about seeking the cooperation of the U.S. government in banning the importation to the United States of their national treasures.

Second, African governments should give serious consideration to the formulation of bilateral agreements among themselves. If much of the potential damage caused by the illegal art business can be contained locally, the battle to stem the international traffic can then be undertaken with greater zest and concentration.

In a world where civilization is defined on the strength of technological achievement, African governments must come to terms with the imperative of preventing their past from being shipped abroad; cultural matters must be accorded the pride of place that they deserve on the political agenda. Since proof of ownership is a critical element in determining the repatriation of illegally exported cultural objects, a standard course of accessioning collections must be embarked upon by museums; a rigorous menu of inventories must be seen as an essential element in museum operations. Museum personnel must be trained and retrained; the public must be educated about the importance of safeguarding cultural property, and a progressive curriculum may have to be developed for use by the police and the customs and excise. Indeed, the excellent and comprehensive programs proposed by Henry Drewal and his Foundation for African Archaeology in this volume are strongly endorsed and recommended as a model to be adopted and implemented by African nations.

Once the domestic front has been taken care of, African nations must then explore every avenue within the international community to push the issue of the erasure of Africa's patrimony to the top of political agenda. What is needed is, in fact, reparation and repatriation. The issue at hand has cultural, economic, moral, and political dimensions, all of which are intertwined. In addition to pressing for the return of illegally acquired artworks, Africa has the right to seek compensation for the unjust deprivation of an essential part of its soul and history. Those who argue against repatriation and restitution of Africa's cultural property emphasize the unrealistic nature of such a demand by pointing out that museums are underfunded and understaffed and that the health of such returned objects will be imperiled. Such arguments are predictable, coming from those who are bent on reinventing the rationale for colonization. Shaw (1986:47) has argued very persuasively that the West must accept the principle of restitution instead of presenting untenable reasons for the status quo: "It is entirely reasonable and natural that emergent nations should feel passionately about these things, and need them to establish their own identity, their own roots, and write their own history. The authorities who cling to these foreign treasures disregard the fact that in many cases these objects hold spiritual, cultural, emotional and aesthetic values for the people of the country of origin."

During the twentieth century, the interests of Africa have been subordinated to those of the West; Europe granted political independence but retained economic and cultural controls. Today, Africa pays an estimated $100 million daily to service its debt to the West. Yet one of the most basic rights—the right to one's heritage—is constantly tampered with in Africa. Cultural hemorrhaging denies the economic potentials of studying African art and culture in Africa. The fundamental question that must be asked and addressed is, Whose cultural property?

NOTES

I am greatly in the debt of friends and colleagues who have donated ideas and shared thoughts as well as sources with me in the course of preparing this paper. In particular, I acknowledge the contributions of Roy Sieber, Ekpo Eyo, Rowland Abiodun, Janet Stanley, Judith Herschman, and Barbara Frank.

1. *Museum* (1987:300–303) contains annotated photographs of the stolen items. The four items from Igbo-Ukwu are: a) a bronze pendant in the form of a leopard's head; b) an ornate bronze hilt; c) a bronze altar stand with male and female figures framed in spiral designs; and d) a bronze pendant depicting an animal's head. The three Benin objects are a) a small terracotta of Benin head, b) a fifteenth-century brass memorial head, and c) a carved ivory horn.

2. The symposium drew participants from academia, the police, the customs, and the national museum. The symposium report appears in a special issue of *African Notes* (1972).

3. Nigeria ratified the 1970 UNESCO convention on January 24, 1972. The ratification became effective three months later, on April 24.

4. Beier makes a strong case for government to stop such "acts of Barbarism," while the symposium recommended the discouraging of willful destruction of cultural property by churches or any religious body. It is likely that the government responded to this by inserting a clause in Decree no. 77 of 1979 that makes it unlawful for any person to willfully destroy, remove, excavate, deface, or alter an antiquity.

REFERENCES

Allison, Philip. "Collecting Yoruba Art." *African Arts* 6, no.4 (Summer 1973):64–68.

Beier, Ulli. "The Preservation and Protection of Nigerian Antiquities." *African Notes* Special No. (1972):33.

Clark, I. C., and Lewis E. Levy. "National Legislation to Encourage International Cooperation. The Cultural Property Export and Import Act of Canada." In *The Challenge of Our Cultural Heritage: Why Preserve the Past?* ed. Yudhishthir Raj Isar, 213–31. Washington, D.C.: Smithsonian Institution Press, 1986.

Eyo, Ekpo, "A Threat to National Art Treasures: The Illicit Traffic in Stolen Art." In *The Challenge of Our Cultural Heritage: Why Preserve the Past?* ed. Yudhishthir Raj Isar, Washington, D.C.: Smithsonian Institution Press, 1986.

———. "Nigeria." *Museum* 31, no.1 (1979):18–21.

———. "Fakes, Fakers, and Fakery: Authenticity in African Art." *African Arts* 9, no. 3 (April 1976):20–31, 48.

Eyo, Ekpo, and Frank Willett. *Treasures of Ancient Nigeria.* New York: Alfred Knopf, 1980.

Hershey, Irwin. "Some Home Truths about Repatriation." *Primitive Art Newsletter* 5, no. 10 (October 1982):1–3.

———. "The Great Nigerian Museum Mystery." *Primitive Art Newsletter* 5, no. 11 (November 1982):1–2.

Isar, Yudhishthir Raj, ed. *The Challenge of Our Cultural Heritage: Why Preserve the Past?* Proceedings of a Conference on Cultural Preservation, April 8–10, 1984. Washington, D.C.: Smithsonian Institution Press, 1986.

jegede, dele. *Art by Metamorphosis: Selections of African Art from the Spelman College Collection.* Atlanta: Spelman College, 1988.

———. Personal communication with Ekpo Eyo. April 4, 1993.

————. "Loss of Nigerian Antiquities." *African Notes* (1970–71):5.

McIntosh, R. J., and Susan Keech McIntosh. "Dilettantism and plunder—illicit traffic in ancient Malian art." *Museum* no. 149 (1986):49–57.

Murray, K. C. "Art in Nigeria: The Need for a Museum." *Journal of the Royal African Society* 41, no. 162 (January 1942):241–49.

————. "Return and Restitution of Cultural Property: The Role of Museums." *Museum* no. 162 (1989): 112–13.

Nicklin, Keith. "Rape and Restitution: The Cross River Region Considered." *Museum* 3, nos. 3/4 (1981):259–69.

Odu, J. O. "?" *African Notes.* 1972.

Plakins, Ava. "A Scandal That Won't Go Away." *The Connoisseur* (January 1983):16.

Posnansky, Merrick. "The Price of Popularity." *African Arts* 4, no. 3 (1975):88–89.

Rubin, Arnold. "A propos." *African Arts* 4, no. 2 (1971):79.

Shaw, Thurstan. "Restitution of Cultural Property: Elements for the Dossier." *Museum* 146 (1986):46–48.

Stanley, J., and Judith Herschman. *African Museums Bibliography.* Washington, D.C.: Fowler Museum of Cultural History and National Museum of African Art, 1991.

UNESCO. *The Protection of Movable Property* (compendium of legislative texts). 2 vols. Paris: UNESCO, 1984.

12

COPING WITH COLLAPSE IN THE 1990s

WEST AFRICAN MUSEUMS, UNIVERSITIES, AND NATIONAL PATRIMONIES

MERRICK POSNANSKY

Africa entered a new era in the 1960s: Independence was proclaimed and with it came a sense of hope and pride. There was hope that each individual country could chart an independent course to prosperity with education, health care, and higher standards of living for all its citizens, and there was a developing pride in their own cultural identity and integrity. There was also a determination to discover a presumed concealed past and promote an awareness of cultural heritage among the population. Universities, museums, ministries of culture, and antiquities services figured strongly in the development plans of the newly emerging states and were created at both the national and sometimes the provincial levels within the first fifteen years of independence. There was a palpable excitement and competition in countries like Nigeria, where every state scrambled to have both a university and a museum.

The late 1970s and the 1980s represented, however, as a 1989 World Bank report noted with regret, a "lost decade," a period when, over most of West Africa, state economies were in tatters, living standards were falling, infrastructures were collapsing, trained personnel were hemorrhaging to the developed world, and cultural institutions were neglected. It was also an era when the demands for "traditional" African art and even for basic crafts like woven textiles, basketry, and wooden stools grew outside of Africa, when research output by national universities in most West African countries declined, when the destruction of sites with salable antiquities, previously unimportant, began to spread, and when the smuggling of antiquities reached epidemic proportions that have alarmed us and stimulated such conferences as the one for which this essay was originally prepared. I will argue that Africa's past will continue to disappear, sites will continue to be degraded, and art will continue to be smuggled out of Africa and into the developed world until the infrastructure of museums, universities, and antiquities is drastically overhauled and until each and every African country designs, commits resources to, and implements what would amount to a comprehensive management plan which includes both research and educational components for the conservation of its historical and cultural patrimony.

BACKGROUND TO THE PROBLEM

Museums are not new creations in Africa, with the first in tropical Africa having been established in Uganda, Kenya, and Zimbabwe more than eighty years ago; they are, however, relatively recent creations in West Africa, a fact that represents an aspect of colonial history. Museums as we know them today are European transplants and as such represented European interests in such matters as big game in Kenya, Islamic silverware in Zanzibar, and ethnography in Uganda and Tanganyika. The museums were a product of European settlement. In East and Central Africa, Europeans made their homes there or at least served long tours of duty with their families. These transplants were also the patrons of the museums, forming the boards of trustees that managed such institutions. They provided their services to the museums primarily on a voluntary basis. Small subventions were provided by the always financially strapped colonial governments to the nascent museums, much as they were to other cultural, social, and educational institutions that largely served the expatriate community. Collections were donated and much of the enthusiasm that they generated furthered the spirit of volunteerism that was a hallmark of such developments. The museums were often aided by associated cultural and scientific societies, as in Nairobi or Uganda, that also published scientific work on materials donated to the museum, such as a piece on the snakes of Uganda published in the *Uganda Journal* in eleven parts between 1935 and 1938.

In West Africa European settlement was discouraged. The higher incidence of disease and generally more trying living conditions led to shorter tours of service, and children were discouraged from staying beyond toddlerhood. Expatriate involvement in local institutions was less evident, and, except for small collections in government departments, such as the geological survey in the Gold Coast or the remarkable archaeological collection built up by Thurstan Shaw at the Gold Coast's Achimota College in the late 1930s, museums were the exception rather than the rule. Nigeria, for instance, with the largest population, did not have a regular museum until the 1950s, and that museum came about only through the enthusiasm of Bernard Fagg, a district officer in Jos. The most important of the exceptions was that of IFAN (the Institut Français d'Afrique Noire), Dakar, which served the whole of francophone West Africa, as well as a smaller IFAN museum with a highly significant archaeological collection in Conakry and a largely ethnographic collection established as a regular museum in Abidjan in 1947. Major government involvement in other countries awaited the post–World War II period.

Conceptually, the colonial museum could be nothing but European, even though created by such vigorous and significant individuals as Margaret Trowell in Uganda, Kenneth Murray in Lagos, Raymond Mauny in Dakar, Bohumil Holas in Abidjan, and Louis Leakey in Nairobi. Each of these remarkable individuals imposed the patterns of her or his individual interests and research. Though such museums were based on European models, the curators fortunately had an African vision, a vision with which we may now disagree with the benefit of hindsight, but a clearly recognizable vision. Some of the exhibitions they created have been criticized for their nonrepresentative nature, but in many ways their coverage was broad for their times, with historical sections in the museums in Dakar and Accra, with music and archaeology included with the basic ethnography. Several museums in the immediate preindependence era had also added modern art to their collections; in Uganda, such practices helped to foster the first independent African art gallery.

The lack of an overriding sense of vision was perhaps the greatest weakness of the museums of the independence era. The communities that created the colonial museums languished and in many cases disappeared; the volunteerism that sustained them was dependent on a leisured, economically comfortable and secure class of colonial functionaries and settlers, and little was done to ensure that the African society that succeeded them had an appreciation or knowledge of museums. Even here, however, there were exceptions, as in the case of Uganda, where there had been a series of dedicated museum trustees drawn from the local African community for at least twenty years before independence in 1962. Most important, however, the personal sense of patronage was lost; there were few functionaries with the means or inclination to collect either for themselves or for a national institution. The overriding state interest was more abstract than a personal, expressed interest; the state sought to discover, protect, and project a national patrimony, a concern that largely fell to government committees and salaried officers to implement.

The expanding numbers of senior museum personnel were appointed on the basis of academic merit and paper qualifications rather than on the basis of expertise or enthusiasm and love for the objects that comprised the museum collections. They were in most cases patrons of neither the ethnographic nor the creative arts. The days of the scholar-administrator had passed; other matters dominated their time—in some cases political development, in other cases personal, family, or community economic enhancement. By the late 1970s and the 1980s, most were troubled by economic worries, when, like other government officers on fixed salaries, their standards of living declined with rampant inflation and stagnant economies. The new generation of African administrators wrote, but they did so predominantly in the realms of politics, history, and creative literature—areas they perceived as being of prime importance for shaping the political, social, and cultural dialectics of their new nations—rather than on material culture and ethnography. Museums had few articulate advocates. As a cultural institution, the university predominated. The more talented scholars were recruited, trained, and sponsored in their research by universities. Such researchers and teachers had a greater access to opportunities both for research and for interaction with their African and international colleagues than did their museum counterparts.

What were some of the problems faced by museums that have led to the present crisis? The problem was certainly not the lack of staff but rather the lack of the right resources, a general lack of stimulation, and a malaise that afflicted virtually all the museums. The West African museums were never understaffed; in fact, the number of senior employees grew quickly in countries such as Ghana or Nigeria after independence. Elsewhere, particularly in francophone West Africa, new museums were being established. In contrast to the Americas and Europe, where there are many one-person museums, most museums in West Africa had a relatively large junior staff but few well-trained technical staff. In Ghana, for instance, at independence the national museum had two senior professionals; within fifteen years that number had quadrupled but less was being accomplished in terms of tangible results such as displays, augmentation of collections, or research on collections or in the field. In Ghana the present displays have altered very little since the opening exhibition of 1957. A lack of change has marked most of the public exhibitions in West Africa museums, and many of them present selected ethnographic items, rather like shoe displays in a shop, that tell a few facts about the objects without any comprehensive attempt to fully represent national culture. In the early days of independence the problem was certainly not material, since vehicles were available, overseas training opportunities existed, and salaries had not yet plummeted. In the first decade and a half of independence, an era of state investment in the culture, an age before the droughts and infrastrutural collapse, underfunding clearly was not the principal problem in museum development that it became in later years.

Over the course of time, however, museum funding did not keep up with inflation. Most of the more enterprising senior staff were siphoned off into other government agencies or were attracted by the research facilities, teaching opportunities, and often higher salaries in the universities. The remaining staff stayed because there was no place else to go as vacancies in other ministries dried up. Agbenyega Adedze, an African museum specialist, returning from a visit to a large number of African museums, wrote in March 1993, "The impression I got from most people working in the museums was that they are not working in the museum out of love or care for the objects but were pushed into the museum because they did not have anywhere else to go" (personal communication). This is a sad indictment of the current situation and reinforces arguments that I have made elsewhere (Posnansky 1992), that the principal problem in African museums is that of the curatorial ethic, of an artifactual myopia, of a lack of vision, problems that have become accentuated in the crisis that we face today.

Some have argued that the problem is in management, but that is too simplistic an answer and is the stock response trotted out to explain most of Africa's contemporary ills. There was certainly and still is mismanagement. Institutions grew too rapidly; they were part of government bureaucracies that controlled too many resources and had to satisfy too many interests, but mismanagement cannot provide all the explanations.

At the heart of every museum is its collection, but all too often the object, or artifact, and everything that such collections of artifacts tell us about the societies that made them and about the cultural heritage of their descendants, has been allowed to become secondary to administrative interests. Most of the world's greatest museums began as collections in search of curation, aggregations lovingly compiled by single-minded collectors for whom each object had a story to tell. The original motive was not the capital appreciation that afflicts so many of today's collectors. The financial value at the time was irrelevant. Good curation ultimately depends on the same interaction between the object and the curator. The curator has the mandate to conserve but the broader mandate is to appreciate, in its broadest sense, the history and particularities of every artifact, whether a simple stone flake or an elaborate work of art. Such appreciation cannot be taught but must be acquired through intimacy. Nothing can replace the intimacy that grows out of and matures during the multifaceted process of collection, documentation, conservation, research, and often communication of the information locked within the object and released with enthusiasm to the visitors to the museum and to the wider community through display and publication.

In Africa, instead of a focused working concern on the national collections, interest was all too often diverted to a broader philosophic rhetoric of protecting and projecting a heritage uprooted from either the artifacts or the context that created them. It was as if African museums had jumped a step, safeguarding concepts while neglecting to document, build up, conserve, and create effective visibility for their collections and monuments. The creation of such a visibility must be an essential building block of a national patrimony, because it enhances national awareness of the importance of conserving the past. Museum curators in Africa became separated from their staffs, reaping the material benefits of trips abroad and the attendant allowances that made such trips so attractive for foreign-exchange-strapped professionals. While museum curators were attending international gatherings, convened by such organizations as UNESCO, the International Council of Museums (ICOM), and the International Commission on Museums and Sites (ICOMOS), to help write or at least sign on to charters for the conservation of the world's greatest treasures, the collections in their own museums suffered, disappeared, and were generally neglected because the same curators were often the only persons with any hands-on experience in the daily chores of museum registration or conservation.

One important factor in the current state of affairs is politics. Museums are parts of ministries, and ministries reflect the patronage of the governing authorities as much as the professional requirements of their constituent components. Appointments to museums and to the administrative echelons of the university are often made on an ad hoc basis related neither to the skills and credentials of the appointees nor to any long-term staffing needs of the institution. This political aspect of museums has all too often been ignored in the literature, though it is all too real on the ground. Heads of museums are appointed at a moment's notice without open application, and just as sudden are the dismissals of senior personnel, sometimes even announced on the radio to take instant effect. Senior personnel have been known to shuffle their staff around according to political or ethnic affiliation. This infusion of politics into the museum results in a lack of continuity, a sense of insecurity, a lack of involvement, and no sense of either direction or mission. These effects run throughout the ranks of museum staffs. Museums become tied to ministry regulations, without control of their own budgets. As a result, far too many personnel are employed, but there is no money for programmatic needs and initiative is stifled. There are no standing funds accumulating surpluses from year to year, as is necessary for equipment replacement or collection building. At the end of the year whatever funds are outstanding go back to the government, which discourages savings on staff or recurrent expenditures to provide money for vital long-term research or collection enhancement. The museum, in this situation, becomes yet another branch of government subject to all the vagaries of an insecure political and economic environment.

Universities and Archaeology

While many museums were disintegrating in their capacity to operate effectively after the early 1970s and were failing to protect Africa's past, universities were developing their capacities both to conduct research and to create awareness of Africa's cultural heritage. In the early 1970s, several departments of archaeology in Nigeria (Ibadan, Nsukka, Ife, and later Zaria) were conducting research and teaching archaeology, and there was a flourishing department in Ghana and smaller research units in both Abidjan and Dakar. Graduates in archaeology were produced in Ghana beginning in 1971 and in 1974 Ekpo Eyo became the first West African to receive an Ibadan doctorate in archaeology. By the early 1980s, West Africans largely staffed the departments, research output was impressive, and all the departments published materials. Several of the archaeologists were also making an impact with the public media in developing a broader awareness of the importance of the archaeological record. In this respect the radio broadcasts of both Professor James Anquandah and Dr. Kofi Agorsah on Ghana Broadcasting's External Service were significant. Most of the major developments occurred in anglophone Africa, although in the early 1980s other countries such as Togo, Benin, and Burkina Faso were developing archaeology at the university level.

If archaeology was successful at the university level in the 1970s, what led to the crisis of the present day? There are many significant factors both internal and external to the area, but foremost must be the economic downturn of the late 1970s and early 1980s, which was compounded by environmental stress with rainfall in 1982–83 over most of West Africa at its lowest level in more than forty years (Posnansky 1984). There were growing population movements caused by both drought and the nationalistic actions of key countries, such as Nigeria, which in 1983 expelled approximately a million Ghanaians. Museums and universities became low priorities when food was scarce and infrastructures, such as roads and health services, were rapidly deteriorating. Archaeologists in Ghana and Nigeria lost their capacity to travel into the field. Projects could rarely be sustained. Key faculty, both African and expatriate, sought jobs outside the country, and graduates sent for overseas training never returned. Of five Ghanaians who went overseas to undertake doctoral research on Ghanaian topics, only one, Kofi Agorsah, returned to teach in Ghana, and he only did so for five years. Though student numbers rose, there were fewer faculty to teach them, and they often had fewer qualifications. Opportunities for long-term student participation in field research dissipated. Few books came into the libraries and virtually none arrived in university bookstores; the few that were available were out of reach of students, who could barely, in some cases, afford one substantial meal a day. Even the standby of duplicated notes prepared by the lecturers was hampered by mimeograph machines bereft of spare parts. Photocopiers, so commonplace in Western universities, were broken or nonexistent. For example, at the University of Ghana in the late 1980s, there were seldom more than three machines available to the public, and the one in the university library, where demand was most acute, was overburdened and often out of commission.

In many universities there was academic inbreeding, with lecturers getting their first, second, and even doctoral degrees from the same department and from a very limited range of instructors. Job mobility was impossible in countries with only a single university teaching archaeology. New ideas were few and far between because of intellectual isolation. Faculty, secure in their tenure but insecure in their economic means, had little incentive to undertake research or to expand or update their repertoires. The frequent closures of universities disrupted normal teaching schedules and made it impossible to take advantage of the opportunities provided by foreign missions.

Endemic economic collapse meant poor roads, which made sites virtually inaccessible to faculty who were all too often required to use their own frequently dilapidated vehicles for fieldwork. Salaries dropped to levels one-fiftieth of what they had been in the 1960s in real spending power in countries like Ghana (Posnansky 1989), whereas in others, like Benin, salaries were low and up to six months in arrears. Libraries were unable to make new accessions, equipment broke down and could not be replaced, and, as in the museums, a state of malaise prevailed. Even so, some significant work was and still is being conducted throughout West Africa by African scholars such as James Anquandah in Ghana, Alexis Adande in Benin, John Baptiste Kiéthéga in Burkina Faso, Bassey Wai Andah in Nigeria, and Angele Aquigah in Togo.

External Factors

While African archaeological activity was decreasing in the 1980s, interest in African art blossomed and, in common with other collectibles, prices rose astronomically. The increased demand for art, stimulated unwittingly and indirectly by such journals as the University of California's *African Arts,* ultimately led to an expansion of smuggling and site despoliation. Museums, antiquities services, and universities—all in a weakened condition—were unable to take any effective action to stem the flow. Many countries, particularly in francophone Africa, still have no effective ordinances defining antiquities or monuments, and even in those countries with ordinances or legislation there is no machinery for effective enforcement. Throughout the 1980s, and particularly at the end of the decade with the end of the cold war, Africa became increasingly marginalized, with donor fatigue affecting grants to African institutions. Equipment levels in major departments are far lower than they were thirty years ago. Departments of archaeology have for the most part been unable to share in the advantages of the electronic revolution and computers that have so transformed archaeology outside of Africa.

All too frequently many of the foreign researchers have been graduate students working with limited funds themselves, using but not always replacing scarce fieldwork equipment and exporting their finds abroad for study. Laboratory classes based on the analysis of finds from sites in Africa, so essential an ingredient for familiarizing undergraduates with archaeological material, have thus not been a staple of archaeological education in West Africa in recent years. Even when larger teams have been in the field, little or no provision has been made for conservation of any kind and there has in some instances been insufficient involvement of local departments or antiquities services in their work. Furthermore, foreign teams often arrive during the period when the African university is in session, from October until June. Academic schedules are too rigid to excuse students from courses, particularly courses in subjects other than archaeology, so field cooperation, although wanted by both parties, is too difficult to arrange. As a result, local institutions believe they do not know what foreign teams are doing and the foreigners are disappointed in the lack of local enthusiasm for their efforts.

We certainly now know much more about West Africa's past than we did a quarter of a century ago, but many countries have paid a price in sites not conserved and an awareness by the wrong groups, for the wrong reasons, of the intrinsic value of the cultural patrimony.

SOLUTIONS

Having all too briefly looked at the problem, how can we improve the situation? There is no single magic bullet. Solutions lie in three directions: independent initiatives by African universities, museums, and antiquities services; long-term bilateral cooperation; and multilateral cooperation involving both inter-African networks, such as those established by the West African Museums Project in Dakar, and international initiatives that may involve completely new organizations, such as the Foundation for African Archaeology, initiated by Henry Drewel, targeted at specific problems for which there is a clearly definable and feasible solution. All these different approaches must become part of a developing strategy or they will be but further examples of the isolated palliatives of the last few years that have brought some small improvements but little sustainable development.

Independent African Initiatives

It is clear at the outset that to achieve success there must be closer working relationships between museums and universities. Each has its role. Universities, having the stronger research capacity in Africa, often have easier access to external foundation funding, have better libraries, and can draw on a larger pool of assistants in the form of student helpers. Museums, on the other hand, possess the collections on which research should depend, have in some instances conservation and display facilities, and also have the opportunity for year-round access to the field. In reality, in the present crisis facilities for adequate research, display, or conservation are all too often nonexistent and the lack of adequate funding leads to a state of paralysis. At the crux of the crisis is a need for a new direction in integrated training at both the university and museum levels with cultural conservation clearly in mind.

New Professionalism

Within Africa one of the principal changes that must take place is the creation of a new professionalism. African museums first must recruit specialists with training—and particularly an avocation—in one or more of the disciplines covered by the museum, rather than offering a career in museology. Similar to underwater archaeology, in which most archaeologists can be taught to dive but not all divers can become respectable archaeologists, most art historians, archaeologists, and ethnographers can learn museum practice, but not all museologists have an avocation for the disciplines within a museum. It is clearly necessary for training, whenever possible, to be undertaken in Africa, on African material, and in African conditions and using the technology appropriate to West African rather than American or Western budgets. There is presently a fair amount of discussion about the future of African education. In this discussion there are many who favor a more practical approach, with professional schools providing technical expertise even at the undergraduate level. This is already the case with law, medicine, and management and business. Proponents of this tactic argue that because professional expertise is at a premium and financial resources are at a minimum, the period of training for a profession should be reduced. But one must make a clear separation between a set of techniques and an academic discipline. Competent museum professionals need a core discipline in which they have expertise and for which enthusiasm is expressed.

Internship Training

Archaeology and the museum profession are not immune to contemporary trends, and many plans are actively being discussed in Africa for postgraduate programs in museum studies and conservation, most recently in Ghana. Though commendable and very necessary, will they solve the present problem of transitory staff and of ineffective and often unmotivated personnel? I think not, since the major problem is not a lack of technical expertise, which can be obtained on the job or from practical work in another institution, but a dearth of disciplinary zeal and of enthusiasm for museum work and scholarship. At a lower level the Jos training school for museum technicians, established by UNESCO and the Museums Association of Tropical Africa in 1962, has trained hundreds of museum technicians. Most of them have, however, left the profession and their training has not had the impact that was anticipated when the school was first established. Rather then separate the professional training from the academic, a better approach would clearly be to integrate it within the degree system.

I have argued elsewhere (Posnansky 1993) for the need for internships as an integral part of a student's training. Internships are undertaken on a voluntary or part-time basis in many American universities; students can use work-study (not necessarily of the formal variety) opportunities to get on-the- job training, and the institution can discover whether the student has any aptitude for museum work and if so in what field. Such opportunities, either paid or unpaid, are rarely available in Africa, but if such a system could be instituted the end result would be the same—a heightened awareness of what museum work and archaeology are all about. The cost of internship programs, of assisting students to participate in Africa in museums and on excavations, is relatively low, measured in hundreds of dollars rather than the tens of thousands necessary for large-scale overseas training. Such internships should be counted toward degree qualifications, with grades reflecting effort and achievement. Several of the finest African archaeologists and museum curators had the advantage of such on-the-job training at the student level.

Transforming the University Curriculum
A corollary to this argument is that the teaching of archaeology in Africa needs to be broadened in scope so that the relevance of the discipline is enhanced for historical and environmental conservation, for public education, and for tourist stimulation and education. I was saddened rather than flattered to discover on a return to West Africa that the courses that I introduced for the first full degree program in archaeology in tropical Africa at the University of Ghana in 1968 were still being taught. Archaeology, like every other discipline, must reflect the needs of the world in which it exists. In the present state of Africa, in response to the crisis of the despoliation of Africa's past and cognizant of the developments in the discipline, this means that courses on public archaeology and on conservation should become standard fare. In West Africa, both at Ibadan and Legon, conservation with regard to the correct procedures for handling material in the field and later in the laboratory had historically been more central to archaeology than in the United States, with both departments maintaining conservation laboratories and including trained conservators on their staffs. It is important that this tradition be strengthened and the curriculum expanded to cover such topics as site conservation and site management. Practical conservation, rather than being regarded as a job for technicians and thus of lesser merit than other skills and knowledge acquired by archaeologists, must be elevated in importance and integrated into the training of all students. For students with a grounding in the sciences, conservation courses could be provided as a postgraduate specialty on a regional basis for those professionals who have already gained an academic background in archaeology and have had the practical experience that will enable them to profit from such training. It is gratifying to note that this option is already being explored by several African universities. Having just benefited from participation in a well-designed academic quarter's training in conservation provided by the Getty Conservation Institute for the University of California at Los Angeles at its Marina del Rey facility and witnessed the eye-opening experiences of a group of international graduate students to such a course, I am well aware of the potential for such courses in Africa. It is in this area that African museums will require the greatest immediate help from overseas organizations.

One of the weaknesses of African universities has been the late appreciation of the special nature of art history. It was not a standard discipline in the new universities, and it has crept in through departments of archaeology, as in the University of Ghana, or through institutes of African studies, as in Nigeria, but it has hardly been institutionalized and is still regarded as a research discipline. It is certainly apparent that the material cultural concerns of the archaeologists do not always do justice to the art historical implications of archaeological discoveries. It is essential that art history be accorded the recognition it deserves and be included as an option at least within archaeology curricula as was initiated, for instance, by the courses of E. N. O. Quarcoopome (now of the University of Michigan) at the University of Ghana. If necessary, priority status should be given to art history's needs in secondments of visiting scholars, such as Fulbright recipients, to teach within Africa. At present most art historians visit Africa for research rather than to teach.

At the time of independence it was possible to appreciate the reasons for excluding anthropology from university curricula, as it was then regarded as an alien discipline that had prospered by highlighting what were perceived as the primitive aspects of African societies. Now, however, anthropology must be integrated into the university syllabus, as has been done at Ibadan. Such integration can be achieved by inclusion of elements in both sociology and archaeology, as has been done at the University of Ghana, but it clearly remains necessary to make sure that material culture receives the attention it requires. It is in this respect that close links between museums and universities are essential to give students the opportunity to handle material. One very obvious way of acquiring a greater integration is for university faculty to hold part-time curatorial posts in their national or regional museums or for the university to have museum professionals appointed as part-time professors. Such cross-employment should be easy, as both institutions often fall within the same ministry. In the past when this has been arranged, as in Uganda in the 1960s when Alan Walker looked after paleontology in both Makerere and the Uganda Museum and I looked after archaeology, it has proved successful, allowing classes to take place in the museum and students to acquire an interest and knowledge of museum practice. Not only is an awareness of ethnography important for students of archaeology and those contemplating museum work, it also clearly has a relevance for promoting appropriate technology that recognizes the relationship between environment and culture. The relevance of archaeology, of art history, and of ethnography to tourism, adult education, and community development must be stressed, as must their intrinsic importance as disciplines concerned with cultural patrimony.

Apprenticeships

Museum apprenticeship programs should be available for further training once the student, with one of the required museum disciplines, is appointed to the museum. The prerequisite for the apprenticeship program should normally consist of having obtained some practical hands-on experience while still a student in an internship program. This apprenticeship program must involve practical experience in all the different departments of the museum. The problem in the past has been that appointment to a museum post meant a professional position with the basic hands-on work of registration, conservation, and display left to technicians appointed for their technical ability rather than for either their academic or their avocational interest. It might be argued by some that this step-by-step training in each of the basic branches of museum work is either impossible or difficult in African museums because there are too few staff members to supervise such an internship or apprenticeship program. Although such might well be the case, the problem could be overcome by a new approach to museum training in Africa that involves carefully crafted programs of bilateral cooperation (discussed below).

For far too long African museums have relied too much on overseas training that has focused on high-tech approaches. Museum personnel return from abroad disillusioned with their own institutions because they do not have the same facilities or support staff as do museums they have enjoyed abroad; they also lack the encouragement of their own ministries to put their ideas into practice. Foreign aid to African museums has too often consisted of travel opportunities that recirculate museum administrators, already out of touch with their own collections, from one philosophical gathering to yet another highly technical conference without materially improving their basic curatorial or collection appreciation skills. Such museum staff, lacking either a basic appreciation of or an intimacy with the potential of their own collections, are neither able nor sufficiently motivated to articulate a vision for their museums. They cannot generate the enthusiasm necessary to galvanize support for museum development from the government or the community or to mount realistic training schedules.

Adult Education and Community Involvement
Although national and local history has been integrated into school syllabi, a general apathy toward conservation of the past remains. Although the need for economic enrichment is clearly at the root of customs officers, shipping agents, and even monument guardians turning a blind eye to site plunder and antiquities smuggling, it is not the whole picture. Many of those involved have never learned to appreciate the importance of their own hidden heritage. There is clearly a problem not only of communication but also of education and of the mobilization of national cultural pride. This situation cannot be changed by a mandate from the government but only through programs of mass public education. Because of limited resources this is presently difficult, but one solution may be to target specific areas of cultural fragility, such as those that have produced terra-cotta figures in Mali, Ghana, Nigeria, and Chad. Many of the plundered sites are in areas where there has been little or no follow-up work by archaeologists. For instance, in the Koma area of Ghana only one season of excavations was conducted. An intermittent presence is a necessity (if a permanent presence is impossible) to build up local pride as a bulwark against personal avarice.

Community pride must be encouraged through constant association with a national university or museum. It is no coincidence that the vandalized sites of Africa are also often abandoned and far from the capitals where the archaeologists are located. The brief climax of local glory has subsided and there is normally no real local vested interest in conservation. Somehow a community cannot escape the conclusion that if the archaeologists leave, they have lost interest, at least for the time being, particularly if there is no conservation of sites. In this respect foreign archaeologists are particularly at fault. Money is requested for fieldwork and for publication but rarely for site conservation or public education. Local officials must be encouraged to maintain museums on the spot and to make pilfering of antiquities not just morally repugnant but socially unacceptable within the community. Communities must be persuaded to protect their own cultural patrimony.

Efforts must take place to educate the public at the local level, which is where adult education comes into the picture. Unlike university education, which is concentrated in capitals or large urban centers, adult education is often decentralized and is undertaken in all branches of the tertiary education system and in some countries through the extension services of government ministries. Adult education, through short courses, courses in the vernacular, and university-of-the-air programs, which began as early as the 1970s in several parts of Africa, is capable of reaching large numbers of people in scattered areas. But first we have to sell the idea of cultural conservation as a topic worthy of adult education. This sale must be made by university archaeologists and by the museums. Graduates of archaeology should be encouraged to seek posts in adult education and colleges of further education. For far too long adult education has been primarily regarded as providing vocational training and civic awareness. Adult education institutes have provided training for mature students who never had the opportunity to complete their education, to obtain their qualifications, and specifically to obtain the certificates needed to advance in the workforce. We now need to convince our colleagues that developing a heightened awareness of one's cultural heritage is a part of civil education. Museums and institutes of adult education could cooperate to their mutual advantage in the promotion of joint courses concerned with cultural patrimony. Adult education centers are in a position to provide courses at projected local museums and promote new museums associated with their own centers.

Traveling recently through West Africa, I was constantly reminded that we need teachers for teachers. The universities are not fulfilling their mandate; there is an urgent need to mobilize universities to spread an awareness of the importance of the tangible record of the past to a wider public. Many universities have a requirement that final honors students write long essays. This is an ideal occasion for students and their home communities to interact. More than thirty years ago the University of East Africa provided funds for faculty to supervise such fieldwork and to actively recruit in the rural areas. This is again a relatively low-cost program that could bring remote areas into the cultural loop. Although it can be argued that focusing attention on an area's cultural resources may invite destruction of those resources, it has been my own experience that broadening knowledge acts as a community safeguard to protect those resources from the less-scrupulous members of the community. There is an old Akan proverb symbolized by a gold weight of a cockroach attacked by two fowls in the compound. The gist of the proverb is that once a cockroach is in the open it can be seen by all and thus is fair game. In the same sense once the cultural resources are revealed to a broader group there is less possibility of their complete disappearance.

There is particular need to keep traditional leaders involved in future archaeological work and to give them a prime role in cultural conservation. The question often posed is, Whose past is it? A case can be made that the past is universal, but this is too philosophical an approach. In the rural areas the chief and his elders are custodians of the past. Though libations are poured and sacrifices made, all too often it is lip service. The involvement of traditional councils is essential. Chiefs with encouragement can be the most effective custodians of shrines; they are often the best informed and most respected within their communities. There are many traditional sites, old towns whose traditions still live within the community. The traditional community must be wooed, encouraged, and brought into active cooperation, ultimately by breaking down the centralizing tendencies of national museums, by spending scarce resources on the upkeep of local sites, and even by developing small collections of artifacts in chiefs' palaces. All too often regalia get lost in interregnal periods, but once the trust is put in the community, as opposed to a single individual, there is hope that the community will have too much to lose, not just in attention from the museum, but also in its regional reputation.

Mass media, of course, play a role in educating a broader public. In Africa the key medium in the rural areas is radio. Even at the village level there is increasing scope for communication using educational video. It is apparent that if African museums, antiquities services, and universities are to get their messages across, a coordination of efforts is necessary: weekend or longer programs must be held in key localities; talks must be filmed on location, and the videos of the seminars and site visits must be used for further dissemination of key messages. But key to the message is the need to carefully explain at the local level why the vestiges of the past need to be conserved. Involving ministries of tourism with local chiefs interested in stimulating local pride and with educators is essential at this level. Cultural conservation must be made cost-effective at the local level. From 1970 to 1979, I was actively involved in the excavation of the medieval and early modern town of Begho in Ghana. Increased cultural visibility, fostered by our archaeological and later ethnological activity, ultimately led to direct government awareness of the community, which in turn led to such small-scale investments as boreholes and water pumps, and more routine visits by government health officers and agricultural extension officers. We could thus demonstrate a direct payoff resulting from our work, and the village developed pride in being the site of an ancient town, which had material as well as psychical advantages.

Broadening the Scope of African Museums

African museums are unique. What is folk art outside Africa may be living culture within Africa. There is a need to break away from static art museum displays and to establish dynamic centers in which the process of manufacture, the nature of usage, and the social context are encouraged over fixed displays. In the 1960s in Niamey, Livingstone, and Dar-es-Salaam such museums were established. To succeed, they require constant encouragement provided by the energy of the peoples whose cultures are being demonstrated. Such folk villages, producing indigenous crafts, rather than the airport art or Europeanized crafts of many present artisanal centers, can provide an important link between museum aspirations and tourist development, but they cannot be allowed to become tired, the equivalent of human zoos or craft boutiques. There is a rapid expansion of demand for authentic crafts in the West. Many of those who profit from the trade have little relationship with museums. It behooves African museums to take a leadership role in this trade, obtaining part of the profit to support their own activities and also helping keep alive important skills. Business managers will constitute a vital ingredient in the dynamic African museum of the future.

Among the innovations of the early days of independence are science and industry museums, which must be revitalized. African museums must be seen as relevant to give them a greater chance of popular acceptance and thus support from both governmental and private sources, which is vital if cultural preservation is to be effective. The African public has far too few outlets for advanced scientific education, either in the schools or in the community. Many countries promote science fairs and displays of industrial development for periodic special exhibitions. In 1987 I was fascinated by one such exhibition in Togo, with its displays on low-priced solar energy and on effective low-cost hearths for rural use. The exhibits were popular; unfortunately, they were also temporary. Museums in this sphere have an unequaled chance to tap the private commercial sector and often the foreign sector of multinational corporations. With structural adjustment programs a reality, government funding is tight, and it behooves African museums to be creative in finding some resources on their own. Museums can through temporary exhibitions attract more visitors and create a dynamic that they all too often lack. They could mount exhibitions in cooperation with government agencies on such topics as good nutrition and traditional diet or, as brilliantly demonstrated recently by the museum in Ouagadougou, on such features of everyday life as the bicycle. I was sorry to observe on a recent swing through West Africa that although the American election prominently figured in the displays inside and outside of American cultural center buildings, African national elections, then being conducted, did not figure in the displays of African museums. Contemporary history existing in special cloths, buttons, posters, and such should not escape the purview of the museums. Today's events are tomorrow's culture.

Museum Empowerment

Currently West Africa's museums lack status; they lack advocates at the highest level as a result of recent history. The solutions discussed above will help museums become effective and dynamic centers for cultural development. Management poses a key problem, however. The governance of museums needs to be altered. Instead of being a small item on an education or sports budget, museums require a sense of integrity—an ability to build up funds for research and collection. There is an urgent necessity to remake the African museum. Many museums were placed under the direct control of government ministries at independence to give them the necessary national support to grow, but as a result they suffered from over-bureaucratization. Existing boards of trustees were scrapped as legacies of colonialism. The baby was thrown out with the bathwater; the idea was not unsuitable, but rather the board members.

Independent boards of management and trustees of distinction will provide the advocacy that museums require if they are to thrive. Independent boards should be made up of retired civil servants, distinguished and successful citizens who may have served their countries overseas, well-respected and published academics, senior clergy, traditional chiefs, and established and financially secure leaders of industry and business. These people are more likely to attract both financial support and government backing than are disillusioned, underpaid curators or minor ministry officials to whom the curators may have to report the museum's affairs. Boards should consist of role models for the society they serve, above the hint of corruption and political intrigue. Museums require advocacy of their needs and achievements. Many excellent exhibitions, small-scale excavations, and school programs too often go unnoticed. With the imprimatur of a distinguished board such achievements can be made to work for the museum. Using such a board gives the museum access to in-country facilities such as the press, philanthropic bodies, and a network with the contacts of the board members which spreads overseas as well as in-country. Active boards made up of dynamic and interested members can assist with both bilateral and multilateral cooperation. Such activity must be a major component of the process of museum regeneration. The public needs to know what a museum does. The presence of a substantial independent board, rather than one appointed by the museum curator or by the minister concerned, should provide a spur to activity.[1] Nothing challenges the lazy as much as a concern for an accounting. Such reorganization could solve the need for both visibility and transparency that so many museums apparently lack.

Bilateral Cooperation

Most museums in West Africa have received external help. In the early days of independence a great deal of assistance came from metropolitan governments in both Britain and France. Many of the first generation of curators and technicians went to Europe for training, some, like Richard Nunoo of Ghana, as early as the 1940s. Unfortunately, many of these early appointees, particularly in Nigeria, were siphoned off to other posts shortly after returning from Europe. Several large foundations and UNESCO also provided assistance. More recently, various embassies and foreign cultural missions have provided gifts of equipment, books, and films. There has, however, been little sustained involvement. Even when bilateral programs have been initiated, as between the University of Michigan and Benin, they have been over a limited period.

Bilateral cooperation should involve as far as possible a greater commitment to African museums, establishing some form of twinning arrangement by which the overseas institution helps with training within the African institution. For far too long staff have left Africa for training opportunities overseas. Selection has been based not on a museum or disciplinary avocation but largely on general academic merit. For others, overseas training has been the reward for long service rather than the recognition of museum potential. Outside training should be limited in nature and confined to those staff who have acquired collection appreciation skills by working on existing collections.

Nothing heightens awareness of a collection better than research on it. Bilateral cooperation in this scenario should support in-house apprenticeship programs under which well-trained museum registrars or conservators commit themselves to long-term secondments (from three to five years) to work closely with African trainees. In this way basic skills can be passed on through the routine of daily work in the milieu in which the trainees will make their future.

Foreign know-how can be adapted to difficult local conditions. A technology appropriate to those conditions should be adopted, based not necessarily on computers or expensive equipment that is difficult to maintain, but rather on common-sense techniques. Maps, pen and India ink, frequent airing of specimens, constant inspection for signs of infestation, homemade fumigation chambers, and museum-constructed angle-iron storage units can all form the basis of such an appropriate technology—appropriate both for the resources available and for the climatic conditions.

In addition to archaeologists, many European, Japanese, Australasian, and American graduate researchers with experience in museums with ethnographic material may be tempted to work in Africa to enhance their own knowledge of African material culture, particularly if there is also the carrot of collection and re-search opportunities. There are many ways of funding such secondments. In the early days of independence, some museum assistance, as in what was then Tan-ganyika, was provided under various overseas volunteer arrangements such as the Peace Corps. We need to approach all the countries with Peace Corps–type arrangements—Japan, Canada, Britain, Scandinavia, and France—to commit a limited number of positions to museums and insist that the volunteers have some practical expertise that they can contribute. Long-term institution-to-institution secondments should be actively explored. From the United States greater con-sideration should perhaps be given to stimulating more applications for Fulbright positions for museum work with encouragement of second-year extensions. Ap-proaches should be made to foundations for a pilot project in which a number of fellowships are granted jointly to foreign and African museums to allow trained personnel to spend a year in the foreign institution both before and after their two years of secondment. This will ensure that participants have a sense of security while in Africa, safe in the knowledge that two years in Africa will not be followed by immediate unemployment. Such a program could be initiated with as few as three to five appointments a year and would result in a far better training program than any presently in place.[2] It would also ensure that personal and enduring networks based on side-by-side hands-on work would be established between African and foreign museums. The six-month or one-year research fellowship is really not long enough to get to know a foreign country effectively, and if the West is to maintain an expertise in African studies, longer stays in Africa are essential. Such secondments could be developed as a way of augmenting and documenting collections in both the institutions. Once staff from two institutions have worked together it will become easier to tailor training programs overseas to meet the spe-cific conditions of the trainee's home museum. Overseas training would be de-layed until the trainee was prepared to take as full advantage of the opportunity as possible, which is not always the case at present.

It is probably necessary to begin with a few centers of excellence, help them build up capacity in cooperation with as many agencies as possible, and use such centers for practical training for museums within their regions. This is proving successful with the West African Museums Project's efforts in Bamako. The big weakness in all aid efforts hitherto has been sustainability.

In the archaeological sphere much closer bilateral cooperation between American and African institutions has been attempted. Though nothing on the scale of the University of Florida's work in Tanzania has yet been attempted, our own university over the past ten years has provided senior doctoral students and professors for teaching at the University of Ghana and has given books to the archaeology library. Similar initiatives involving books, equipment, the dating of specimens, and joint fieldwork have been made in Togo and Benin on a smaller scale. It is clear that such bilateral networking is valuable and must be encouraged by foundation and government sponsors. In times of economic stress, when foreign universities are short of resources, it would be of advantage if such organizations as the U.S. Information Agency were more flexible in granting extensions of university linkages that have success records or if the agency could encourage multiple secondments under Fulbright to ensure the sustainability of programs.

Because equipment is clearly a major problem in West Africa, particularly for surveying, analysis, and basic slide presentations, a concerted program must be created to improve such facilities in West Africa. Many universities and museums in the West have already replaced computers several times; consequently, many older computers still exist that are surplus to requirements but still serviceable. The same applies to audiovisual equipment, with electronic and automatic models having replaced earlier manual varieties. Much of this older equipment is easier to maintain than more recent sophisticated machines. Many West Africans have already learned to use such equipment. One of the major problems is to ship items to West Africa. Some instrumentality or a group of agencies including the Arts Council of the African Studies Association, the Society of Africanist Archaeologists, and the Foundation for African Archaeology should be urged to maintain a register of equipment needed in West Africa and available in the United States. The same grouping of organizations could attempt to match research possibilities and museum priorities in West Africa with overseas institutions able to help and with volunteers who have the skills and resources ready to participate in those projects suggested by our African colleagues as priorities.

Multilateral Cooperation

It is often difficult for a single museum or university to sustain a support program for an African museum or department. Departmental interests and staff change and new emphases are developed. For this reason, it is essential to have help coming from larger organizations. In the past UNESCO has played a leading role, providing training, and sending out consultants for on-the-spot advice and country assessments leading to plans of action to guide many institutions. In recent years the funding for such work has been limited; UNESCO does not always have employees with the appropriate regional expertise or the resources to keep staff members in the field for long periods. Other organizations have stepped into the breech, of which the West African Museums Project in Dakar has been the most effective.[3]

The future looks promising for broader multilateral help, with the World Bank's foray into the cultural field and the establishment of a five-year program under the capacity-building initiative, which aims to improve substantially the capability of African institutions to undertake and evaluate major new research programs. For a long time most help came from American, French, British, and German sources. In recent years both the Swedes and other Scandinavians have been more actively involved, and the growing cooperation between Japanese and American Africanists has included discussion of work by nationals of both countries in the field of material culture. Japan's interest in particular has expanded, and Japan has surpassed both the United States and Great Britain as an aid donor and provider of development money. New agreements must include museum cooperation programs, which will help build up the African collections of Japanese museums while providing capital equipment for the degraded African institutions. Professionals on both sides can learn from one another. A heightened appreciation of African culture within Japan and later within other countries in East and Southeast Asia with expanding economies (South Korea, Taiwan, Malaysia, and Singapore) will hopefully lead to expanded interest and aid. It is important to integrate this work into a more coherent program, to establish consortia, and to avoid the ad hoc policies and exploitation that have led to many of today's problems.

SUMMARY

It is all too easy to speak of the problems and outline some solutions, some of them feasible, most of them plain common sense, and many of them previously suggested. It is just as essential to acknowledge the winds of change that are already blowing in West Africa, fanned by such organizations as the West African Museums Project, but owing much to West African initiatives themselves. Several exciting developments have occurred in Nigeria. In early December 1992 the national museum opened a new custom-built facility in Ibadan on spacious grounds and with enough room for development and provisions for such services as conservation. In early 1993, the first issue of *Nigerian Heritage*, the new journal of the National Commission of Museums and Monuments, appeared. The national commission has also initiated two one-year schools—for training their own graduates—at Idumu in Kwara State for archaeologists and at Jos for museologists. That all this is taking place at a time of economic depression and uncertainty at the end of the period of military rule is a very reassuring development.

It has also been a considerable achievement on the part of Bassey Wai Andah to have produced the *West African Journal of Archaeology* on a relatively regular basis: Twelve volumes appeared between 1981 and 1992, although some were delayed or were double issues. The focus on an African dimension for cultural resource management at the conference honoring the life achievements of Thurstan Shaw at Ibadan in 1989 and the prompt publication of the conference papers in book form in 1990 indicate a vitality among Africa's researchers that is sometimes overlooked. That the West African Archaeological Association met in 1994 in Benin after having met in 1992 in Bondoukou is again a clear sign of active involvement and many West Africans are sorry that there has not been greater participation by Western archaeologists. Ghana has more than one hundred district planning centers for national culture that will network with the national museum. The new building for the science museum, started in 1973, is now at last nearing completion with new grants from the government for work in 1992–94. In Benin the director of culture has taken a personal interest in museum development and the museum curators and archaeologists are working closely together and have secured several grants from overseas sponsors for new fieldwork and the documentation of existing collections. There are similar encouraging stories from other West African countries and it behooves American scholars to support these initiatives in a much more aggressive and generous fashion.

In conclusion, although for various reasons Africa's museums have not lived up to the high expectations they had at independence, a new will exists within West Africa for conserving cultural heritage. The implementation of an effective program depends both on a change of emphasis and on a new ethic based on an enthusiasm for the collections. A new generation of more realistic professionals who have witnessed the realities of the 1980s has emerged, and they are willing to adopt appropriate strategies.

Clear basics in university and museum training must be mastered before moving to a high-tech new world. Artifactual myopia and root training must be firmly rejected by African museums. Foreign cooperation cannot consist only of providing travel opportunities, short conferences, or joint collection and research programs, but must involve a willingness to commit people and time within Africa and to provide hands-on training. Too many projects have been far too short in duration, raising hopes and leaving behind no funds for conservation of either objects or sites. Only when departments and museums in West Africa are put on a stable footing, when job satisfaction is secured, and when cooperation with overseas bodies is established in a spirit of mutuality can other problems regarding research and the implementation of an effective cultural resource management policy be implemented. Site destruction and smuggling cannot be tackled without making sure that there are effective bodies in Africa to form the vanguard of conservation in its broadest sense. At present many of those bodies are weak, and change can only come from active participation by both African and overseas organizations.

Rather than concentrating on the minutiae of smuggling and case histories of conservation, museum management must be restructured to effectively protect the cultural history of the nations they serve, a process that involves advocacy at the highest level and greater visibility for museums within the national agenda. The priorities for action, however, must come from within Africa. The West African Museums Project in particular deserves credit for putting museum personnel in touch with international organizations. The Council for the Development of Social Science Research in Africa has supported the field research and manuscript preparation of African graduate students. The master's theses of West African students provide a particularly rich resource for West African archaeology. Equally important has been the continued support in the cultural field of the U.S. Information Agency, which brought African specialists to the United States in

1992 for interaction with their American colleagues under a program on "Cultural Preservation: Art and Archaeology in Africa," initiated by their Office for Citizens Exchange. Foreign friends can make helpful suggestions based on experience. Our concern can hopefully leverage aid, particularly in terms of long-term commitment, for those countries and institutions that have shaped and enriched our personal and professional lives.

NOTES

1. Though such a board would initially have to be established by the government in consultation with the museum directorate, further appointments would be made by the board itself in consultation with both the museum directorate and the ministry concerned.

2. A program lasting up to five years and involving five appointees for four consecutive years, lasting seven years and providing for a limited amount of equipment would cost on the order of $3-4 million, depending on the level of fellowship remuneration and administrative overheads.

3. Established in 1982, the West African Museums Project has been funded by both the Ford and the Rockefeller Foundations. The project has conducted workshops on textiles and wooden objects in Bamako and on aspects of storage in Dakar. It has also convened local conferences throughout West Africa and has involved many other international agencies, such as ICCROM in Rome, in its work. Grants have also been obtained from museums (1991 West African Museums Project unpublished proposal document).

REFERENCES

Posnansky, Merrick. "The 1982–1983 Drought in Ghana—Impact and Aftermath: The Village Perspective." Paper presented at the African Studies Association, 1984.

———. "Towards Excellence in Higher Education." Lecture given at the University of Ghana, February 19, Summarized in *West Africa*, (1989):829–31.

———. "Museums, Museology, and Artifactual Myopia: Recollections and Reflections of Forty Years of Museum Development in Africa." Paper presented at the Ninth Triennial Symposium on Africa Art. University of Iowa, April 22, 1992.

———. "The Archaeologist and the African Community." *Akan Studies Council Newsletter* (1993):8–11.

13

HOW ACCURATE ARE INTERPRETATIONS OF AFRICAN OBJECTS IN WESTERN MUSEUMS?

Francis B. Musonda

Museum curators in the Western world have long been tormented by the strange and often unique African objects that find their way into their museums. However, to enable patrons to appreciate and enjoy exhibitions on African materials, and at the same time to fulfill the museum's responsibilities, these curators tend to label objects with inadequate information. The curators cannot tell the whole story about those objects, so they tend to provide a general narrative that would place the pieces in a cultural system instead of treating them as merely inanimate museum pieces.

Partly as a result of this lack of a meaningful interpretation of objects and their value, African scholars have recently decried the magnitude of the plundering of Africa's cultural heritage since the continent opened up trade with Europe. After several decades of dormancy as a result of colonial oppression, African countries are using both national and international forums to demand the restitution of their cultural property. Decades of colonial rule have, unfortunately, left yawning gaps in Africa's cultural heritage. African countries argue, perhaps rightly, that few museums in the West are unable to boast of possessing some of Africa's priceless cultural objects.

I do not argue here for the return of Africa's cultural objects to their places of origin. Rather, I would like to emphasize that a cultural object has more compelling meaning when it is displayed in its natural environment. However, because the African objects under discussion are already in Western museums, the majority of African museum curators believe that their Western counterparts should make every effort to present correct information in order to ensure that the true culture of the object's country of origin is seen.

HOW OBJECTS LEFT AFRICA

The majority of the African objects discussed here are ethnographic. The people responsible for their manufacture were highly trained professionals working in a complex traditional society. It must be stressed that since these works of art were not an expression of individual imagination or skills but of the traditions of an ethnic group, we have an obligation to understand the customs of the group as a prelude to the correct interpretation of the object's meaning.

Recent studies of non-Western societies have revealed one important thing about human civilization—namely, the study of human beings and their traditions cannot be reduced analytically as easily as can the study of automobile engines. Any scholarly investigation of traditions of a cultural group requires some intimate familiarity with the people being studied (e.g., Lee 1979).

The majority of African objects in Western museums date from the seventeenth to the nineteenth century. Through colonization, large parts of Africa that had been remote to Europeans were opened up, not only to European-style administration but to the collection of African cultural objects.

The advent of colonial rule took place in stages, with each stage characterized by an unprecedented removal of cultural objects in varying ways. The Portuguese-Spanish sailors were the first Europeans to explore the African coast, followed by curious explorers who penetrated the hinterland. Next came traders interested in slaves and ivory, then missionaries, and colonial administrators. Each category had people interested in African objects. While some of these people may have obtained these free of charge, some may have paid for them, and others may have obtained them through use of force or intimidation. Cases of theft cannot be completely ruled out. Traders were primarily interested in the conduct of trade and most likely completely ignored details of cultural activity. Many colonial administrators conducted anthropologically oriented research and collected cultural objects, many of which were provided to museums along with interpretations of their uses.

The advent of colonialism subtly introduced an influx of scholars and students who, through their researches, removed hundreds of objects from Africa that eventually found their way to museums. Unlike dealers, whose abilities were restricted to recognizing artistic qualities of African sculpture, these collectors took good care of their acquisitions and paid attention to their context.

Many Westerners have set off for Africa to learn about the people's traditions, customs, and religious beliefs, much like the desire to see the world that inspired the early travelers. This category of collector—commonly referred to as tourist—has enjoyed the support of local Africans in the airlifting of cultural objects to the West.

For whatever purpose these objects were collected, it is unlikely that the collectors took the trouble to record proper information about them. As modern scholars have come to realize, many African objects tend to have several and varied cultural functions. One must understand that African sculpture, for example, is functional and religious in character. African masks, which are familiar objects in American and European museums, may be used in ritual dances symbolizing specific characters, purposes, and spirits that a Western museum curator not exposed to African traditions may be unable to appreciate or comprehend.

Pearce (1988:57) has made interesting observations on current British curatorial views and practices with regard to collections that originated outside Europe: "Relatively few curators who find themselves responsible for ethnographic collections have formal training in social anthropology and most come from the fields either of European history or archaeology." As a result, ethnographic collections at the Museum of Mankind, the Victoria and Albert Museum, and other museums in Britain that are quite considerable in extent and important in content, have tended to be badly under-curated.

CONTEXT/INTERPRETATION

The majority of African cultural objects found in Western museums were collected from Africa during the period of exploration, when literacy on the African continent was at its lowest ebb. This was the era of missionary and commercial expansion, geographic discovery, and military conquest. The coming of Europeans to Africa undoubtedly introduced Western influences into indigenous representational art, either through direct communication of Western art to African artists or through observation by African artists of the new elements in their environment. In either case, traditional art must have been substantially affected. (We see this phenomenon clearly in hunter-gatherer rock painting in South Africa.)

Since the circumstances under which early Europeans acquired African cultural objects are not clear to us, it can only be assumed that they recorded what they saw and encountered for a nonprofessional audience. Most of the observations reflected European perceptions about Africa and Africans, and thus represent factually incorrect information because of prejudices. Take, for instance, the Exeter City Museum in Devon, Britain, which has a large ethnographic collection arising from activities of British colonial administrators, missionaries, and military officers. It is highly unlikely that all African objects in the museum had the appropriate information attached to them, if only because the majority of such objects would have been collected as a result of their beauty and craftsmanship. Those that failed to fit in the well-known spectrum of everyday Western arts and crafts were treated only as curiosities (Gerbrands 1990:14).

It is also true that the explanatory information that usually accompanies such museum objects may have been obtained from visiting scholars or illegal traders, people who may have been eager to offer information relating to such objects, even if such information was not corroborated. Noting the way African objects have been displayed in Western museums and the authenticity attached to the so-called remarkable accounts given by explorers and missionaries of Africa's native inhabitants and their way of life, it is absolutely necessary to reexamine these interpretations. We must adopt a more radical approach to ensure that information of high quality is attached to each object.

It is therefore not strange that curators of the National Museum of African Art, with its abundantly rich collection of African art objects, concede that their objects have complex individual histories that limit our understanding of art history, particularly because some traditions were not exposed to outside observers. It is not uncommon in some Western museums to encounter expertly executed displays of African cultural objects accompanied by such descriptions as "The objects in the exhibition were created by people whose cultures and traditions are in many respects quite different from those of the Western world." For example, in an exhibition on the mother and child in African sculpture organized by the Los Angeles County Museum of Art between December 5, 1985, and July 6, 1986, the museum curator bemoans the lack of specific data on the meaning of the positions and poses represented by the majority of the sculptures. This problem arises because the collectors tended to gather very little or superficial information about the objects. The collector's major concern was the search for other things, such as ivory, slaves, and so forth. The so-called elaborate accounts found in numerous museum brochures written before the 1960s were mere descriptions with very little, if any, meaningful interpretation attached to them. These have proven inadequate for museum purposes. Curators in some of these museums seem reluctant to examine and appreciate the works of African antiquity from a modern African point of view.

Depiction of culture as it was when the material was collected is a fundamental cause of suspicion about the display of overseas material in Western museums. Such practices lack regard for the fact that traditions change and that the same material may serve different functions in a changing society. For example, in 1986 Britain's Museum of Mankind held an exhibition of the material culture of the Amazonian people of South America. The exhibition emphasized the culture of the early years of the twentieth century rather than at the time of the exhibit. This approach perhaps confirmed the long-standing suspicion that curators in the West are unaware that cultural traditions of so-called primitive societies are not static but dynamic. As if to confirm this, a year earlier an exhibition on primitivism in twentieth-century art had been mounted at the Museum of Modern Art. Art historians were not impressed by the dominant mystique of primitivism that permeated the treatment of the African and other non-European arts on exhibit (Blier 1990:95). The exhibition was accused of lacking serious scholarly treatment of the African artworks and of providing labels and entries that did not illuminate the objects' meanings and contexts of use.

The purposes of mounting museum exhibitions may vary, but ultimately such exhibitions must provide visitors with information on humanity's accomplishments. Many museums in the West have strengthened their exhibitions by publishing excellent brochures that carry vivid descriptions of the displays. But curators have only been able to identify individual objects in a general way according to style or function, employing analogy. It is unlikely that the meaning of such objects can be interpreted correctly, because African objects and their meanings were not traditionally exposed to outside observers. Therefore, once it is established that the recorded information on an object is incorrect or inconsistent, a museum's function as a source of information is defeated. Because such an object cannot be used in research to discover the truth and educate the public, it has no benefit to the museum or to society at large and therefore has no value to a people's cultural heritage. Objects collected by amateurs and nonscholars in collaboration with untrained and unskilled Africans that are now proudly displayed in Western museums should not be expected to carry labels bearing correct or representative information about their cultural meaning.

We are not advocating destroying such objects or removing them from museums. Their value may be appreciated if museums realize that a dynamic culture does not disintegrate with the loss of one of its functional objects. The culture often survives the disruption and reemerges, albeit in a slightly different form. This sentiment should give hope to our colleagues in the West that interpretations of those objects locked up in cupboards and lacking proper information may still benefit from pieces that have been preserved elsewhere.

Once curators begin to correct the contextual information of African objects in their museums, visitors will be provided not only with firsthand information on the uses, manufacture, and significance of such objects, but also with their true meaning as well. This achievement will make it possible for the country of origin to be proud of the dissemination of its cultural heritage outside its borders.

It should be noted here that some European and American museums have solicited assistance from curators in African museums in mounting their exhibitions. These scholars offer important sources of information on a wide and varied range of cultural objects. For example, the Ethnographical Museum in Stockholm continues to support and emphasize international cooperation between museums of the North and those in Africa. Others organize field trips to collect ethnographic materials for purposes of display. For example, members of the anthropology department at Brown University's Haffenreffer Museum in Rhode Island have undertaken field collections in Kenya, Sierra Leone, Nigeria, Botswana, and Sudan (Gentis 1985:44).

THE PROBLEM OF ACCESSIONING AND DOCUMENTATION

Because of the manner in which African artifacts found their way to European and American museums, the process of documentation has not been properly carried out. This has rendered accessioning and documentation of these objects highly suspect. Museum curators confronted with rare ancient African objects have had to decide whether to acquire such objects. Most displays suffer not only because of inaccurate or misleading text but also from inadequacy in accessioning procedures because of insufficient information. For example, the Haffenreffer Museum has a Djenné terra-cotta head discovered in 1943 and dated to circa A.D. 1100–1500 that illustrates both of these concerns. Its function is not clearly known, although it is believed to be associated with funerary practices (Gentis 1985:44).

Any museum that wants to build an African ethnographic collection should attempt to document the role of an object in the context of its African society instead of emphasizing only its aesthetics. An updated information system requires some historical perspective through research in all aspects of African traditional life. Africa has a lot of potential for fieldwork on the study of traditional art forms that are in danger of disappearing through infiltration of Western lifestyles, urbanization, or neglect. Strict regulations must be formulated concerning authentication of natural history and cultural objects for purposes of identification. This process will help control illegal trade in antiquities.

There are museums, of course, such as the Field Museum of Natural History in Chicago, that have developed procedures and guidelines for accessioning and deaccessioning museum collections. But policy statements on acquisition of antiquities fall short of banning completely those cultural objects (specimens) that fail to comply with laws and regulations of countries of origin. Emphasis is usually placed on the lack of context of acquisitions and not on the illegal trade in them.

To conclude, the nature of acquisitions of African objects by museums in the West has posed problems for curators, who have the onerous task of being as objective as possible in the interpretation of such objects. Scholars must grapple with nineteenth-century descriptions of Africans, their traditions, and their institutions because these are the only sources of data on museums' African collections. Noting past deficiencies in how collections were built up in most museums in the West, curators must pay particular attention to field data and document the function of each object in the context of its African society. Cultural programs must be initiated between African and Western museums that will emphasize learning from each other and cooperation among institutions.

These programs should seriously consider offering support to African museum curators so that they can work with their American and European colleagues in the quest for correct information on cultural objects hidden in the museums of the West. Most African museum curators want, first and foremost, to see that each cultural object, wherever it may be on display, has its functional meaning correctly presented. This is a better way of creating and conveying a correct understanding of the African continent.

The problem created by lack of strict acquisition policies and guidelines for accessioning museum collections directly leads to Western museums' inabilities to remove the erroneous notions still held in the Western world about the African people and their institutions. A proper understanding of Africans' cultural backgrounds is obliterated through shady accessioning policies. The prejudices that limited acquisitions have continued to shape curator's perceptions about African cultural heritage. This lack of concern has made it possible for trade in antiquities to continue unquestioned.

REFERENCES

Blier, S. P. "African Art Studies at the Crossroads: An American Perspective." In *African Art Studies: The State of the Discipline*. Washington, D.C.: National Museum of African Art, 1990.

Gentis, T. "African Art at the Haffenreffer Museum." *African Arts* 18, no. 3 (May 1985):44–51.

Gerbrands, A. A. "The History of African Art Studies." In *African Art Studies: The State of the Discipline*. Washington, D.C.: National Museum of African Art, 1990.

Lee, R. B. *The Dobe !Kung*. New York: Holt, Rinehart and Winston, 1979.

Pearce, S. N. "Developing Approaches to Non-European Material in British Museums." In *Museology and Developing Countries—"Help or Manipulation."* ICOMFOM Study Series no. 15. Hyderabad, Varanasi, New Delhi, 1988.

14

WHOSE CULTURAL HERITAGE?

CONFLICTS AND CONTRADICTIONS IN THE CONSERVATION OF HISTORIC STRUCTURES, TOWNS, AND ROCK ART IN TANZANIA

AMINI AZA MTURI

The need for each country to develop and maintain a comprehensive national inventory of its cultural resources or property has been advocated and accepted by cultural resources management experts (Taboroff 1992). However, to many countries in the developing world, including Tanzania, this objective remains a mere aspiration, for the distant future. Despite this lack of a comprehensive national inventory, the limited research and documentation undertaken by both local and foreign researchers in Tanzania have resulted in the identification of rich and diversified cultural resources that must be conserved and managed as a national heritage. These resources include Plio-Pleistocene sites, Upper Pleistocene and Holocene sites, rock shelters with rock art, Early and Late Iron Age sites, varying architectural and urban complex sites, historic quarters and towns, ethnological and historic sites, and unique natural features.

LEGAL AND INSTITUTIONAL FRAMEWORK

The first legal measure to protect Tanzania's cultural heritage, the Monuments Preservation Ordinance, was promulgated by the British colonial government in 1937. The ordinance empowered the governor to declare and gazette structures of historic significance as monuments, and sites of archaeological, scientific, and historic significance as reserved areas. This ordinance was repealed and replaced by the Antiquities Act of 1964, which remains the principal legislation for cultural resource management in the country despite its being amended by the Antiquities (Amendment) Act of 1979.

The Antiquities (Amendment) Act of 1979 defines ethnographic objects as any movable object made, shaped, painted, carved, inscribed, or otherwise produced or modified by human agency in Tanganyika after 1863 for use in any social or cultural activity, irrespective of whether it is still used by any community in Tanganyika. The category does not include any object made, shaped, painted, carved, inscribed, or otherwise produced or modified by human agency in Tanganyika for sale as a curio.

The 1979 act empowers the appropriate minister, after consultation with the minister for lands, to declare as a conservation area any area or site that (a) is a valuable national heritage for its aesthetic value; (b) contains a homogeneous group of monuments; or (c) contains buildings, structures, or other forms of human settlement that constitute a valuable national heritage for their historical, architectural, social, or cultural value. Besides identifying and offering legal protection to the cultural resources of the country, the Tanzania antiquities legislation also establishes the regulatory regime for monitoring research, trade, and exchange as well as the export of protected resources.

Since 1957, Tanganyika and now Tanzania has had a central government agency responsible for cultural resource management, but since independence in 1961 the agency's status and efficacy have been in a state of flux. What started as the Department of Antiquities in 1957 has since 1962 been merged with culture or archives; since 1984 the agency has operated as the Antiquities Unit. The national museum was established in 1937 as the King George Memorial Museum and is responsible for the preservation of movable heritage; this museum and the archaeology unit of the University of Dar es Salaam, established in 1985 with teaching and research responsibilities, are other relevant institutions.

Protection exists for a wide range of cultural resources; the regulatory mechanism, if properly and effectively enforced, should be adequate to control the sale, exchange, trade, and export of cultural objects. During the late 1950s and early 1960s, cases of theft and possible illegal export of Chinese bowls and plates found in tombs of eighth- to eighteenth-century port towns were reported, but this practice seems to have stopped. There have recently been a number of thefts of objects in the custody of the national museum. Although there are incidents of hawkers selling coins, some of them historic, to tourists in Bagamoyo and Kilwa (Karoma, this volume), it would be safe to posit that the illegal trafficking in cultural resources protected under the law is not yet a significant problem in Tanzania.

Another category of cultural heritage that has been reported to have been bought and exported illegally are the carved doors that are protected objects under the legislation and are found on buildings in all the historic towns, including Dar es Salaam. In 1970 all such doors and their owners were registered; owners received detailed guidelines about acceptable practices with the carved doors. This registration or inventory has proved to be very effective: a 1985–86 re-registration indicated that only one door is no longer with its owner—it was removed and illegally exported to Germany.

The absence of illegal trafficking in cultural resources does not mean that the cultural heritage in Tanzania is not threatened. Other factors, especially the absence of good policies and programs, a weak socioeconomic base, and the attitudes of the policymakers, administrators, professionals, and the public at large are all equally major threats, and they contribute to the erasure of cultural heritage. This essay will examine conflicts and contradictions in how people perceive the significance of cultural heritage and how these perceptions affect involvement in the conservation of cultural heritage. The conservation of historic structures and towns, with special emphasis on Bagamoyo, and the conservation and management of rock-art sites in Tanzania will be used as case studies.

HISTORIC STRUCTURES, TOWNS, AND BUILDINGS

The first historic structures to receive attention in terms of both research and conservation were the ruined remains of coral stone mosques, palaces, residential houses, and tombs of port towns that grew and prospered along the Tanzanian coast during the ninth to eighteenth centuries. This historic and architectural heritage has been referred to either as Arabic or Islamic architecture (Chittick 1974; Garlake 1966), but archaeologists and historians believe that the architectural heritage should appropriately be described as Swahili architecture (Mturi 1974, 1982).

Surveying and documentation of the sites containing such historic structures was undertaken in 1957–59 by the newly established Antiquities Department (Chittick 1958, 1959, 1960), while major conservation work occurred between 1958 and 1962 and centered on the important site of Kilwa Kisiwani. However, the future of this UNESCO World Heritage site is in jeopardy because of conflicts between the existing village and the need to preserve both the monuments standing aboveground and those buried below. Because a substantial part of the village is built over the collapsed remains of ancient Kilwa, any socioeconomic activity by the villagers, including building activities and agriculture, directly threatens buried cultural resources. To resolve these conflicts a land-use plan was prepared in 1984 (Mturi 1987), but it has yet to be implemented, and the site remains threatened (Karoma, this volume).

The measures to protect and preserve the historic structures of the eighth- to eighteenth-century port towns were not extended to include the historic towns of the nineteenth century. These towns grew primarily because of the restructuring of the trading and commercial relations between the eastern coast of Africa and the countries bordering the Indian Ocean. The Portuguese, who had interfered with trading relations during the sixteenth to eighteenth centuries, were finally defeated by the Oman sultanate, which became the dominant power along the eastern coast north of Mozambique between 1800 and 1890. In 1840 Sultan Sayyid Said shifted his capital from Muscat, in Oman, to Zanzibar. He encouraged and supported trading and commercial contacts, especially the expansion of the slave and ivory trade into the interior, thus creating an economic boom. New port towns grew on the mainland to service the caravans traveling to and from the interior. In mainland Tanzania, Bagamoyo, Kilwa Kivinje, Mikindani, and Pangani were the most important such towns, and they, therefore, have important historic quarters of coral-built houses based on early Swahili architectural forms with added Indian and Arabic architectural elements.

With the scramble for Africa, the Zanzibar sultanate surrendered the Tanzanian mainland to Germany, while Zanzibar itself became a British protectorate. The Germans added several administrative and residential houses to the already prosperous port towns, some of the new structures incorporating Swahili architectural idioms combined with neoclassical and Teutonic architectural elements.

The Germans initially used the existing port towns as administrative centers; for example, Bagamoyo, the primary port town on the mainland, became the capital of German East Africa until early in 1891, when the capital was transferred to Dar es Salaam, a settlement about fifty kilometers to the south that was established in the 1860s by Sultan Majid of Zanzibar. The Germans, however, developed communication infrastructures that bypassed the established port towns and subsequently undermined their economic viability. For example, the central railway line to the interior, which roughly followed the main caravan route from Bagamoyo to Ujiji on Lake Tanganyika, started from Dar es Salaam, which had a deep natural harbor. The railway line to Moshi and Arusha in the northeast roughly followed the caravan route from Pangani, bypassed the town and started from the new harbor of Tanga. Kilwa Kivinje was used as an administrative center for a short period, but the colonial authorities established a new center in Kilwa Masoko about thirty kilometers to the south. The Germans also used Mikindani as an administrative center, but the British established a new port and town in Mtwara, twelve kilometers to the south.

These developments affected the economic viability of the nineteenth-century port towns. Most of the merchants who were involved in the slave and ivory trade that was the economic mainstay of the port towns either moved and established new businesses in the new towns or scaled down their operations in the old towns. Moreover, new businesses that were established following the European colonial administration bypassed these old towns for the new ones. Consequently, the old port towns, although they remained important urban settlements during the European colonial period and although their historic centers remained largely intact, became socially and economically depressed, and this period was one of gradual but sure decline.

This social and economic decline has adversely affected the historic and architectural heritage of the towns. The towns cannot generate enough wealth for the maintenance of the historic buildings, and the buildings are often owned by absentee landlords and rented to tenants who have no historic or cultural link to the buildings. Even when the structures are owned by resident businessmen and rented, the rents are too low and owners have no incentive to invest in the proper upkeep of the buildings. Consequently, most of the historic buildings are in a state of disrepair and are underutilized; a few of them are abandoned.

Under such conditions, it is obvious that the weak socioeconomic base represents the main threat to this type of national heritage. Therefore, any successful conservation strategy must resolve the two main issues: regenerating the economic base, which should provide enough wealth to enable the owners and users of historic buildings to ensure their proper maintenance, and educating the present owners and users, whose social-cultural link with the heritage is ambiguous, to ensure their involvement in conservation and management.

As noted, no measures were taken during the colonial era to ensure the protection and preservation of these nineteenth-century port towns. One probable explanation for this inaction was that the colonial administration believed that the towns in question were recent and were associated with the notorious slave and ivory trade and were therefore archaeologically and historically not worth preserving. Another reason is that those responsible for formulating conservation policies and deciding which historical structures were worthy of preservation practiced the policies of the time, which were aimed at conserving monuments and sites deemed to be of exceptional historical, architectural, archaeological, and artistic value.

Another possible explanation is that although the historic and architectural significance of these towns was appreciated, the colonial administration believed it more prudent politically not to conserve them and accord them the status of national heritage. If the colonial administration adopted this cautious approach, what would one expect of the newly independent countries? Would not the nationalistic feelings of such countries be hurt if they were advised to conserve a heritage that reminded them either of their dehumanization or of their recent colonial past? This seems to be the stand taken by the expatriate conservators who continued to head the Antiquities Department after Tanganyika became independent in 1961. Thus, during the period 1961–1968 no measures were taken for the conservation of the historic towns or the colonial buildings that were regarded as having historic and architectural significance, although the study and publication of the history and architecture of such towns and buildings received support and encouragement (Brown 1970; Cassoon 1970). The following two cases illustrate the thinking of policymakers and the Antiquities Department on these issues.

In 1963, the White Fathers' building, one of the oldest buildings in Dar es Salaam, was threatened with demolition and the then conservator of antiquities noted that

> Enquiries concerning the future of the White Fathers' House elicited the information that plans were afoot for the building to be demolished to make way for large and modern buildings. When however the Archbishop of Dar-es-Salaam learnt that there was a possibility that the building might become a monument, he reluctantly abandoned his plans for the development of the site. Negotiations concerning the future of the building are still in hand. In the meantime, Mr. P. S. Garlake, a student of the British Institute of History and Archaeology in East Africa has surveyed both buildings and produced excellent plans and elevations. (Sassoon 1965)

In the following year it was noted that "The negotiations on the future of the building were abandoned in 1964 on the instructions of the Ministry responsible for Antiquities" (Sassoon 1966). The White Fathers' building is still standing and being used, although it is yet to be protected, and renovation work undertaken in the 1980s did not respect the historic and architectural character of the building.

Since the 1960s, the Antiquities Department used as its offices one of the oldest buildings in Dar es Salaam, constructed by Sayyid Majid and completed in 1866 and known as the Old Boma. In 1968 the department obtained funds to build a new headquarters. Instead of using the funds to conserve and renovate the Old Boma, a historic building, and continuing to use it as its headquarters, the department acquiesced to a condemnation order and to the allocation of the area for the construction of an ultramodern civic center. The civic center was never built, but the Old Boma was abandoned and fell into a state of disrepair between 1970 and 1980, when it was again threatened with demolition, this time for the construction of a tourist hotel. On this occasion, however, the Antiquities Department stood firm and the building was saved; with the support of Tanzania Publishing House, conservation and rehabilitation work was initiated. To date the work is incomplete and at a standstill, and the building therefore remains vacant and unused.

Without disregarding the philosophical issues discussed above and the then prevailing sociopolitical climate, the Department of Antiquities in the period 1969–73 started to redefine its conservation philosophy and policies and gradually adopted the policy of conserving and managing buildings of historic and architectural significance in urban areas, not as monuments or museum pieces, but as historic building resources that should continue to be used within the community. The conservation and management of historic towns, urban quarters, and other buildings should be integrated within the overall urban planning and development process. The following rationale was advanced to support the new thinking and approach:

1) Although the towns and buildings are associated with historic processes and events that are degrading and dehumanizing, there is no way to erase these events and exclude them from the national history. Some of the tangible remains of this history must, therefore, be protected and preserved for the benefit of present and future generations.

2) The historic buildings of these towns testify to how people of the time adapted to the local environment and exploited local building materials and developed new building techniques. The structures therefore represent a pool of knowledge that if properly studied can be adapted and developed further to suit modern needs and thus contribute to the development of local or national construction and technologies. This strategy is more appropriate and sustainable than the wholesale importation of foreign building materials and technologies.

3) The architectural significance of the buildings is the product of local building expertise and especially local craftsmen, who were commissioned and employed by the owners. Conserving these buildings pays tribute to local skills and craftsmanship, which can be further developed and employed in the modern construction industry.

4) The historic buildings represent a major investment in terms of materials, labor, and money and they are therefore a major resource. If properly conserved and managed, historic buildings may continue to contribute to the social and economic development of the nation, especially in meeting the housing needs of the community and in acting as a tourist resource. When combined with other tourist attractions, such as climate, beaches and aquatic resources, and sports, such buildings can greatly contribute to the development of the tourist industry.

Besides the philosophical issues that generated negative attitudes, there was also the problem of different development philosophies and approaches. To many economists, urban planners, architects, and others development equaled modernization, which was interpreted to mean copying the development models of the industrialized West. With this approach conservation was regarded as the antithesis of development. An intersectional and interdisciplinary approach was created to resolve this dichotomy (Mturi 1982). For Bagamoyo an ad hoc committee was appointed in 1972; it included representatives of the ruling party, the urban planning division, the University of Dar es Salaam, and the ministry responsible for local government. The Dar es Salaam Committee was established in 1973 and consisted of representatives of the urban planning division, the Ministry of Works, and the Dar es Salaam region and architects, most of them expatriate (Mturi 1978). It must be emphasized that these ad hoc committees sought to develop a consensus among the key players, whose activities either as institutions or as professionals have a direct bearing on the conservation or destruction of the towns and buildings of historic and architectural significance in an urban environment. A major omission in this strategic approach is the representation and participation of the general public—the owners and users of the historic buildings. This omission was tactical rather than a failure to realize the need for public understanding, awareness, support, and involvement in the conservation endeavor.

The main goal at this juncture was to formulate appropriate reasoned statements to convince the policymakers of the importance of conserving the towns and buildings as a national heritage, thereby obtaining official backing for such actions. Public support and involvement were considered crucial to the implementation phase rather than at the policy decision level. In the case of Bagamoyo, however, deliberate steps were taken to ensure that the committee consulted the local residents and authorities by visiting and staying in the town and meeting with elders, who identified main areas of historical interest and the related history of the buildings, and with local political leaders.

THE BAGAMOYO CONSERVATION PROJECT

The Bagamoyo ad hoc committee recommended that the whole historical center of Bagamoyo should be protected and preserved as a living historic town; the highest policy-making authorities endorsed this plan, and appropriate legal, administrative, and technical measures had to be formulated and implemented.

To widen the scope of the Bagamoyo conservation program and solicit both national and international support, the services of a UNESCO consultant were obtained in 1978. The consultant was charged with assisting the Tanzanian authorities (Department of Antiquities) in compiling an inventory of historic monuments in the old quarter of Bagamoyo, in preparing a restoration plan for the old quarters of Bagamoyo, and in planning a training center for specialists in coastal monuments preservation.

The consultancy resulted in the issuing of a special report (Watson 1979) that dealt with the town's historical background, geographical situation, architectural heritage, and present economy and with objectives and proposals for conservation—conservation areas and listed buildings, proposed development plan, cultural and tourist potential, and training. The report was submitted to the Tanzanian government in November 1979 and was endorsed in a meeting held in Bagamoyo on January 17–19, 1980, attended by representatives of several ministries and state bodies—antiquities, culture, urban development, tourism, the coast region, Bagamoyo district—and of the mass media. Subsequently the conservation areas were gazetted by the minister as provided for in the Antiquities (Amendment) Act of 1979 and these were incorporated for specific land uses in the

Bagamoyo Township physical master plan prepared by the Ministry of Lands, Housing, and Urban Development in 1980.

Despite the implementation of these legal and planning measures, the conservation and management of the historic town did not begin until 1988, when the Bagamoyo Conservation Project, agreed upon and financed by the Tanzanian government, the Ford Foundation, and the Norwegian Agency for International Cooperation, began to be implemented. Why did such a delay occur? The most common answer is that in a country faced with socioeconomic problems, the conservation of the national heritage will be relegated to the background, and budgetary provisions will be minimal. Beginning in 1980, Tanzania's economy began to collapse and the government was forced to cut down on new projects and investments and even the financing of ongoing projects declined. The government adopted a number of structural adjustment programs whose net result was a drastic decrease in resources allocated to the social sector and what was referred to as nonproductive activities. Under such an economic regime financing the conservation of the national heritage will be problematic, if not impossible.

Although this general scenario is appealing there are other reasons why the conservation and management of national historic resources are not accorded priority in social and economic planning and development. First, conservation and management of the national heritage have not been integrated with the planning and development of other sectors. For example, although the importance of historic towns, buildings, sites, and other cultural heritage resources in the development of tourism is acknowledged by many, there is to date not a single development plan on tourism that includes the conservation of cultural heritage. Bagamoyo is a particularly good example. All brochures on Tanzanian tourism, especially those dealing with the coast, will mention Bagamoyo as one of the most important tourist attractions, but not a single tourist organization has included conservation of the town in its development plan.

Second, the government has failed to articulate policies and programs that will attract and allow other actors, including the public, to participate in the conservation and management of the national heritage. Although this is true in cases of monuments, sites, and historic buildings owned by the state, when it comes to living historic towns, the government is only the custodian and its main responsibility is the establishment of an environment conducive for the conservation and management of the historic towns. The key players here are the owners, both private and public.

The experience in Tanzania shows that unless the role of the owners of buildings in historic towns is clearly defined and policies and programs are articulated to involve the public and owners in the conservation endeavor, historic towns will continue to be threatened by negligence and decay and will eventually collapse. Studies undertaken when preparing the Bagamoyo Conservation Project revealed that the owners of the buildings in the historic town considered their buildings either as a future building plot for a more modern house or as a source of building material—the coral stone can be sold or used in other construction activities. With this outlook, there is no need to repair and maintain the buildings, and, in fact, the sooner they collapse the better.

Another problem is that the owners view the government as the custodian of the historic and architectural significance of the buildings; if the government wants to conserve the buildings, then it is the government's responsibility, and not the owners'. In the resulting dependency syndrome, everyone—the district political and government leaders, building owners, and the public at large—expects the central government to plan, finance, and undertake the necessary conservation and rehabilitation work.

Activities of the Bagamoyo Conservation Project

Taking this state of affairs into consideration, the Bagamoyo Conservation Project was designed not only as a national program aimed at the conservation and management of the Bagamoyo historic town but also as a model to develop and test the philosophies, policies, and methodologies to be used in the conservation of other historic towns and buildings. The project also sought to resolve some issues at the local level, especially how to sensitize and involve the owners and the general public, the imparting of local skills necessary for conservation work, and the rehabilitation of the socioeconomic base. Consequently, the first three years of the project narrowed its scope to training, studies, documentation, the preparation of conservation and development plans, and community education.

Training
One major bottleneck in the conservation of historic towns and buildings in Tanzania is the lack of trained and qualified personnel in architectural conservation at both the professional and the subprofessional levels. In addition, the traditional skills and materials used for the construction of these buildings have fallen into disuse. The training component for the project was therefore designed to educate architectural conservation technicians who would be employed by the Antiquities Department and deployed at historic sites. A nine-month module was designed, covering both theoretical and practical training. It was also designed to train local craftsmen in the conservation work, especially in repairing and consolidation of structures and in the use of traditional skills and materials. Such education would be practical by attachment to ongoing conservation work, thereby creating a pool of knowledgeable self-employed craftsmen who could be contracted by owners of historic buildings to undertake conservation work.

Up to 1990, thirty architectural conservation technicians had been trained for both the Antiquities Unit and the Zanzibar Stone Town Conservation Authority. Most of those employed by the Antiquities Unit have remained in Bagamoyo to continue with conservation and rehabilitation work. This, however, defeats the project's objective of creating local employment. This state of affairs results primarily from the fact that the training of local craftsmen has not been successful initially, mainly because the government wages were low relative to private construction pay. However, this initial lack of participation by the local craftsmen seems to have been resolved and several local craftsmen are now engaged in the rehabilitation of the old fort.

Studies and Documentation

The project sought a detailed evaluation of the historic buildings in terms of ownership, use, condition, and state of preservation. Each building's conservation needs would be ranked, land use and availability and adequacy of public utilities would be evaluated, and a conservation and development plan for the historic center of Bagamoyo would be prepared. The plan would include 1) the nature, type, and urgency of conservation and rehabilitation work for all historic buildings; 2) proposals for undeveloped areas within the historic center; 3) conditions for the development of areas surrounding the historic center to ensure that future buildings harmonize with the character of the historic center; 4) improvement/development of public amenities; 5) detailed guidelines for owners of historic buildings as well as for future developers; 6) definitions of the responsibilities of the various agencies—the Antiquities Unit, the district council, and the coordinating machinery.

The preparation of the conservation and development plan was regarded not only as an essential professional and technical requirement but as an educational tool. One of the problems encountered during the preparation of the project was the confusion on the role and responsibilities of the various agencies and actors. For example, what is the role of the district council in allocating building plots within the conservation area? Where should an owner of a plot in the conservation area go to get the necessary permits for building, and so forth? Does an owner of a historic building need a permit before he can repair or demolish his building? Is the owner of a collapsed building allowed to quarry for the coral stone? The plan should answer all these questions and define the procedures and regulatory machinery.

The conservation and development plan was completed in 1990 and submitted to public scrutiny and review. However, as of late 1995, the plan has not been published, and the guidelines have not been prepared and given the necessary legal backing. The confusing situation narrated above therefore still prevails, a situation that will no doubt have adverse effects on conservation as the project personnel stationed in Bagamoyo have no legal and administrative authority over activities in the conservation areas. The legal and administrative machinery for executing the plan exists, and the failure to implement it can only be attributed to a lack of professional leadership within the Antiquities Unit.

Community Education and Development

This component was originally to consist of two parallel activities: development of public understanding, appreciation, and involvement and a community development aspect concerned with creation of income-generating activities for selected target groups to improve the social and economic status of residents of the historic center. The preparation of the income-generating activities, which the Ford Foundation was prepared to finance, was entrusted to the Community Development Department. Because of management problems this aspect of the component was never finished and was excluded from the project. The component was therefore narrowed to community education and participation and included public exhibitions on the history, the architecture, and the need to conserve the architectural heritage of Bagamoyo; seminars for owners of historic buildings, political and governmental leaders, and functionaries at different levels; and conservation and rehabilitation work to demonstrate the efficacy and viability of conserving the architectural heritage.

A photographic exhibition outlining the history of Bagamoyo, the historic and architectural character of the buildings, and the activities of the project was mounted for public viewing during the inauguration of the project. Two seminars were also organized, one for political and governmental leaders and functionaries at the district and regional levels and the second for owners of historic buildings, district councilors resident in Bagamoyo Township, and local political leaders. During the seminars, the objectives and activities of the project were discussed in detail, as were general conservation issues, the need and benefits of conserving the national heritage, and the role and responsibilities of building owners, the government in general, and the various agencies and functionaries.

Several conservation and rehabilitation projects have been undertaken to serve two main objectives: to offer practical training to the architectural conservation technician trainees and local craftsmen and to act as demonstrative or pilot models to show the owners and the public at large that the use of traditional building materials—coral stone, mangrove poles, lime mortar, and so forth—and skills is a viable and appropriate alternative to the use of modern building materials, especially cement mortar and cement blocks. It was expected that such demonstrations would convince the owners in particular to start treating their historic buildings as an investment and resource that, if properly maintained, could contribute both to the protection and preservation of the national heritage and to the social and economic well-being of the owners.

The German blockhouse was gazetted as a monument during the colonial period but had been neglected and had reached an advanced stage of decay. The monument was repaired and consolidated and the surrounding area was developed into a small park, thus demonstrating the possibility of using traditional skills and materials to reclaim a structure that many people had thought beyond repair. The development of a park for public use demonstrated that a monument is not only for the enjoyment of tourists but also for the local people. Such public use should generate understanding and support. Although the project completed the necessary works, the Antiquities Unit was expected to take over routine maintenance, presentation, interpretation, and park management. As of late 1995, little has been done, and if the unit does not become more serious and professional in managing the monument, this important historic structure might revert to a state of disrepair.

The project also undertook the conservation and rehabilitation of a privately owned building that had been abandoned for more than a decade and was in an advanced state of disrepair. The building was chosen to demonstrate to the owners and the public that such a building can be rescued and rehabilitated into a useful and profitable housing resource. Second, by choosing a privately owned house the government sought to establish the machinery for state–private owner partnerships that will be used in the future in supporting private owners. Although the conservation and rehabilitation work was financed using project funds, on completion of the work the cost was to be shared—25 percent to be treated as a grant to the owner and 75 percent to be treated as a loan to be repaid from the rental of the building. The repaid money would be used to support other owners of historic buildings.

On completion of the work, the building would be used as a guest house with a restaurant and bar. The management of the guest house would be privately contracted; it was expected that this would generate enough rental money to convince private owners that, with proper care and maintenance, their historical buildings were a profitable investment. Because of management problems, the conservation work has not been completed; consequently, the success of this plan cannot be evaluated.

The German Boma remains the district headquarters and was repaired and consolidated as part of the training for the second course for architecture conservation technicians. The fort, one of the earliest of the landmark buildings, is currently being conserved and rehabilitated through a European Economic Community (EEC) grant provided under the Lome III agreement between the EEC and represented African countries.

Evaluation and Conclusions

It might be too early to evaluate the Bagamoyo Conservation Project. However, it can be said that the undertaking of the project has generated interest and awareness among the owners, as is demonstrated by the fact that a number of buildings have been repaired, although the owners remain skeptical about the use of traditional materials and continue to use cement mortar. The implementation of the Conservation and Development Plan is essential to make the use of traditional material a legal requirement. Owners' interest and commitment is also shown by their support in principle of the establishment of an association of owners of historic buildings. A meeting convened in 1992 supported such a move, but to date the association has not yet been formed. This delay probably reflects the project's failure to develop the necessary local professional leadership to sensitize and coordinate the activities of the owners. It seems as if the project personnel have concentrated on conservation and rehabilitation work and have neglected their role in developing and supporting public involvement and participation. If this proves to be the case, it would be a very unfortunate development and will undermine the future of the project.

To conclude, the Bagamoyo Conservation Project demonstrates several points. With qualified, committed, and dynamic professional leadership it is possible to formulate and implement a conservation project with the support of the government and foreign donors even in a situation where the country is in a social and economic crisis. With minimum infrastructure and using existing facilities, it is possible to plan and implement a fairly specialized training program and develop the necessary expertise and skills required for the technical conservation of the national heritage. And it is possible, despite the attitudes of the owners and the public, to sensitize them and develop the necessary awareness, support, and involvement. To sustain such support, however, those responsible at the official level must abandon some of their attitudes and practices and stop planning from the top. The operational module should be for the conservation authority to work with the owners of historic buildings, organize them to plan and undertake their own conservation work, and offer the owners the necessary professional and technical support.

THE CONSERVATION AND MANAGEMENT OF ROCK-ART SITES

The most impressive concentration of rock-art sites in Tanzania, mostly rock shelters, is found in central Tanzania in Kondoa District of Dodoma region (Leakey et al. 1950; Leakey 1983; Fozzard 1966; Ten Raa 1974), Iramba District (Ordner 1971), and Singida District (Masao 1976, 1979). However, rock-art sites are also found in other parts of the country, notably in the Lake Victoria zone in Mwanza and in Bukoba rural district (Turner 1953; Chaplin 1974), in the Ikimbu area (Shorter 1967), and in Yaeda Plain in Mbulu District. A few sites have also been reported in Tabora (Collinson 1970), Masasi, Lindi, and Iringa.

An analysis of the rock art of eastern, central, and southern Africa by Anati, who as a UNESCO consultant in 1980 visited 102 sites with two hundred decorated surfaces in central Tanzania, indicates that the rock art of the area is probably among the oldest, dating from between forty and fifty thousand years ago (Anati 1986). If this proves accurate, central Tanzania has not only the oldest prehistoric art in the world but also one of the longest artistic traditions, spanning a period of more than thirty thousand years. This might also mean that central Tanzania was a major center for the origin and evolution of prehistoric art.

The State of Preservation of the Rock Art

If the interpretative scheme and chronology advanced by Anati is proven, then the earliest rock art in central Tanzania was probably executed long before European Upper Palaeolithic art and certainly before any other art known in northern Africa, the Near East, or Europe. The rock art of central Tanzania is very rich and diversified and therefore represents a national as well as a world heritage. This heritage witnesses, documents, and provides study material for some forty thousand years of cultural history, thus giving a deeper insight into and understanding of the evolution of humanity and its intellectual adventures. The art also contributes to a new understanding of the formation and early evolution of African societies. It is therefore a heritage that must be protected and preserved for the benefit and enjoyment of everyone.

Taking into consideration the number of rock-art sites already known, the number of painted figures, the age of the paintings, and therefore the time they have been exposed to the elements, it would be reasonable to say that, on the whole, the rock art of Tanzania is fairly well preserved. However, there is ample evidence that decay and deterioration have existed for a long time. The last major evaluation of the rock-art sites occurred in 1980, when Anati and I visited 102 sites with two hundred decorated surfaces. Another inspection was made in August

1992, when about twenty sites in the Kondoa area were visited. It became clear that the processes of decay and deterioration have accelerated in the past thirty to forty years, for reasons yet unknown. In some cases sites that were visited and were in a good state of preservation in 1980 had greatly deteriorated twelve years later, with paintings fading and hardly visible or in a few cases completely faded. Thus, this unique and important heritage is endangered and urgent conservation and management measures must be formulated and implemented to safeguard the art. In particular, immediate and urgent measures should be taken to study and understand the processes of decay and deterioration and to identify the causes. Such studies are indispensable in successfully formulating and implementing appropriate conservation and management measures to arrest or mitigate the processes.

Many factors are known to contribute to the decay and deterioration of rock art. In the case of Tanzania, no detailed and systematic studies and analyses have been undertaken to identify the agencies involved. However, taking into consideration observations made by Anati during his UNESCO consultancy mission, the observation of other researchers and the author during the past thirty years, and studies undertaken in other countries (e.g., Gillespie 1983), the factors affecting the rock art of Tanzania can be grouped under two main categories—those due to human activities and those due to natural agencies [not discussed in this chapter, ed.].

Damage from Human Activities

Human activities affect rock art in two ways: directly by destroying the paintings themselves, or indirectly by destroying the archaeological resources in the deposits of the shelters that house paintings. Although human damage to the rock art is not widespread, it has occurred in several shelters and it can be ranked as one of the most serious threats to the art because it is irreversible and results in the destruction of the art. The rock shelters with paintings are not now inhabited, though in 1980 one shelter was being inhabited by a family and a blacksmith occasionally used another shelter—Hanje (Lindi) in Singida District—as a workshop. However, there is evidence that in the past the shelters were more frequently used for habitation, for refuge, or for religious and other ceremonial activities. Such past use has resulted in the destruction of the paintings by smoke and soot from fires. Modern damage to the paintings results mostly from human vandalism—modern paintings superimposed on ancient paintings, names and other characters scribbled over painted surfaces, marks made on paintings, and painted surfaces pecked or rubbed. Tourists' use of water to make the paintings more visible has also been claimed as one of the causes for the decay of the paintings, but this has not yet been proven. Chalk and charcoal are the main materials used for the execution of modern paintings or for retouching, although modern paints have been used in a few cases. These acts of human vandalism are evident in all areas with paintings. Most of these activities are probably the work of children, although the participation of adults cannot be ruled out.

Illegal excavations in the rock shelters constitute another widespread activity. Although such excavations do not damage or destroy the paintings, they result in the destruction of the archaeological resources contained in the deposits of the shelters, an irreparable loss because the evidence so destroyed cannot be retrieved. Such illegal diggings were rampant in Kondoa District in the 1950s and 1960s. Another spate of illegal excavations occurred in the 1970s in Kondoa and Iramba Districts. The reasons for these excavations are not known, but the most plausible explanation is that the people responsible are either looking for minerals or treasure hunting. During the early 1950s it was rumored that the paintings were the work of the Portuguese. The illegal excavators claimed that they were looking for Portuguese treasures that were buried in the shelters. It is difficult to explain this myth since the Portuguese never visited the interior of Tanzania, although they were active on the coast between the sixteenth and eighteenth centuries. This myth likely originated when members of the Pan African Congress of Prehistory and Quaternary Studies visited the paintings in 1948 and from the Leakeys' work in the area during 1950–51. It is likely that people misinterpreted the comparisons made between the Kondoa paintings and those of Portuguese by members of the congress and by the Leakeys.

The excavations of the 1970s were prompted by another myth, this time connected with the Germans. It was rumored that before the Germans were defeated in World War I they buried many valuables, including German coins. Some people regarded rock shelters as the most likely places for the Germans to have buried their treasures. Another possible explanation for such excavations is the search for minerals. Some people may not be convinced that the archaeologists who excavate in these shelters are looking only for pottery shards, stone artifacts, bones, and the like. The public has generally been skeptical that a government would allocate resources for such archaeological work. Thus, it is likely that some of the local people believe the archaeologists to be geologists looking for minerals. Understanding the motives behind these illegal excavations is necessary to formulate an effective educational program to eliminate such activities.

Conservation and Management

As of late 1995, no detailed and comprehensive measures have been formulated and implemented to conserve and manage the rock-art sites of Tanzania. The only action taken was the construction of protective structures in fourteen rock shelters with paintings in the Kolo-Kisese cluster of sites. These protective structures— cages of wire mesh on a timber framework resting on a stone foundation—represented a reaction to the spate of illegal excavations in the 1960s. The cages allow people to see and photograph the paintings without entering the shelters, and it was expected that such measures would prevent illegal excavations and damage to the paintings. Construction of the protective structures was followed by the opening of the sites to visitors through the construction of access roads and the employment of guides. Although no illegal excavations have been reported in these fourteen rock shelters, the effectiveness of the protective cages is dubious, because the cages have been vandalized and wire mesh, nuts and bolts, doors, and timber have been stolen. Unless such protective structures are indestructible by humans, they cannot offer 100 percent protection to the sites.

That this unique but fragile artistic heritage is threatened by human abuse and by complex natural mechanisms (geologic, biological, chemical, and mechanical) is common knowledge, and Tanzanian authorities were alerted to this situation by a UNESCO consultant in 1980. Anati's report, which was primarily aimed at evaluating the significance of the rock art of Tanzania and its possible nomination under the World Heritage List, attempted to systematically evaluate and analyze the reasons for deterioration of rock art and to put forward conservation and management proposals, including further study, training of the requisite scientific and technical manpower, and establishment of a rock-art conservation and research laboratory. It is unfortunate that the Tanzanian authorities *have not yet implemented these proposals* and that Tanzanian rock art, though it meets all the criteria for nomination to the World Heritage List, remains unlisted because Tanzanian authorities *have not completed* the required procedures.

The nomination of the rock-art sites would not only put the rock art of Tanzania on the world map but would also attract both technical and financial assistance from the World Heritage fund. The nomination and listing would also make it easier for UNESCO to formulate and launch an international campaign to safeguard the Tanzanian rock art. The 1976 UNESCO general conference passed a resolution authorizing the director general of UNESCO to study the possibility of launching an international campaign to assist Tanzania in safeguarding its national heritage. After consultation with appropriate UNESCO officials, it was agreed in principle that the rock-art sites of Tanzania would qualify for such an international campaign. A proposal entitled "International Campaign for the Safeguarding of Tanzania Cultural Heritage: The Conservation of the Rock Art of Central Tanzania" was prepared by the author in 1986 and submitted to the Tanzanian authorities, *but the international campaign has yet to be launched.*

In 1988–89, the author, in consultation with Mary Leakey and Stephanie Kuna of Chicago, explored other ways of initiating a program for the conservation of the rock art of Tanzania. The Preservation Trust for Rock Art Limited was established and incorporated in Chicago to raise funds for the conservation of rock-art sites in Tanzania. A meeting held on August 16, 1989, in Arusha agreed on a program of action, with both short-term and long-term objectives and activities. The short-term plan of action seeks to address issues related to threats from human vandalism, while the long-term plan includes studies, the development and testing of appropriate conservation measures, and the conservation and management of the rock-art sites.

The Short-Term Plan of Action

The short-term plan of action concentrates on measures to improve the policing and surveillance of rock-art sites to minimize human vandalism and to educate the public and engender understanding, support, and involvement in the protection and management of the sites. The following measures are therefore proposed:

1) Establishment of posts for guards/guides in areas with numerous rock-art sites, especially at Kisese, Masange, Pahi, and Tlawi.

2) Strengthening of the Kolo guards/guides post by expansion and employment of a mid-level cadre to take charge of monitoring and supervisory services.

3) Increasing the number of guards/guides from two to ten.

4) Training of the guards/guides to improve their proficiency in guiding visitors and to educate them about their responsibilities as guardians of the sites.

5) Improving the mobility of the guards/guides by providing them with reliable transport—bicycles for the guards/guides and a motorcycle for the supervisor—thereby enabling them to undertake regular site inspections. The staff should also be provided with uniforms, boots, and raincoats.

6) Organization of seminars, public meetings, and discussions at schools and with village and district leaders to educate the general public about the significance of the rock art, the need to protect and preserve the heritage, and the public's role and responsibility in conserving and managing the rock-art sites.

7) Production of a documentary film that will highlight the significance of Tanzania's rock art, relate it to prehistoric art in general, and demonstrate the measures necessary to ensure its protection and preservation. The film would be used as an educational tool in schools, colleges, and villages as well as to sensitize and educate the international community, generating support for the preservation trust.

8) Incorporation of rock-art research results and knowledge in all levels of the education system.

The Long-Term Plan of Action

A long-term plan of action will concentrate on the following areas:

1) Recording and documenting the rock-art sites.

2) Documentation and identification of the causes of decay and deterioration.

3) Developing and testing appropriate conservation measures.

4) Establishment of the necessary conservation and research facilities, including the training of scientific and technical personnel at a rock-art research and conservation laboratory.

5) Protection and interpretation of a selected sample of sites for the enjoyment of the public, including tourists.

The detailed and systematic recording and documentation of the rock-art sites is an essential conservation and management tool that should permit evaluation of the rock art and the compilation of a national inventory. Such documentation should also result in the creation and maintenance of a data bank, an important research and conservation facility. Whatever conservation and management measures are adopted, however, the number of sites involved, with thousands of painted figures, is such that no conservation strategy can guarantee the protection and preservation of all rock-art sites. Only a representative sample of sites, especially those of great significance, can be accorded priority in terms of conservation and management; many sites, though not completely neglected, will receive limited attention, depending on the availability of resources. Thus it is essential that each site should be recorded and documented in detail for future reference and research. These records should include site locations, maps and plans, photographs and high-quality tracings, and photogrammetric surveys, especially for the important sites.

The study and research program will identify the causes and processes involved in the decay and deterioration of rock art and develop and test appropriate conservation measures and techniques. Areas of study would include: 1) the chemical composition of the paint pigments, their properties and behavior, and the chemical and physical processes involved in their destruction; 2) petrographic, geomorphological, and other studies to elucidate the mineralogical composition of the host rock and its properties and behavior when exposed to the elements; 3) chemical and other studies of the properties and behavior of the encrustations, salt, and other contaminants deposited on the painted surfaces and of how these processes contribute to the chemical and physical weathering of the host rock and the disintegration of the paint; and 4) climatological, hydrological, and other studies to elucidate the processes involved in water-induced damage.

Such studies require highly specialized personnel and should be interdisciplinary, involving different specialists—geochemists, petrologists, mineralogists, hydrologists, conservation chemists, and so forth. The research also requires the use of highly specialized techniques and technology, among them infrared spectroscopy, x-ray diffraction, petrographic microscopes, and scanning electron microscopes. Tanzania lacks both the specialized personnel and the facilities. The training of scientific and technical personnel and the establishment of the rock-art research and conservation laboratory will redress this shortfall; however, the participation of foreign researchers and experts will be essential and should be encouraged.

Ultimately, these studies seek to develop and test appropriate conservation measures and techniques to mitigate and arrest the decay and deterioration of the paintings, thereby ensuring the future of the rock art. Subsequent conservation and management measures should be formulated and implemented to safeguard the sites and to interpret them for public enjoyment.

Public Participation and Involvement

Although the scientific and technical conservation measures to be formulated and applied will remove the natural threats to the rock art, the threat from human activities must be addressed when formulating and implementing conservation and management measures. It has been argued that public understanding, support, and involvement are essential in the conservation of the national heritage. The rock-art sites of Tanzania are located in inhabited areas, and human vandalism has occurred. As pointed out, the short-term plan seeks to educate the public about the significance of the rock art and to define the public's role and responsibility in protecting and preserving it.

Because of deficiencies in the educational system, the rock art of Tanzania and its significance as a cultural and tourist resource are unknown to the inhabitants in the areas with rock-art sites and to the public at large. Even at primary schools situated near rock-art sites, teachers and pupils were unaware of the existence of the sites. This lack of awareness is difficult to explain because most schools teach the history of the "people of the caves," which should include the communities that used the rock shelters and executed the paintings. For the educational component of the short-term plan of action to succeed, it must therefore:

a) Educate the villagers living in the areas with rock-art sites, developing the necessary awareness and support and enlisting their involvement in the protection and preservation of the sites. This awareness and support would make it easier for the strengthened monitoring and supervisory field staff to undertake their policing duties and to work closely with the villagers in preventing acts of vandalism.

b) Restructure the educational programs at all levels to integrate the nature, significance, and role of the national heritage in the social and economic development of the nation, creating a knowledgeable and informed public that can be easily organized and involved in the conservation and management of the national heritage.

Because of the lack of awareness and support, the Tanzanian public is not organized to lobby the government to adopt policies aimed at conserving the national heritage even in those cases where the cultural resources concerned are directly relevant to the history and culture of specific communities. Although measures to educate and sensitize the public may in the long term resolve this bottleneck, deliberate measures must be taken to encourage and support the formation of societies that will provide such pressure. Thus, in implementing the short-term plan of action, the Preservation Trust for Rock Art, in collaboration with the government agency responsible for cultural resources management, should seek the formation of societies for the conservation of rock art at both the local and the national levels.

Public participation and involvement should not confine itself to duties and responsibilities on the part of the villagers but should also include public benefits from the conservation and management of the rock-art sites. Ensuring such benefits could make it easier to obtain support to protect and preserve the sites. Several measures can be taken to achieve public benefits.

Priority should be given to employing local people in those jobs that do not require specialist skills. For example all guards/guides should be recruited from villages in areas with rock-art sites. Seasonal work such as repair and maintenance of access roads should be contracted to villages. Project work that does not require expertise should be contracted to skilled local residents. For example, the construction of new guard/guide posts proposed under the short-term plan of action can include contracting with villagers to make burnt bricks for the buildings and employing local craftsmen and laborers in construction. This will help to make the communities stake-holders in the preservation project.

When properly conserved, interpreted, and promoted, rock-art sites can be a major tourist attraction. How can the villages benefit from this new economic activity in their area? Possibilities include ensuring that priority is given to hiring local people; ensuring that a percentage of the revenue realized is paid to the villages to finance their social and economic activities and the servicing of tourists and tourist facilities; and developing local handicrafts as well as agricultural activities, especially horticulture.

Both the short-term and long-term plans of action formulated by the Preservation Trust for Rock Art have yet to be implemented. Tanzanian authorities have not reacted positively to attempts to make the trust operational. The trust only received the official backing of the Tanzanian government in April 1992, and initial reactions are encouraging. It is therefore hoped that the activities of the trust will greatly contribute to the conservation of the rock-art sites of Tanzania, including the development of mechanisms for public support and involvement.

REFERENCES

Anati, E. "The State of Research in Rock Art: The Rock Art of Tanzania and the East African Sequence." *Bollettino del Centro Camuno di Studi Priestoriei* vol. 23 (1986):15–68.

Brown, T. W. "Bagamoyo: An Historical Introduction." *Tanzania Notes and Records* 71 (1970):69–83.

Cassoon, W. T. "Architectural Notes on Dar es Salaam." *Tanzania Notes and Records* 71 (1970):181–84.

Chaplin, J. H. "The Prehistoric Rock Art of Lake Victoria Region." *Azania* 9 (1974):1–50.

Chittick, H. N. *Annual Report of the Department of Antiquities for the Year 1957.* Dar es Salaam: Government Printer, 1959.

———. *Annual Report of the Department of Antiquities for the Year 1958.* Dar es Salaam: Government Printer, 1959.

———. *Annual Report of the Department of Antiquities for the Year 1959.* Dar es Salaam: Government Printer, 1960.

———. *Kisiwani Mafia: Excavations at an Islamic Settlement on the East African Coast.* Occasion Paper no. 1. Dar es Salaam, Government Printer, 1961.

———. *Kilwa: An Islamic Trading City on the Eastern Coast of Africa.* 2 vols. Nairobi: British Institute in Eastern Africa Memoir no. 5., 1974.

Collinson, J. D. H. "The Makolo Rock Paintings of Nyamwezi." *Azania* 5 (1970):55–63.

Fozzard, P. M. H. "Some Rock Paintings of Western Usandawe." *Tanzania Notes and Records* 65 (1966):57–62.

Garlake, P. S. *Early Islamic Architecture of the East African Coast.* Memoir no. 1 of the British Institute of History and Archaeology in East Africa. Oxford: Oxford University Press, 1966.

Gillespie, G., ed. *Rock Art Sites in Kakadu National Park: Some Preliminary Research Findings for Their Conservation and Management.* Australian National Park and Wildlife Service, 1983.

Leakey, L. S. B., et al. "Tanganyika Rock Paintings." *Tanganyika Notes and Records* 29 (1950).

Leakey, M. D. *Vanishing Art: The Rock Paintings of Tanzania.* Hamilton/Rainbird, 1983.

Masao, F. T. "Some Common Aspects of Rock Paintings of Kondoa and Singida." *Tanzania Notes and Records* 77 and 78 (1976):51–66.

———. *The Later Stone Age and the Rock Paintings of Central Tanzania.* Wiesbaden: Franz Steiner Verlag, 1979.

Mturi, A. A. *A Guide to the Ruins of Kaole with Some Notes on Other Antiquities on the Coast to the North of Dar es Salaam.* Dar es Salaam: Antiquities Division, Ministry of National Culture and Youth, 1974.

———. *Annual Report of the Antiquities Department for the Year 1972 and 1973.* Dar es Salaam: Government Printer, 1978.

———. "The Designation and Management of Conservation Areas in Tanzania with Case Studies of Kilwa Kisiwani, Bagamoyo, and Dar es Salaam." Unpublished dissertation. University of York: England, 1982.

————. "Land Use Planning and the Conservation of World Heritage Site of Kilwa Kisi-wani." ICOMOS Eighth General Assembly International Symposium, vol. 11. Washington, D.C.: US ICOMOS, 1987.

Ordner, K. "An Archaeological Survey of Iramba, Tanzania." *Azania* 6 (1971):151–98.

Sassoon, H. *Annual Report of the Antiquities Division for the Year 1963.* Dar es Salaam: Government Printer, 1965.

————. *Annual Report of the Antiquities Department for the Year 1964.* Dar es Salaam: Government Printer, 1966.

Shorter, A. E. M. "Rock Paintings in Ukimbu." *Tanzania Notes and Records* 67 (1967):49–55.

Taboroff, J. "Bringing Cultural Heritage into the Development Agenda: Summary Findings of a Report of Cultural Heritage in Environment Assessment in Sub-Saharan Africa." In *Culture and Development in Africa.* ed. I. Serageldin and J. Taboroff, vol. 2, 322–39. Washington, D.C.: World Bank, 1992.

Ten Raa, E. "A Record of Some Prehistoric and Some Recent Sandawe Rock Paintings," *Tanganyika Notes and Records* 75 (1974):9–27.

Turner, R. E. S. "A Series of Rock Paintings Near Mwanza." *Tanganyika Notes and Records* 34 (1953):62–67.

Watson, T. N. *Conservation of Bagamoyo.* Serial no. FMR/CC/Ut/79/190. Paris: UNESCO, 1979.

15

THE DETERIORATION AND DESTRUCTION OF ARCHAEOLOGICAL AND HISTORICAL SITES IN TANZANIA

N. J. Karoma

The deterioration and destruction of historical heritage is a worldwide phenomenon, and Tanzania is no exception. Two main causes account for much of the deterioration and destruction of such resources in most of the world. The first cause is natural agents, the wear and tear of time resulting primarily from exposure to the elements, such as humidity, heat and cold, erosion, and biological and chemical action. The other cause is human-related, such as uncontrolled industrial, rural, urban, and agricultural development, rural underdevelopment, mass tourism, and irresponsible human action, especially vandalism and neglect. Of all these, the last is the least known and discussed.

This chapter draws on experiences of historical heritage management in Tanzania during the past twenty years. I will argue that there is a disparity between official policy as presented in the country's antiquities legislation and public statements and the actual day-to-day management practices. I will show that the presence of protective legislation is not enough to ensure effective management of historical heritage sites and that a well-trained and committed management team is an essential ingredient to the success of good management.

TANZANIA'S HERITAGE RESOURCES

Tanzania is custodian of an impressive array of globally significant cultural heritage resources, some dating as far back as the Pliocene era, about four million years ago. One example is the 3.85 million-year-old hominid fossil footprint at Laetoli in northern Tanzania. Providing evidence of full bipedalism among hominids at least one million years before the appearance of stone tools and expanded brains, this site is considered to "rank among the great palaeontological discoveries of our century" (Tuttle 1990:61).

Let us quickly review some of the other singular heritage resources in Tanzania's custody. The Plio-Pleistocene to Holocene site at Olduvai Gorge, where hominid remains, fossil bones, and stone tools document the story of humankind during the last two million years, has been described as the "Grand Canyon of human evolution," the "Mecca of palaeoanthropologists," and the "cradle of mankind." There are also several important Later Quaternary sites like Mumba in the

Eyasi Basin, as well as Nasera, Ndutu, and Loiyangalani on the Serengeti Plain. Some of the sites contain biological evidence for the emergence of anatomically modern humans and all of them contain the cultural evidence for the earliest members of our species, *Homo sapiens sapiens*.

The Later Pleistocene to Holocene rock-art sites of Central Tanzania are of global importance (Mturi, this volume). Some of the rock-art styles represented at these sites are thought to be the oldest in the world, as they may date from between fifty thousand and forty thousand years ago (Anati 1986; Mturi, this volume). We also have a wide array of important Iron Age sites, the earliest of which date to the second half of the last millennium B.C. They are important because they include early evidence of complex metallurgical skills involving the production of carbon steel by a distinctive process almost two thousand years ago (Schmidt and Avery 1978).

There are also numerous coastal sites that are the remains of early ninth to eighteenth century Swahili urban societies (see Kusimba and Wilson and Omar, this volume). These magnificent sites attest to trade and commercial contacts between the East African coast, the Persian Gulf, and other Indian Ocean coastal locations. Finally, there are historic sites of both indigenous and foreign origin, including those that contain traditional architecture and those that remind one of the colonial period. These date from the late nineteenth century to the present.

Clearly, there are very few countries in the world with a cultural record that is as long, varied, and complete as that found in Tanzania. As a poor Third World nation, Tanzania has the unenviable task of managing a long and priceless human heritage. As D. N. Mwakawago, a former Tanzanian minister for information and culture, pointed out in 1983 in an opening address to participants in a seminar on conservation of historic towns and monuments along the coast of Kenya, Mozambique, Somalia, and Tanzania, "the cultural heritage of a country is a nonrenewable resource and once destroyed or lost it cannot be recreated. Every effort must therefore be taken to preserve it."

A legal and institutional framework for the conservation and management of these and numerous other heritage resources began to take shape in Tanzania during the British trusteeship period. In 1937 the British colonial administration passed the Monuments Preservation Ordinance, which empowered the governor to declare and gazette structures of historic significance as monuments and areas and sites of archaeological, scientific, and historical significance as reserved areas. Not until 1957 did the government establish an agency, the Antiquities Department, to handle the conservation and management of immovable cultural property. In 1964 the Monuments Preservation Ordinance was repealed and replaced by the Antiquities Act of 1964. The latter remains the principal legislation for cultural resources management in Tanzania, although it was modified by the Antiquities (Amendment) Act in 1979. In 1937 the King George VI Memorial Museum opened and established another agency for cultural resource management in Dar es Salaam. It was renamed the National Museum in 1962, two years after independence. The museum is responsible for conservation of the movable property, primarily archaeological, palaeontological, historical, and ethnographic objects. Its main task is to collect, preserve, display, and interpret these objects for the nation.

Conversely, the Antiquities Department (now a unit) was charged with the task of conserving immovable property, especially sites and monuments, and with administering the legal provisions of the antiquities legislation (Mturi, this volume). But many of the legal provisions of the antiquities law are routinely violated, often by officials of the very agency established to administer them.

EXAMPLES OF HERITAGE DESTRUCTION AND DETERIORATION IN TANZANIA

The Case of Songo Mnara

While conducting an archaeology field school in the Kilwa Coast area between July and September 1992 for first- and second-year undergraduate students at the University of Dar es Salaam, we visited the antiquities of the area, including the famous sites of Kilwa Kisiwani, Songo Mnara, and Kilwa Kivinje, three sites that are facing deterioration and destruction. The destruction we encountered at Songo Mnara seems to be a classic case of the disparity between official policy and actual management of resources.

According to Chittick (1965), Songo Mnara is one of more than eighty ruined coastal sites. It is an important fourteenth- to sixteenth-century trading port, closely allied with Kilwa and with impressive remains of a palace complex, which is made up of seventeen buildings, five mosques, and other domestic buildings. The settlement consists of a number of residences, some of great complexity. The ruins of Songo Mnara are interesting because, unlike Kilwa Kisiwani, most of the stone domestic buildings from a rich settlement of the late medieval period are still preserved. At Kilwa no houses of this time period still survive aboveground because their ruins were demolished for the stone around the late eighteenth century.

Legally, Songo Mnara is listed as a protected monument under the antiquities rules in 1980, which stipulate that, "subject to a permit first sought and obtained from the Director of Antiquities or any person authorized in that behalf, no person shall, within the area of protected objects or monuments—displace or in any way interfere with any object whether artificial or non-artificial from its proper positions; cause fire to any grass, undergrowth, or tree of the surrounding area."

One of the first things we noticed at the Songo Mnara ruins was that someone had been burning trees and brush growing among the ruins. The branches of several fallen trees were also burned close to the coralline stones that form the walls. As a result, large parts of the ruins had been reduced to a white powder of lime, and whole walls had been completely destroyed. One of the official guides at the ruins explained that the guides set fire to the brush and trees because it was a less energy-consuming technique of brush and bush clearing. Moreover, the guide added that he was not motivated to do the hard work of bush clearing because of his low pay.

At other places along the walls we noticed a variety of other bushes growing, but the guides had not done anything to remove them. Many walls at Songo Mnara seem to be collapsing as a result of uncontrolled vegetation growth. Yet there are legal provisions established to deal with this problem, and enforcing them is definitely within the means of the government agency charged with the duty of managing and protecting this site. But instead of managing Songo Mnara, the Antiquities Unit is mismanaging the site by acts of omission in which unattended vegetation slowly but surely leads to deterioration and eventual destruction, and it is also involved in the direct destruction of the ruins through burning. In a nutshell, by destroying sites it is supposed to protect, the Antiquities Unit is involved in the violation of the very law it is supposed to administer.

The Case of Kilwa Kisiwani

The ancient ruined trading city of Kilwa Kisiwani is yet another case of the disparity between official policy and management of resources. A ninth- to eighteenth-century port town that reached its zenith between the thirteenth and fifteenth centuries, it was a center of maritime power that controlled the coast from Mafia in the north to Sofala in Mozambique. There are major monumental remains of mosques, palaces, and tombs, extensive local and exotic antiquities, and remains of fallen and buried buildings and many movable objects. Kilwa Kisiwani is also a gazetted national monument. But unlike Songo Mnara, Kilwa Kisiwani is also registered under the World Heritage List established under the UNESCO Convention on the Protection of the World Cultural and Natural Heritage. The site was included on the World Heritage List because of its historical and archaeological significance. This site provides the best evidence of the growth of civilization and commerce of the East African coast from the ninth to the nineteenth century, in terms both of archaeology and of documentary history. This area provides a vivid insight into the way of life, both social and economic. It is architecturally important because it provides a unique example of the growth of the distinctive Swahili tradition in architecture over time. No other site on the East African coast provides more clues to the building techniques used in Swahili architecture and their chronological periods.

Legally, Kilwa Kisiwani is a protected monument as defined in the principal legislation of 1964 and as amended in section 2 (a) of the Antiquities (Amendment) Act of 1979:

> Any building, fortification, interment, midden, dam or any structure erected, built or formed by human agency in Tanganyika before the year 1863. The same legislation also establishes the regulatory regime for monitoring research, trade and exchange as well as the exportation of protected resources. Under this law, no person except the Director or a person acting on his behalf shall, whether on his own land or elsewhere:
> (i) Excavate, dig or probe for monuments or relics, or
> (ii) Remove or collect any relic or object he supposes to be a relic from the site of discovery, except for the purpose of protecting it and reporting the discovery.

In 1986 I noticed that some island inhabitants were in the habit of digging up the foundations of the ruins (fig. 15-1) for the stone, which they used to build new, albeit less elegant, houses (figs. 15-2, 15-3, 15-4). On my return to Dar es Salaam, I reported the matter to the relevant antiquities officers, but little has been done to stop this destruction, despite the fact that, many years before, elaborate plans had been laid out for the conservation of this important site as a protected area (Mturi 1982:110) and for mobilizing and educating the inhabitants of the island concerning the value of conserving their heritage.

Another disparity in the official policy and the management of the heritage resources at Kilwa Kisiwani concerned the trade in protected objects. We were approached by people who wanted to sell us protected objects, especially old Arab coins and beads (fig. 15-5). Ironically, they did so in the presence of the antiquities official who had accompanied the field school, apparently to monitor its activities and movements. We did not buy the objects, but other people, especially tourists, did so with an ambivalent antiquities official looking on in utter amusement.

Site Deterioration and Destruction at Bagamoyo

The coastal town of Bagamoyo grew and prospered during the second half of the nineteenth century because of the expansion of the trade in ivory and slaves which was encouraged and supported by the Sultan of Oman, who shifted his capital from Muscat to Zanzibar in 1840. The growth of trade and commerce resulted in the proliferation of traders, merchants, craftsmen, and laborers, and following a population boom, building activities increased considerably and resulted in edifices built primarily by Arab and Indian traders. European traders, explorers, and missionaries and finally German colonization followed. Between 1889 and 1897 a number of buildings were constructed based on the Swahili traditions of the coast but with recognizable Teutonic elements (Mturi 1982:113).

Most of the buildings situated in the old quarter of Bagamoyo near the shore have survived. In addition to their historic and architectural significance, they form a distinctive townscape with two-storied buildings fronting narrow and sometimes winding streets. Following the shift of the capital of German East African from Bagamoyo to Dar es Salaam in 1891 and the subsequent growth of Dar es Salaam as the main port and industrial and commercial capital, Bagamoyo was unable to maintain its prosperity. It declined and stagnated socially and economically, resulting in the neglect of most of the houses and the under-utilization and/or total abandonment of the buildings.

During the mid-1970s, an ad hoc committee was formed under the auspices of the Antiquities Department to look into the possibility of conserving Bagamoyo. The committee recommended that the whole historical center of Bagamoyo should be protected and preserved as a living historic town. This recommendation was endorsed by the highest policy-making authorities at both the political and the governmental level. Legal, administrative, and technical measures were formulated, although the conservation and management of the historic town did not begin until 1988, when the plan received funding from the Tanzanian government, the Ford Foundation, and the Norwegian Agency for International Development.

I visited Bagamoyo a number of times between 1969 and 1991, and as far as I can recall, the situation had changed very little over that time despite the substantial government and donor funding. For example, small trees growing on walls were

Figure 15-1. The ruins of Kilwa Kisiwani, a UNESCO World Heritage Site, are being mined by local residents for coral rag, which was the ancient building material. Note in the left foreground a pit where materials have been removed.

Figure 15-2. The ancient coral rag after being removed from the walls of ruins is then used to build local mud and wattle homes, as illustrated in this photograph.

Figure 15-3. A newly constructed home, with the ancient coral rag clearly in evidence. This home belongs to an official of the Antiquities Unit of the Republic of Tanzania. Official participation in the destruction of the ancient Kilwa ruins is an index of the crisis in failures to manage the cultural heritage in Tanzania.

Figure 15-4. An older home in the contemporary community at Kilwa Kisiwani, showing that the tradition of using ancient walls from the ruins dates back many years.

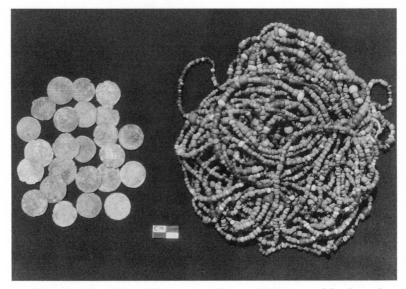

Figure 15-5. A visitor to Kilwa can purchase ancient coins and beads, such as these pictured here (photographed while documenting the destruction of Kilwa). These artifacts have been looted from the Kilwa ruins with impunity under the scrutiny of government representatives charged with cultural heritage management.

the rule rather than the exception. Young trees, especially of the fig type, which has an aggressive root system, soon grow into large trees. The roots attack the coralline rock-and-lime plastered walls, quickly pulling the walls down.

Hence, despite external and internal central government support, little has been accomplished in the conservation of this historic town. The local press has taken up the matter with the responsible government agency. *Sunday News* staff writer Balinagwe Mwambungu (1987) wrote: "A lot of noise has been made about Bagamoyo and the ministry responsible for antiquities asked for external help to conserve the old town. How far has the project gone is not the subject under discussion. But it would be interesting to hear from the authorities concerned how they have faired in this project." The availability of funds does not necessarily guarantee more efficient management of cultural heritage resources: Good planning and commitment are also essential.

The Deterioration and Destruction of Other Important
Heritage Sites in Tanzania

Because the antiquities legislation does not require developers to conduct heritage impact assessment surveys and mitigation measures prior to construction, a staggering amount of heritage resources have been destroyed in the course of development activities, especially since the 1970s. During this period, major construction works involving railways, trunk roads, dams, pipelines, airports, large farms, harbor expansion projects, urban growth, and industry took place in Tan-

Figure 15-6. Visiting scholars gaze dejectedly at the wretched conditions at the oldest habitation site documented for prehistoric times, the DK site of Olduvai Gorge. The artifacts once on display have been scattered and grass is growing in the display area. Note the missing roof, removed by vandals five years before this 1993 photograph.

zania. On rare occasions, significant sites were located by chance, although this is the exception rather than the rule. This situation represents yet another disparity between the legal provisions and the management of the heritage.

Nature also takes a toll on many of the country's heritage sites, including the unique footprint site of Laetoli, which was colonized by a growth of acacia trees. The rock paintings of central Tanzania are yet another example of the disparity between official policy and management. A UNESCO expert sent to study the state of central Tanzanian rock art recommended that the rock art be placed on the World Heritage List, thereby attracting external advice and funding. All that was needed was the completion of application forms for listing by the responsible agency. Almost a decade has elapsed since the recommendations were made, but the authorities have yet to complete the requisite forms (see Mturi, this volume). Is this not a case of what an article in *African Events* (March 1993) characterizes as "Official Lethargy"?

Perhaps another case of official lethargy can be seen in the destruction of the DK site at Olduvai Gorge. In 1989 vandals stole the corrugated iron sheets from the shed that had for many years protected what was billed in the *Guiness Book of Records* as the oldest human structure in the world. As of late 1994, nothing had been done to restore protection or to reconstruct the site, which was destroyed by vandals cooking their food on it and by exposure to the elements (fig. 15–6).

In the case of Olduvai, arguments have been advanced that the destruction there is not a simple case of vandalism but that those responsible for the destruction were making a political statement. One theory holds that the Masai have lived in Olduvai since time immemorial and that the word *olduvai* is a corruption of the Masai term *oldupai*, which refers to a type of wild sisal that grows in the area. For many years, the Masai had grazed their cattle around the gorge, often taking their herds to drink at its bottom. According to antiquities regulations, the Masai are forbidden to take their cattle into the gorge, but under the regulations governing the Ngorongoro Conservation Area, which also administers Olduvai, the Masai are allowed to take their cattle into the gorge. This disparity in the conservation policies of the two heritage-management organizations has led to frustration on the part of some Olduvai Masai, who think the Antiquities Unit regulations constitute an infringement on their traditional grazing rights. It was allegedly in an attempt to externalize their feeling of frustration that some anonymous Masai tribesmen vandalized the BK and DK sites at Olduvai.

CONCLUSION

Although Tanzania has a legal framework for the protection of its historical heritage, this legislation is rendered almost meaningless by the institution that is supposed to enforce it. Thus, the existence of protective legislation is not enough. Trained manpower, an enlightened population, and, above all, an active and committed leadership are clearly essential if the disparity between official policy and heritage management practices in Africa is to be corrected.

REFERENCES

Anati, E. "The State of Research in Rock Art: The Rock Art of Tanzania and the East African Sequence." *Bollettino del Centro Camuno di Studi Preistorici* vol. 23 (1986):15–68.

Brown, T. W. "Bagamoyo: An Historical Introduction." *Tanzania Notes and Records* 71 (1970):69–83.

Chittick, H. N. *A Guide to the Ruins of Kilwa with Some Notes on Other Antiquities in the Region.* Dar es Salaam: National Culture and Antiquities Division, Ministry of Community Development and National Culture, 1965.

Garlake, P. S. *Early Islamic Architecture of the East African Coast.* Memoir no. 1 of the British Institute of History and Archaeology in East Africa. Oxford: Oxford University Press, 1966.

Mturi, A. A. "The Designation and Management of Conservation Areas in Tanzania with Case Studies of Kilwa Kisiwani, Bagamoyo, and Dar es Salaam." Unpublished diploma dissertation in conservation studies, University of York: England, 1982.

———. "Top-Down or Down-Top Planning and Management: Public Awareness and Involvement in the Conservation of Historic Towns, Buildings, Rock Art Sites in Tanzania." Paper presented at the Carter Lecture Series, Gainesville, Florida, 1993.

Mwambungu, B. "Historical Sites Disregarded." *Sunday News.* 1 March 1987.

Schmidt, P. R., and D. H. Avery. "Complex Iron Smelting and Prehistoric Culture in Tanzania." *Science* 201 (1978): 1085–89.

Tuttle, R. H. "The Pitted Pattern of Laetoli Feet: Who or What Walked on the Ancient African Plains?" *Natural History* 3, no. 90 (1990):61–65.

16

KENYA'S DESTRUCTION OF THE SWAHILI CULTURAL HERITAGE

C. M. KUSIMBA

Kenya's population growth rate is 4.1 percent and doubles the population every twenty years. The 1979 population census indicated that Kenya had a population of about 21 million people. The Kenya government population figures for the 1989 census indicated that the population then was between 28 and 30 million. More than 50 percent of the country's population is under the age of fifteen. Only 17 percent of Kenya's land is arable, and the country has few valuable minerals (see Harden 1990).

Population pressure threatens to spill over to rangeland areas that hold Kenya's world-famous wildlife sanctuaries. These national parks and game reserves are Kenya's leading source of foreign exchange. Because tourism earns more foreign exchange for the country than both coffee and tea combined (Opala 1993b), the Kenya government has aggressively expanded its tourist industry (see also Wilson and Omar, this volume). Thus Kenyans have found themselves at the mercy of global economic trends. Tourism provides short-run benefits from small investments and creates jobs. Various studies have shown that development initiatives aimed at Kenya's high economic potential areas tend to be socially destructive and culturally alienating to the areas' inhabitants (e.g. Rigby 1992). One example of such development initiatives is being carried out on the coast with culturally and economically disastrous results for the local coastal populations. The destruction of Swahili cultural heritage and identity has been deliberate and has been supported by the administrative and political establishments.[1]

This chapter has five sections. The first introduces the world of the Swahili of Kenya and discusses the ecological heritage of the Kenya coast and its role in the evolution of the Swahili cultural heritage. The second examines perceptions of Swahili cultural history that have contributed to the current practices of destruction of the Swahili heritage. The Third examines the primary role of the National Museums of Kenya as guardian of the Swahili cultural heritage both in principle and in practice. The fourth uses several cases to illustrate the various forms of destruction of the Swahili heritage. The final section discusses the relationship between heritage management programs and government development initiatives in Kenya. The chapter's conclusion reminds us about the importance of preserving the Swahili cultural heritage and warns us not to be the generation to complete the plunder of Africa's past.

THE SWAHILI COAST OF KENYA

Swahili peoples have traditionally inhabited the eastern and southeastern African coast as well as adjacent islands in the Indian Ocean, including the Comoros and northern Madagascar. Their language, Kiswahili, is a Bantu language that is now spoken by many people in East and Central Africa. It is a national language of Kenya and Tanzania and is presently taught in some European and American universities. This essay concerns only the Swahili people who live on the Kenya coast and the adjacent islands of Wasini, Funzi, Mombasa, an the Lamu Archipelago. They speak Kiswahili as their first language and culturally identify themselves as being Waswahili, although they prefer to identify themselves with the town or village from which they hail (Allen 1993; Middleton 1992; Nurse and Spear 1985; Wilson 1980).

About four hundred archaeological sites, many of which have coral mosques, houses, and defensive walls, are known on the East African coast (Horton 1988). More than eighty such sites are known on the Kenya coast, and others are still being found (Abungu 1993; Wilson 1978, 1980). These sites have collectively been linked with ancestors of the peoples who presently inhabit much of the coastline, including the Mijikenda, the Segeju, and the Swahili (Fosbrook 1957; Gillman 1944; Kusimba 1993). Ethnographic and archaeological evidence supports the view that the ancestors of present-day Swahili may have built many of the archaeological settlements on the coast.

The coastal historical and monumental ruins were built beginning in A.D. 800 by the ancestors of the present-day Swahili (Horton 1987; Middleton 1987, 1992; Nurse and Spear 1985; Pouwels 1987). The ruins include mosques, elite residences, stone houses, dressed wells, wall enclosures, and defensive town walls, all built of cut coral and coral rag in lime and mud mortar (Fawcett and LaViolette 1990). Historical and archaeological evidence confirms that Swahili settlements developed gradually from small fishing, farming, and ironworking settlements (Nurse and Spear 1985). It is now known that most of the sites were also filled with humbler dwellings made of unfired mud bricks and parked clay on wooden frames (Horton 1988; Killick and Kusimba 1992; Middleton 1992; Pouwels 1987). The spatial organization of the settlements and the design of the houses have exhibited continuity up to the present both in Swahili towns and in non-Swahili towns in the vicinity of the coast (Kusimba 1993; Wilson 1982).

Most people on the Kenyan coast are Muslims. The existence of Islam has tentatively been traced to the settlement of Shanga on Pate Island on the northern Kenyan coast. Horton has uncovered a mosque at Shanga that was built and rebuilt through five phases. The earliest phase, Shanga I, has been dated to A.D. 810 on the basis of "fragments of eggshell wares, Sassanian Islamic pottery, and sherds of Chinese stoneware, Dusun, Changsha, and a rim of Yue greenware" (Horton 1988:311). On the basis of this evidence, the expansion of mosque size through time, and mosque distribution supported by written records by the local intelligentsia and foreign travelers, it is now known that Islam was established on the Swahili coast relatively early but was a religion of a minority population over much of the time. The conversion of most African people to Islam was a slow process of compromise and adaptation to fit Islam into an African context (Mazrui 1980).

PERCEPTIONS OF SWAHILI CULTURAL HISTORY THAT INFORM PRESENT DESTRUCTION

One common misconception about the Kenyan coast is that the Swahili are not its legitimate inhabitants. Other groups consider them *wageni*, immigrants or visitors who may have settled the coast but whose original homeland is elsewhere. Nothing could be further from the truth: In terms of seniority, the ancestors of the Swahili have been in Kenya longer than many other ethnic groups in Kenya. A radiocarbon date of a crucible steel specimen from Galu dated to A.D. 630–890 suggests that the ancestors of present-day Swahili and other coastal communities settled the land and exploited its resources many centuries before the ancestors of so-called original Kenyans set foot on the coast (Kusimba 1993; Kusimba, Killick, and Creswell 1994).

The other misconception—a most damaging one—is that most Kenyans and visitors to the coast perceive the Swahili as different from other Kenyans in both cultural and racial terms (Allen 1976a, 1976b, 1979, 1993). These views arise from a misread past of the Swahili people. A recent article about Malindi (Mwandam 1991) reads:

> The town's history goes back to the 9th century. In the 13th century, it was inhabited mostly by Arabs whose dominance was not taken by the locals lying down. Also, fierce battles broke out between different Arab tribes as they tried to oust each other from the region. There were also the Portuguese, Ottoman Turks and the fierce Wazimba who had swept up the east coast from the southern African region leaving a trail of blood.

In talking to many Kenyans, both in the United States and in Kenya, I have been surprised that a significant percentage espouse Mwandam's views.

In Kenya, most people get their information from newspapers, which often profess personal opinions with little or no empirical basis, but which are nevertheless persuasive. Misconceptions about Swahili cultural roots and identity have significantly influenced government policy toward the coast, especially with regard to Muslim Swahili (see, for example, *Daily Nation* 1993b; Majtenyi 1993). The blame for these misconceptions about the Swahili, their history, and their cultural heritage rests squarely with the work of scientists—primarily linguists, anthropologists, archaeologists, and historians—and the ignorance of the Kenyan elite, including teachers, journalists, and even top government civil servants working among the Swahili, who are the primary public policy makers and implementors. Such officials have callously endorsed programs that are antithetical to Swahili communities' basic needs and harmony.

The work that found its way into the Kenyan curriculum and that many believe to be truly representative of Swahili cultural history was based on research carried out during the colonial period. This work served colonial interests and was based on an imagined and invented Swahili past (see Hobsbawm and Ranger 1992; Mudimbe 1988). Yet this work is still taught to Kenyan schoolchildren, many of whom do not pursue history at higher levels. The Swahili example thus demonstrates that once a falsified past finds a niche in popular literature, the damage caused is often very difficult to undo.

THE NATIONAL MUSEUMS OF KENYA AS GUARDIANS OF THE SWAHILI CULTURAL HERITAGE

The National Museums of Kenya (NMK), founded in 1927, is one of the most important research institutions in Kenya.

> [NMK] is a statutory body with legislative authority to regulate all archaeological and paleontological sites and monuments in Kenya. As the national repository of prehistoric, cultural, and biological specimens, the National Museums falls under the umbrella of Ministry of Home Affairs and National Heritage. The National Museums currently employs over 600 staff and has an operating budget of Kshs 50 million. The central government provides 28 percent and the rest is made up from revenues, donations, and project support. (*Weekly Review* 1990:33)

According to this *Weekly Review* report (the accuracy of which was verified by Omar Bwana, deputy director of the NMK), the NMK has seven research departments. The report details functions of both research and nonresearch departments. The report is vague on NMK's role in the conservation of sites and monuments:

> The National Museums of Kenya also plays an important conservation role in environmental, monumental, architectural, and material culture conservation. Several sites have been gazetted and restored, the most significant of these being the 18th century Lamu Fort which until 1984 had served as a prison. The historic Lamu town is already declared and gazetted as a national monument and a similar program is underway in Old Town Mombasa.

Kenya, despite being world-famous for its contributions in the study of the evolution of humankind, has not ratified the 1970 UNESCO Convention on the Means of Prohibiting and Preventing the Illicit Import, Export, and Transfer of Ownership of Cultural Property (see Papageorge Kouroupas, Prott in this volume). In 1995 the staff of the Antiquities, Sites, and Monuments Department numbered less than ten in all the museums in the country. The coast had three ICCROM-trained conservators, who were stationed in Mombasa. The conservation department had neither support staff nor a departmental vehicle; consequently, its activities were confined to laboratory conservation work and visits to nearby sites, usually those that are considered significant sources of revenue for the museums.

The Kenya Coastal Museums

The activities of the Kenya Coastal Museums are distributed among four departments: the curator's office, education, archaeology, and conservation. There are two museums on the Kenya coast, the Fort Jesus and the Lamu museums. Both are headed by curators who ensure that all the archaeological sites in their area are systematically surveyed, mapped, and protected and that all ethnographic and archaeological material is properly inventoried, curated, stored, and exhibited. They see to it not only that visiting research associates get access to resources and materials available at the museum but also that their research is in league with the objectives of the NMK, one of which is to promote the cultural and national heritage of Kenya through research on the cultural, social, technological, and political achievements of its people. The curators ensure that all museum visitors, both foreign and national, are well received, their questions answered, and their suggestions taken into consideration. They ensure that the material culture housed at the museums is jealously protected from piracy, especially by art dealers; and they ensure that knowledge is spread through exhibitions and displays.

As guardians of Kenya's cultural heritage, the curator's duty is to ensure that all archaeological sites and excavated artifacts are protected from vandalism by the treasure hunters who, in league with art dealers, are operating an international multimillion-dollar business (but see chapters in this volume by Brent, Jegede, McIntosh, Nkwi, and Sidibé).

The archaeology department is the main research section of the Kenya Coastal Museums. Headed by a resident archaeologist, the department conducts research into various aspects of coastal cultures; it also focuses on the dissemination of cultural information, the promotion of culture, and the development of culture (Odak 1988:150). Compared to the colonial period, archaeological research carried out by the department since the 1970s has been minimal.[2]

The present resident archaeologist is Dr. George Abungu, who took office in 1990. He has a technical staff of nine, who are high school graduates and have received no specialized archaeological training but are reported to be highly skilled and trained.[3] Abungu repeated Tom Wilson's 1978-80 survey of the entire coast to assess the state of preservation of the archaeological sites and monuments (Abungu and Katana 1991; Abungu 1991). Realizing the importance of keeping a record and aware that the successful conservation of most coastal sites was like chasing a mirage, Abungu collaborated with the Film Department of the Ministry of Information and Broadcasting to document most of the sites along the coast (Abungu 1991). Abungu's project results were horrifying: Sites had been demolished, had been bought and privatized, or had simply disappeared. Some have been destroyed since the museum launched this survey program.

The conservation department's duties include the inspection of sites and monuments and ensuring that gazetted sites and monuments are properly protected and that all ethnographic and archaeological equipment is well treated and stored. The department reconstructs archaeological artifacts for exhibition and regularly monitors their condition. Conservators work with museum archaeologists by advising them on the treatment and conservation of artifacts in the field.

The Fort Jesus conservation department recently completed the reconstruction and treatment of artifacts from the excavation of the *Antonio de Tanna*, a Portuguese ship that was sunk by Omani Arabs when they took Fort Jesus from the Portuguese in 1698 (Mwadime 1991; Sassoon 1978).

Ideally, museum conservators should visit sites and monuments in the area to ensure that they are well preserved and protected from vandals as well as from natural deterioration due to fallen trees and branches or to roots that damage standing ruins. In practice, they do so only when the resident archaeologist is visiting the site to conduct research. Only one conservator knows all the coastal sites, and this is because he participated in Wilson's 1978–80 project and has been codirecting the recently completed project (Abungu and Katana 1991). The other two conservators are involved primarily in the treatment of archaeological artifacts, in particular artifacts from the Mombasa wreck excavations of 1977 and 1980 (Mwadime 1991).

THE DESTRUCTION OF SWAHILI CULTURAL HERITAGE

Between 1989 and 1992 I carried out anthropological fieldwork among coastal fishers, boat builders, blacksmiths, and elders with the view of understanding the social and economic context of Swahili crafts. The project covered the four districts of Kwale, Mombasa, Kilifi, and Lamu. I was unable to conduct research in the Tana River District and mainland Lamu because of widespread banditry.[4] The cases that follow represent my personal experiences of the destruction of the Swahili heritage during the project.

Case 1: Appropriation of Swahili Land through Illegal Land
Transactions—Wasini Island

Wasini is located several hundred meters off the southern Kenyan coast in Kwale District. Two communities live on this island: the Wavumba of Wasini village and the Wachifundi of Mukwiro village. A. C. Hollis (1900) collected oral traditions of Wavumba, and W. F. McKay (1975) visited the island and reportedly found thirteenth- to sixteenth-century ceramics. Wilson surveyed Wasini and reported that the present town was probably settled in the early eighteenth century, when Diwani Ruga moved there with his people from Vumba Kuu (1980:6).

I collected oral traditions from Mohamed Bin Abubakr in 1989. Abubakr was then ninety years old and very frail. (He died in 1990). According to Abubakr, most people on the island of Wasini were farmers, mangrove harvesters, fishermen, or sailors. During the mid-nineteenth century, when Omani Arabs ruled the East African coast, large coconut plantations were established on the mainland along most of the coast. Once the Arabs established settlements on the coast, they controlled most of the economic and political spheres of the society. The local elite, including that of Wasini Island, began to lose their power to the Arabs. Some became employed as caretakers of the expanding Arab economic empire. The late nineteenth century also saw a considerable influx of Indian immigrants to the coast, many of whom started business enterprises.

At the turn of the century, most people on the Kenyan coast were employed in Arab or Indian business concerns—plantation agriculture, fishing, sailing, and long-distance trade in the interior. According to Abubakr, sailing was most popular because side businesses would provide enough money to set up other businesses or to pay off debts. Fishing was for local consumption and export to the Persian Gulf, the Arabian Peninsula, and the Indian subcontinent. For example, a well-planned and successful voyage to Oman was enough to change one from a pauper to a landowner. It was rare for local people to organize caravans and voyages because Arabs collaborated with Indian financiers to deny Swahili and Giriama credit facilities. Swahili, Segeju, and Mijikenda merchants ended up losing their cargo on the high seas or to pirates. When this happened they could be forced to sell their property—land, houses, or slaves. This trend resulted in the loss of political and economic power to foreigners, mainly Arab and Indian.

Ironically, Abubakr lamented that Arab and Indian merchants no longer come to the coast in large numbers. He pointed out four reasons for the decline in Indian and Arab dhow trade on the East African coast. First, tariffs on international trade were introduced after independence. Customs duties were imposed on foreign vessels reaching Kenyan ports. Immigration regulations required that all foreigners have valid visas to enter the country, and most sailors from the Indian and Arab countries did not have passports and thus were discouraged.

Second, the overthrow of the Zanzibar sultanate in 1964 and the merging of Tanganyika, Zanzibar, and Pemba to form a united nation of Tanzania increased anti-Arab sentiments in East Africa. Nationalists emphasized the Arab role in enslaving African people and the Arab alliance with European colonialists. These anti-Arab sentiments discouraged foreign Muslim merchants from coming to East Africa.

Third, Kenya and Tanzania have cracked down on illegal maritime trade. The governments' ban on the export of ivory, rhinoceros horns, cat skins, and ostrich eggshells and the introduction of quotas in the harvesting of mangrove fueled the decline.

Finally, the discovery of oil in the Middle East resulted in the modernization of the economy in Arab countries. They presently prefer steel from Western European countries to East African mangroves for house construction. In fact, this newfound wealth has reversed fortunes; the people of Kenya and Tanzania today travel to Arab countries to seek wealth, much as Arabs previously came to East Africa.

The major transformations on Wasini Island have been directly related to changes in ownership of land. According to Abubakr, there was little need to look after cattle, goats, and sheep in the past. People needed only to ensure that all livestock had fresh water. Since the 1970s, Wasini has seen an influx of new settlers and an exodus of natives from the island. Settlement and displacement followed the government land adjudication program of 1968–69. Two hotels on the island have attracted newcomers in search of employment opportunities.[5] It is apparent that recent changes in the land tenure system have destabilized the community. Residents now have title deeds to their property and can do as they please with it. Some, as expected, have sold their land to developers eager to exploit the tourist potential of the island. Others feel that they have been unfairly displaced from ancestral lands by the program.

Traditional farming practices have declined because of privatization. Most of the land bought by outsiders is lying fallow. When Wasini and Funzi Islands and most of Kwale District were surveyed by the government in 1968–69, most of the land, previously referred to as crown land although it had owners, was given to outsiders.[6] Outsiders failed to understand the traditional system of land tenure and land use practices in the area and chose to introduce new methods of land utilization. Consequently, even as land lies fallow, most of the native inhabitants are either landless idlers or wage laborers in fishing and mangrove cutting.[7] Some natives have moved to other villages, like Vanga, Shimoni, and Gazi, and to Mombasa, where they live in poverty.

The land adjudication program at Wasini was conducted very unfairly, as it pitted the island clans against each other. Independence brought ill feelings against those perceived as foreigners and especially those who had received preferential treatment during colonial times. Consequently, many descendants of Arab parents found themselves isolated. The plight of the family of Abdulrahaman Saggaf Alawy represents only the tip of the iceberg. Since 1968 Abdulrahaman Saggaf, the head of his clan, and fifty-six others have been involved in a land dispute case. Having been displaced, they now live scattered among relatives in Vanga, Shimoni, Gazi, and Mombasa. I read more than one hundred letters that Saggaf and his displaced relatives wrote to relevant administrative structures in the country, including the president. An example is the letter addressed to the provincial commissioner, Coast Province, dated April 3, 1986, in which Saggaf provides a detailed history of grievances while also passionately lamenting the illegal land grabbing and the failure of the government to answer legitimate complaints.[8]

The letter to the provincial commissioner was never answered! One of the officers who was allegedly involved in the acquisition of land on Wasini Island was the district commissioner of Kwale District, from whom these people expected justice. Saggaf objected to the development of plot 435 and received a court order preventing it. The commissioner's letter of February 17, 1988 (ref no. PNM/1/17), to the land registrar in Kwale reads:

Objection to Caution

I have decided to raise an objection to the caution placed on my parcel Kwale/Wasini Island/435 by Mr. Abdulrahaman Saggaf Alawy of P.O. Box 81402 MOMBASA.

1) The Adjudication Act is clear on the procedures of lodging appeals under the Adjudication Act which Mr. Alawy does not appear to have complied with.

2) The person who sold me the parcel Mr. Feisal [the area chief and the commissioner's subordinate] had been issued with the title deed to his parcel back in 1984 and there was nothing in the Land Registry to indicate that there was any outstanding dispute when I bought the parcel [but see following letter].

3) I do not understand the justification of the caution and the grounds of placing it years after the adjudication work was completed and Titles issued.

4) If there is any dispute it should be between Mr. Alawy and Mr. Feisal who sold me the land.

5) The transaction of the sale and sub division was done legally according to the relevant laws.

6) I was not informed as is required under the Law when caution was placed until I got information from other sources from copies written by some people from Wasini calling the transaction illegal.

District Commissioner, Kwale [Name Withheld]

Although this letter was written by the commissioner as a private citizen, I find it disturbing that he used government stationery and signed it in his official position. This action confirms the extent to which government officials will go in abusing the powers allocated to them as civil servants. By using his position, the commissioner affirms his power vis-à-vis his accuser.

Letter no. LA.5/1/25 vol. IV/45 dated March 21, 1981, written by F. R. S. Onyango on behalf of the director of land adjudication in Nairobi to Nassir Mohamed Kiboga and copied to the land adjudication officer in Kwale and to the provincial land adjudication officer in Mombasa, not only confirms that the district commissioner's defense is falsified but also shows the extent to which corruption in government is tolerated (see also jegede, Schmidt, this volume).

Illegal Sale of Land in Kidimu-Wasini-Majoreni

I refer to your letter dated 15/10/80 and regret the delay in replying it. I have to inform you that the process of land adjudication in Kidimu, Wasini, and Majoreni is carried out strictly under the provisions of the Land Adjudication Act, Chapter 284. This Act lays down clearly the procedure to be followed when one is claiming an interest in land and when one is aggrieved by the manner a demarcation/recording officer, the adjudication officer committee, the arbitration board or the adjudication officer has dealt with one's claim to that interest. It is important that the procedure is adhered to by the claimants to interests in land, as there is no other way of going about the matter. Land complaints arising from the procedure of land adjudication cannot be solved outside the provisions of the Land Adjudication Act aforesaid.

Yours faithfully, F. R. S. Onyango

A letter, ref no. 116/011/vol.II/143, from J. K. Kaguthi dated December 16, 1980, on behalf of the permanent secretary of the provincial administration and of internal security, office of the president, to whom Mkuku Ahamed had appealed after having exhausted all provincial channels, reads:

Illegal Acquisition and Sale of Land in Pongwe Location

I acknowledge yours dated 7th December, 1980 addressed to the head of Civil Service on the above Subject. I note that your complaint is against land transactions in your location by some officials and politicians in Kwale District. Please do raise your complaints with the Provincial Commissioner Coast for advice and necessary action.

Yours faithfully, J. K. Kaguthi

It seems unlikely that such land claims will ever be adequately addressed in view of the emerging evidence that the then provincial commissioner of Coast

Province was himself allegedly involved in questionable land transactions in the area (*Daily Nation*, November 11, 1992).

Case 2: Illegal Acquisition of the Mayungu Fishing Camp from Local Fishermen for Tourism Development

Mayungu is a small fishing village of 150 people eight miles south of Malindi along the beach. My first visit to Mayungu occurred on December 24, 1991. I sought to collect data on fishing techniques, the tool kit, the types of fish caught, and the fishing way of life. Most of the houses in the village were temporary structures of makuti and poles. Mayungu fishers come from all over the coast, from Lamu to Shimoni and as far as Kisumu in western Kenya. Most of the fishermen are migrant workers, but six are permanent settlers of Mayungu: Faquik Kahale Shekuwe, Lali Swaleh Lali, Khaled Bwanah Mbere, Omar Kombo Fadhili, Mohamed Athman Rehi, and Lali Musa Abdalla. When I arrived at Mayungu, I found the fishermen anxious and in the midst of a land dispute with Omar Khamisi Balleth, a businessman in Malindi. According to the villagers, Balleth had bought the village from Stephen Wachira Mathenge of Nairobi and was planning to sell it to an Italian hotel developer who would build a hotel worth U.S. $10 million.

I returned to Mayungu on January 11, 1991, to meet Faquik Kahale. The house in which the Kahales live is built of mud and poles and thatched with makuti. It is strengthened in the corners with coral beams. The other approximately thirty houses in the village were also built of makuti. There were two permanent structures in the village, the mosque and the fisheries department office, where fishermen pay their taxes and get their licenses. It also serves as a collection center for fish-buying companies.

The village is devoted exclusively to year-round fishing. The village's daily catch provides a large proportion of the seafood sold in Malindi. Given Mayungu's proximity to Malindi and its rough edges, both the entrepreneurially minded and the ecologically minded liked the village, but for very different reasons. An Englishman called Mr. Philip established a tourist restaurant, Sun and Fun, nearby. Tourists could get away from Malindi and at the same time visit an African village next door. According to Faquik, Mr. Philip was friendly and was helping them to ensure that the village was protected. Mr. Philip had even helped Faquik and his colleagues secure the services of a lawyer. In a 1992 interview, Faquik recalled:

> I came to Mayungu from Kizingitini, Lamu, in 1955 with some people [*wazee*] to fish.[] I decided to bring my family along to Mayungu. This was in 1959. Mayungu was then a forest. Here I set up camp and continued fishing as well as clearing the forest for building a house and for a garden to plant food crops.[]
> During the last thirty-two years we succeeded, through hard work and devotion, in making this place our home. Our livelihood is derived from the sea. [] Our future and that of our children was assured until two years ago [1990]. [] In 1989 we heard a rumor that the land we occupied belonged to one Mathenge [Stephen Mathenge Wachira] of Nairobi. This rumor came as a surprise because we had lived in this plot and developed it for more than thirty years and never seen anyone claiming that it belonged to them. [] It was an outrage!

Recently [1991] Omar Khamisi bin Balleth came to the village and claimed that he had bought this land from Mathenge. He then ordered us out of what he claimed was his private property. We refused to leave . . . this land belongs to us and is our very lifeline. We derive all our livelihood from the sea. To evict us from this—our home—would be tantamount to disconnecting our lifeline. [] In the meantime we are prepared to fight over this land in a court of law. []

The rest of us have refused to be coerced into moving because to move would be to accept the verdict that we are squatters. How can anyone be a squatter on one's own motherland? To leave the beach would be suicidal. All our boats are on the beach. We clean our fishes, repair our boats, and hold our celebrations and ceremonies on the beach. It would be unthinkable to leave this our home. []

Over the years we have witnessed many fishermen rendered jobless and homeless because of allocation of beach properties to private holdings in the name of progress. What sort of progress denies local people the opportunity to earn a decent livelihood from their natural resources? We have heard that Omar Balleth has plans to sell this property to an Italian developer for ten million shillings. The Italian has bought that plot over there but since it does not have a beach, he wants to buy this plot and put up a multimillion shilling hotel. Now, tell me how we shall continue to fish here once this process is finalized. [] We are prepared to fight for this place because this is our life. []⁹

Faquik further explained that Balleth was biding his time and using the local authorities, including the chief and district officer, to intimidate the villagers. The police had visited the village, harassing, detaining, and interrogating the residents. The area chief, an accomplice of Balleth, had threatened to evict them, arguing that the land did not belong to them and that they were squatting on private property. Gifts and promises of retirement benefits to some villagers were weakening village solidarity. Ouko and Ghali Musa had already given up the fight and moved to the houses across the road.

The Mayungu and Wasini cases outlined here are but the tip of the iceberg. Government officials have collaborated with local and international businesspeople to take over all the open spaces in the country under the guise of national development and job and foreign-exchange generation. The trouble is that most of the so-called open spaces are also historical sites and monuments. When developers acquire land, they usually fence it and put in cottages, restaurants, and hotels to cater to the tourist market. To develop the land, much of the vegetation is cleared and the ruins are demolished (see also Karoma; Mturi; Wilson and Omar; jegede, this volume). The NMK's Antiquities, Sites, and Monuments Department never learns about these reports until it is too late. Also, since the purpose of the department has not been clearly defined, the responsibility of protecting monuments is often given to the Archaeology Department.¹⁰ The following case illustrates the role of the NMK.

Case 3: The Destruction of the Historical Site of Galu in Kwale District

Between October and November 1991, I carried out an archaeological excavation at the settlement of Galu, Kwale District. I sought to investigate the development of iron-making technology on the Swahili coast. My excavations focused on a locality with large amounts of iron slag, tuyeres, and low-fired clay pottery sherds. The area was located by the western gate of the site and is now known to be the earliest smelting site on the Kenya coast, having yielded a calibrated radiocarbon date of A.D. 630–890 (Kusimba 1993; Kusimba, Killick, and Creswell 1994).

Galu is a rectangular stone-walled enclosure of about five to six acres. It has two gates, located on the eastern and western ends, with a large well located in the center. The settlement of Galu is a coral-enclosed village on the coast of southern Kenya and northern Tanzania of the type that used to be called "Maasai walls." Gillman (1944) noted that the walls of the enclosures were between 2 to 2.5 meters high. These settlements were presumably built by the Segeju and Digo to protect themselves from raids by the Maasai between the seventeenth and nineteenth centuries. Galu was one of these settlements. Similar settlements may have included Tumbe, Munje, Moa, Zingibari, Petugiza, Kigirini, Manza, Tawalani, Kichalikani, Monga, Kwale, Kizingani, Chomgoliani, Mvuhuni, Gomani, and Mtimbani (Fosbrook 1957:32).

When I began research in 1991, Galu was covered by scrub and bush, with thick overgrown grass. A 1971 aerial photograph shows that much of the area from the shoreline was forested. There were no habitation structures in the vicinity of the site. Indeed, the nearest hamlet was Mwabungu, three kilometers away. In general, the immediate area around Galu is still an uninhabited area waiting to be exploited. In truth much of the area has been surveyed by the government and is probably privately owned.

While I was engaged in excavations of Galu, a private company, Zimmerlin and Company, based in Mombasa, was surveying the area. The surveyors had knocked off a section of the northern wall to permit their work. I brought the matter to Dr. Abungu's attention when he visited the site. Such incidents make it clear that interest in the development potential of the area is increasing; this development will affect archaeological and historical sites like Galu.

I also met a man cutting down the forest in the site to make charcoal, which he sold to the tourist hotels nearby. He had been engaged in this work near Galu for twelve years. According to him, it takes two large trees that have probably taken fifty years to mature to build a charcoal furnace that will eventually yield ten charcoal bags of about thirty-five or forty kilograms each. This man cut down trees at the rate of two every week; at such a pace he would fell 104 mature trees each year for 1,040 sacks of charcoal. From this he earns a total of Kshs 52,000. Considering that this man has been living at Galu since 1980, he might have felled a total of 1,248 mature trees, some of which were probably more than one hundred years old, for a total of 12,480 bags of charcoal. For this labor he would earn Kshs 624,000. I cannot explain why this respectable sum of money is at odds with the indigent condition of this man and his family.

The destruction of the forest in the enclosure has been systematic, fast, and professionally executed. After observing this man at work over a period of three days, I could not help but respect him. I thought that in another six months there would be hardly any trees left at Galu, and then he might move to more lucrative grounds or devise other survival options. I wondered, as he carried his sacks of charcoal away, how long before he would turn to the ruin wall if some developer moved into the area and needed building materials. Only time would tell.

On November 28, 1992, a year later, I received a letter from a colleague in Kenya that read: "Galu is no more! Completely vandalized. No wall, No nothing!!" I was dumbfounded. This was one of the few sites that provided evidence for early Iron Age iron smelting and smithing on the coast. I could not believe the news, especially when I had brought the matter of the surveyors to the museum's attention.

On January 29, 1993, while attending the World Archaeological Intercongress in Mombasa, I accompanied Peter Schmidt to the site. We found that the wall of the enclosure had been cleanly demolished and the materials were gone, presumably sold to a developer in the area. We both agreed it was a professionally executed job. The only person I knew capable of this feat was the charcoal burner. I still had heard no official word from the conservation or archaeology departments on the action that had been taken.

On February 8, I accompanied Jimbi Katana, one of the museum conservators, to the site to take pictures. I saw the charcoal burner but was unable to talk with him because he ran away upon seeing the museum truck. On February 12, an article appeared in the *Daily Nation* that decried the destruction of the sixteenth-century monument in Galu. Because I was not in Kenya at the time of the destruction of the monument, I was not sure whether this was the first report or a follow-up. The report was typically sensational, stating that the site had been destroyed by area residents, that the site was a major tourist attraction, and that the residents also cut down trees in the *kayas* (Mayoyo 1993).

This report can be disputed in several respects. First, anyone who is aware of the high esteem in which old settlements are held by local residents knows that it is unthinkable for local residents to pick so much as a stone from holy shrines or old settlements. The ruins of Galu are referred to by local people as *Mizimuni*, "where the spirits [of the dead ancestors] reside," or *Kwa mashekhe*, "the residence of the sheikhs" (see, for example, Giles 1987, 1989). Second, it is not clear whether these ruins are *kayas* (precolonial settlements of the Mijikenda peoples), and it was not the residents who cut down the trees but a lone man, and the museum authorities were aware of his activities and did nothing to prevent the site's destruction. Finally, very few people even in the area knew about the existence of the site, and few if any tourists went there. It is two kilometers from the sea and in a forested area. When I left Kenya on February 14, I knew no further information except that steps were being taken to apprehend the culprits. To my knowledge, nothing has changed since Galu's unceremonial demolition.

Case 4: The Destruction of the Historical Ruins of Mtwapa

The ruins of Mtwapa are located fifteen kilometers north of Mombasa along Mtwapa Creek, which is navigable for at least twenty kilometers inland. This area of north coast is the heart of tourist activity, with many hotels and restaurants. Mtwapa area is thus attractive in many respects. The creek offers fishing and other water sports. The ruins could offer an excellent tourist attraction if they were well developed (Wilson 1980).

The ruined town of Mtwapa appears to have consisted of approximately twenty acres of ruins. Most of them were built of mud, and there is little evidence above ground except for scattered pottery. Much of the stone town was built inside a defensive wall. At the southeast corner of the site lies approximately nine acres of forest. Within this forest is a section built of coral stone where sixty-four house ruins remain standing. The houses in this forest area were last occupied in the late sixteenth and early seventeenth centuries and a remarkable wealth of architectural and archaeological information has been recovered from them (Kusimba 1993).

Since 1986, the archaeology team from Fort Jesus Museum has been carrying out archaeological excavations at the ruins. Much of the preliminary work was completed by Richard Wilding and the author and is being prepared for publication. Excavations have uncovered a rich archaeological sequence. Mtwapa had a total of five mosques, three of which were outside the town wall. All the mosques outside have been destroyed by cultivation and settlement since the 1980s. Within the stone walls were thirteen wells; sixty-four stone houses; twenty-two mounds, presumably of collapsed houses; seven houses with distinct graffiti; and forty-two pit latrines, fifteen of which were in open spaces, indicating that the structures to which they belonged had collapsed (Kusimba 1993).

The land on which the Mtwapa ruins stand is privately owned by Vernon Colpoys and Mama Biimu, the granddaughter of Hamisi bin Kombo, leader of Tisia Taifa, who had extensive lands at Mtwapa.[11] But the ruins are the responsibility of the museum. All the land around the area belonged to Khamisi Kombo, leader of Watwafi, and has now passed on to his great-grandchildren, of whom Mama Biimu is one. Between 1986 and 1993, all the land except the forest on which the ruins stand was sold or leased to developers. The areas along the creek and beaches have long been developed, and their occupants, despite destroying the ruins in the initial stages of settlement in the 1930s and 1940s, have ensured the protection of the remaining part of the ruins. Many of these owners are now elderly and these properties may pass on to owners with less honorable intentions.

The pressure of land and real estate development in Mtwapa has meant that the walls of the ruins are vandalized and the materials are sold to developers for construction. Since the only forest left in Mtwapa is the space where the ruins stand, the trees are being destroyed for firewood, charcoal, and boat construction. Some neighbors of the ruins have goats and cows that graze in the ruins, especially during the dry season, causing many walls to collapse. The forest around the ruins has been cleared, exposing the wall and the ruins to more vandals. Three paths among the ruins provide access to the sea for the increasing number of seagoers. The forest outside the ruins formerly provided some natural protection for the ruins and its wildlife, including baboons, monkeys, antelope, duikers, dik-diks, and snakes. Expansion of human settlement has placed obvious constraints on wildlife. Some neighbors have found it necessary to invite members of the Kenya Wildlife Service to shoot the baboons and monkeys for destroying their crops (Justus Mweni, pers. comm. 1991).

Since 1986 the museum has permanently employed two security guards at the site. Vandals have been arrested and some have been jailed for between three and six months. Boat builders have periodically cut trees and built their boats at the beach. One man chopped down some trees from Mtwapa forest in 1991 and the museum took no action. He died immediately after his boat was completed, and rumor had it that his death was a punishment for abusing the sacred forest (Mama Biimu interview). Some tourist businesses in the neighborhood are conducting guided visitations to the ruins, apparently with the blessing of the museums, despite protests by the owners of the ruins, who would like to maintain the natural ecology of Mtwapa (Colpoys interview; Mama Biimu interview).

Tourist visits to the site conducted by the nearby Claudios Restaurant have been authorized by the curator's office at Fort Jesus Museum. These visits have certain ethical and scientific implications for the site. First, archaeological investigations are still in progress and there are as yet no publications, which is generally a prerequisite for public visits to such sites. Second, the restaurant operator is no authority on Swahili history. Although he was provided with materials on the site by the museum, the information was based on very preliminary hypotheses that are not yet fully tested. Third, there are no clear-cut paths, so many of the visits to the ruins are done randomly. Fourth, cultural objects are picked up by the tourists. Surface collections at the site usually include ivory, rock crystal, pink coral, bronze, iron tools, glass vessels, carnelian, and Indian and Persian beads as well as considerable quantities of Islamic and Chinese ceramics. Finally, the restaurateur, who has received authorization from the museum administration, has ignored protestations by the owner, Vernon Colpoys, to stop the visits into his property. This has discouraged Colpoys, who accuses the museums of holding double standards.

Other Cases of Destruction

Many other cases of destruction of historical sites and monuments are known on the Swahili coast. In 1987 the private owner of the Kilepwa settlement ruins bulldozed the entire site. He was arrested and tried but never sentenced. In 1991, the domed mosque at Jumba la Mtwana was destroyed a day after a team from the museums visited the mosque, which is on private property. Arrests were made, but as far as I know the case has never gone beyond preliminary stages despite receiving high publicity. Although I am a witness and have recorded a statement with the police, I have never been summoned to appear in court. I can assume that the case was thrown out (see also Wilson and Omar, this volume).

In 1992 an Italian real estate developer in Malindi bought a large area immediately north of Mambrui for a tourist complex. The area in which this hotel has now been built contained five mosques and an extensive settlement. Little is known about this area archaeologically. I visited the site in April 1992 on directions from the curator, who had been advised that the sites were being bulldozed. I took pictures and recorded a video of the site. I talked to the owner, Armando, and explained the historical and scientific importance of the area. His response was brutally frank. His major concern was the welfare of the families of the thousand people he had employed building the hotel complex; once the complex was finished he would employ more than three thousand people. When reminded that his actions would be unacceptable in his native Italy, he responded that if

Kenyans were interested in preserving their cultural heritage they should follow Italy's footsteps and protect ruins by placing them in government hands before they had been bought by foreigners. His indictment could not have been more honest. The meeting was reported to the museum authorities (Tinga 1992). A rescue archaeological operation was undertaken in the Sabaki-Ngomeni area (Abungu 1993), but the tourist hotel was completed in 1994.

A similar rush has been reported at Kipini, where a complex of tenth- to fifteenth-century towns of fifteen to forty-five acres was under threat. The government had allocated twenty thousand acres at the Tana River Delta to a private developer for a ranch. The irony is that this area had previously been set aside as a tropical wetland reserve, the first of its kind in Africa. After vigorous protest by scientists, conservators, and government and non-governmental agencies to the commissioner of lands, the government eventually reversed its decision, and the Tana Delta is for the present moment safe (East African Wildlife Society 1993; Hanseen 1993; Opala 1993a, 1993b; Sunguh 1993).

These few cases illustrate Kenya's destruction of the Swahili cultural heritage and the powerlessness of those charged with the responsibility of protecting this natural and cultural heritage. More examples are provided by Wilson and Omar (this volume).

SWAHILI HERITAGE MANAGEMENT AND DEVELOPMENT

These cases reveal several interrelated problems. A general breakdown in accountability among civil servants and politicians has encouraged the abuse of power for private gain (see Schmidt, this volume). The laws of the land have been broken with impunity. Perhaps because present laws benefit those in power, there has been little motivation to correct the situation. For example, in the Kenya Development Plan (1989–93) the government plans to establish a land use commission to oversee land allocation and use practices. However, no such commission has yet been appointed, leaving the commissioner of lands enormous power to allocate, adjudicate, and register land without regard to its history of ownership and ecologically sound use (Opala 1993a). The Land Planning Act (Cap 303 of 1970) empowers the minister of lands and settlement to determine land use without consulting other parties. The act has not been repealed, although it is outmoded. The displacement of Abdulrahaman Saggaf and his family, the Mayungu fishermen, and others from their ancestral homes should be seen from this perspective.

Private investors have capitalized on loopholes in the Land Planning Act to exploit the situation. The general economic recession of the 1980s coupled with the decline on the world market of coffee and tea prices has worsened the situation. The country's increasing dependence on tourism has made it easy for foreign investors to make handsome investment deals. I do not think that the situation is going to improve in view of the government's refusal to fully implement structural adjustment programs (Jegede, this volume).

The present NMK personnel involved in the protection of antiquities, sites, and monuments are inadequate because the main focus of the museums is research, much of which is dependent on foreign funding. The museum infrastructure for dealing with the vast land under its jurisdiction is minimal. Frustration and general apathy presently reigning at the NMK incapacitate those committed to the ideals of museums as defined by the Eleventh General Assembly of the International Council of Museums at Copenhagen in 1974. Merrick Posnansky's analysis in this volume of the collapse of West African museums and universities is in most respects applicable to much of sub-Saharan Africa (see also Jegede, Karoma, Mturi, Nkwi, and Schmidt, this volume).

In general the NMK supports high-profile projects that promote international funding and public interest. The world-famous paleontological research at Koobi Fora, the UNESCO project on the preservation of the Swahili towns of Lamu and Mombasa, and the Ford Foundation's reconstruction of the Lamu Fort are cases in point (see Bwana 1985). These projects were attractive because they required very little local money. They also generated media attention and this boded well for the publicity-minded museum administration (Crary 1986).

Less glamorous scientific projects, such as Early Iron Age archaeology in eastern Africa, have never been enthusiastically supported by the NMK (Wandibba 1989). Similarly, sites and monuments deemed less grand and from which the Museums will not gain revenue through collections by tourist visits have, in general, been left to decay (Odak 1979). For example, the protection of the inland sites of the Mijikenda received little attention until they were almost completely destroyed. It is disconcerting that the Museums only became interested in saving the endangered *kayas* and indigenous forests when they were almost wiped out (Robertson 1992:20–21; Luke 1992:24–27). Rather than creating the so-called Giriama village at Gede, the Museums should have used their knowledge of the rich cultural heritage of the Mijikenda to protect sacred burial and precolonial settlement sites. Instead the Museums, amid protests from the local community, created a Giriama village at the Gede historical site and encouraged local families to live there to entertain tourists. Some Museums officials still think this a novel idea—having people idly sit around waiting for convoys of tourists in order to entertain them with traditional African dances. Many Kenyans and Western tourists with whom I have discussed the matter have found the whole idea of creating a living museum at Gede repugnant if not disturbing. The NMK continues to support this village because it generates revenue, regardless of whether the general consensus is against the idea.

The argument commonly used for lack of attention to most coastal sites and monuments is that they are privately owned and the Museums therefore do not have authority to develop them. Ironically, the Museums voluntarily ceded their responsibilities over monuments, some of which have been transferred to private concerns; these include Mbaraki Pillar and Ndia Kuu Mosque, both on Mombasa Island, which were ceded to a local welfare organization to rebuild into a mosque and a community center. Kongo Mosque in Diani has also been given to the same group for development into a holiday/conference center. Although welfare organizations have played an important role in community development in recent years, I question the wisdom of ceding the few acquired sites to other agencies for development for their own exclusive purposes at the expense of many unclaimed sites. It should be worthwhile for such organizations to assist the NMK in acquiring new sites.

The biggest losers are indigenous coastal people, who have lost both private and public lands and the resources available in them. Privatization of land has created a landless and homeless community. Beach areas that used to be held communally have been fenced off, excluding fishers and sailors from cleaning and repairing their boats and canoes (see also Graham 1989; Rigby 1992). Tourism led to the creation of marine national parks on the coral reefs. Fishermen are restricted from these zones lest they over-fish the tourist areas. Ironically, it is the tourists who have caused the most damage to the coral reef through snorkeling, diving, and shell collection (Brown 1975).

Because many Swahili people are Muslims, they do not seek employment in hotels that serve alcohol and pork. Consequently, local people have not been the major beneficiaries from the tourist expansion program. Many Swahili, Pokomo, and Mijikenda peoples of the coast have been displaced from their lands both through illegal land deals and by the so-called Shifta bandits. Ethnic unrest in northeast Kenya caused by Somali nationalism in the 1960s and 1970s forced many people out of their homes over much of the mainland Lamu and Tana River districts. Many people who fled their homes are still living in the towns of Lamu, Malindi, Mombasa, and Kilifi, where they are engaged in wage labor. Many have lost their land and have become permanently displaced. Following a decline in banditry and insecurity, many people are returning to these places to claim their ancestral lands (Kusimba 1993). George Abungu, however, does not think that these people are true claimants, for most of them are young men who were born away from Kipini and other areas on the coast. A statement attributed to him reads:

> For the last few months we started seeing people, mainly from Malindi, claiming that their ancestral lands are within the sites. . . . Scientific evidence does not support these claims. . . . The sites were deserted centuries ago. Claims by people that their grandparents lived on the sites therefore contradict scientific explanations availed by archaeological facts. . . . There is no evidence whatsoever that the people who settled at Kipini actually originated from Mwana, Ungwana, and Shaka, last inhabited 350 years ago. (Sunguh 1993)

With this kind of scientific proof who needs the natives to justify their claim to their property? Ethnic identities are rarely directly imprinted in the archaeological record (Haaland 1977). This is a classic case in which the archaeologist gathers the data and the media award the interpretation to the winner. What other proof does an investor need?

Because newcomers to the coast are ignorant of traditional land tenure and land use practices, they have improperly used the land. Others buy or acquire land in anticipation of selling it to real estate developers for a profit, as, for example, in Mayungu. Much of the land is left fallow because the new owners do not usually develop it immediately. Fallow land is unknown in some agricultural societies in Kenya; consequently, such lands on the coast are considered proof of coastal peoples' indolence and idleness. Appropriating these lands is deemed a necessary action for the general good of the people. Unemployment is high among young people nationally and is worse on the coast because most of the young people have not had secular education. Displacement of their parents since the 1960s and 1970s coupled with the lack of government investment in education in the area during the last thirty years has created a generation of marginal, unemployable people. Many young people have settled for working in tourist-related enterprises, the most popular being beach combing (Peake 1989).

Museum media publicity aimed at increasing public awareness of the country's cultural heritage—in particular the Swahili sites and monuments—has increased real estate speculation and investment. Although many people in Kenya are at present aware of Swahili sites and monuments other than Fort Jesus in Mombasa, a Portuguese fortress, the downside of this program (Abungu 1991) has been an increase in the destruction of sites and monuments by people on whose property these ruins sit; for example, Jumba Ia Mtwana, Munge, Tumbe, Galu, Kilepwa, Pate, and Mjana Kheri. Many people in Lamu and Mombasa demolished their houses and built new modern ones months before the towns were gazetted. They were probably silently protesting the gazetting of their town. Hostility and suspicion surrounds many visits by museum staff to privately owned archaeological sites. Many people perceive the museum as an adversary. Once I was told in Pate of the fallacy of trying to educate people on preserving their past. "Doesn't the museum know that if traditional pride in the monuments was lacking the museum would not have found a single stone here?" (see also Mturi; Wilson and Omar, this volume). It is important to realize that dealing with the media is a double-edged sword. For the moment, media hype has benefited investors and prospectors searching for pristine, undeveloped, untamed, high-potential areas for investment. The media have not been involved in the reinterpretation of Swahili history for the community and the schoolchildren.

CONCLUSION

The destruction of people, their cultural history, and their heritage has taken many forms throughout the history of humankind. Some forms have involved distortions and fabrications. Some have been inventions of the past to justify and legitimate the present (Mudimbe 1988). Some have employed racial and ethnic arguments to justify domination of others. History is replete with examples of incarceration, isolation, extermination, detention, evacuation, and murder of peoples whose views questioned established notions of truth (e.g., Gartrell 1986).

It is the right of every individual and community to participate freely in production mechanisms that will enhance their happiness. This ensures the reproduction of that community in a manner in balance with the laws of nature. For this reason, it is morally wrong for one individual or a group of individuals to engage in activities that are antithetical to the realization of collective harmony, personal freedom, and the prosperity of others.

Careful exploitation of the basic resources of the Swahili coast can benefit those who have found on the coast a place to call home as well as be respectful of most peoples who have lived in the area for the last two millennia. It is morally wrong to exclude the people whose ancestors created that which all of us have found attractive—the richly laden Swahili heritage (e.g., Allen 1993; Knappert 1989; Middleton 1992). In discussing the plight of the Swahili and the destruction of their cultural heritage, I have brought to the fore problems that arise from exclusion of the so-called underprivileged members of society on the basis of religion, race, ethnicity, and gender. I do not seek to indict or banish anyone; however, if this essay can inspire the feelings of shame evoked by the work of McIntosh (this volume) and others and cause those responsible for the destruction of these and many other important archaeological sites the world over to rethink their actions, I shall consider my work a worthwhile contribution.

ACKNOWLEDGMENTS

I would like to thank my wife, Sibel Barut, for patiently reading and editing several drafts of this paper and for her support during the many anguishing moments I have experienced as I learned of the continued destruction of Swahili archaeological sites. Peter Schmidt provided a travel grant to the University of Florida in Gainesville, where this essay was first presented. His commitment to Africa goes beyond mere scholastic interest. I would thus like to dedicate this essay to Peter Schmidt for his courage in organizing the 1993 Carter Lecture Series.

NOTES

1. B. Gartrell's 1986 piece on conflicts arising from state expansionist policies and indigenous needs during both the colonial and the contemporary periods is applicable to the present Swahili people's predicament with respect to Kenya's national economic policies.

2. Contrary to public opinion and media reports, much of the published work on the coast has been done by the British Institute in Eastern Africa and by foreign researchers (for example, Chittick 1967, 1984; Garlake 1966; Horton 1984, 1988).

3. Little attempt has been made to train two of the three longest serving and those who are, in my view, the most experienced.

4. Cattle rustling and general banditry have existed in northern Kenya since the 1960s. Government action has been dismal; despite the presence of permanent security personnel in the area since the 1960s, private property and lives continue to be lost to the extent that many townspeople in Lamu and in the Tana River districts have fled their homes since the 1960s, leaving villages in ruins. Much of this land had not been adjudicated, and consequently many people, especially those in high places, have returned to these areas and taken over the land, thereby permanently displacing the inhabitants.

5. Because many hotels and restaurants serve beer and pork, coastal Muslims often do not seek employment in these enterprises; consequently, the immediate community does not directly benefit from them. See below.

6. Outsiders was used to refer to all people not originally from the immediate coastal area. To be more precise, an outsider is anyone who is not a Swahili, a Segeju, or a Mijikenda.

7. Ironically, these outsiders and the political establishment have used the under-utilization of coastal land to argue that coastal people are lazy. There is overwhelming evi-

dence that these arguments have favored the seizure of land from coastal natives. See below.

    8. An April 3, 1986 letter to the Provincial Commissioner, Coast Province:

> "Complaint and Inquiry on the Adjudication of Wasini Shinoni Communal Reserve, Kwale District by Land Adjudication Department.
> [The letter poignantly concludes]: "I am a victim of a syndicate of a group of land agents working in a beautiful network within the official circle and outsiders [foreign investors]. However, I beg you to help me and others regain our land that are presently in the hands of the illegal land grabbers.
>   Yours faithfully A. Abdulrahaman Saggaf Alawy."

    9. Editors' note: This is part of a much longer text that has been reduced for this publication. The [] symbol indicates sections of missing text.

    10. Omar Bwana served as the head of sites and monuments until 1990, when he was appointed deputy director of the NMK. His office was not filled until 1993 when Abungu was appointed to head the coast museums program (Mayoyo 1993:5).

    11. I am grateful to Justin Willis of the British Institute in Eastern Africa for sharing valuable oral data he collected from Mtwapa and for bringing to my notice earlier sources on Mtwapa and other sites along the Kenyan and Tanzanian coasts.

REFERENCES

Abungu, G. H. O. "Survey of Swahili Ruins on the East African Coast." *The National Museums of Kenya, Biennial Report, 1989–91*. Nairobi: Majestic Printing Works, 1991:49.

———. "New Finds Along the Kenya Coast: 'The Mosque Complex' of the North Sabaki-Ngomeni Region." Paper presented at the World Archaeology InterCongress, Mombasa, January 1993.

Abungu, G. H. O., and J. Katana. "The Swahili Coast Revisited: An Archaeological Survey of Kenya Coastal Sites." Unpublished manuscript. Fort Jesus Museum, Mombasa, Kenya, 1991.

Allen, J. de Vere. "Swahili Culture and Identity." Seminar paper presented at the Institute of African Studies, University of Nairobi, 1976a.

———. "The Swahilis in Western Historiography." Seminar paper presented at the Institute of African Studies, University of Nairobi, 1976b.

———. "Swahilization: A Cultural Concept and Its Significance in Kenya Today." Seminar paper presented at the Institute of African Studies, University of Nairobi, 1979.

———. *Swahili Origins: Swahili Culture and the Shungwaya Phenomenon*. London: James Currey, 1993.

Brown, L. *East African Coasts and Reefs*. Nairobi: East African Publishing House, 1975.

Bwana, O. "Conservation and Tourism: The Case of Lamu." *Build Kenya* 8, no. 1 (1985): 14–18.

Chittick, H. N. "Discoveries in the Lamu Archipelago." *Azania* 2 (1967):37–67.

———. *Manda: Excavations at an Island Port on the Kenya Coast*. Memoir no. 9. Nairobi: British Institute in Eastern Africa, 1984.

Crary, D. "Preservation Plan for Ancient Lamu Island." *Business Times*, May 10, 1986.

Daily Nation. "Lamu: Land Here Is the Major Issue." November 11, 1992.

Daily Nation. "Environmental Abuse." January 28, 1993a.

Daily Nation. "Give Muslims More—Nassir." February 19, 1993b.

East African Wildlife Society. "An Open Letter to the Commissioner of Lands." *Daily Nation*, January 20, 1993.

Fawcett, W. B., and A. LaViolette. "Iron Age Settlement around Mkiu, South-eastern Tanzania." *Azania* 25 (1990):19–39.

Forsbrook, H. A. "The Masai Wall of Moa: Walled Towns of the Segeju." *Tanganyika Notes and Records* 30–37, 1957.

Garlake, P. S. *Islamic Architecture on the East African Coast.* Nairobi: The British Institute/ Oxford University Press, 1966.

———. *The Kingdoms of Africa.* New York: Peter Bedrick Books, 1990.

Gartrell, B. "'Colonialism' and the Fourth World: Notes on Variations in Colonial Situations." *Culture* 6, no. 1 (1986):3–17

Giles, L. "Possession Cults on the Swahili Coast: A Reexamination of Theories of Marginality." *Africa* 57, no. 2 (1987):234–58.

———. "Spirit Possession on the Swahili Coast." Ph.D thesis, University of Texas at Austin. University Microfilms, Ann Arbor, 1989.

Gillman, C. "An Annotated List of Ancient and Modern Indigenous Structures in Eastern Africa." *Tanganyika Notes and Records* 17 (1944):44–55.

Graham, O. "A Land Divided: The Impact of Ranching on Pastoral Society." *The Ecologist* 19, no. 5 (1989):184–85.

Haaland, R. "Archaeological Classification and Ethnic Groups: A Case Study from Sudanese Nubia." *Norwegian Archaeological Review* 10 (1977):1–83.

Haas, J. *The Evolution of the Prehistoric State.* New York: New York University Press, 1982.

Hanseen, N. "Experts Urge Probe." *Daily Nation*, February 22, 1993.

Harden, B. *Africa: Dispaches from a Fragile Continent.* Boston: Houghton Mifflin, 1990.

Hobsbawm, E., and T. O. Ranger (eds.). *The Invention of Tradition.* Cambridge: Cambridge University Press, 1992.

Hollis, A. C. "Notes on the History of the Vumba, East Africa." *Journal of the Royal Anthropological Institute* 30 (1900):276–77.

Horton, M. "The Early Settlement of the Northern Kenya Coast." Ph.D. dissertation, Cambridge: University of Cambridge, 1984.

———. "The Swahili Corridor." *Scientific American* (September 1987):86–93.

———. "Early Muslim Trading Settlements on the East African Coast: New Evidence from Shanga." *Antiquaries Journal* 68 (1988):290–323.

Killick, D. J., and C. M. Kusimba. "Imported Metals at the Swahili Town of Ungwana, Kenya." Paper presented at the Fifty-seventh Annual Meeting of the Society for American Archaeology. Pittsburgh, Pennsylvania, April 1992.

Knappert, J. "Swahili Arts and Crafts." *Kenya Past and Present* 21 (1989):20–28.

Kusimba, C. M. The Archaeology and Ethnography of Iron Metallurgy, Ph.D. dissertation, Bryn Mawr College, 1993.

———. "Wither Lamu?" Review paper in possession of author.

Kusimba, C. M., D. Killick, R. G. Creswell. "Indigenous and Imported Metals among Swahili Sites on the Kenya Coast." *MASCA Research Papers in Science and Archaeology*, Supplement 2, Philadelphia, University Museum, 1994.

Luke, Q. "Preservation of the Kayas." In *The National Museums of Kenya Biennial Report 1989–91.* Nairobi, Government Printer, 1992.

Majtenyi, C. "In High Places: Youthful MP with a Vision for his People." *Daily Nation*, February 3, 1993.

Mayoyo, P. "Sixteenth Century Monument Destroyed in Kwale." *Daily Nation*, February 12, 1993.

Mazrui, A. A. *The African Condition.* Cambridge: Cambridge University Press, 1980.

McKay, W. F. "A Precolonial History of the Southern Kenya Coast." Ph.D. dissertation, Boston University, Boston, Massachusetts, 1975.

Middleton, J. "The Towns of the Swahili Coast of East Africa." In *The Diversity of the Muslim Community: Anthropological Essays in Memory of Peter Lienhardt*, A. al-Shahi, ed. London: Ithaca Press, 1987.

———. *The World of the Swahili: An African Mercantile Civilization*. New Haven: Yale University Press, 1992.

Mudimbe, V. Y. *The Invention of Africa: Gnosis, Philosophy, and the Order of Knowledge*. Bloomington: Indiana University Press, 1988.

Mwadime, W. "The Conservation of Movable Cultural Property from Underwater Sites: The Case of the Mombasa Wreck." Unpublished manuscript. Fort Jesus Museum, Mombasa, Kenya, 1991.

Mwandam, I. "The Paradise Thousands Dream About." *Daily Nation*, December 21, 1991.

Nation Correspondent. "In High Places: Prof's Vision of the Coast." *Daily Nation*, February 10, 1993.

Nurse, D., and T. Spar. *The Swahili: Reconstructing the History and Language of an African Society, 800–1500*. Philadelphia: University of Pennsylvania Press, 1985.

Odak, O. "Kenya's Historic Sites: Their Record and Some Problems of Preservation." Seminar Paper, Institute of African Studies, University of Nairobi, Nairobi, Kenya, 1979.

———. "Kenya: The Museum Function of KAERA (The Kenya Archaeological and Ethnographic Research Agency)." *Museum* 40, no.3 (1988):150–54.

Opala, K. "Special Report: Two Years on, Leakey's Wildlife Crusade Goes On." *Daily Nation*, February 23, 1993a.

———. "Special Report: Land Use Practices that Are a Threat to Wildlife." *Daily Nation*, March 2, 1993b.

Peake, R. "Swahili Stratification and Tourism in Malindi Old Town, Kenya." *Africa* 59, no. 2 (1989):209–20.

Pouwels, P. L. *Horn and Crescent: Cultural Change and Traditional Islam on the East African Coast, 800–1900*. Cambridge: Cambridge University Press, 1987.

Rigby, P. *Cattle, Capitalism, and Class*, Philadelphia: Temple University Press, 1992.

Robertson, A. "Researchers Campaign to Save Kayas, Mangea Hill, and Tana Wetlands." *National Museums of Kenya: Biennial Report 1989–91*. Nairobi: Majestic Printing Works, 1992:21.

Sassoon, H. "How Old Is Mombasa?" *Kenya Past and Present* 9 (1978): 33–37.

Sunguh, G. "Scramble for Kipini Plots in Full Swing." *Daily Nation*. February 24, 1993.

Tinga, K. K. "Report on the Visit to Mambrui-mjana Heri Area." Unpublished manuscript. Mombasa, Kenya: Fort Jesus Museum, 1992.

Wandibba. S. "Archaeology and Education in Kenya." Paper presented at the World Archaeology Congress 1, Southhampton. 1989.

Weekly Review. "National Museums of Kenya." *Sixtieth Anniversary Issue*. September 21, 1990.

Wilson, T. H. *The Monumental Architecture and Archaeology North of the Tana River*. Nairobi: National Museums of Kenya, 1978.

———. "The Monumental Architecture and Archaeology of the Central and Southern Kenya Coast." Nairobi: National Museums of Kenya, 1980.

———. "Spatial Analysis and Settlement Patterns on the East African Coast." *Paideuma* 28 (1982):201–19.

INTERVIEWS

Abubakr, Mohamed Bin, Wasini Island, Kenya, 1989.

Alawyr, Abdulrahaman Saggaf, Mombasa, Kenya, 1992.

Biimu, Mama, Mtwapa, Kenya, 1991.
Claudios, Mtwapa, Kenya, 1992.
Colpoys, Vernon, Mtwapa, Kenya, 1991–92.
Maamun, Rashid Said, Mombasa, Kenya, 1991.
Shekuwe, Faquih Kahale, Mayungu Village, Kenya, 1992.
Swaleh, Ustadh Harith, Lamu Town, Kenya, 1989 and 1992.

17

PRESERVATION OF CULTURAL HERITAGE ON THE EAST AFRICAN COAST

THOMAS H. WILSON AND ATHMAN LALI OMAR

This chapter examines problems and suggests solutions concerning the disappearance of Africa's cultural heritage. It focuses on the coast of eastern Africa, especially Kenya, but many of the issues span the continent and some are truly worldwide. The examples of cultural preservation on the East African coast illuminate larger issues that must be addressed by African peoples and states as well as by the international community.

Themes in cultural preservation on the East African coast include the tensions between the dual needs of development and preservation; private individuals, corporations, and governments as agents inhibiting the preservation of cultural heritage; problems of looting and collecting; trafficking and the art market; theft from museums; the removal of regalia from cultural contexts; the importance of site surveys and museum inventories; legal frameworks for preservation; economic and educational reasons for preserving cultural heritage; and the role of organizations outside Africa in preservation. This essay concentrates on human agency and does not address the major preservation problems arising from chemical and mechanical weathering, including the actions of animals, and it does not address the issue of historic preservation. However, with its focus on human agency we will also explore some of the distinctive tensions that exist within poor but growing subsistence communities and the historical monuments that are sometimes in their midst. For example, the dilemma that faces heritage managers on the island of Pate—where local farmers are harvesting the walls of ruins for building materials—is characteristic of the conflict between local needs and national interests (also see Karoma this volume).

THE COAST OF EASTERN AFRICA

Acheulian hunters and gatherers visited what is now the coast of eastern Africa perhaps as many as 250,000 years ago (Kato, Omi, and Adachi 1977) and much later Late Stone Age peoples appeared sporadically along the coast (e.g., Isaac 1974). In the first millennium, Iron Age peoples approached the East African coast along its length, but only in the last decade have archaeologists begun to understand the relationships between these peoples and the later Swahili civilization on which this essay focuses (Sinclair 1990, 1991; Schmidt, Karoma, and LaViolette 1992). The *Periplus of the Erythraean Sea* and Ptolemy's *Geography* indicate occupation of the coast of eastern Africa and trade relations with the classical world almost two thousand years ago (Huntingford 1980; Freeman-Grenville 1962a). Archaeology confirms a site of this period in the Horn of Africa at Hafun (Chittick 1979, 1983; Smith and Wright 1988), and tantalizing evidence from Chibuene in Mozambique (Sinclair 1990:10; 1991) and Ngazidga in the Comoro Islands (Sinclair 1992:1) suggests possible contemporary early occupation farther south along the coast.

Beginning in the late eighth or early ninth century, sites were founded from the Lamu Archipelago to Mozambique, which suggests rapid development and florescence of the coast over a broad area (Chittick 1967, 1974, 1984; Horton 1980, 1984, 1986, 1987; Sinclair 1982; Stiles 1992; Wilson 1982b, 1992). By the twelfth century, many communities were established along the mainland coast and offshore on Pemba, Zanzibar, Mafia, the Comoros, and northwestern Madagascar that may be considered progenitors of the culture that we now call Swahili (Chittick 1982; Horton and Clark 1985; Vérin 1986; Wright 1984). This essay concentrates on Swahili cultural heritage, but it should be stressed that many other peoples participated in coastal cultures during the period under discussion, including Cushitic speakers in the north and speakers of numerous Bantu languages elsewhere (Nurse and Spear 1985; Prins 1952, 1967).

The archaeological record suggests that at its widest expanse the Swahili coast extended for more than three thousand kilometers. Sites range from complex urban situations over twenty-seven hectares (seventy acres) in extent to isolated structures or other evidence of occupation (Garlake 1966; Horton 1984; Wilson 1978, 1980, 1982a, 1982b, 1992). A typical site with standing architectural remains might include one or more mosques, houses, tombs, and specialized features such as wells or town walls. Construction was typically of coral rag set in a mortar of lime and sand, although archaeological deposits sometimes reveal the remains of structures of mud and wood. Sometimes towns with long histories, deep archaeological deposits, and many surviving historical structures remain inhabited, as in Lamu, Pate, and Mombasa. Systematic archaeological surveying on mainland Tanzania suggests that many smaller sites exist in addition to those with obvious building remains (Fawcett and LaViolette 1990).

The sites and monuments of the Swahili coast, developed over a thousand years, are today threatened from many directions. This essay first focuses on some of the threats to cultural heritage on the East African coast, and then considers some solutions that local, national, and international communities can implement to arrest the disappearance of Africa's past.

DEVELOPMENT AND THE LOSS OF CULTURAL HERITAGE

In any nation, tension often exists between the need for development and the need for preservation. All countries have the sovereign right to develop their natural and human resources, but each also should recognize the paramount importance of preserving cultural heritage. Sometimes peoples and governments successfully reconcile these potentially conflicting forces into unified development policies, but divergent priorities often lead to unfortunate consequences. The next few sections explore several examples from the East African coast.

Nowhere is the potential for misunderstandings greater than along coastlines, where population centers, desirable land, sensitive environments, and remains of cultural significance create competing pressures. This is certainly the case in eastern Africa. On the Kenyan coast between Malindi and the Tanzania frontier and in certain areas of the Lamu Archipelago, the demand for beachfront property has been intense for years. Individuals and commercial concerns, the government, and multinational corporations compete with preservation needs along the coast. With adequate planning, use of coastal resources can accommodate competing needs, but the following examples illustrate problems arising from a variety of contexts and agents.

Social Services and Cultural Heritage: Coast General Hospital

Mombasa is one of the largest cities on the East African coast and has one of the longest histories. In the twelfth century, al-Idrisi described Mombasa as a small place and a dependency of the Zanj, where the principal economic activities were mining iron and hunting big cats (Freeman-Grenville 1962a:20). By the sixteenth century, Mombasa was sufficiently significant to become a principal focus of the Portuguese on the coast (Strandes 1971). With the exceptions of Fort Jesus and Mbaraki Pillar (Kirkman 1964:130–52, 1974, 1975a; Sassoon 1981), most of old Mombasa now lies buried beneath the streets and buildings of the present city along the northern sweep of Mombasa Harbor.

In the modern city, Coast General Hospital is the largest public health facility serving eastern Kenya. In the late 1970s, efforts by the Kenyan Government to expand Coast General Hospital exposed the site of old Mombasa, which immediately presented the choice of halting or delaying construction of a greatly needed medical facility or building over one of the earliest sites on the coast of eastern Africa. Ultimately the contractor, not the government, halted work while archaeologists investigated the site, generally following the lines of the construction trenches.

These excavations uncovered complex deposits more than four meters deep and revealed a possible workshop, street, and mosque. A radiocarbon date in the late tenth century suggests the period of earliest occupation, with building beginning perhaps as early as the thirteenth century (Sassoon 1978, 1981). The need for such salvage archaeology could have been avoided by protecting the site and developing the hospital extension elsewhere or allowing more time for excavations. At the time, the Kenyan government showed little interest in stopping construction to investigate or preserve the site. As a result, an important section of early Mombasa is now beneath Coast General Hospital. No one knows how much was unnecessarily destroyed, but the situation underscores the desirability of avoiding placing site preservation and social services at odds.

Endangerment of Sites from Resettlement: Luziwa

In the 1970s the government of Kenya, with the assistance of foreign aid, developed an agricultural settlement project at Mpekatoni on the mainland opposite Lamu Island. As part of the development of the area, the administration built roads, dug wells, and allotted plots to farmers, mainly those from central Kenya. There are at least six sites in the area, some of which might have been associated with larger communities on the islands (Wilson 1980:121–27; Ylvisaker 1979).

One of the most significant sites at Mpekatoni is Luziwa (sometimes Uziwa). Luziwa was inhabited by the late sixteenth century, when the Portuguese captain of Malindi took refuge there briefly (Kirkman 1964:75), and the site was mentioned in 1635 in the inscription over the entrance to Fort Jesus as being in alliance with and paying tribute to the Portuguese. Kirkman reported house remains and two mosques surrounded by a town wall (1971:296). Most prominent are the remains of a large mosque with an elaborate mihrab (the feature on the eastern wall of the mosque that serves to orient the direction of prayer), which is protected under Kenyan law. Nevertheless, the site was assigned to a farmer, who cultivated much of the area, including the immediate vicinity of the mosque. When the national museum informed the authorities, they did not rectify the situation, even though the farmer agreed to move. The district officer could have reassigned the farmer to a new location but did not. Perhaps the problem arose because of ignorance of the ordinance, but it continued because the resettlement authorities held political power from the central government and had little interest in preservation.

Development projects must be preceded by an environmental impact study, which could have prevented the situation at Luziwa, if indeed the study revealed the problem and there was sufficient intergovernmental communication. Funds for compensation and land for relocation should be available if similar problems arise.

Wetlands Development and Threats to Sites

Three major sites of the Kenyan coast are located just north of the mouth of the Tana River near Kipini: Ungwana, Mwana, and Shaka (Abungu 1990; Allen 1983; Kirkman 1964, 1966; Wilson 1978:46–74). All three sites are architecturally and historically significant, and Mwana (fig. 17-1) is known for its domed mosque and a group of outstanding tombs (Garlake 1966; Wilson 1979a).

Proposed development of wetlands in the Tana River Delta potentially endangers these extraordinary sites. In 1988 there was broad consensus in Kenya to establish the Tana Delta Wetlands National Park. Kenya is a signatory of the Ramsar Convention and of the Convention on Wetlands of International Importance and became a contracting party to the convention in 1990, obliging Kenya to protect wetlands of national and international importance. Contrary to the spirit of creating the national park, the commissioner of lands allotted twenty thousand hectares at the mouth of the river to Coastal Aquaculture Ltd., which sought to develop shrimp farming in the area. The issue was finally resolved when the

Figure 17-1. The domed mosque at Mwana, near Kipini, on the north Kenya coast. Oil exploration crews bulldozed a road across the site, missing the mosque but hitting many other structures. Any development of wetlands in the area may threaten Mwana and other nearby sites, including Ungwana and Shaka.

president of Kenya, under intense pressure from environmentalists, announced the revocation of the land allotments in July 1993. However, the problem and the hot debate that it generated in the Kenya press (see the *Weekly Review*, February 19, 1993:20 and March 5, 1993 and the *Daily Nation*, December 31, 1992, and March 5, 1993) illustrate that only high-level political involvement and intercession can protect valuable areas from development.

Multinational Corporations and Cultural Heritage

All countries hope for natural resources that will alleviate financial difficulties and provide needed services. Precious metals, minerals, and oil have this potential. In the 1970s the Kenyan government encouraged exploration for oil in the northeastern part of the country, and these surveys adversely affected coastal sites on the mainland and islands.

Takwa is located at a strategic position where a mangrove channel running east from Lamu Harbor almost bifurcates Manda Island. About 150 structures of coral rag survive at Takwa, including a single central congregational mosque (fig. 17-2), numerous houses, a pillar tomb, and a town wall (Kirkman 1957; Wilson 1979b, 1982b:203–09, 1992:87–90; Connah 1987:164, 167, 175). The National Museums of Kenya developed the site as a national monument, and it was protected under the laws of Kenya.

During the oil explorations, a multinational company plowed a road through the western environs of Takwa, destroying perhaps 10 to 15 percent of the site

Figure 17-2. The mosque at Takwa, on Manda Island in the Lamu Archipelago. Now a national monument, Takwa, like Mwana, was damaged by crews looking for oil.

down to the foundations of buildings. This situation is not completely revealed on the site maps, but one sees it on the ground (Wilson 1982b:204, 1992:88). With this wanton destruction, this company reduced the scientific importance, educational potential, and architectural significance of Takwa National Monument.

The same corporation bulldozed a road across Mwana, one of the most signifi- cant sites on the north Kenyan coast, near the mouth of the Tana River, cutting a straight line across the site irrespective of buildings or the town wall (Garlake 1966:39–40; Ghaidan 1976:27; Wilson 1978:63–74; Allen 1983). The same explora- tion appears to have razed Bui, an early site on Pate Island, to build a bridge at Mtangawanda (Wilson 1978:103).

Problems of Private and Commercial Development

There are many reasons for competing interests on an attractive coastline. Indi- viduals want to build houses at scenic locations, business associations seek to establish tourist hotels, or local residents want to develop the land. Chapurukha Makokha Kusimba discusses in this volume the destruction of Mtwapa, a few ki- lometers north of Mombasa (Garlake 1966:97, figs. 35, 39, 77; Wilson 1980:52–54), and similar situations occurred at Jumba la Mtwana and Kilifi (Wilson 1982a; Kirkman 1975a). The mosque at Kilindini and the site of Kitoka also illustrate how fragile sites can suffer from inadequately controlled development.

Kilindini was one of several communities that developed on Mombasa Island. Located on the south side of the island, above the harbor of the same name, Kilin- dini was settled from the south mainland in the early seventeenth century and abandoned about two hundred years later. Until recently one of the landmarks of

Figure 17-3. Panel of wall niches in a house at Kitoka, on Takaungu Creek near Kilifi. The owner of Kitoka has destroyed the mosques, houses, and most of the standing remains to cultivate the land.

the area was the mosque of the Kilindini, which excavations revealed dated to the late seventeenth century, with subsequent renovations (Kirkman 1964:156–57, 1971:301; Garlake 1966: figs. 59, 60). In 1974 the coast archaeologist, Hamo Sassoon, discovered to his horror that the mosque had been demolished to make room for a modern construction. The Kilindini mosque was a site of architectural and historical significance, unprotected by law, that was completely destroyed unbeknownst to museum personnel.

Kitoka is located on the north bank of Takaungu Creek, near Mnarani, Kilifi, and Kioni on Kilifi Creek (Kirkman 1958:95, 1975b:227, 240–41). Kitoka might have been one of the communities sighted by Vasco da Gama in 1498 (Freeman-Grenville 1962a:53), and when Garlake visited in the mid-1960s the site covered about 2.5 hectares and comprised two mosques and numerous houses (1966: figs. 35, 36). Kitoka houses (fig. 17-3) displayed some of the most complex panels of decorative niches on the East African coast (Allen 1979; figs. 4, 5; Wilson 1980: 83–88, 1982a:6). When teams from the National Museums of Kenya visited Kitoka in the late 1970s and early 1980s, the small mosque had already disappeared. The site, located on private property, was threatened by the owner, who was clearing and cultivating the area and was hostile to the concept of preservation. Since then, major destruction has apparently occurred at Kitoka, the owner perhaps believing

Figure 17-4. Overview of Pate, showing tobacco cultivation among the ruined houses.

that the faster he removed the standing architecture the less trouble he would have. He seems to have been correct.

These examples illustrate how the state's competing aims of providing services, resettlement projects, wetlands utilization, industrial opportunities, commercial expansion, and development for individual rather than state or corporate reasons can imperil sites and monuments. The next example shows the complexities and tensions inherent when local needs seem to conflict with preservation policies of the state.

PRESERVATION ISSUES AT PATE

Pate, covering about twenty-seven hectares within the town wall, is perhaps the largest site on the coast (fig. 17-4). There are two contemporary villages at Pate, Kitokwa to the west and Mitaayu to the east. The ruins at Pate include at least six collapsed mosques, two mosques that the people of Pate have restored, numerous tombs and cemeteries, many elaborate houses, and the remains of the vast town wall with several gates and redoubts (Chittick 1967, 1969b; Garlake 1966; Wilson 1978:88–99; Kirkman 1964; Strandes 1971). There are numerous inscriptions at Pate, not all of which are published (Freeman-Grenville and Martin 1973; and see also below), and there are many decorative carvings in the mosques. Houses often contain elaborate decorative panels of niches.

Test excavations by Wilson and Lali Omar in a house in eastern Pate exposed five meters of complex urban stratigraphy, and another excavation at the south side of the Bwana Bakari Mosque (fig. 17-5) yielded a ceramic sequence compar-

Figure 17-5. The mosque of Bwana Bakari at Pate, below which a National Museums of Kenya excavation revealed a ceramic sequence dating from the late eighth or early ninth century. The people of Pate restored and use the seventeenth-century mosque.

able to the earliest deposits elsewhere on the coast (Horton 1984; Chittick 1974). In the very deepest levels were earthenware ceramics of the earliest Tana River Tradition. Slightly above were Sassanian-Islamic and tin-glazed wares, above which were crosshatched, hatched, and champlevé sgraffiato. The lowest three meters of deposits in central Pate, therefore, represent a classic early coastal ceramic sequence that probably dates from the ninth to the middle of the thirteenth century and establishes Pate as one of the oldest continually occupied sites in eastern Africa.

The historical, cultural, architectural, and archaeological significance of Pate and the fact that the town is still inhabited perhaps make it inevitable that many serious preservation issues arise there. The people of Pate regard it as their right to remove stones from the ruins for building purposes, thereby dismantling the site, and to cultivate tobacco as a cash crop over much of the area, stirring up the archaeological deposits and weakening the ruined buildings.

The Kenyan government originally protected by law (gazetted) the entire ruin field. Attempts to enforce the ordinance caused ill feelings toward the National Museums of Kenya from the people of Pate. A study by Usam Ghaidan on conservation in Lamu District recommended that Pate be degazetted and only specific areas be protected by law (1976:34). This recommendation was implemented, and five areas of Pate have currently been regazetted. Ghaidan, an architect, was more interested in preserving architectural integrity than the archaeological record. It is difficult to argue that the Kenyan government should deprive the people of Pate of their ability to make money from growing tobacco, because other economic opportunities on the island are few. On the other hand, it is hard to condone the slow destruction of a major site. In any case, the people of Pate continue to harvest building materials from the ruins to construct new houses.

Pate exemplifies some of the themes and tensions in cultural preservation: the right to earn a livelihood versus the need for cultural preservation; the need to preserve communities as well as monuments and sites; the relationships between preservation authorities and the people affected; the role of government consultants; the obligation to educate the local people about preservation programs; the need for economic alternatives; and redevelopment and reuse of ruined structures. Another example from Pate illustrates how conceptions of private property rights potentially deny the larger community its culturalheritage.

Removal of Architectural Elements: A Tombstone from Pate

Whether someone removes an object from a monument or site with the intent of selling it, keeping it, or "preserving" it, the effect on the site is the same. Removal and recovery of a tombstone from Pate illustrates the potential for serious historical, architectural, and aesthetic loss and the ways museums can recover objects of cultural significance.

In 1913 C. H. Stigand recorded a dated tombstone at Pate that listed three sultans of Pate whose names also occur in the Pate Chronicle (Stigand 1913; Freeman-Grenville 1962a; Werner 1914). The Pate Chronicle is an indigenous document, occurring in several versions, and cross-referencing its text and the inscription could be valuable historical verification of the existence of these sultans. Stigand recorded the date, incorrectly, as A.H. 1024, A.D. 1616 (1913:163), further complicating the already challenging task of interpreting the historical significance of the Pate Chronicle (Chittick 1969b).

The tombstone (fig. 17-6), probably still attached to its tomb in 1911, disappeared sometime thereafter, and it remained lost to scholars until it was discovered in a workroom of the district commissioner's office in Lamu in spring 1981. Maawaiya bin Muhammad brought the tombstone of the sultan Fumomadi to Lamu sometime before his death in 1928, and it remained in the possession of his family until, after negotiations, they donated it to the Lamu Museum in May 1981.

Rediscovery of the tombstone allowed us to retranslate the inscription and correct the reading of the date:

1) There is no God but God; Muhammad is the Messenger of God; God bless him and grant him peace.
2) In the year of the Hegira of the Prophet Muhammad, God bless him, one thousand two hundred twenty-four.
3) This is the grave of Sultan Muhammad bin Sultan
4) Abu Bakr bin Sultan Bwana Mkuu
5) Al-Nabahani, al-Batawi, forgive him and have mercy on him.
6) His death was Wednesday 22 Jumada II.[1]

The correct date for the death of Sultan Fumomadi, therefore, was August 4, 1809, the exact date recorded for this event in the Pate Chronicle. The tombstone also confirms two previous sultans in the chronicle's list.

Figure 17-6. The tombstone of Sultan Muhammad (Fumomadi) from Pate. An important historical monument, it was incorrectly translated by Captain Stigand in 1913, removed from Pate before 1928, and recovered by the National Museums of Kenya in 1981.

Sultan Fumomadi's tombstone illustrates the potential historical, architectural, and aesthetic loss from removal of individual objects and underscores the importance of recovering such objects. It demonstrates how cooperation between governmental agencies and individuals can lead to repatriation and perhaps to reuniting the tombstone with the tomb. National press coverage helped to emphasize the significance of the donation, possibly deterring such acts of removal or encouraging others to return cultural property to the museum. The success was not complete, however, because the donor still possesses another historical tombstone from Pate.

LOOTING AND COLLECTING

In many parts of the world, including Africa, vandals loot sites for gain from the sale or exchange of the stolen objects. In Egypt, thieves have robbed tombs since antiquity, and looters have caused major damage to sites in Peru, Mesoamerica, and the southwestern United States. To our knowledge, the coast of eastern Africa has not experienced concerted theft on this scale. Serious damage to monuments and sites nevertheless occurs when persons remove objects from sites or monuments for whatever reason.

On the coast of eastern Africa, by far the most serious threat to the monuments is not so much from harvesting antiquities as from collecting building materials.

The coral rag and cut coral used in the stone towns can be reused as is or burned to make lime for mortar or plaster. This problem has been ongoing throughout the coast for years, partly because local people think, as at Pate, that they have a right to use the old materials. The most recent example of destruction is from Galu on the south Kenya coast (Kusimba, this volume). Galu and Tumbe are the only two examples in Kenya of the so-called Segeju defensive walls, although other such enclosures occur on the northern Tanzania coast and a similar compound is found at Bur Gao in Somalia (Wilson 1980; Chittick 1958–59, 1969a; Allen 1993). Destruction like that documented by Kusimba at Galu can happen so quickly that, if authorities cannot post local guards or educate local communities, developers can ruin sites extraordinarily fast—indeed, it is in their best interests to do so. Perhaps the next step is recourse under the new Kenyan antiquities law (see below) to deter such behavior in the future.

Ironically, persons without criminal intent who simply seek mementos or pick up interesting objects can cause serious damage to sites. For example, there is a small site eroding from the dunes above a beach near Lamu that is a route used by tourists and local people. Periodically Sassanian-Islamic and other interesting ceramics dating from the ninth century appear on the side of the dune or on the beach, and passers-by, attracted by the glassy greenish-blue glaze of the Sassanian-Islamic ware, often thoughtlessly remove the ceramics. Over time, this activity is removing evidence of early occupation at the site. Posting at the site might be a simple solution that would somewhat deter collecting, but it also calls attention to the site.

Trafficking in the Art Market

In eastern Africa, the problem of plundering sites to harvest antiquities has not reached the destructive scale it has elsewhere, for example in Mali, where the extraordinary level of plunder and the cancerous tentacles of the trade are documented in this volume by R. J. McIntosh, M. Brent, and S. Sidibé. Although less serious than intentionally looting sites, collecting mementos from sites or monuments nevertheless damages the integrity of cultural heritage. Illicitly removing objects from their country of origin to make money can be much worse because the activity is more intense and often repeated. Even though archaeological sites are not systematically plundered in eastern Africa, other objects are being removed with alarming persistence. On the coast the problem has been particularly pernicious in regard to Lamu carved doors, Mijikenda grave markers, and holy Korans.

Carved doors occur widely on the East African coast, at least from Mogadishu to Zanzibar (Allen 1973, 1974a, 1974c), and in Kenya they are specifically protected by law (Antiquities and Monuments Act, 1983, at 13). Art dealers covet these carvings and seek to remove them from Kenya and to sell them to museums and collectors. An experience of the National Museums of Kenya illustrates the problem. A man in Lamu owned a structure in which there was a protected carved door. Approached by a foreign agent, he agreed to sell the door for export to Europe, and, informed of the transaction, museum officials intervened. The man explained he was moving the door to another structure for installation. Later, when informed that the door was on a boat in Lamu Harbor, the man explained that the new location was in Mombasa. Intercepted before export in Mombasa, the door is now back in Lamu, although it is not installed in its original structure. One lesson is the need for more effective enforcement procedures, and another is the need to protect the architectural integrity of structures as well as architectural features of buildings.

The Mijikenda comprise several ethnic groups that live along the central Kenyan coast (Prins 1952; Spear 1978, 1981). Some Mijikenda groups, such as the Giriama, carve abstract grave posts (*vigango*) associated with sacred compounds, or *kaya* (Parkin 1991; Mutoro 1987). Nobody except Giriama are supposed to enter their sacred precincts, and removal of the grave markers defiles both the grave and the sacred area. Collectors highly prize the grave posts, which are often remarkable works of art, and many have been removed and exported. Because of the economics involved, the situation undoubtedly encourages Mijikenda themselves to remove the grave markers and sell them for profit. Nobody knows how many grave posts survive in situ.

Regalia: Removal, Recovery, Preservation, and Use

Regalia often play a significant role in religious and civil ceremonies and in the political process, and sometimes their presence is necessary for rituals to proceed (Nkwi, this volume). Loss of regalia may preclude ceremonies crucial to the survival of social institutions, with serious consequences for those involved. If the activities requiring regalia have lapsed, it is important to preserve the regalia as a material record of previous practices and to permit reinstitution of the ceremonies in the future. Two examples from the coast of Kenya illustrate some of the issues.

The historic old site of Vumba Kuu straddles the Kenya-Tanzania border near the coast. According to tradition, Vumba Kuu was founded in A.D. 1204, but archaeology has yet to reveal evidence much earlier than the fifteenth century (Chittick 1958–59; McKay 1975; Wilson 1980:1–4). In the first half of the seventeenth century, one Mwana Chambi Chande Ivor is remembered as the man who, with the assistance of Segeju and probably Digo allies, conquered eight Shirazi (or Dabuli) towns nearby (Hollis 1900; Allen 1993:151–55; McKay 1975). Special ceremonies with specific regalia were necessary for the enthronement of each *diwan*, or leader, of the Vumba confederacy, and, interestingly enough, people from the defeated towns were forbidden to wear sandals or turbans, to carry umbrellas, to veil women, to install wooden doors, or to possess large drums (Hollis 1900:282).

Investiture of a *diwan* of Vumba Kuu was a lengthy and costly business that entailed complex ceremonies and use of regalia, including wooden sandals, silver necklaces, turbans, special bedsteads, drums, cymbals, and *siwas* (side-blown horns). At other times, drums and horns were played for feasts, for births or deaths of important persons, or when praying for rain. A short carved-ivory *siwa*, perhaps a gift from the ruler of Pate to Diwan Hasan at Ozi in the mid-eighteenth century, survived in 1980 at Vanga, although its end is missing and it has been used as a chopping block (Wilson 1980:146; Dickson 1921). In 1980 we also located

Figure 17-7. Two of three carved drums at Wasini in 1980. Possibly carved in the early nineteenth century, these drums may have been used in enthronement ceremonies for the *diwans* of the Shirazi Confederacy, originally at Vumba Kuu and later at Wasini.

three beautiful drums (fig. 17-7), carved in the early nineteenth century, in the possession of Saggaf bin Hassan bin Nasir, grandson of Sayyid Nasir bin Alaui bin Diwan Kikambala, who died in 1885, before he could be enthroned at Vumba Kuu. After negotiations, Saggaf bin Hassan placed the drums in the care of the Fort Jesus Museum. We located three other drums at Vanga and another at Shirazi, all of them deteriorating through exposure to the elements (Wilson 1980: 46–49).

The Vumba/Wasini regalia are the visual and material evidence of an extraordinary history on the coast. The *diwanate* ceased to exist in 1897, and the condition of the regalia precludes their recent use. Those items in possession of the National Museums of Kenya will serve as a unique record of those times, whereas the survival of the others is in question.

The *siwas* of Pate and Lamu are examples of incredible works of art and objects of historical significance from the north Kenyan coast (Allen 1976, 1977; Sassoon 1975). The ivory *siwa* of Pate and the brass *siwa* of Lamu, dating from the seventeenth and eighteenth centuries respectively, were used on state occasions and for private ceremonies with public implications. These horns are now on display in the Lamu Museum, and they constitute two of the major artistic and historical treasures in Kenya.

THE FOUNDATIONS OF CULTURAL PRESERVATION: SITE SURVEYS

A threshold issue in cultural preservation is knowing what survives to preserve (Mturi, this volume). Site surveys and museum inventories are necessary to determine preservation and conservation needs. Surveys of cultural property require trained and experienced personnel, a survey plan, materials, access, transportation, capacity to analyze data, financial support, and a plethora of other prerequisites based upon the local situation (McIntosh 1992). Without the information provided by surveys, however, preservation and conservation efforts will be ineffectual no matter how well intentioned. For example, Kenya law incompletely protected some sites because their full extent was unknown. Therefore, even if the political will to preserve them existed, action would be ineffective, because officials had inadequate knowledge of the parameters of preservation.

The quality and extent of site survey along the coast of eastern Africa vary considerably. In Somalia there has never been a consistent site survey from Mogadishu southward, although there have been significant contributions (Brenner 1868; Cerulli 1957; Chittick 1969a, 1982; Elliot 1925–26; FitzGerald 1898; Grottanelli 1955a and b; Prins 1967; Sanseverino 1983; Wilson 1984). There needs to be a comprehensive survey of the sites and monuments of the coast of Somalia in relation to the hinterland (Dualeh Jama 1990).

In Kenya, the National Museums of Kenya established a registry of all the sites in the country. On the Kenyan coast, serious archaeological survey has progressed since 1948 (Allen 1974b, 1980, 1981, 1993; Chittick 1967; Kirkman 1957, 1975b; Wilson 1978, 1980, 1982b, 1992). Relations with the hinterland have been investigated by Horton (1984), Abungu (1989), and Mutoro (1987). In addition to the published materials, the archives of the National Museums of Kenya and the British Institute in Eastern Africa contain important collections of unpublished manuscripts and photographs relating to monuments and sites, for example, the Hollis photographs at the National Museums. Geological surveys (Caswell 1953; Thompson 1956), air photos, and satellite imagery are all useful tools in determining location of sites and relationships to natural features.

In Tanzania, Chittick (1958–59) and Freeman-Grenville (1962b) conducted pioneering surveys along the coast, to which Mturi has added much information. In the past few years, archaeological surveys on the coast of Tanzania have progressed significantly. Horton and Clark have provided the first systematic survey on Zanzibar (1985), and Fawcett and LaViolette (1990), and LaViolette, Fawcett, and Schmidt (1989) have completed the first scientific surveys using transects that indicate the relationships of all types of sites in the survey area. Sinclair (1990, 1991), and Schmidt (1988), Schmidt and his associates (1992), and Collett (1985) have addressed the issue of linking first millennium Iron Age sites with the coastal settlements. UNESCO completed technical reports on Zanzibar town, Kilwa, and Bagamoyo (see, for example, United Nations 1983).

Surveys in the Comoro Islands reveal occupation from the ninth and tenth centuries (Kus and Wright 1976; Wright 1984, 1986; Allibert, Argant, and Argant 1983), as has work on the coast of Mozambique (Sinclair 1982, 1990:8–12, 1991). Vérin (1986), among others, has investigated sites on the northern coast of Madagascar.

Recently, the Urban Origins in Eastern Africa project, sponsored by the Swedish Agency for Research Cooperation with Developing Countries, has developed comprehensive plans for site survey, standardization of terminology, comparative chronologies, training, institutional development, and other initiatives coast-wide

(Sinclair and Wandibba 1988; Sinclair 1988; Sinclair and Pwiti 1990). This ambitious program could serve as a model of North-South cooperation as well as a framework for developing and implementing regional archaeological programs.

LEGAL PROTECTION OF CULTURAL HERITAGE

It is crucial for international organizations and nations to promulgate effective legislation to protect cultural property. Enforcement of protective legislation is a problem everywhere in the world, but strong preservation laws provide the legal means to protect heritage (Karoma, Mturi, Papageorge Kouroupas, and Prott, all in this volume).[2]

In Kenya calls for the preservative of the coastal sites were made as early as the first decade of this century, and in 1927 some of the sites were protected by law under the Ancient Monuments Preservation Ordinance, which was repealed and replaced in 1934 by Chapter 215 of the Laws of Kenya, The Preservation of Objects of Archaeological and Paleontological Interest Ordinance. This legislation protected sites and monuments demarcated and published in the *Kenya Gazette*, and about thirty monuments and sites were gazetted by 1980. Lack of adequate site survey sometimes led to protecting only portions of sites, perhaps because of misunderstanding the distinctions between monuments and sites. For example, gazetting protected only one tomb at Kiunga and solely the large mosque at Kitoka, instead of the sites where these monuments occur. The situation underscores, among other things, the relationship between proper surveys and effective legislation and the desirability of including specialists in the drafting of preservation legislation.

In 1983 Kenya enacted new legislation concerning the national museum and protection of cultural heritage (the National Museums Act, 1983, and the Antiquities and Monuments Act). Under the acts, the government may protect monuments and sites above or below ground, including surrounding land, as well as objects of historical or cultural interest. The laws provide for access to and excavation of sites on private land and compensation to owners for damages incurred, making it much tougher than legislation in the United States. Objects cannot be removed from sites without license. The government minister may restrict access to the site and forbid agricultural or livestock use on it. The acts provide for compulsory purchase of endangered monuments and assesses fines and/or imprisonment for anyone who imperils a monument. They declare any antiquity to be the property of the government, and no one can sell, part with, or exchange a protected object without a permit.

The law requires export permits and prohibits export except through a customs port of entry. It gives museums or other authorities the right to inspect monuments without warrant and to order cessation of work thereto, authority to enter premises without warrant and to demand production of antiquities or protected objects, and the authority to search any person reasonably suspected of acquiring ownership or possession of a protected object. Such materials may be seized or forfeited to the government for deposit with the museum. The acts provide penalties of fines and/or imprisonment for persons breaching the various sections. This legislation has considerable teeth.

ECONOMIC ARGUMENTS FOR PRESERVATION

Museums, sites, and monuments are tremendous economic, educational, and cultural resources. Tourism is consistently one of the top industries in Kenya, bringing a great deal of foreign exchange into the country. For the Kenyan coast, Burrows (1975) has explained the economic potential of cultural tourism, which attracts visitors to the coast through a combination of museums, monuments, game and marine parks, and the usual beach attractions. Such a package can provide the rationale for the preservation and development of monuments and sites because there are clear economic benefits.

There are several museums and national monuments along the Kenya coast. In the north, the Lamu Museum comprises the old district commissioner's residence on the seafront, Lamu Fort, and a Swahili house museum (Allen 1972, 1974a). In Mombasa, Fort Jesus Museum (fig. 17-8) includes the fort and the old law courts building (Kirkman 1974). National monuments include Gedi (Kirkman 1954, 1963, 1975b), Mnarani (Kirkman 1958), Jumba la Mtwana (Sassoon 1980), and Takwa (Wilson 1979b).[3] In fiscal year 1988–89, 804,532 people visited Kenyan museums; of these, 246,497 visited coastal museums and monuments. During the same period, coastal monuments and sites reported revenues of K£ 477,745 and expenses of K£ 364,287 (Okoth 1990:66–67). Even including a grant-in-aid of K£ 68,000, a surplus of K£ 113,458 leaves many Western museum administrators envious.

The economic impact on museums is not the same as the economic impact of museums. The National Museums of Kenya tracks nonresidents as well as residents in its visitation statistics. Of visitors to coastal museums and monuments in 1989, 167,000 were tourists, who stayed in hotels, shopped, used transportation, and did all the other things that tourists do. This represents a major impact on the Kenyan economy, and coastal museums and monuments are a major element in attracting tourists to the coast. Cultural tourism pays, but only if governments preserve sites and monuments and develop museums.

THE EDUCATIONAL MISSION OF MUSEUMS, MONUMENTS, AND SITES

There are significant educational reasons for preserving sites and monuments and developing museums (see Posnansky, this volume; Mturi, this volume). In 1989, 24,126 schoolchildren and organized groups visited museums and monuments on the Kenyan coast, and 3,760 children of Kenyan residents went though the same facilities on unguided tours (Okoth 1990:61). The Fort Jesus and Lamu museums have education departments that provide tours and special programs that provide educational experiences to complement classroom learning. Visual images

Figure 17-8. Fort Jesus, Mombasa, was constructed in 1593 and has featured prominently in the history of the coast. A prison in the British colonial period, Fort Jesus was excavated by James Kirkman and is now an interpreted historical monument and museum.

facilitate learning and encourage lasting memories of the associated lesson. In addition, coastal museums provide opportunities for adult education that are often unavailable elsewhere, such as programs for Muslim women or handicapped children. If the experience in the United States is any indication, museums will have increasingly important roles in public education. Ministries of education in Africa should fund programs in museum education as well as schools.

Museums hold objects that can be used for scholarly research, for public education through exhibitions and publications, and for academic or museum training. The story of a country's past often can be told through objects, and, for earlier periods, archaeology can be one of the principal sources of African history. Museums are also repositories of historical, ethnographic, and contemporary collections, and governments and private sources should support African museums' efforts to collect in these areas. Museum libraries and archives can be major repositories and research facilities duplicated nowhere else in the country (Wilson and Parezo 1992). The library in Fort Jesus houses manuscripts and publications rare or unavailable in much of Europe and the United States, and is one of the best collections of its kind.

There are also political and religious arguments for preservation of monuments and sites (Drewal, this volume). Objects in museums can be visual images of a country's past, powerful national symbols, and important symbols in nation building. Ruined monuments also sometimes serve as places of worship. On the Kenyan coast, people still use old tombs and mosques at Omwe, Takwa, Lamu, Siyu, Ukunda, Kongo, Munje, and other locations for prayer and ritual.

Conservation of Monuments and Sites

The foregoing establishes some of the social, cultural, educational, and economic reasons to preserve monuments and sites and demonstrates that a tough antiquities act can establish the legal framework for their protection (see also Mturi, this volume). For standing monuments and historic structures, governments must initiate conservation programs to ensure that cultural preservation exists in fact as well as in theory.

In Kenya, conservation of coastal monuments dates at least to the 1930s, when the Public Works Department undertook stabilization work at sites such as Gedi, Mnarani, and Kongo. Conservation was an integral part of the Lamu special project in the 1970s and has remained so ever since (Wilson 1982a; Ghaiden 1976; Abungu and Katana 1990). A thorough conservation plan for monuments and sites must include surveying, written plans for conservation treatment, and implementation of the plan. Establishing priorities is imperative, because conservation needs of monuments and sites, whether in Africa or in the developed world, characteristically exceed funding capacity and available trained personnel.

Once a conservation plan is in place, conservation treatment should proceed, using appropriate traditional building techniques and materials. The National Museums of Kenya spent considerable time and money testing building techniques to discover the most effective conservation methods, to train staff, to support conservation research, to undertake field conservation, and to establish a conservation laboratory in Mombasa. Money for conservation projects is hard to get in any country, but perhaps more revenues from Kenyan monuments and sites could be earmarked for their conservation. For major monuments, the World Monument Fund can be a source of support.

The Role of Museums Outside Eastern Africa

There are many ways that museums outside eastern Africa can assist with the sort of projects and needs outlined in this essay. The International Council of Museums establishes the international standard with its code of ethics, which states that it is highly unethical for a museum to support the illicit market in objects, mandates that museums not acquire objects without valid title or those that were exported from their country of origin or an intermediate country in violation of law, and requires that museums not receive excavated materials if there is "reasonable cause to believe that their recovery involved the recent unscientific or intentional destruction or damage of monuments or sites, or involved a failure to disclose the finds to the owner or occupier of the land, or to the proper legal or governmental authorities."[4] An example of fruitful international cooperation is the American Association of Museums/International Council of Museum's program, International Partnerships among Museums, which encourages staff exchanges between U.S. museums and museums in other countries. Although the program does not support conservation training, it does promote joint or complementary projects in most other areas of museum activities.[5]

There are many things that museums outside Africa can do to help preserve cultural heritage. They can help African museums set up collections management policies and procedures, security systems, and systems of registration. They can become involved in training of all kinds and can assist in building libraries, like the book project of the Arts Council of the African Studies Association. Western museums can ensure that African museum professionals are invited to conferences and that funding is available for such participation. Museums can and do assist U.S. customs agents in stopping illicit importation of objects of cultural heritage, and they can adhere closely to the ethical codes that will do much to stop such trade. In these and many other ways museums outside Africa can help preserve Africa's past.

CONCLUSION

Surveying the potential to arrest the disappearance of Africa's past on the coast of eastern Africa yields feelings of optimism and challenge. The countries of the littoral have made great progress in many areas. In the spirit of offering constructive suggestions to governments, agencies, philanthropic organizations, and individuals, we recommend commitment to and financial support for 1) site surveys and museum inventories; 2) conservation plans, surveys, and treatment programs; 3) intergovernmental communication among agencies whose spheres impact preservation; 4) controlling corporations whose activities threaten cultural heritage; 5) requiring environmental impact studies before any development that could endanger cultural heritage; 6) monitoring sites and monuments on public and private land for their preservation; 7) strictly enforcing cultural preservation laws, and closing loopholes in them; 8) educating the public about the economic, social, and cultural reasons for cultural preservation; 9) fostering cooperation among museums, police, customs agents, and district, provincial, and national governments; 10) publicizing thefts from museums in international art publications and among international police authorities; 11) encouraging relationships between institutions and individuals in Africa and abroad; 12) training staff in all areas of museum operations and programs, including conservation, archaeology, art history, ethnology, folklore, history, exhibitions, libraries and archives, collection management, education, and administration; 13) establishing and adhering to national and international ethical standards and enforcing breaches with penalties.

These suggestions do not exhaust the needs and requirements of maintaining cultural heritage in Africa, but they will considerably advance the goal of preserving sites, monuments, and communities, which will make a better world for us all.

NOTES

1. Translation by Athman Lai Omar and Thomas H. Wilson in collaboration with Wilfred Lockwood, Rex Smith, and James Kirkman.

2. UNESCO is publishing the national laws and regulations governing the protection of movable cultural property. Copies may be obtained free of charge from the Division of Cultural Heritage, UNESCO, 1 rue Miollis, 75015 Paris, France.

3. The government of Kenya gazetted the old towns of Lamu and Mombasa as national monuments in 1986 and 1989 respectively, and established town planning and conservation offices in both places, but unlike the other national monuments, there is no fee to enter (Abungu and Katana 1990).

4. International Council of Museums, *Code of Professional Ethics*, Paris.

5. For information about International Partnerships among Museums, call the Department of International Programs and AAM/ICOM, 1225 I Street NW, Washington, D.C. 20005 (202/289–1818); museums outside the United States should contact the U.S. Information Service post at the U.S. embassy or consulate nearest them regarding the possibility of being nominated into the competition.

REFERENCES

Abungu, G. H. O. "Communities on the River Tana, Kenya: An Archaeological Study of Relations between the Delta and the River Basin, 700–1890 A.D." Ph.D. diss., Cambridge University, 1989.

Abungu, G. H. O., and P. J. Katana. "Development of Urban Settlements along the East African Coast and the Introduction of an Integrated Conservation Approach." Paper presented to the Zanzibar Stonetown Workshop, 19–20 November 1990.

Allen, J. de V. *Lamu*. Nairobi, 1972.

————. "Swahili Ornament: A Study of the Eighteenth Century Plasterwork and Carved Doors of the Lamu Region." *Art and Archaeology Research Papers* 3 (1973):1–14; 4 (1973): 87–92.

————. *Lamu Town: A Guide*. Mombasa, 1974a.

————. "Swahili Architecture in the Later Middle Ages." *African Arts* 7 (1974b):42–47, 66–68, 83–84.

————. "Swahili Culture Reconsidered: Some Historical Implications of the Material Culture of the Northern Kenya Coast in the Eighteenth and Nineteenth Centuries." *Azania* 9 (1974c):105–38.

————. "The *Siwas* of Lamu and Pate: Two Antique Side-Blown Horns from the Swahili Coast." *Art and Archaeology Research Papers* 9 (1976):38–47.

————. "Two Antique Musical Instruments from Central Kenya." *Kenya Past and Present* 8 (1977).

————. "The Swahili House: Cultural and Ritual Concepts Underlying Its Plan and Structure." In *Swahili Houses and Tombs of the Coast of Kenya*. J. de V. Allen and T. H. Wilson, eds. London: Art and Archaeology Research Papers, 1979. 1–32.

————. "Settlement Patterns on the East African Coast, c. 800–1900." In *Proceedings of the Eighth Panafrican Congress of Prehistory and Quaternary Studies*. ed. R. E. Leakey and B. A. Ogot, 361–63, 1980.

————. "Swahili Culture and the Nature of East Coast Settlement." *International Journal of African Historical Studies* 14 (1981):306–34.

————. "The Names of the Tana Delta Sites." *Azania* 17 (1983):165–72.

————. *Swahili Origins: Swahili Culture and the Shungwaya Phenomenon*. London: James Currey, 1993.

Allen, J. de V., and T. H. Wilson. *Swahili Houses and Tombs of the Coast of Kenya*. London: Art and Archaeology Research Papers, 1979.

————. *From Zinj to Zanzibar: Studies in History, Trade and Society on the Eastern Coast of Africa.* *Paideuma* 28 (1982). Wiesbaden: Franz Steiner Verlag.

Allibert, C., A. Argant, and J. Argant. "Le site de Bagamoyo (Mayotte)," *Etudes Océan Indien* 2 (1983):5–40.

Anonymous. *Museo della Gareso Catalogo.* Mogadishu: Regio Governo della Somalia, 1934.

Brenner, R. "Richard Brenner's Forschungen in Ost-Afrika." *Petermann's Mittheilungen* (1868):175–79, 361–67, 456–65.

Burrows, G. S. *The Development of Cultural Tourism.* Paris: UNESCO, 1975.

Caswell, P. V. *Geology of the Mombasa-Kwale Area.* Nairobi: Geological Survey of Kenya, report no. 24, 1953.

Cerulli, E. *Somalia, scritti editi ed inediti.* 3 vols. Rome, 1957.

Chittick, H. N. *Annual Reports of the Department of Antiquities, 1957–59.* Dar es Salaam: Government Printer, 1958–1959.

————. "Discoveries in the Lamu Archipelago." *Azania* 2 (1967):37–68.

————. "An Archaeological Reconnaissance of the Southern Somali Coast." *Azania* 4 (1969a): 115–30.

————. "A New Look at the History of Pate." *Journal of African History* 10 (1969b):375–91.

————. *Kilwa: An Islamic Trading City on the East African Coast.* Nairobi: British Institute in Eastern Africa, 1974.

————. "Early Ports in the Horn of Africa." *The International Journal of Nautical Archaeology and Underwater Exploration* 8, no. 4 (1979):273–77.

————. "Mediaeval Mogadishu." *Paideuma* 28 (1982):45–62.

————. "Ancient Ports of Northern Somalia: Excavations at Hafun." Paper presented to the Second International Congress of Somali Studies, Hamburg, 1983.

————. *Manda: Excavations at an Island Port on the Coast of Kenya.* Nairobi: British Institute in Eastern Africa, 1984.

Cobelj, S. "The Provincial Museum of Hargeisa." *Museum* 38, no. 151 (1986):150–54.

Collett, D. P. "The Spread of Early Iron-Producing Communities in Eastern and Southern Africa." Ph.D. diss., Cambridge University, 1985.

Connah, G. *African Civilizations.* Cambridge: Cambridge University Press, 1987.

Dickson, T. A. "The Regalia of the Wa-Vumba." *Man* 20 (1921):33–35.

Dualeh Jama, A. "Urban Origins on the Southern Somali Coast with Special Reference to Mogadishu A.D. 1000 to 1600." In *Urgan Origins in Eastern Africa: Proceedings of the 1990 Workshop, Harare and Great Zimbabwe,* ed. P. J. J. Sinclair and G. Pwiti, 106–12. Stockholm: The Central Board of National Antiquities, 1990.

Elliot, J. A. G. "A Visit to the Bajun Islands." *Journal of the African Society* 25 (1925–26):10–22, 147–63, 245–63, 338–58.

Fawcett, W. B., and A. LaViolette. "Iron Age Settlement around Mkiu, Southeastern Tanzania." *Azania* 25 (1990):19–26.

FitzGerald, W. W. A. *Travels in the Coastlands of British East Africa and the Islands of Zanzibar and Pemba.* London, 1898.

Freeman-Grenville, F. G. S. *The East African Coast: Select Documents from the First to the Later Nineteenth Century.* Oxford University Press, 1962a.

————. *The Medieval History of the Coast of Tanganyika.* Oxford University Press, 1962b.

Freeman-Grenville, F. G. S., and B. G. Martin. "A Preliminary Handlist of the Arabic Inscriptions of the Eastern African Coast." *Journal of the Royal Asiatic Society* 2 (1973):98–122.

Garlake, P. S. *The Early Islamic Architecture of the East African Coast.* Nairobi: Oxford University Press, 1966.

Ghaidan, U. *Lamu: A Study of the Swahili Town.* Nairobi: East African Literature Bureau, 1975.

————. *Lamu: A Study in Conservation.* Nairobi: East African Literature Bureau, 1976.

Grottanelli, V. I. "A Lost African Metropolis." *Afrikanistische Studien* 26 (1955a):231–42.
———. *Pescatori dell'Oceano Indiano.* Rome, 1955b.
Hollis, A. C. "Notes on the History of Vumba, East Africa." *Journal of the Royal Anthropological Institute* 30 (1900):275–97.
Horton, M. C. *Shanga 1980.* Cambridge: Cambridge University Press, 1980.
———. "The Early Settlement of the Northern Swahili Coast." Ph.D. diss., Cambridge University, 1984.
———. "Asiatic Colonisation of the East African Coast: The Manda Evidence." *Journal of the Royal Asiatic Society* 2 (1986):201–13.
———. "The Swahili Corridor." *Scientific American* (September 1987):86–93.
Horton, M. C., and C. Clark. *The Zanzibar Archaeological Survey, 1984–85.* Zanzibar: Ministry of Information, Culture, and Sport, 1985.
Huntingford, G. B. H. *The Periplus of the Erythraean Sea.* London: Hakluyt Society, 1980.
Isaac, G. L. "Notes on the Stone Age Industries." In *Kilwa: An Islamic Trading City on the East African Coast.* Vol. I. Nairobi: British Institute in Eastern Africa, 1974.
Kato, Y., G. Omi, and K. Adachi. "On the Acheulean Site of Mtongwe, Mombasa." In *Third Preliminary Report of African Studies (Archaeology 1).* ed. G. Omi, 13–17. Nagoya University: Association for African Studies, 1977.
Kirkman, J. S. *The Arab City of Gedi: Excavations at the Great Mosque. Architecture and Finds.* London: 1954.
———. "Historical Archaeology in Kenya 1948–1956." *The Antiquaries Journal* 37 (1957): 16–29.
———. "Mnarani of Kilifi: The Mosques and Tombs." *Ars Orientalis* 3 (1958):95–112.
———. *Gedi: The Palace.* The Hague: Mouton, 1963.
———. *Men and Monuments on the East African Coast.* London: Lutterworth Press, 1964.
———. *Ungwana on the Tana.* The Hague: Mouton, 1966.
———. "Topographical and Historical Notes." In *The Portuguese Period in East Africa,* trans. J. S. Wallwork, ed. J. S. Kirkman, 289–317. Nairobi: East African Literature Bureau, 1971.
———. *Fort Jesus: A Portuguese Fortress on the East African Coast.* Oxford: Oxford University Press, 1974.
———. "Some Conclusions from Archaeological Excavations on the Coast of Kenya 1948–1966." In *East Africa and the Orient,* ed. H. N. Chittick and R. I. Rotberg, 226–47. New York: Africana Press, 1975a.
———. *Gedi.* Mombasa: Rodwell Press, 1975b.
Kus, S., and H. T. Wright. "Note préliminaire sur une reconnaisance archéologique de l'île de Mayotte." *Asie du Sud-Est et Monde Insulindien* 8(2–3)1976:123–35.
———. "Survey archéologique de la région de l'Avaradrano." *Taloha* 10. Antananarivo: Musée d'Art et d'Archéologie, Université de Madagascar, 1986.
Kusimba, C. M. "Iron Working in Eastern Africa: Archaeological and Archaeometallurgical Approaches to the Study of the Early Settlement of the Swahili Coast." Master's thesis, Bryn Mawr College, 1989.
LaViolette, A., W. B. Fawcett, and P. R. Schmidt. "The Coast and the Hinterland: University of Dar es Salaam Archaeological Field Schools, 1987–1988." *Nyame Akuma* 32 (1989): 38–46.
Loughran, K. S., J. L. Loughran, J. W. Johnson, and Said Sheik Samatar, eds. *Somalia in Word and Image.* Washington, D.C., and Bloomington: Foundation for Cultural Understanding and Indiana Universtiy Press, 1986.
McIntosh, S. K. "Archaeological Heritage Management and Site Inventory Systems in Africa: The Role of Development." In *Culture and Development in Africa,* ed. I. Serageldin and J. Taboroff, 2:391–414. Washington, D.C.: World Bank, 1992.

McKay, W. F. "A Pre-Colonial History of the Southern Kenya Coast." Ph.D. diss., Boston University, 1975.

McMahon, K. "The Former Museums of Somalia." Unpublished manuscript, 1991.

Mutoro, H. W. "A Contribution to the Study of Cultural and Economic Dynamics of Historical Settlements of the East African Coast with Particular Reference to the Ruins of Takwa." Master's thesis, University of Nairobi, 1979.

————. "An Archaeological Study of the Mijikenda Kaya Settlements on the Historical Kenya Coast." Ph.D. diss., University of California, Los Angeles, 1987.

Nurse, D., and T. Spear. *The Swahili: Reconstructing the History and Language of an African Society, 800–1500*. Philadelphia: University of Pennsylvania Press, 1985.

Okoth, A. J. *Report of the Auditor-General (Corporations) on the Accounts of the National Museums of Kenya for the Year Ended 30th June, 1989*. Nairobi: 1990.

Parkin, D. *Sacred Void: Spatial Images of Work and Ritual among the Giriama of Kenya*. New York: Cambridge University Press, 1991.

Posnansky, M. *Somali Democratic Republic: Museum and Antiquities Development*. Paris: UNESCO, 1979.

Prins, A. H. J. *Coastal Tribes of the North-Eastern Bantu*. London: International African Institute, 1952.

————. *The Swahili-Speaking Peoples of Zanzibar and the East African Coast*. London: International African Institute, 1967.

Sanseverino, H. C. "Archaeological Remains on the Southern Somalia Coast." *Azania* 18 (1983):151–64.

Sassoon, H. *Fort Jesus Newsletter*. Mombasa: National Museums of Kenya, 1974–75.

————. *The Siwas of Lamu*. Nairobi: National Museums of Kenya, 1975.

————. "How Old is Mombasa?" *Kenya Past and Present* 9 (1978):33–37.

————. "The Coastal Town of Jumba la Mtwana." *Kenya Past and Present* 12 (1980):2–14.

————. "Excavations at the Site of Early Mombasa." *Azania* 15 (1981):1–44.

Schmidt, P. R. "Eastern Expressions of the 'Mwitu' Traditions: Early Iron Age Industry of the Usambara Mountains, Tanzania." *Nyame Akuma* 30 (1988):36–67.

Schmidt, P. R., N. J. Karoma, A. LaViolette, W. Fawcett, A. Z. Mabulla, L. N. Rutabanzibwa, and C. M. Saanane. *Archaeological Investigations in the Vicinity of Mkiu, Kisarawe District, Tanzania*. Archaeological Contributions of the University of Dar es Salaam, Occasional Paper no. 1. Dar es Salaam: 1992.

Sinclair, P. J. J. "Chibuene, an Early Trading Site in Southern Mozambique." *Paideuma* 28 (1982):149–64.

————. *Urban Origins in Eastern Africa: Phase I Progress Report and Phase II Research Outline* (Paper no. 2). Stockholm: The Central Board of National Antiquities, 1988.

————. "Archaeology in Eastern Africa: An Overview of Current Chronological Issues." In *Urban Origins in Eastern Africa: Proceedings of the 1990 Workshop, Harare and Great Zimbabwe*, ed. P. J. Sinclair and G. Pwiti, 2–40. Stockholm: The Central Board of National Antiquities, 1990.

————. "Archaeology in Eastern Africa: An Overview of Current Chronological Issues." *Journal of African History* 32 (1991):179–219.

————. "Urban Origins in Eastern Africa: A Brief Summary of Results to November 1991." In *Mvita: Newsletter of the Regional Centre for the Study of Urban Origins in Eastern and Southern Africa*. Mombasa: National Museums of Kenya, 1992.

Sinclair, P. J. J., and G. Pwiti, eds. *Urban Origins in Eastern Africa. Proceedings of the 1990 Workshop. Harare and Great Zimbabwe*. Stockholm: The Central Board of National Antiquities, 1990.

Sinclair, P. J. J., and S. Wandibba. *Urban Origins in Eastern Africa: Project Proposals and Workshop Summaries*. Paper no. 1. Stockholm: The Central Board of National Antiquities, 1988.

Siravo, F., and A. Pulver. *Planning Lamu*. Nairobi: National Museums of Kenya, 1986.

Smith, M. C., and H. T. Wright. "Notes on a Classical Maritime Site: The Ceramics from Ras Hafun, Somalia." *Azania* 23 (1988):115–42.

Spear, T. T. *The Kaya Complex*. Nairobi: Kenya Literature Bureau, 1978.

———. *Traditions of Origin and Their Interpretation: The Mijikenda of Kenya*. Athens: Ohio University Press, 1981.

Stigand, C. H. *The Land of Zinj*. London: Constable, 1913.

Stiles, D. "The Ports of East Africa, the Comoros and Madagascar: Their Place in Indian Ocean Trade from 1–1500 A.D." *Kenya Past and Present* 24 (1992):27–36.

Strandes, J. *The Portuguese Period in East Africa*. Trans. J. F. Wallwork, ed. J. S. Kirkman. Nairobi: East African Literature Bureau, 1971.

Thompson, A. O. *Geology of the Malindi Area*. Report no. 36 Nairobi: Geological Survey of Kenya, 1956.

Trone, A. "Somalia: Aspects of Conservation at the National Museum." Unpublished manuscript, 1979.

United Nations. *The Stone Town of Zanzibar*. UNCHS Technical Report, 1983.

Vérin, P. *The History of Civilization in Northern Madagascar*. Rotterdam: Balkema, 1986.

Werner, A. "Swahili History of Pate." *Journal of the African Society* 14 (1914):148–61, 278–97, 392–413.

Wilson, T. H. *The Monumental Architecture and Archaeology North of the Tana River*. Nairobi: National Museums of Kenya, 1978.

———. "Swahili Funerary Architecture of the North Kenya Coast." In *Swahili Houses and Tombs of the Coast of Kenya*. by J. de V. Allen and Thomas H. Wilson, 33–46. London: Art and Archaeology Research Papers, 1979a.

———. "Takwa: An Ancient Swahili Settlement of the Lamu Archipelago." *Kenya Past and Present* 10 (1979b):6–16. Reprinted as site guide.

———. *The Monumental Architecture and Archaeology of the Central and Southern Kenya Coast*. Nairobi: National Museums of Kenya, 1980.

———. "Conservation of the Ancient Architecture of the Kenya Coast." *Kenya Past and Present* 14 (1982a):6–19.

———. "Spatial Analysis and Settlement Patterns on the East African Coast." *Paideuma* 28 (1982b):201–19.

———. "Sites and Settlement Patterns of Coastal Jubaland, Southern Somalia." In *Proceedings of the Second International Congress of Somali Studies, Vol. 2: Archaeology and History*. ed. T. Labahn, 73-106. Hamburg: Helmut Buske Verlag, 1984.

———. "Settlement Patterns of the Coast of Southern Somalia and Kenya." In *Proceedings of the First International Congress of Somali Studies*. 76–112. Scholar's Press, 1992.

Wilson, T. H., and N. J. Parezo. "The Role of Museums in Preserving the Anthropological Record." In *Preserving the Anthropological Record*, ed. Sydel Silverman and Nancy J. Parezo, 61–72. New York: Wenner-Gren Foundation, 1992.

Wright, H. T. "Early Seafarers of the Comoro Islands: The Dembeni Phase of the IXth-Xth Centuries A.D." *Azania* 19 (1984):13–59.

———. "Early Communities on the Island of Maore and the Coasts of Madagascar." In *Madagascar: Society and History*, ed. C. P. Kottak, J.-A. Rakotoarisoa, A. Southall, and P. Vérin, 53–87. Durham, N.C.: Carolina Academic Press, 1986.,

Ylvisaker, M. *Lamu in the Nineteenth Century: Land, Trade and Politics*. Boston: African Studies Center, Boston University, 1979.

18

STARTING FROM SCRATCH

THE PAST, PRESENT, AND FUTURE MANAGEMENT OF SOMALIA'S CULTURAL HERITAGE

STEVEN A. BRANDT AND OSMAN YUSUF MOHAMED

There are many causes of Africa's "disappearing past." The destruction of archaeological sites from development, looting, farming, and nature, or the disappearance of art and historical objects into the illicit antiquities/art market come to mind. However, few people may be aware of the devastating effects of civil strife on a country's cultural heritage (Fay 1994).

Somalia is in the midst of a savage civil war that not only has caused divisiveness and disintegration of Somali society at an unprecedented scale (Samatar 1991) but also has resulted in substantial destruction of Somalia's cultural heritage, which already faced threats from nature, development, and neglect. This essay will outline the effects of Somalia's civil war on its cultural properties and provide an introduction to the history of cultural heritage management in Somalia prior to the civil strife of the 1990s. Drawing from the lessons of the past and present, we then suggest a comprehensive national cultural heritage program for Somalia's future that also could play an important role in the postwar reconstruction of Somalia.

SOMALIA'S CULTURAL HERITAGE—A BRIEF REVIEW

Somalia is the easternmost country on the African continent, occupying the physiographic region known as the Horn of Africa. With a variety of climates and environments, Somalia's 640,000 square kilometers encompass mountains, deserts, hills, and rivers as well as the longest coastline of any continental African country. The more than six million Somali people share a common religion (Islam) but, contrary to popular belief, are surprisingly diverse in language, culture, history (precolonial and colonial), and economy (Cassanelli 1982).

Somalia's cultural heritage is as diverse as its geography and people and includes resources valued for their archaeological, historical, architectural, symbolic, and religious significance. Unfortunately, Somalia's cultural heritage is poorly documented compared to that of neighboring African countries. For example, of the thousands of archaeological sites that dot Somalia's landscape, few have been adequately described, and fewer than thirty have been excavated (Brandt 1992; Brandt and Gresham 1991; Clark 1954; Wilson 1982).

Archaeological sites are undoubtedly the most numerous cultural resources in Somalia. They date from more than 300,000 years ago to the last few hundred years and are found in open-air, rock-shelter, and cave contexts. Although Early Stone Age (Acheulian) sites are restricted to northern Somalia (Clark 1954; Seton-Karr 1896), Middle and Later Stone Age archaeological sites are scattered throughout Somalia's countryside, documenting the evolution of a hunting and gathering way of life and the physical makeup of the prehistoric populations (Brandt 1986; 1988; Brandt and Gresham 1991; Coltorti and Mussi 1987).

Neolithic sites providing evidence for the establishment of farming and nomadic pastoralism are also found throughout Somalia. These locales include caves and rock shelters whose walls display spectacular painted or engraved scenes of cattle, goats, sheep, camels, and herders, as well as open-air village sites (Brandt and Carder 1987; Carder 1988). Many of the ubiquitous stone cairns or *tallo* found throughout most of the country may also date from the Neolithic.

Archaeologists have yet to discover Iron Age sites in Somalia. However, test excavations at Ras Hafun (near the tip of the Horn in northeastern Somalia) reveal contact with the Greco-Roman world (Chittick 1982; Smith and Wright 1988). Ras Hafun is also likely to be one of many ports situated along Somalia's Gulf of Aden and Indian Ocean coastline that formed part of the extensive maritime trading system described in the *Periplus of the Erythraean Sea* (Huntingford 1980).

Numerous archaeological sites dating from the introduction of Islam (perhaps as early as the seventh century A.D.; Hersi 1977) to the nineteenth century attest to the rise of urbanism and extensive trade networks throughout Somalia and neighboring countries. These networks include towns and cities with standing walls, tombs, mosques, and other shrines, as well as pastoral and farming settlements (Cassanelli 1982; Chittick 1969, 1976, 1982; Curle 1937; Jonsson 1983; Wilson 1982).

Foreign colonization of Somalia began in the early nineteenth century when various areas came under the political and military control of Egypt and the Sultanate of Oman. Subsequently France took control of Djibouti, Great Britain took control of the northwest (Somaliland) and far south, Italy occupied northeastern, central, and southern Somalia, and Ethiopia seized the Ogaden (Laitin and Samatar 1987; Lewis 1988).

Although all of these countries contributed to the creation (or destruction) of Somalia's cultural heritage, the Italians were particularly influential because they left behind numerous architectural legacies ranging from Catholic cathedrals to Fascist monuments (Hess 1966). Somalis were also busy during the colonial period and after independence in 1960, constructing forts, monuments, tombs, shrines, and other public and private buildings important to the country's heritage (Hess 1964; Loughran et al. 1986).

PAST CULTURAL HERITAGE MANAGEMENT

Unlike other former European colonies, such as India, Kenya, and Zimbabwe, which had the fortune of inheriting relatively sound antiquities laws and cultural heritage management practices at independence, Somalia inherited virtually nothing to protect its diverse resources.

In 1933 the Italian colonial administration in Muqdisho established the country's first museum in a building originally constructed in the late 1800s by the Sultan of Oman. The Garesa Museum was one of the earliest museums in sub-Saharan Africa and the first in eastern Africa to publish a comprehensive catalogue of its collections (Posnansky 1979). The museum's 1934 catalog contained more than 3,500 objects, including historical and ethnographic documents; photographs; industrial objects; archaeological, geological, and botanical specimens; traditional and modern weapons; and numismatics (Museo Della Garesa 1934; McMahon 1991:39).

In spite of their interest in museums, the Italians never introduced antiquities laws to Somalia. This task fell to the colonial administration of British Somaliland, which instituted the Antiquities Ordinance in 1946 in response to a rapid increase in the export of archaeological and historic artifacts by foreign individuals and scientific expeditions (Posnansky 1979). Adopted from the penal code of British India, the Antiquities Ordinance was far from perfect. For example, it imposed insignificant statutory penalties when a site or monument was destroyed. Thus, landowners and developers found it easier to pay the small fine rather than disrupt their development plans. Furthermore, the governor had the last word on granting research or export permits, even though there was no one on his staff who could professionally advise him on such matters. Finally, the law did not state how long archaeological objects could be outside the country. Consequently, many archaeological objects from Somalia ended up permanently in other countries, mostly in Europe. In spite of these inadequacies, the Antiquities Ordinance played an important role in the protection of British Somaliland's cultural heritage.

When Somalia gained its independence in 1960, the government chose not to adopt the Antiquities Ordinance or to create an antiquities law of its own. The reasons for this decision (or oversight) remain unknown, but the end result was that at independence Somalia's cultural resources were left completely unprotected.

Soon after independence the Garesa Museum became the Somali National Museum. Administered by the Ministry of Education, the museum received little financial, logistical, or administrative help, and it rapidly declined. In 1966 the Somali government requested that UNESCO provide a consultant to advise the Ministry of Education on how to improve management of the Somali National Museum, and B. G. R. Reynolds of the Zambia National Museum visited Muqdisho on UNESCO's behalf. He described in detail the museum's unfavorable situation, and offered a comprehensive system for the management of Somalia's cultural resources. Unfortunately, the Ministry of Education chose to disregard his recommendations (Posnansky 1979).

In 1972 the Somali government established the Ministry of Culture and Higher Education, with the ministry's Department of Culture given sole responsibility for the country's cultural resources, including administration of the national museum. At the request of the ministry, UNESCO sent Nazimuddin Ahmed to Somalia in 1977 to assess the state of the museum. Ahmed described the grim situation and made several recommendations, ranging from facilities improvement and staff training to the construction of a new museum. In particular, Ahmed emphasized the need for the establishment of an Antiquities Department to oversee all cultural heritage operations (Posnansky 1979).

The following year P. Cole-King, another UNESCO representative, visited the Somali National Museum. In addition to recommending structural improvements to the building as well as new storage and artifact maintenance facilities, Cole-King (1979) also strongly advised the ministry to establish an Antiquities Department within the museum. In 1979 Merrick Posnansky, yet another UNESCO consultant, visited the museums of Somalia. Like the UNESCO consultants before him, Posnansky made detailed suggestions for the improvement of the museum in Muqdisho and also the new museum at Hargeysa, the latter built by the city government and local citizens through a self-help program. Recognizing the expense involved in establishing a new administrative organization and the lack of trained personnel to work for such an organization, Posnansky (1979) lent further support to Cole-King's recommendation for the establishment of an Antiquities Department within the national museum.

Unfortunately, the Ministry of Culture and Higher Education did not act on any of UNESCO's recommendations. However, in 1979 the Somali government finally recognized their legal responsibility toward the nation's cultural heritage by stating in article 51, section 3, of the revised constitution that the state "shall protect and preserve the nation's historic objects and sites." Responsibility for preparing specific legislation for the protection of the country's cultural properties fell to the Somali Academy of Sciences, Arts and Literature. The academy was established in 1978 and fell under the purview of the Ministry of Culture and Higher Education. The academy was responsible for initiating, planning, coordinating, and financing research within the country and establishing links with foreign research institutions. At the top of the academy's administrative pyramid was the president, followed by the deans of the Institute of Sciences and the Institute of Arts and Literature. The Institute of Sciences was further divided into a natural sciences department and a social sciences department, with the latter chaired by a director who supervised several sections, including a history section. The academy soon recognized the need for an archaeology program within the history section, subsequently changing its name to the History and Archaeology Section.

The academy's archaeology program received two major responsibilities: to protect and manage the cultural heritage, which included the preparation of legislation, and to conduct archaeological research. Unfortunately, the archaeology program was largely unable or unwilling to live up to these responsibilities. One major problem was financial support.

The Ministry of Finance was responsible for allocating funds to all governmental agencies, including the academy. Its judgment in approving a proposed budget was generally conditioned by the availability of funds and the socioeconomic importance attached to the academy's activities. Archaeological research and cultural heritage management received no separate budget; instead, these activities formed just one part of the academy's annual budget for its various research projects and administrative programs. Usually archaeological projects and cultural heritage management received lower priority than other projects.

Consequently, the academy's expenditures for archaeology and preservation were confined exclusively to salaries for personnel, transportation, and office expenses. Usually no funds at all were allocated for archaeological research and conservation. Beginning in 1983 and continuing until the fall of the government in 1991, the Swedish Agency for Research Cooperation with Developing Countries (SAREC) signed an accord with the academy agreeing to provide funds for archaeological research and training. However, it appears that after 1985 much of the SAREC money for archaeological research (and for that matter other academy programs) was squandered or perhaps even embezzled.

As for protection and management of the cultural heritage, the archaeology program's hands were effectively tied because cultural heritage legislation—even a basic antiquities law—was never enacted. In 1984 the academy submitted to Parliament an antiquities bill based, ironically, on the 1946 Antiquities Ordinance for British Somaliland. Unfortunately, the bill was tied up in Parliament from 1984 until the fall of the Siad Barre government in 1991. Reasons for the bill's failure to be enacted are undoubtedly complex but include the following:

1) Parliament generally lacked awareness of and/or interest in the country's preservation problems.

2) Because Parliament was basically a puppet of Siad Barre's dictatorial regime, if the president was not concerned about Somalia's cultural heritage, neither was Parliament.

3) Following the defection of the president of the academy (Ali Hersi) to Canada in 1985, the government appointed a new president who was a member of the same clan as Siad Barre and was ineffective and corrupt. The new president also did little to push the proposed legislation through Parliament, even though she was a member of the legislature.

4) The public had little interest in the protection and management of its cultural heritage, and there were no Somali archaeologists or preservationists skilled and/or interested enough in educating the public and Parliament about the importance of cultural heritage management.

This lack of skilled and/or interested Somali archaeologists requires further elaboration. Unfortunately, the Somali National University did not participate in the development of Somalia's cultural heritage because the history department did not offer any courses in archaeology until the mid-1980s when the coordinator of the academy's archaeology program began to offer a general survey course in African archaeology. Furthermore, only four students traveled overseas to obtain postgraduate education in general archaeology, and only one received specific training in cultural heritage management. Therefore, from 1984 until the fall of the government in 1991, there were only two archaeologists in the academy (and for that matter the whole country) who had postgraduate training.

Lack of personnel, combined with the general dearth of financial and logistical support (including salaries) from the academy and government, severely restricted the activities of the archaeology program. Nevertheless, it seems that the academy, if it had so desired, could have undertaken a number of archaeological or cultural heritage-related activities that would not have required extensive logistical support or financing. On more than one occasion the authors suggested that the academy develop a plan to monitor the many international development agency-funded construction projects in and around Muqdisho, but this proposal fell on deaf ears.

One of the many examples of the consequences of this inaction is shown in a 1988 incident; after returning from two months in the field, Steven Brandt attended an expatriate party where he met a German engineer. After the engineer learned that Brandt was an archaeologist, he proceeded to tell him that his company was undertaking a major sewage project funded by the German government in Xamar Weyn, the historic Early Islamic section of Muqdisho. When told that the project was uncovering "lots of stones, bones, and pottery," Brandt informed Osman Yusuf Mohamed, who was in Somalia conducting doctoral research on the establishment of a cultural heritage program for Somalia.

Mohamed agreed to monitor the project, which unfortunately by then had reached its final stages. To his horror, he found a trench two meters wide and five meters deep from which a vast array of archaeological remains, including ceramics, metal objects, stone walls, animal bones, and human remains, were being unearthed. When asked what they had done with the previously recovered artifacts and bones, the workers stated they had dumped it all into the sea.

The absence of any laws or regulations governing research meant that all archaeologists, and particularly foreigners, were at the mercy of the academy's administrators for their research and travel clearances as well as permission to export material (which was usually a necessity given the absence of laboratories and storage facilities). This situation deteriorated after 1985, when the academy's archaeology coordinator seized from a disinterested and ineffectual academy president virtually complete control over archaeological research. As a result, archaeologists were confronted with ever-changing demands and requirements of permits. Needless to say, it became very difficult for foreigners to conduct research in Somalia, and those who did so rarely returned.

In 1987 the government constructed a new and much bigger Somali National Museum in Muqdisho. However, much to the surprise and disgust of many individuals, the government chose to ignore the carefully thought-out and professionally drafted plans of the academy, and the new museum was built by the Somali army using secret plans drafted by an army officer.

With the opening of the new museum, relations between it and the academy deteriorated markedly, primarily because of a behind-the-scenes power struggle between the academy president and the museum director. The president wanted to bring the museum under academy control, while the museum director wanted to keep it under his purview. Furthermore, it was no secret that the museum director had grand plans, including the establishment of its own archaeology program. The ensuing power struggle raged until the end of the Siad Barre regime.

In summary, Somalia's cultural heritage remained effectively unprotected and unappreciated from the beginning to the end of Somalia's sovereignty. As a result, numerous cultural resources were destroyed (unintentionally or otherwise) at the hands of individuals, the Somali government, and international donor agencies or simply by neglect and the hand of nature. One shudders to think of the further destruction that might have occurred if a tourist industry had flourished in

Somalia. However, this all pales when compared to the death and destruction Somalia has witnessed since 1991.

THE PRESENT

Our knowledge of the extent of material destruction in Somalia is incomplete, especially for areas outside the urban centers. However, firsthand information from a number of sources about the cities shows that in northern Somalia, much if not all of Hargeysa, Erigaabo, and Burao have been destroyed or damaged. The Somali National Museum in Hargeysa and its collection of thousands of essentially ethnographic artifacts have been completely destroyed (Ali Hersi, pers. comm.).

In the south, Braawa evidently suffered little destruction but was repeatedly looted, and items of any historical value were stolen, including carved wooden doors and window frames and all items stored for safekeeping in the mosques. Fortunately, Marka was able to quickly muster its own militia and therefore remained largely free from looting and destruction.

Not surprisingly, Muqdisho has suffered the most damage of any southern city. Both the new Somali National Museum and the old Garesa Museum remain standing, although the Garesa Museum took some direct hits and is severely damaged. However, both museums were entirely vandalized, and what was not stolen was thrown into the streets.

Muqdisho has two major historic districts dating to the ninth century A.D. or earlier. Shaangaani is approximately three square kilometers in extent, but unfortunately is situated in the northern part of the city, which forms the dividing line between two major rival clans. Approximately 50 percent of the buildings have been destroyed and another 30 to 40 percent damaged, while the whole district has been looted repeatedly (John Marks, pers. comm.).

Xamar Weyn, also about three square kilometers in dimension, is located along the oceanfront in the central part of town. Fortunately, it has suffered relatively little destruction, with 20–25 percent of the buildings sustaining damage. However, Xamar Weyn has suffered extensive and systematic looting, with virtually everything of value stolen, including many historic objects.

We do not know what has become of the looted archaeological and historical treasures. However, we have heard reports that some objects were smuggled out of Somalia to neighboring countries, perhaps destined to enter the illicit art and antiquities market.

THE FUTURE

So what does the future hold for Somalia's cultural heritage? Not only does the country lack a government and a historical foundation in cultural heritage management upon which to rebuild, but much of its cultural heritage has been destroyed or damaged. But although the future of Somalia and its cultural heritage may seem hopeless, the situation can be seen as a unique opportunity for Somalis and the international community to develop and build, from scratch, a country's cultural heritage management program. We propose that Somalia become an international test case (and hopefully a showcase) for the establishment of a truly integrated and practical cultural heritage program for a developing country.

As soon as Somalia's civil war ends, we can expect to see government and international agencies immediately undertaking operations that include 1) clearing of rubble, 2) demolition of damaged buildings that are unsafe, unsightly, or in the way of new construction, 3) repair and/or construction of roads, and 4) the digging of trenches to repair or lay down new sewage and water systems. We should also expect to see government bureaucracies reestablished at the local, regional, and state levels.

Drawing upon recommendations of Somalis who formerly represented institutions engaged in cultural heritage management (i.e., the academy and museum) or were interested in but prevented from participating in cultural heritage administration, we suggest that a two-stage cultural heritage management program be initiated. The first stage should be put into effect as quickly as possible and involve Somalis, assisted by an international team of experts in archaeology, historic preservation, and remote sensing, undertaking a rapid but systematic inventory and photo/video documentation of destroyed, damaged, or missing buildings, monuments, and objects. Those damaged resources that are deemed to be significant and salvageable should be monitored to prevent unintentional (or intentional) destruction at the hands of clean-up and construction crews.

Similarly, a crew should be established to monitor any repair or construction activities involving subterranean excavations in sensitive areas. The team should also attempt to retrieve missing art and historic objects and to find a safe place to store material recovered.

First-stage operations should also include meetings with government officials to decide how and where cultural heritage management should be administered and funded within the newly established bureaucracies. Drawing on past experiences in Somalia and other African countries, a Department of Cultural Heritage (DCH) should be established immediately as an independent branch of the government or as an autonomous section within the Ministry of Culture (or perhaps the Office of the President). The rebuilding and administration of the national museums should also be placed within the DCH to create a more cohesive and dynamic institution.

In addition to overseeing and coordinating the emergency cultural heritage programs, the DCH should quickly put together a declaration for the protection of cultural resources that would act as a provisional set of rules for governing and funding cultural heritage activities in the country until the proposed second stage of operations is completed.

The second stage would be a long-term operation involving a multidisciplinary team of Somalis and international experts engaged in developing a practical cultural heritage program for the country. This team should comprise 1) the DCH; 2) Somalis formerly engaged in or interested in cultural heritage management; 3) representatives from relevant Somali ministries and institutions (e.g., the Ministries of Education, Culture and Higher Education, and Finance, and the Somali

National Museum, among others); 4) cultural heritage managers from Africa and other continents; 5) representatives from international organizations concerned with managing Africa's cultural heritage (e.g., UNESCO, ICOM, ICOMOS, ICCROM, SAfA); and 6) representatives of international donor agencies.

The team should be prepared to tackle the drafting and enactment of legislation that establishes an integrated and practical administrative structure; a national policy on cultural properties (e.g., import, export, development, research fees, qualifications of researchers, and so forth); a national register and inventory; and individual and government land rights. Most importantly, innovative, practical, and specific methods of enforcing such legislation will be needed. In addition, the team should address issues of domestic and foreign training programs in archaeology, preservation, and museology; policies for the selection of trainees; and the critical need for increasing public awareness of and participation in cultural heritage management.

CONCLUSION

Many people may argue that cultural heritage management should receive low priority in Somalia's reconstruction because of the urgent need to restore law and order and to provide basic necessities for the population. We respond that Somalis have, for various cultural and historical reasons, never been a particularly nationalistic society. What bonded people together were socio-politico-kinship systems that have now been considerably weakened, if not destroyed, by the civil war.

Once law and order and basic necessities are returned, what will unite Somali society? The development of a sense of pride and ownership in Somalia's cultural heritage will be needed to revive Somali patriotism and the establishment of a new Somali order. The cultural heritage program outlined here should ensure that Somalia's nonrenewable cultural resources will always play an indispensable role in the rebuilding and evolution of Somali society.

ACKNOWLEDGMENTS

The authors would like to thank Dr. Ali Abderahmen Hersi and John Marks for sharing their many personal observations.

REFERENCES

Brandt, S. A. "The Upper Pleistocene and Early Holocene Prehistory of the Horn of Africa." *African Archaeological Review* 4 (1986):41–82.
———. "Early Holocene Mortuary Practices and Hunter-Gatherer Adaptations in Southern Somalia." *World Archaeology* 20 (1988):40–56.
———. "The Importance of Somalia for Understanding African and World Prehistory." In *Proceedings of the First International Congress of Somali Studies,* ed. C. Geshekter and H. Adam. Atlanta: Scholars Press, 1992.

Brandt, S. A., and N. Carder. "Pastoral Rock Art in the Horn of Africa: Making Sense of Udder Chaos." *World Archaeology* 19 (1987):194–213.

Brandt, S. A., and R. Fattovich. "Late Quaternary Archaeological Research in the Horn of Africa." In *A History of African Archaeology*, ed. P. Robertshaw, pp. 95–108. London: Curry/Portsmouth, N.H.: Heinemann, 1990.

Brandt, S. A., and T. H. Gresham. "L'age de la Pierre en Somalie." *L'Anthropologie* 93 (1991[1989]): 222–33.

Carder, N. "Modeling the Evolution of Pastoral Rock Art in the Horn of Africa." M.A. thesis. University of Georgia, 1988.

Cassanelli, L. *The Shaping of Somali Society: Reconstructing the History of a Pastoral People, 1600–1900*. Philadelphia: University of Pennsylvania Press, 1982.

Chittick, H. N. "An Archaeological Reconnaissance of the Southern Somali Coast." *Azania* 4 (1969):115–30.

———. "An Archaeological Reconnaissance in the Horn: The British-Somali Expedition, 1975." *Azania* 11 (1976):117–33.

———. "Mediaeval Mogadishu." *Paideuma* 28 (1982):45–62.

Clark, J. D. *The Prehistoric Cultures of the Horn of Africa*. Cambridge: Cambridge University Press, 1954.

Cole-King, P. A. *Museum Organization*. Serial No. FRM/CC/CH/130. Paris: UNESCO, 1979.

Coltorti, M., and M. Mussi. "Late Stone Age Hunter-Gatherers of the Juba Valley, Southern Somalia." *Nyame Akuma* 28 (1987):32–33.

Curle, A. T. "The Ruined Towns of Somaliland." *Antiquity* 11 (1937):315–27.

Fay, S. "Dubrovnik Rising." *Conde Nast Traveler* August (1994): 86–94, 114–15.

Hersi, A. "The Arab Factor in Somali History." Ph.D. dissertation. University of California, Los Angeles, 1977.

Hess, R. L. "The 'Mad Mullah' and Northern Somalia." *Journal of African History* 3 (1964): 415–33.

———. *Italian Colonialism in Somalia*. Chicago: University of Chicago Press, 1966.

Huntingford, G. W. (trans.). *The Periplus of the Erythraean Sea*. London: Hakluyt Society, 1980.

Jonsson, S. *Archaeological Research Cooperation between Somalia and Sweden*, Stockholm: Civiltryck, 1983.

Laitin, D., and S. Samatar. *Somalia: Nation in Search of a State*. Boulder, Co.: Westview Press, 1987.

Lewis, I. M. *A Modern History of Somalia: Nation and State in the Horn of Africa*. Boulder: Westview, 1988.

Loughran, K., J. Loughran, J. Johnson, and S. Samatar (eds.). *Somalia in Word and Image*. Washington, D.C.: Foundation for Cross Cultural Understanding, 1986.

McMahon, K. "The Former Museums of Somalia." Unpublished manuscript, 1991.

Museo Della Garesa. *Catalago del Museo Della Garesa*. Mogadiscio, 1934.

Posnansky, M. *Museum and Antiquities Development*. Serial No. FRM/CC/CH/79/129. Paris: UNESCO, 1979.

Samatar, S. *Somalia, a Nation in Turmoil*. London: Minority Rights Group, 1991.

Seton-Karr, H. W. "Discovery of Evidences of the Paleolithic Stone Age in Somaliland." *Journal of Royal Anthropological Institute* 25 (1896).

Smith, M. C., and H. T. Wright. "The Ceramics from Ras Hafun in Somalia. Notes on a Classical Site." *Azania* 23 (1988):115–41.

Wilson, T. H. "Spatial Analysis and Settlement Patterns on the East African Coast." *Paideuma* 28 (1982): 201–19.

STATES PARTY TO THE 1970 **UNESCO** CONVENTION ON THE MEANS OF PROHIBITING AND PREVENTING THE ILLICIT IMPORT, EXPORT, AND TRANSFER OF OWNERSHIP OF CULTURAL PROPERTY

(NOVEMBER 1995)

AFRICA

Algeria
Angola
Burkina Faso
Cameroon
Central African Republic
Côte d'Ivoire
Egypt
Guinea
Libya
Madagascar
Mali
Mauritania
Mauritius
Niger
Nigeria
Senegal
Tanzania
Tunisia
Zaïre
Zambia

ASIA AND THE PACIFIC

Australia
Bangladesh
Cambodia
Democratic People's
   Republic of Korea
India
Mongolia
Nepal
Pakistan

People's Republic of
   China
Republic of Korea
Sri Lanka

EUROPE

Armenia
Belarus
Bosnia–Herzegovina
Bulgaria
Croatia
Cyprus
Czech Republic
Georgia
Greece
Hungary
Italy
Poland
Portugal
Romania
Russia
Slovak Republic
Slovenia
Spain
Tadjikistan
Turkey
Ukraine
Yugoslavia

THE MIDDLE EAST

Iran
Iraq
Jordan
Kuwait
Lebanon
Oman
Qatar
Saudi Arabia
Syrian Arab Republic

THE WESTERN HEMISPHERE

Argentina
Belize
Bolivia
Brazil
Canada
Colombia
Cuba
Dominican Republic
Ecuador
El Salvador
Grenada
Guatemala
Honduras
Mexico
Nicaragua
Panama
Peru
United States of America
Uruguay

CONTRIBUTORS

Steven A. Brandt is Associate Professor of Anthropology at the University of Florida. He has done research in the Horn of Africa, including Somalia, Ethiopia, and Eritrea, as well as in Kenya, Tanzania, India, and the United States. He is interested in the origins of food production, the protection of cultural heritage, the effects of war, and the international aspects of training and funding of heritage programs.

Michel Brent was trained as a lawyer and is a journalist with the Belgian weekly magazine *Le Vif/l'Express*. He has devoted several years to covering the pillaging of terra-cotta statuettes from Mali and the movement of these objects through the French and Belgian networks. Recently he has looked more broadly at illicit trafficking networks worldwide.

Henry John Drewal is Evjue-Bascom Professor of Art History at the University of Wisconsin–Madison. He is the author of several books, catalogues, and numerous articles on African and African-diaspora art. He recently coordinated the preparation of a proposal for a Foundation for African Archaeology.

dele jegede is an art historian, critic, and artist. He teaches African art and African American art in the Department of Art, Indiana State University, Terre Haute. His interest in the arts of Africa, with particular focus on popular culture and contemporary art, has led to his concern with the increased rate of theft from Nigerian museums.

N. Jonathan Karoma is Lecturer in History at the University of Dar es Salaam and co-founder of the Archaeology Unit at the University of Dar es Salaam. One of the first professional archaeologists in Tanzania, he specializes in the Stone Age of the Tanzanian coast.

Chapurukha M. Kusimba is Assistant Curator of African Archaeology and Ethnography at the Field Museum, Chicago. His research interests are in African prehistory and ethnography, ethnicity, anthropological theory, and technology and culture change. He has excavated or surveyed several threatened Swahili and colonial monuments and towns.

Robert R. LaGamma is former Director of African Affairs for the United States Information Agency. He is currently Public Affairs Officer for USIS in Pretoria, South Africa. He has served in Zimbabwe, Zambia, Zaïre, Togo, Senegal, and Nigeria, where he worked closely with museum directors and ministry officials and witnessed the difficulties African nations have in trying to preserve their cultural heritage.

Roderick J. McIntosh is Professor of Anthropology at Rice University. His research interests include the Late Stone Age and the Iron Age (particularly of West Africa), origins of urbanism, settlement patterns, palaeoclimates and responses to environmental changes, symbols and belief systems, and the history of archaeology. He has excavated in Ghana, Mali, and Senegal.

Osman Yusuf Mohamed was formerly an archaeologist with the Somali Academy of Sciences and has recently received his Ph.D. from the University of Georgia. His research is on the establishment of a cultural heritage program for Somalia.

Amini Azu Mturi is former Director and Chief Conservator of Antiquities, Tanzania, and Senior Lecturer in the Archaeology Unit of the University of Dar es Salaam. His research interests are in the excavation and architectural restoration of later Swahili towns. He has pioneered work on the conservation of standing stone walls at sites such as Bagamoyo.

Francis B. Musonda is Director of the Lusaka Museum, Zambia, and a member of the Zambian National Museums Board. As an archaeologist, he focused his research on the transition from the Late Stone Age and the beginnings of food production. As a museum official, he is involved in protecting and promoting Zambia's cultural heritage.

Paul Nchoji Nkwi is Professor of Anthropology at the University of Yaounde and President of the PanAfrican Association of Anthropology. His research interests have focused on political anthropology, medical and environmental anthropology, and art and culture. The removal and eventual repatriation of the Afo-a-Kom inspired his interest in the issue of theft of cultural heritage.

Athman Lali Omar was Curator of the Lamu Museum in Kenya until 1988. He is currently enrolled in the Ph.D. program in archaeology at the University of Florida. He has supervised the excavation and conservation of monuments along the Kenyan coast and has a particular interest in the collapse and abandonment of settlements in coastal regions from Kenya northward.

Maria Papageorge Kouroupas is Executive Director of the Cultural Property Advisory Committee, USIA, which advises the President with respect to prospective actions in implementing the 1970 UNESCO convention on illicit trade in cultural property.

Merrick Posnansky is Professor (Emeritus) in the Department of History at the University of California, Los Angeles, and past director of the UCLA Institute of Archaeology and African Studies Center. He formerly headed archaeology programs at the University of Ghana and at Makerere University College in Kampala. He has excavated in seven African countries and has been concerned with the state of African museums.

Lyndel V. Prott is Chief of the International Standards Sections of the Cultural Heritage Division of UNESCO and is Professor of Cultural Heritage Law at the University of Sydney, Australia. Her duties at UNESCO involve the administration of international conventions, encouraging nations to ratify these conventions, and assisting in the drafting of implementation legislation.

Peter R. Schmidt is former Director of the Center for African Studies and Associate Professor of Anthropology at the University of Florida. He is known for his research into the conjunction of archaeological evidence with oral history, as well as for his groundbreaking research into African iron technology. He has conducted archaeological inquiries in Tanzania, Uganda, Gabon, and Cameroon.

Samuel Sidibé is Director of the Mali National Museum. He is a Sorbonne-trained archaeologist who has conducted settlement and remote sensing research in the northern sector (lakes region) of the Middle Niger. He was an author of Mali's request for the bilateral accord with the United States to suppress the traffic in Malian antiquities.

Thomas H. Wilson is the former Executive Director of the Southwest Museum (Los Angeles) and former Museums Program Officer for the National Endowment for the Humanities. As Coast Archaeologist for the National Museums of Kenya during the 1970s he conducted a complete survey of sites of all periods along the Kenyan coast and was responsible for gazetting appropriate sites for protection.

INDEX